Quality teaching

Discussion of teacher education too often degenerates into a false dichotomy between the claims of theory and those of practice. In this timely
and important book, Edgar Stones breaks through that sterile debate by
focusing on teachers as inquirers trying to solve pedagogical problems
and drawing on all the resources – educational and psychological theory,
practical teaching experience, knowledge of their subject – at their disposal
in order to do so.

By detailed analysis of numerous case studies of novice and experienced
teachers grappling with real classroom problems, Stones shows that true
quality teaching is achieved only by sensitivity to the interplay between
the processes by which children acquire knowledge, the structure of
knowledge within the subject being taught and the context in which the
teaching is being done. He makes available to teachers and student teachers
a whole body of empirically based psychological knowledge, on concept
learning, problem solving and the learning of physical skills and shows
for the first time how this knowledge can inform and at the same time be
refined by what happens in the classroom. Throughout his aim is to support
teachers as explorers in pedagogy and active problem solvers, guided but
not limited by theoretical insights from the study of human learning.

Edgar Stones is a Fellow of the British Psychological Society, Emeritus
Professor and former Director of the Institute of Education of Liverpool
University, Honorary Senior Research Fellow in the School of Psychology
and Fellow of the Institute for Advanced Research in the Humanities at
Birmingham University. He is the founder and former president of the
British Educational Research Association and the founder of the *Journal
of Education for Teaching*, which he edits. He has taught in primary and
secondary schools, in further education and in teacher education, and has
written extensively on teaching and teacher education.

Quality teaching

A sample of cases

Edgar Stones

London and New York

First published 1992
by Routledge
11 New Fetter Lane, London EC4P 4EE

Simultaneously published in the USA and Canada
by Routledge
a division of Routledge, Chapman and Hall, Inc.
29 West 35th Street, New York, NY 10001

© 1992 E. Stones
Typeset by Selectmove Ltd, London
Printed in Great Britain by Clays Ltd, St Ives plc

British Library Cataloguing in Publication Data
Stones, E. (Edgar), *1922–*
    Quality teaching: a sample of cases.
    I. Title
    371.102

    ISBN 0–415–01659–2

Library of Congress Cataloging in Publication Data
0–415–01659–2

For Beatrice with thanks

Contents

Figures

1 Learning of quality

'When *I* use a word', Humpty Dumpty said in a rather scornful tone,
'it means just what I choose it to mean – neither more nor less.'

'The question is', said Alice, 'whether you *can* make words mean
different things.'

'The question is', said Humpty Dumpty, 'which is to be master –
that's all.'

(Lewis Carroll, *Through the Looking-glass* 1871)

QUALITY THROUGH THE LOOKING GLASS

Like Humpty Dumpty, the British Department of Education and Science
(DES) has a way with words. One example for the connoisseur was the
title of a Government White Paper *Education: A Framework for Expansion*
(DES 1973), which led to a sphincteral contraction in educational provision
in Britain. A decade later this was followed by another masterpiece:
Teaching Quality, also a White Paper (DES 1983), which is doing for
quality what *Framework for Expansion* did for quantity. Humpty Dumpty
would have approved not only the title, which maintained the tradition of
Education: A Framework for Expansion in meaning what they wanted it
to mean, but also in a central theme echoing Humpty Dumpty's clinching
assertion about the nature of the real question: 'which is to be master?'

In an attempt to get out of this looking-glass world I have found myself
turning around not only the title of the 1983 White Paper, which purported
to be a programme for improving the quality of teaching, but also its
central theses. Thus in *Quality Teaching* I argue that the prescriptions in
the Government's *Teaching Quality* are likely to achieve the opposite of its
declared intentions.

The reasons for the apparent paradox of my suggestion that the
prescriptions of *Teaching Quality* are likely to produce effects the opposite
of those promulgated, are complex. Some of the more potent ones, such as
'which is to be master?', are beyond the scope of this book. However, at the
heart of *Teaching Quality* is a view of teaching that sustains and gives it life.
Since its enunciation, this view of teaching has thrived and has, in recent

years, permeated education in many countries. It is a view that seems to regard education as a commodity and teachers as the people who deliver it.

Lest it be thought I imply that the British have a monopoly on pedagogical sophistry, or that the 1983 White Paper was a passing cloud, let me draw readers' attention to recent trends in teacher education worldwide. In the USA *Tomorrow's Teachers*, purportedly a prospectus for the professionalisation of teaching, has been seen more as a mask for its 'ongoing "proletarianisation"' (Gottleib and Cornbleth 1989). Current trends in Britain have fulfilled the threats of *Teaching Quality*, and, to rub salt into the wound, the Government reprinted the report in 1985. This renewal of the message was followed by an upsurge in comment on the subject, well illustrated by a collection of papers edited by Carr on the subject in 1989. Gilroy (1991), comparing current trends with changes beginning to emerge in the USSR, sees a deep irony in the contrast between attempts to discard a failed 'system of overwhelming social control and management' and British attempts to introduce just such a system.

A recent international colloquium on teacher education found participants from many countries grappling with very similar problems (Stones 1990). They recognised that teacher education was in need of improvement but found that Humpty Dumpty had put his finger on the key question. No matter how assiduously teacher educators worked to develop effective methods of teaching, or how diligently they tried to remedy the deficiencies in their practice, their efforts seemed doomed to frustration in the face of a *force majeur* imposing its own version of teaching on them.

The collection of papers by Carr analyses the reasons for the current predicament of teacher education in which the idea of 'quality' in teaching has been defined in terms calculated to lead to the derogation of theory of teaching and an elevation of control mechanisms (Carr 1989). This echoes the appraisal of the White Paper in the *Journal of Education for Teaching* (Stones 1983) which saw the paper as more a mechanism of control than a serious grappling with the complexities of teaching and teacher training.

One problem over the years has been the too-ready acceptance by teachers and teacher educators of the meanings imposed by politicians and administrators. Thus, centrally inspired versions of 'appraisal' of teaching have been embraced, and in many countries conferences about appraisal reached epidemic proportions in the 1980s with virtually no examination of its content or methods. 'Quality' is receiving similar treatment in the early 1990s. There may now be somewhat more hope, however, for a principled and informed resistance to the central imposition of a mechanistic view of teaching and an insistence on the participation of teachers and teacher educators in defining such things as 'teaching', 'appraisal' and 'quality'. Professionals are beginning to resist and even, on occasion, defy non-professional impositions that fly in the face of their pedagogical understanding. I discuss this question in a later chapter. However, as a brief example, let me cite the case of the Papua New Guinea teacher trainers who opposed the bureaucratic imposition on the colleges of a method of examining English as a second language that lacked validity and reliability and fostered rote learning (McLaughlin 1991). They defended an approach stressing language for communication with great force and energy. Whether they will eventually carry the day has still to be seen. But the significant development is the scale of their resistance. This example is a microcosm of conditions in many countries as is attested by comments from other contributors to the same issue of the journal in which the Papua New Guinea report appeared. Their analyses examined the relationship of the Papua New Guinea experience to the plight of teacher education in their own countries (Alarcão *et al.*, 1991).

A fundamental thesis of *Teaching Quality* which is still alive and thriving in many parts of the world is that it is sufficient for teachers to have a thorough knowledge of subject matter and practical classroom experience: the former, to ensure that they are up-to-date on the product they are to deliver, and the latter to ensure that they know how to deliver it. Subject study in higher education, it is averred, will equip teachers with the material to transmit, and practical classroom experience will equip them with effective transmission skills. There is no suggestion in this outlook that there is a place for theoretical knowledge about the nature of teaching. When educational theory is mentioned by those who espouse this view of teaching, it is usually to denigrate it as irrelevant to practice. It is rare, however, to find any substantiating analytical argument. (See, for example, Cox 1989.)

Few, surely, would disagree that teachers should have a good grasp of subject knowledge and should also be familiar with schools and classrooms. However, the 'delivery' view of teaching grossly oversimplifies its true nature, and the prescriptions intended to improve it are doomed to fail because of the lack of understanding of its complexities.

To substantiate my appraisal of this view of teaching I shall examine what seem to me its key misconceptions. Then I shall propose methods of enhancing our understanding of its complexities to enable us to take steps that really do offer hope of improving teaching. In the discussion I draw on theoretical understandings that relate to practical teaching. I also present and analyse examples of actual teaching by student teachers and by experienced teachers using a theory-informed approach to their teaching. I hope that this way of discussing and analysing teaching will be useful to teachers and student teachers wishing to improve the quality of their teaching and their ability to reflect on their practice with the insight afforded by a grasp of theoretical principles. I also hope that it will interest educationists wishing to explore the possible nature of pedagogical theory and its relationship to practical teaching.

Writing for such a wide and disparate readership is a difficult task, especially when one is considering a topic as complex as teaching. This difficulty is compounded by the widespread underestimation of this complexity. Thus the writer needs to relate sufficiently closely to the concerns of serious-minded practising teachers to suggest to them that the message holds promise of genuine improvement in their teaching and also to engage researchers and teacher-educators interested in rigorous and analytical approaches to theoretical issues. Thus, one travels between the Scylla of explicating the obvious to one population and the Charybdis of blinding the other with science. All the time one is trying to expound one's views on some very complex concepts and establish convincing links with practical teaching in a context of mutual misunderstanding and sometimes deprecation by both groups of the other's main activities.

I am referring here both to the widespread distrust of theory among teachers and to the low regard of practical teaching manifested by the inferior status it is accorded in many training institutions in many countries. A recent example of the former may be found in the address to a British teachers' union by its general secretary (Dawson 1990). He called for a two-year course with less theory and an emphasis on learning to 'control' the pupils. He asserted that there was evidence to demonstrate that training courses had little impact on the quality of teaching. An illustration from the USA of the low esteem of practical teaching in academe may be found in an article by Clark (Clark 1988). Here he comments on the inferior status accorded in teacher training institutions to clinical supervision in which graduate students act as overseers and on the speculation as to who should be responsible. Similar attitudes are found outside the USA. As I commented in a discussion of supervision, when I first started to work in teacher education in England, I received no induction to the practice of supervision but a great deal to the organisation of transport of student teachers to teaching practice schools (Stones 1984a). No mention was ever made of a theory that might be relevant to supervision, nor have I heard it mentioned since, except when I have raised the subject.

Despite the difficulties of the task it is essential that an effort be made to navigate the straits of sterile theorising and blind practice. Quality teaching cannot be a-theoretical, nor can it be nurtured by disquisitions on the nature of teaching by theorists with their feet in the clouds. Both theory and practice are essential. Indeed, they are inseparable. Quality teaching is more properly conceived of as a unified field embracing both theory and practice in which teachers, teacher educators and researchers are jointly responsible for the development of theoretical understanding and the improvement of teaching (Stones 1986a, Erickson 1988). I develop this theme in the pages that follow. In so doing, I shall not be reporting, in conventional ways, outcomes of experiments or reviews of work on teaching as it is now, but on explorations of teaching as it might be.

VIEWS OF TEACHING

Current orthodoxy in the 'delivery' camp often supports its view that good teaching results from a combination of subject study and practical experience by citing the procedures in British 'public' schools (i.e. expensive private schools). The claim is that these schools are noted for the excellence of their teaching largely because they have traditionally recruited teachers who have *not* had formal teacher training and, therefore, have not been influenced by educational theorists (Cox 1989). This argument contains several fallacies that need to be clarified by anyone who wishes to make a serious study of teaching.

The first fallacy is to assume that there is a consensus about the nature of 'good teaching'. The nature of much current argument on this question is unequivocally ideologically partisan which, in itself, is enough to make the point that the idea of 'good teaching' is a value-laden concept. This kind of argument is rarely well informed, and the field of teaching and teacher training is no exception. In fact a considerable body of research in the field suggests that there is no general consensus on what constitutes good teaching. (See Leinhardt 1990 for a discussion of various approaches to the problem. See also Medley 1987.) The second fallacy, that subject expertise and not teacher training makes for good teachers, falls if there is no agreement about what 'good teaching' is.

Other factors to be considered in this line of argument are that the British public schools, especially the most expensive and prestigious ones, recruit from a very privileged stratum of society, have small classes, are well equipped compared to most state schools and enjoy a network of connections within the state apparatus and the country's élite universities. The success of these schools is commonly measured by the number of their pupils who obtain entrance to these universities, particularly Oxford and Cambridge. Even if we accept this criterion as an indicator of good teaching, the assertion that this is because the teachers are uncontaminated by teacher training can be no more than opinion. Is it beyond the bounds of possibility that the other factors mentioned may influence these schools' success far more than the lack of training enjoyed by the teachers? One could equally well argue that they achieve success despite their teachers' lack of training and that they would perform even better if the teachers were knowledgeable in pedagogical theory.

A further illustration of the value-laden nature of the idea of 'good teacher' may be taken from attitudes to corporal punishment. Many people who have held political office in recent years in the British educational system are, or were, in favour of corporal punishment and would presumably not exclude people who beat children from the category of 'good teacher'. The European Community takes a different view of 'good teacher' and bans corporal punishment in member states, and Britain has had to fall into line. Interestingly, the 'public' schools held up as paragons of good teaching in some quarters, being outside the state system, are currently allowed to carry on beating. Many states in the USA permit teachers to inflict corporal punishment. Presumably they see no conflict between the idea of a good teacher and the use of corporal punishment. Any teacher who used it, however, would fail the European test of a good teacher.

Should anyone argue that the public schools get their 'superior' results *because* they beat the pupils, I doubt that they would persuade many people nowadays to accept beating as a means to this end. I think people in most countries would prefer unbeaten children who had had less of the curriculum delivered to them to those who had had it beaten into them.

In fact, there is an extensive literature that indicates that punishment does not encourage learning. I have to admit, however, that anyone who finds being beaten pleasurable would probably learn better. This could well be the reason for the continuation of the practice in the British 'public schools'.

The problematic nature of defining 'good teaching' has not deterred a large number of people involved in education from devising schemes for appraising teachers' performance. In English-speaking countries teacher appraisal schemes have proliferated in recent years. In practically all such schemes, teaching is conceived of in the sense of 'delivering the curriculum'. Teacher appraisal schemes of this type became so prevalent in Britain in the mid-1980s that in 1986 the British Educational Research Association mounted a conference to draw to the attention of educationists the degree to which the schemes ignored the complex nature of teaching (Stones and Wilcox 1986).

There is one other current pressure on teaching that reinforces the view of teaching as 'telling' or 'delivering'. This pressure is towards focusing attention on the teaching of 'facts', rather than processes and problem solving. It may be characterised as a 'back to basics' movement. This is an abiding influence in education in many countries. In nineteenth-century Britain the education of the populace was restricted to the learning of sufficient facts and simple processes for them to be able to cope with the demands of industry, but no more, for fear that learning to think might lead to revolution. In the twentieth century the necessary skills may be more complex, but judging by the words and deeds of many people with influence over education in many countries, the kind of learning favoured is little different. Later, I shall examine the nature of this type of learning and explain why I believe it necessary to avoid it wherever possible.

Even the modicum of instruction proposed in the early nineteenth century was too much for some, whose views were encapsulated in 1807 by the words of Giddy in Parliament:

However specious in theory the project might be, of giving education to the labouring classes of the poor, it would teach them to despise their lot in life, instead of making them good servants in agriculture and other laborious employment to which their rank in society has destined them; instead of teaching them subordination, it would render them factious and refractory as was evident in the manufacturing counties; it would enable them to read seditious pamphlets, vicious books, and publications against Christianity; it would render them insolent to their superiors; and in a few years the result would be that the legislature would find it necessary to direct the strong arm of power towards them and to furnish the executive magistrate with more vigorous laws than were now in force.

(Barnard 1952)

The same sentiments appear to be abroad at the end of the twentieth century. There are those who believe this to be the case. In Britain this is expressed by critiques of government-inspired divisions in education with 'training' for one group and 'education' for an élite (Hextall 1988). Hextall, in fact, quotes a British teacher who describes recent developments in British education in terms not dissimilar to Giddy's but with opposite intent: 'Education is being reduced to a mechanistic process for turning out well-programmed, but unquestioning, operatives for the Thatcherite New Jerusalem' (Hextall 1988: 74). Berman, writing about recent developments in the USA, describes similar processes with a track for a privileged group to be educated in new technological skills and a 'slow' learner track (Berman 1988). Berman also comments on the implications of the factory view of schooling for the way teachers are perceived. Teachers are seen as assembly line workers implementing programmes decided upon at higher levels. In both Britain and the USA there is an increasingly overt penetration of representatives of business interests in the making of those decisions. Pressure for the learning of facts fits in well with this view of teaching. Facts can easily be dispensed or 'delivered'. Little is demanded of teachers except compliance.

However, Berman goes on to draw attention to an important possible counteracting force. Teacher-educators may take the call for 'excellence', which he sees as a code word for more emphasis on sciences, mathematics and technical subjects and decreased emphasis of everything else, and interpret it differently. They might endeavour to build greater intellectual rigour into the teacher training courses to equip student teachers with the tools for critical thinking and critical literacy.

Once teachers possess these intellectual tools rather than merely the technical skills of classroom management and teaching from prepackaged instructional kits, they might impart these same tools of critical literacy and critical thinking to their students. If indeed this comes to fruition. If students are taught how to analyse social and political issues . . . will they remain content to receive training or education that consigns them indefinitely to positions of economic subordinacy? Or will they insist that their education be reconceptualised to provide at least a modicum of control over their lives?

(Berman 1988: 54)

It is unlikely that everyone would accept teacher-educators of this ilk into their classification of good teachers. For my part, I consider the development of the skills Berman refers to entirely desirable and part of being fully human. These skills are those towards which the teachers whose work I report were working. The achievement of this goal by all teachers is an enormous undertaking. It is not merely that teachers and teacher-educators are constrained by outside forces. The history of education since the beginning of industrialisation is characterised by the 'delivery of facts' view of teaching. It is bred in the bone of pupils, parents and student teachers. It is another factor that makes the task of introducing new approaches difficult. I have found it prevalent in my experience both with graduate student teachers embarking upon a course of teacher training and with experienced teachers starting work on in-service courses or on teaching-research projects. It is encapsulated for me in two experiences. The first occurred when a teacher was watching a videotape of my attempts to discuss with another experienced teacher, a trainee supervisor of student teachers, a lesson she had taught. I was doing my best to help the teacher to appraise her own recorded performance with the minimum of guidance. Missing the point of this exercise, the viewer asked: 'What are you trying to *tell* her?' The second is a more general phenomenon. Rejoinders made by student teachers when invited to explain how they would teach a subject of their choice to someone, have commonly been of the type: 'First I would tell them this, then I would tell them that, then I would tell them the other'. Assessment of learning is in the same mould. Pupils and students at all levels and ages of schooling routinely get good grades for merely repeating, frequently without understanding, what the teacher has previously told them.

People trying to improve teaching of the 'telling' type have, over the years, adopted many different methods. These have tended to vary according to fashion and the current state of technology. In the nineteenth century and well into the twentieth, one aid to teaching and learning was to beat pupils who failed. Teaching Latin 'through the seat of the pants' was not a joke for generations of children. In recent times, solutions to pedagogical problems have very often been sought by the use of various types of technology. Enthusiasm for aids such as language laboratories, teaching machines, closed circuit TV and currently, computers, video-disks, lasers, multi-media 'presentations' have promised the pedagogical holy grail. In due course some of them have been absorbed into the teacher's armamentarium, others gather dust in stock rooms. None has brought the prophesied pedagogical millennium.

Nor was there ever the slightest chance that these aids on their own could do so, since they all took as given the 'telling' view of teaching. Some writers of teaching programs fully understood that teaching machines, as such, could accomplish nothing. The thing that mattered was the program in the machine. Some of these programs, in fact, did make use of knowledge of learning theory in their approach to teaching for meaningful learning, so that, to an extent, they were able to transcend straightforward 'telling'. Any improvement in pupil learning, however, was a consequence of the programmers' pedagogical thinking, not the medium. This point is made by Clark (1983) in a survey of the effects of all kind of media on pupil learning.

However, few teachers in any stage of education have grasped this point. Huge amounts of information are 'delivered' through lectures and other types of exposition uninformed by pedagogical principles. Given this state of affairs, one might imagine that teacher training institutions would be doing their best to teach their pupils pedagogical principles to enable them to transcend mere 'telling'. Unfortunately this has not happened, for a number of reasons that I have discussed elsewhere (Stones 1989a). 'Educational Theory' in these institutions, has, in the main, dealt with academic studies similar to the 'parent disciplines' such as sociology, philosophy and psychology. Staff of these institutions rarely attempt to relate these studies directly to teaching, so, in effect, no theory of teaching is taught.

Instead, teaching is commonly seen as a craft subject that should be learned on the job (O'Hear 1989). Neophyte teachers will learn to teach by observing other teachers. Neither neophyte nor old hand is likely to have any formal knowledge about the way people learn, so that all that a new teacher can learn is what other teachers have learned largely through trial and error or folk wisdom. I do not intend to denigrate the knowledge that teachers learn 'on the job'; it is very important, as I shall try to show later. But it is restricted in scope to teachers' experience and it is not systematised. It is therefore limited in its general accessibility. Teachers are, thus, doubly constrained by the view of teaching as a craft in which the main function of practitioners is passing on information. On the one hand, current practitioners' skills and knowledge are confined to their own experience and, therefore, limited. On the other hand, the lack of an underlying theory confines any discussion between experienced and beginning teachers to surface activities of teaching. A theory of teaching should help both to remove these constraints and to establish a more accurate view of teaching as an extremely complex human activity.

Some people argue for the systematising of the 'craft knowledge' of teachers as a way towards establishing theory. There are, however, problems with this view. Its unqualified espousal is deeply conservative, since it confines our attention to what teachers do now, whereas we should have our eyes on what they might do to improve what they are doing now. The systematising of the craft knowledge approach is a version of 'modelling the master teacher' whose limitations are outlined by Stolurow (1965) and Stones and Morris (1972). I prefer the 'master the teaching model' approach. This approach does not dismiss 'craft knowledge' but accepts it as one element to be considered in exploring the nature of pedagogical theory and practice. To fail to take into account the work done in the field of human learning seems to me to be blinkered or even perverse when we seek to improve teaching. Thus the fact that the title of this book is *Quality Teaching*, not *Quality Teachers*, is not insignificant.

Leinhardt (1990) discusses questions related to the use of craft knowledge in the assessment of teaching. Many of the problems identified, however, apply in non-assessment situations. Leinhardt argues that since not all craft knowledge is likely to be accurate, we are faced with the problem of distinguishing between superstition and valid and useful teacher understanding. Among Leinhardt's recommendations for tackling this problem is to derive the knowledge from recognised 'expert' teachers and gradually assimilate the derived knowledge into a cumulative corpus accessible to all. But the outcome is not to be the sole consideration. Craft knowledge and theory need to be integrated.

I would not dissent from this view. However, I should like elucidation about the nature of the 'theory' involved. This is not made particularly clear, but craft knowledge is discussed in distinction to 'general, subject-based, principled knowledge in a discipline'. Later discussion refers to theory acquired in the professional training of teachers which emphasises its value 'as an efficient, universal, cohesive truth filter for disorganised, practical experience', and the use of 'theory of instruction of teachers and assessment of their performance'.

I have already mentioned my misgivings about the likely efficacy of the theory taught in teacher training institutions. In Britain, in any case, theory of education, related or unrelated to actual teaching, has virtually disappeared, and the question of its relevance is irrelevant. In the USA, given the low status that teacher education has been accorded, the idea of a theory that could possibly provide a theory of instruction capable of providing a truth filter of the type described by Leinhardt seems dubious in the extreme. What may be offered is the *pedagogical content knowledge* first raised by Shulman (1986) and pursued with vigour by numerous US authors since, with a recent attempt to capture it occupying a whole issue of *Journal of Teacher Education* (May–June 1990). One of the authors in that issue concluded that the concept of pedagogical knowledge was difficult to pin down (Mark 1990). He offers a practical definition as a class of knowledge central to teachers' work that 'would not typically be held by nonteaching subject matter experts or by teachers who know little of that subject'. We now know what it is *not*. We approach a view of what it *is* when the author suggests two elements, teacher's awareness of pupil misconceptions and the use of analogies. Beyond that we learn no more.

The editorial summary of the topic (Ashton 1990) is more helpful. The writer's view of pedagogical content knowledge sees it as one element in a wider conceptualisation of teacher education in which pedagogy and content knowledge are integrated. The elucidatory element in her comments refers to

> programs that systematically examine the structures of the disciplines and how students come to understand them. This includes the study of the organisation of concepts and principles in the disciplines and the strategies used in the disciplines to discover new knowledge as well as the development of strategies and materials that enable students to understand those concepts and processes. In addition, teacher education strategies are needed to help prospective teachers develop their understanding of pedagogical content knowledge and skill in pedagogical reasoning. To be effective this work requires the collaboration of specialists in subject matter and pedagogy, developmental and cognitive psychologists and classroom teachers.

This comment encapsulates much of the orientation of the work that I have been engaged in with practising and pre-service teachers since the early 1970s, some of which is reported in this book. While Ashton's comment does not, to my mind, clarify definitively the nature of pedagogical content knowledge, I can live with that ambiguity in view of the suggestion that it is part and parcel of a variety of approaches to developing systematic approaches to teaching. The work described in the pages that follow suggests to me that 'pedagogical content knowledge' is a term that is of little functional help in analysing and practising teaching and could actually be counterproductive by isolating one aspect of pedagogical theory and practice. I understand the reasons for its origins in an attempt to redress the balance in favour of a neglected element in teacher education, but regret the way it became a decontextualised buzz word. When I first encountered it I discovered to my amazement that I had been helping teachers and student teachers to examine and develop 'pedagogical content knowledge' for quite a long time, just like Molière's 'Bourgeois Gentilhomme' who suddenly learned that he had been speaking prose all his life.

There is one other aspect of the discussion of craft knowledge that I believe unhelpful. There is an undue focus on the interactive aspect of teaching. Some who argue for the primacy of craft knowledge in the study of teaching seem to consider what goes on in the classroom as the sole concern. Yet what goes on before the teacher enters the classroom and after leaving are both important. A currently fashionable topic in the literature on teaching that touches on these matters is the exploration of teacher thinking.

One theme receiving attention is the way teachers plan their lessons and their reasoning during the process (Clark 1988). Most teachers spend time planning their teaching, so this is clearly an aspect of teacher activity that merits inclusion in our conception of teaching. The teacher's thoughts and actions after leaving the classroom has received less attention. However, this seems to me to be equally as vital as other aspects of teaching and also worthy of inclusion in the use of the term 'teaching'. Apart from the paucity of comment on the before and after of the interactive aspect of teaching there is virtually no mention in the literature of pedagogical intervention by teacher-educators to enhance student teacher or experienced teacher competence in either field. In my view, this is a serious deficiency that needs to be addressed. I describe attempts to do this later in this book.

I have spent time discussing the idea of craft knowledge and related concepts such as pedagogical subject knowledge because they are of central concern in much of the current discourse in the academic educational community and because they touch on some of the issues I raise later when I consider the work of teachers exploring their own teaching. As I suggested, I am more sympathetic to views such as those of Ashton, who seeks to draw on a plurality of sources for a theory of teaching than those suggesting that a theory can be constructed from the practice of 'expert' teachers and then used to train teachers to do likewise (Brown and McIntyre 1988). However, I think it important to stress that the idea of craft knowledge as promulgated by many educationists (and certainly those mentioned here) does not consider teaching to be a simple skill, easy to acquire, as do the people such as Cox whom I mentioned earlier. On the contrary: most of them see teaching as a very complex skill, very difficult to describe and analyse.

There is one other thing that is rarely mentioned in discussions about teaching, but which is of utmost importance – not, perhaps, in its practical application, but in its implications for our understanding of the nature of teachers' work. This is the principle that a teacher's fundamental task is to change the functioning of learners' brains in some way. Few people would dispute the view of the brain as 'the most complicated and sophisticated thing on the planet' (Churchland and Churchland 1990). Most people would also agree that the profession of brain surgeon has a high prestige, certainly higher than that of the teaching profession. Yet a brain surgeon merely modifies the structure of the brain, whereas a teacher attempts to change its functioning. Moreover, a brain surgeon operates on one brain at a time, whereas teachers are expected to work with large numbers of brains. Presumably the Churchlands' assertion was intended to refer to the functioning of the brain as well as its morphology, and by that token, it seems to me, the functioning of the brain should be viewed as at least as complex as its structure.

I put these questions quite starkly precisely because they are so often overlooked. I do not, however, thereby espouse a mechanistic approach to education – as I think will become clear. I do think it important that the complexity of teaching be not overlooked or underestimated.

The daunting complexity of the pedagogical vistas that open up when one considers the implications of this view of teaching is likely to inspire flight or fight reactions among teachers. Half a century ago many psychologists took the former course and forsook the classroom for the laboratory, where they worked with rats or psychology students examining the most simple types of learning. In recent years there has been a very modest movement back to the classroom. In the pages that follow I take the fight alternative but argue for the involvement, not just of the psychologists and other interested academic researchers, but of teachers also. The approach I propose will, thus, have the potential of drawing on a very large population of investigators, i.e. the teachers themselves, to explore and improve the nature of human learning and teaching since, whatever else can be said about teachers, it cannot be denied that they are numerous.

This is encouraging and also very important. The history of attempted innovations in education demonstrates that attempts to innovate run into the sand if teachers do not accept, understand and become committed to them. Advances in education and teaching, in distinction from adminis-trative and bureaucratic changes, are totally dependent upon a highly skilled teacher force with real understanding of theory – especially of learning but also of the impact of wider social pressures.

THEORY

In view of the questions I have raised about the elusive nature of a theory of teaching, I must first present the reader with some indication of my own views on theory. In the process of elaborating these views I shall also be making clear what I consider to be good teaching. The rest of the book spells out these views in detail. As a working definition of theory, I suggest: 'bodies of principles that have explanatory power and the potential of guiding teacher action'. This still leaves considerable scope for interpretation according to one's value position about the nature of appropriate 'teacher action'. It certainly does not rule out craft knowledge, but it certainly does not accept that craft knowledge is sufficient. However, the process of constructing a theory of teaching should open that proposition to scrutiny by others in a way that a-theoretical approaches cannot.

Thus the argument of this book, since it discusses very specific approaches to theory and practice, will fill out the working definition and attempt to make explicit the nature of appropriate teacher action which it espouses. In the process I shall examine the 'telling' view of teaching and endeavour to reveal its inadequacies. An alternative view of teaching will be developed – one that argues the importance of a theory of pedagogy to inform teacher action of a different type from merely 'telling' pupils. If I succeed in my attempts to make my approaches, methods, theoretical position and methods of evaluation clear and detailed, they should be available to the type of scrutiny I have advocated.

Briefly stated, my view of teaching is that of teachers as inquirers attempting to solve pedagogical problems. The pedagogical problems are not of the type commonly addressed in teacher training courses, such as the use of audio-visual aids, or how to write on the chalkboard, or how to use one's voice; rather they are concerned with more fundamental questions such as the conceptual structure of the subject under study or the most appropriate approach to teaching for meaningful learning. The apex of this work is how best to help pupils to solve their own problems, either in relation to work in school or in their lives outside. To help them to solve their own pedagogical problems, teacher inquirers will draw on any information that offers guidance in their activities. This information may come from any source, but I suggest that one of the most fruitful sources is likely to be those fields that have traditionally related to the study of education and, in particular, of psychology related to pedagogy. Another will be teachers' practical teaching activity and, yet another, their understanding of their particular subjects. However, neither educational studies nor practical teaching, as they are normally conceived, will suffice. One of the key aspects of the work of teacher inquirers will be the transformation of both. This book considers ways in which this might be accomplished.

The ability to solve problems depends on learning. Thus information from the study of human learning should be of help in improving teaching. The potential does exist, since there is a considerable body of knowledge on the psychology of human learning. However, few attempts have been made to connect this information with practical teaching, so there is little that is directly relevant to teachers' work. As a consequence, few teachers explicitly and consciously attempt to relate their practice to theoretical principles of human learning.

The way in which pedagogical theory and practical teaching relate is implicit in the view of teachers as inquirers. The certitudes of the 'delivery' approach are replaced by a realistic recognition of the tentativeness of our understanding of how teachers' actions influence pupils' learning. There is no body of theory that teachers can 'apply' in their teaching in the way that they might 'tell' pupils about various subjects of study. Theoretical insights from the study of human learning can guide teacher action but not prescribe its exact nature.

This follows because of the enormous complexity of the usual teaching set-up. With one teacher and many pupils, it is impossible, given our current knowledge, to apply simple prescriptive procedures. Teachers will comprehend theory in their own personal ways, according to their experience and their grasp of the underlying principles. Pupils differ in very complex ways because of their unique genetic endowments and life experiences. The physical environment of every lesson is also unique – not only because some lessons take place in well-equipped and congenial buildings, while others take place in buildings lacking basic facilities and equipment, but also in such things as the time of day, the time of year and the weather.

Other very important factors are such things as the social and political conditions existing inside and outside the classroom. Clearly the learning environment of pupils in a school in a quiet rural community is very different from that in a school in a densely populated run-down urban area – as are learning conditions during civil strife or war as compared with those in the same school in peaceful times.

Psychological studies make it clear that human learning can be hindered or enhanced by relatively minor changes in learning conditions, either within the learners or in their environments. Variables such as I have just mentioned are, therefore, all likely to have significant effects on learning. But teachers are one of the most potent variables of all. If they have some knowledge of the way in which the other variables affect learning they will be in a position to influence the effects of those variables. Knowledge from other fields of educational studies similarly affect the way teachers relate to their pupils and thereby influence their learning. I am thinking of such things as teachers' knowledge of the way teaching has been and currently is conceived by historians, philosophers and sociologists. This knowledge will complement teachers' understanding of how they might manipulate variables to enhance pupil learning with insights about the values they would wish to inform their approach to pupils and what they would wish to teach them.

Inquiring teachers will see teaching as an activity of great complexity which we hardly yet begin to understand. They will see it as open-ended exploration in which they express their pedagogical knowledge in action that will not only improve the conditions of learning for their pupils, but also enlarge their own theoretical understanding. This follows from the view of teaching as inquiry informed by a self-consciously held body of principles in which the principles are put to the acid test of practice. In fact, the theory and the practice are best conceived of as two aspects of the same process, so that it might equally be said that practice is also tested in the light of theory. The two are mutually refining. An important aim of this book is to discuss ways in which exploration and inquiry in theory and practice might be made more effective.

Those who argue against theory in relation to teaching deny to teachers the insights into practice I have just discussed. By focusing on the subject to be taught and the practice of teaching, they also deny the complexity of teaching and reduce it to a non-problematical activity. They thus foreclose the discussion and effectively rule out any scrutiny of teaching aimed at improving it. They lead teachers into a pedagogical dead end.

PRACTICE AND THEORY

Prospectuses for teacher training institutions in most parts of the English-speaking world contain syllabuses for lecture courses in a wide variety of subjects, giving specific details about their coverage. In the case of teaching practice, however, few give any details at all. Usually all that is mentioned is the amount of time to be spent in school and the dates or days that student teachers will be working there.

This is an interesting phenomenon. It implies that the subjects of study, commonly seen as 'theory', are problematic and in need of explication, whereas practice is non-problematic. It assumes that a prospective student teacher, will immediately comprehend what teaching and teaching practice comprises. This assumption justifies the attitudes referred to above that denigrate the place of pedagogical theory in teacher education and see teaching as nothing more than a relatively simple skill to be learned by imitation. It also undermines the claim of educational studies to a place in teacher training. If teaching can be learned on the job, why do we need a theory of teaching in training institutions?

This view of teaching and teaching practice implies a process of delivery such as I have discussed earlier. Teachers are to 'deliver' the curriculum by 'telling' their pupils. Pupil learning is equated with their absorbing the teacher's message. There is no suggestion that there are 'pedagogical' skills pertaining to the encouragement of pupil learning. Implicit in the delivery mode of teaching is an essentially passive view of pupils. The process of absorption, assuming it actually takes place, is equated with learning. This reasoning is implicit in recent developments in various countries where untrained people enter teaching and acquire qualifications later mainly as a consequence of having taught.

I do not wish to imply that lecturing or telling cannot lead to learning. Expository teaching has its place in teachers' repertoires. But even expository teaching, which is one of the simplest pedagogical skills, can be improved if teachers have an understanding of the principles of human learning. Other, more complex and more interesting kinds of learning, demand a more thorough grasp of those principles. Questions such as these are rarely discussed in relation to practical teaching in training institutions.

My earlier suggestion, that one of the main aims of teaching should be the development of problem-solving skills in pupils, implies an approach to teaching practice in teacher training that is radically different from those currently in favour. Unlike current practice, it accepts that teaching is a highly complex activity that cannot be learned merely by watching others. It takes a view completely at variance from those which see teaching as a process of delivery that does not need explication. It takes a view of human learning that is equally at variance from the one which sees pupils as passive receivers of teachers' messages. Worthwhile learning cannot be a one-way process. The learner must be engaged with the world and not just with the teacher's talk. Being able to remember the teacher's words is the shadow of learning. The substance demands experience of reality as well as words.

QUALITY LEARNING

Quality teaching should aim for quality learning. The nature of that learning has already been alluded to. Let us now consider further some of the processes that seem to be crucial for worthwhile human learning. I cannot hope to present here a comprehensive account of current views on the subject. However, I shall try to give an outline of what seem to me to be those aspects of human learning that impinge directly on our consideration of teaching.

First let us consider those features of learning that seem to be universal in animal species, since the basic features of learning in our species resemble those of other animals. However, we should bear in mind that human learning transcends learning in other species in extent and in kind. Very primitive animals depend almost entirely on instinct, rather than learning, for their survival. Even apparently complex activities such as may be observed in some species owe little or nothing to learning. For example, web making in spiders and the dance of bees indicating the direction of the source of pollen are chains of instinctive responses to stimuli from the creatures' environment. As such they are stereotyped and inflexible.

More complex animals such as mammals depend much more on learned behaviour for their much more flexible adaptation to their environment. This adaptation can be observed in the way animals develop new behaviours in response to changes in their environment made by humans. We are familiar with the ability of domestic animals to learn various tasks, such as herding sheep, drawing ploughs and running races. Wild animals also learn to adapt in unusual ways to a human-dominated world. For example, foxes learn to overturn rubbish bins to get at the contents, and tits learn to remove the caps from milk bottles.

This learning, as in most species, is almost entirely dependent upon interaction with the physical world. The activities acquired by the animals just referred to developed in response to the changes made to the material world by human technology. Human learning also responds to changes in the material world, but, also, more than in any other species, changes the material world itself. Those changes in turn demand still further changes in human learning. Human learning is thus the key factor in a cycle of change that crucially affects life on the planet. It would seem reasonable, therefore, for us to devote a fair amount of time and resources to studying human learning, with a view to improving it for the benefit of the planet and life upon it. I do not think that at the moment humankind is taking that study very seriously.

The reason that humans have such a disproportionate influence on the material world is that we also inhabit an immaterial world. This is the world of ideas, theories, ideologies, metaphors, music, poetry and countless other kinds of abstraction. This world of abstractions is unimaginably more complex than the material world, although ultimately derived from our interactions with it. It is the dominant influence in human learning. It is manifested in our use of language, which in turn, influences human learning, as I shall be discussing shortly.

One of the most important influences on learning in all species is what is often referred to as the 'affective' outcomes of specific actions. 'Positive affect' may be thought of as roughly equivalent to pleasant emotions and 'negative affect' as equivalent to unpleasant emotions or pain. With some rather esoteric exceptions, animals, including humans, will take action to avoid negative affect and to increase positive affect. Interactions with the environment that increase the former and reduce the latter are likely to be repeated, and vice versa. Interactions that persist and become part of habitual behaviour are what we refer to as learning.

It is unlikely that new behaviour will persist if its links with positive affect are unperceived. Thus, in general, the two must more or less coincide in time and space for the learning to occur. This contiguity has a further fundamentally important aspect. When a new activity is linked to an existing one, which has led to positive affect in the past, the new activity normally becomes part of the routine activity of the individual. Whatever gives rise to the positive affect is usually referred to as a 'reinforcer'. The term 'reinforcement' is used to refer to the process of action followed by a reinforcer. (See Chapter 10 for further discussion of this construct.)

The important thing about these linkages is that they are fluid, unlike instinctive reactions, which are rigid and unchanging. Learned activity can wax and wane as it is seen by the individual to be useful or not useful. Actions can become more elaborate or more refined.

Different linkages among activities may be made and develop. Thus behaviour becomes more complex and versatile as a result of learning. Pavlov (1941, 1955) referred to simple learned behaviour as 'conditional responses', 'conditional' because they are provisional, in the sense that they can be acquired and discarded according to the needs of the individual.

For learners to come to a decision as to whether a particular action is useful or not useful, they need information about its effect. Information of this type is usually referred to as 'feedback'. An example of feedback in human learning is observing the discrepancy between one's aim at a target and the location of the actual hit. The observation enables one to adjust one's aim so as to reduce the discrepancy between aim and achievement. If one were unable to see the results of one's attempt to hit the target this adjustment would be impossible. The same can be said about all kinds of learning and indeed, most continuing activity, including learning to teach and teaching itself. Only the most unprofessional and disenchanted teachers would be totally uninterested in the outcome of their teaching on their pupils. Most teachers will take note of their pupils' reaction to their teaching and adjust their approach to improve their 'aim'; this is a topic we shall be considering in the next chapter.

Feedback and reinforcement are frequently confused, but they are not the same. Reinforcement is an event that increases the probability that an activity will be repeated, without necessarily being logically connected to it. Thus domestic animals or animals used in experiments may learn behaviour essentially at the whim of the trainer or the experimenter. There is no logical connection between a dog's sitting when hearing the word 'sit' and the appearance of a reward or reinforcer. Nevertheless the animal does sit when it hears the sound because of regular past connections between the action and the reward. This is the functioning of positive affect.

Undoubtedly some school learning is of this type. Children blindly do this or that because teacher approves and not because they see a causal or logical connection between their action and the appearance of a reinforcer. Sometimes when this kind of learning takes place, the teacher is under the impression that the pupils have seen the connection between their actions and the results of the actions, whereas, in reality, they have not. This kind of mistake is likely to take place when the teacher's analysis of the nature of the learning task is faulty. However, teachers can help themselves to avoid this error by building into their teaching some form of information-producing device that will give them feedback about the results of their own actions. They will thus increase their chances of getting clear evidence whether or not their pupils have seen the vital connections.

Human learning is pre-eminently concerned with seeing logical connections between phenomena. We are almost certainly the only terrestrial species that can have ideas about 'causality', as well as being affected by it. The more accurate our ideas about causality are, the less we are its victims. It thus behoves teachers to do all they can to equip their pupils more accurately to discern logical connections between their actions and the outcomes of their actions.

The very ideas of 'causality' and 'logic' assume the process of abstraction referred to earlier. Abstraction is a little-understood aspect of brain function. By its agency humans classify their physical environment so that they are able to respond to the general idea of things as well as to their physical manifestation. For example, we can think and talk about trees, foxes, stars, spoons and an infinite number of other things, even when they are out of range of our physical senses. In fact, of course, these abstractions, more or less by definition, are extra-sensory; that is, they are not perceptible by our physical senses. 'Instances', or 'exemplars' are perceptible to one or more of our senses, so that we are able to see, hear, touch, smell and, in some cases, even taste, physically existing individual trees, foxes and spoons. Sight, for most of us, is the dominant sense, and we are able to see examples of all the things I mentioned. The other senses, however, are also important. Our idea of stars, depending as it does entirely on vision from an enormous distance, can be only rudimentary, as compared with our idea of trees.

Indeed, we are able to acquire abstractions of this type only through physically experiencing specific examples of the real, materially existing 'things'. The 'real things' are normally referred to as 'exemplars' of the abstractions. The abstractions themselves are referred to as 'concepts'. Concepts such as 'spoon', 'stars', 'trees' are relatively simple, since they refer to classes of concrete objects. Other concepts refer to more complicated things such as abstract qualities and relationships among phenomena. My earlier comments on 'causality' and 'logic' refer to this type of concept.

Concepts of this type, despite their complexity, seem to obey the same laws in human learning as the simpler ones. Although they may have no actual physical existence themselves, we learn them through experiencing them by observing exemplifications of the concepts in some way through our senses. If we can't experience a phenomenon we have great difficulty in imagining it. For example, one cannot experience one's own death; and thus our concept of our own death is, so to speak, second-hand from the concept of death we have obtained by observing the death of others, human and non-human. To turn to more congenial abstractions, we acquire the concept of horses galloping by seeing, hearing, and, if we are horse riders, feeling the actual act of what we refer to as 'galloping'. Many urban children, however, will get the idea of galloping entirely from looking at pictures and watching TV. Their concepts will be very different from those of a professional jockey, all of whose senses will be involved in his learning the idea of galloping. However, the basic core of the concept, a particular type of rapid movement normally associated with horses, is accessible to both, so that a jockey could talk to an urban child about galloping.

EXPERIENCE, ABSTRACTION, CONCEPTS

The jockey example raises several fundamental questions about human learning that relate to teaching. The disparity between the jockey's concept of galloping and that of an urban child reflects their different life experiences. By the same token, the different life experiences of teachers, as mature and more experienced persons than their pupils, will inevitably lead to disparity between teachers' concepts and those of their pupils. Were a jockey to talk to the child about galloping in the same way jockeys talk to each other, there is little doubt that the level of the child's comprehension would be low. The same can be said about teachers' discourse with children; an important fact that is often overlooked.

The fact that we all have widely different life experiences implies that our concepts must also differ in some way. Edward Sapir, a linguist, puts it like this: 'Experience lodges in an individual consciousness and is, strictly speaking, incommunicable' (Sapir 1963). The fact that human communication is flawed in this way is not just a tragic philosophical fact to be lamented by dramatists and poets, but a pedagogical truth of singular importance. Any teacher who forgets this truth will fail to enable pupils to learn concepts.

Although the brain activity related to abstraction is obscure, we have some understanding about the conditions that facilitate it. If one never encounters exemplars of a concept there is no basis for abstraction. Thus, to continue the example of galloping, children who had never seen or heard horses or other similar animals galloping, either in real life or in some representative form as in TV or film, could never acquire the concept. Any attempt to explain galloping to those children could give only a vague idea of the process, and that idea would itself be dependent on their having learned the concepts used in the explanation.

It is true that a child lacking the experience might make some sense out of a dictionary definition, for example: 'gallop (of a horse or other quadruped) to run fast with a two-beat stride in which all four legs are off the ground at the same time'. However, unless the child had already had experiences relating to the abstractions used in the definition – for example, 'quadruped', 'two-beat' and 'stride' – learning might well involve very little abstraction. Instead of the concept of 'galloping' being learned, all that would happen would be the learning of a word that symbolises it.

Dictionary definitions present teachers with interesting and important questions. The definition we have just considered is an example of what was earlier referred to as the 'core' of a concept. The core of a concept is developed by usage in a given speech community so that its members can actually converse with each other. It is the irreducible minimum of elements necessary for mutual comprehension. In learning theory the elements constituting this core are referred to as the 'criterial attributes' of the concept. All exemplars of the concept must include this basic core, its 'criterial attributes'. The child and the jockey could speak to each other because the child had acquired the criterial attributes of galloping (horses running fast) through watching TV and films. But for the jockey, there is more to galloping than the horse's running fast, as I have already suggested. These additional elements, the sights, sounds, smells and other sensations, complicate and enrich the jockey's concept of galloping. However, for most people within a given speech community, this richness is not essential for basic communication. Everything apart from the idea of running quickly with a particular action can be dispensed with.

All elements other than the basic core of concepts, the criterial attributes, are referred to, not surprisingly, as 'non-criterial attributes'. The interesting and important questions then are: 'How can we ensure that pupils acquire the criterial attributes of concepts and avoid rote learning?' and 'What should our attitude be towards non-criterial attributes?' Should we be content when pupils have acquired the essential core of the concept? Or should we do all we can to build on it so that the personal concepts of children, while all including the common core of criterial attributes agreed by their speech community, also embody a variety of other, non-criterial, attributes derived from a wide experience of exemplars of the concept in many different contexts?

I believe most people would share my view that the richer an individual's concepts are, the better. However, since that richness depends upon experience, realism dictates that teachers will have to decide how best to allocate the time available in the teaching of concepts. The decisions arrived at will depend upon current attitudes in the educational system about curriculum matters and ideology. The greatest pedagogical problems will arise when insufficient time is allocated to provide the basic experience essential for the learners to learn the criterial attributes of the concepts they are intended to learn. When this happens, rote learning will ensue.

Some politicians and administrators who have power over schooling think there is nothing wrong with rote learning and will not see a problem. I have never seen the point made, but one additional, and possibly unconscious, attraction of rote learning for such people is that it is far cheaper than providing the resources necessary for true learning. Anyone engaged in teaching, in my view, should reject views of this type and press for learning that at least embodies the criterial attributes of the concepts to be learned. I enter a caveat here. Some very simple learning can only be rote. Where there are no logical connections among things, there can be no criterial attributes and therefore no concepts. Examples of this type are learning the alphabet and vocabulary in foreign language learning. I shall consider other situations in which rote learning might be appropriate in later discussion.

In the main, however, my approach will be to try to avoid rote learning and to foster meaningful learning. Current views about how this might be done relate to the way in which learners encounter exemplars and non-exemplars of concepts. A non-exemplar is a phenomenon that does not possess the criterial attributes of the concept; a stationary horse or a horse walking is a non-exemplar of galloping. A knife is a non-exemplar of a spoon. The first obvious point in concept learning, therefore, is that learners must encounter positive exemplars.

LANGUAGE AND LEARNING

In everyday life we might well encounter novel positive exemplars of concepts more or less randomly. Such exemplars could range from concrete objects to abstract ideas. Obviously, young children are likely to encounter many such novel concepts, in view of their limited experience. Infants, in fact, start from scratch. They react to things not as exemplars of concepts but as particular concrete objects. A very young child may respond to a feeding bottle or a cup because it has been accompanied in the past by drink. It would not respond in the same way to a cup or bottle of a different shape or colour, because its response is to the physical properties of the container. It only gradually learns to respond to the idea of 'cup' in general, in part because it has encountered a variety of cups in connection with the presentation of drink. When this stage is reached a child will respond in much the same way, and no matter from which angle it is looking at them, to cups of different shape, size, or colour. The child now responds to the abstract notion of 'cup' and accepts objects that are physically dissimilar as members of one category. It has learned the concept of 'cup'.

This is a much simplified view of the process of concept learning. It does not refer to the most important element in human learning: the role of language. In the case of the child learning the concept of 'cup', an adult introduces an invariant into situations that are in other respects quite different. The invariant in English-speaking communities is the word 'cup'. Thus when an adult says 'cup' while holding one for a child to drink, he or she introduces into the learning situation what amounts to an extra criterial attribute: the word naming the concept.

This role of the words that name concepts is frequently unappreciated. Many people think of the names of things as labels affixed to ideas, as though we all agree to call an already existing class of things 'cups'. This is a fundamental misconception. In fact the names of things are the most important elements in our learning of the concepts. They are crucial to the process of abstraction that enables us to see dissimilar objects as belonging to the same class.

Part of the power of language in early learning in hearing children is that it uses sound. Vision, touch and taste are all fundamental to early concept formation, but all have their limitations as criterial attributes. For example, although sight may be the dominant sense in our interaction with the physical world, strong colour differences between two things of the same class may prove so overwhelming perceptually that a learner may have difficulty in accepting that they are, indeed, in the same category. A brilliantly red cup may be responded to differently from a blue one. Colour has a particularly potent effect on the way young children see their world. Other things such as shape, texture and size commonly assume more importance according to children's experiences and the teaching they get. All these perceptions of the material world at times present problems in concept learning. The apparent shape and size of an object will vary according to its orientation: a cup seen from the top looks different from one seen from the side or upside down, but it is still a cup. It cannot be felt unless it is within reach.

The sound that stands for, that is, symbolises, the concept, however, does not change except insofar as the speaker's accent or intonation varies. The sound (i.e. the word) can also be perceived from all angles and even in the dark. Since it is always present and easily perceived (when other attributes may be difficult to distinguish), the sound signals to the learner that the object is a member of a particular class.

I have used the word 'symbolise' in connection with the use of words to stand for concepts. A symbol is something that stands, by convention, for something else. There need be no logical connection between the two things. Sounds used as symbols, i.e. words, tend to be linked quite arbitrarily with the concepts they represent. This is attested by the variety of words used in different languages for one concept. This arbitrariness is, in itself, important. If the linkage of symbol to concept were not arbitrary the symbol would have some logical connection with the thing it symbolised. Few words have such a logical connection. The main category of such words is formed by onomatopoeia, in which the logical connection is between the name of an object or action and a sound that seems to suggest its qualities. 'Cuckoo', 'babble', 'zip' and 'croak' are examples of such words. Were all words to have such links with the things they symbolised, language as we know it would be clearly impossible. Arbitrariness, which allows us to use any sound to symbolise a concept, gives language an enormous flexibility. Since language is a complex set of symbols of concepts (crudely, ideas), it enables human beings to learn to manipulate the abstractions language symbolises in the activity we refer to as 'thinking'. This is not to say that once learning has taken place we need to 'talk to ourselves' internally in order to think.

It is probably useful to make the point here that it is the *symbolic function* of spoken language that is crucial, not the fact that it makes use of sound. Sound is more important than the other senses in this context because it happens to be the most flexible medium for humans to communicate symbols to each other. However, vision and touch can also serve as channels of communication, as in normal reading, in sign language used by deaf people and in the use of Braille. Any medium that can be used in symbolling has the potential for use as a language and thus to enable humans to form abstractions and to think.

In learning concepts, therefore, words constitute criterial attributes of a totally different kind from the physical properties that constitute the criterial attributes of simple concepts such as that symbolised by the word 'cup'. In the case of more complex concepts, such as those symbolised by the words 'energy' or 'honour', there may be few or no concrete attributes. The criterial attributes may be other concepts. 'Honour', in one sense, for example, has a dictionary definition of 'personal integrity'. The two words symbolise the criterial attributes of 'honour'. Any discussion of human characteristics that touches on the integrity of an individual will be discussing 'honour'. If one of these qualities is missing, the discussion is not concerned with 'honour'.

This example attempts to illustrate the way in which concepts and the words that symbolise them make possible discourse among humans entirely in abstract terms. Teaching often takes the form of one-way discourse using abstractions, and this is often referred to as 'explaining'. A moment's thought about the example of 'honour' will indicate the dangers inherent in this kind of teaching. Anyone who had not learned what 'individual' and 'integrity' were would not be able to discuss 'honour'. By the same token, a person learning about 'honour' would be unable to follow a talk that used the two words and would make no progress until the criterial attributes had been learned.

The same logic can be applied to the learning of the criterial attributes of 'honour'. The learning of their defining attributes will depend upon the learner's prior experience. 'Integrity', in one dictionary, is defined as 'adherence to moral principles; honesty'. While we should not take it for granted that dictionary definitions will always include the criterial attributes of the concepts they purport to define, there is little doubt that no-one is likely to learn the concept without the prior learning of the concepts proposed by the definition. And so on. As we pursue the analysis we approach ever more closely the world of concrete experiences.

The message for teachers here is that, in the last analysis, learning depends upon experience of the material world. This is not to say that all new learning depends on direct interaction with the material world. Provided that the criterial attributes of new concepts are concepts that are familiar and well understood by the learner, it is possible to use this existing knowledge to build new abstractions. However, without the foundation in the familiar, the new learning is likely to be rote rather than meaningful.

Much of the material world is inaccessible to us. My earlier reference to the limited nature of our concept of 'star' illustrates this point. Nevertheless, adults normally do acquire a concept of 'star' as one dictionary definition puts it: 'one of a vast number of celestial objects visible in the clear night sky as points of light'. This learning is abstracted from many experiences of looking at the night sky. The exact nature of the concept will depend upon the individual experiences accompanying our looking, for example whether we live in the country or the town, whether we are interested in astronomy and know something about the constellations, and whether we know the difference between planets and stars. With deeper and more extensive experience our concept of 'star' might be such that it embraces the attributes set out in another dictionary definition: 'A hot gaseous mass, such as the sun, that radiates energy esp. as heat and light, usually derived from thermonuclear reactions in the interior, and in some cases as radio waves and x-rays. The surface temperature can range from about 1500 to 100,000 degrees Celsius'.

While all readers may have a rudimentary grasp of the concepts constituting this definition, the way specialists in nuclear physics conceptualise 'star' will be more complex because of their more extensive experience of thermonuclear reactions. Astronomers' concepts of 'star' will be different again because of their own specialist experience. Thus three groups of people using the same word, 'star', are likely to have very different ideas about it because all have had different types of experience. The same applies to relationships within teaching groups. The concepts learners have formed in relation to the words they use will differ according to their individual experiences; all are likely to differ more pronouncedly from those of the teacher. Teachers will need to bear both these important points in mind if they are to establish their teaching on firm foundations.

Two important aspects of pedagogy arise from the need to establish a firm base for learning. One is the need to ascertain that learners have previously acquired the subordinate concepts essential for new learning. The other point is that once it is clear that the learners have acquired the subordinate concepts, the teacher can build on those concepts to expand the learners' understanding without their having additional direct sensory experience. This can be done through the use of language. The teacher reminds the learners of the nature of the existing concepts and draws attention to their relationships with the new learning. It should be noted that new concepts may well include not only previously unencountered concrete phenomena but also unfamiliar abstractions and relationships.

Successful learning follows from the integration of the new with the existing concepts in a more complex and inclusive way of thinking. In our current knowledge of human cognitive processes a useful way of visualising learning is in terms of a movement towards increasingly inclusive abstractions. These abstractions derive ultimately from direct sensory experience. New learning involves the restructuring of existing thought processes, not just the piling up of new ideas. Learners demonstrate that they have successfully integrated their new with their previously learned concepts into new, more complex cognitive structures by applying the new learning successfully in ways they could not have done previously.

More complex and abstract concepts are sometimes referred to by researchers in the field as 'schemas' and the relationships among concepts as 'schematic systems' (Tennyson and Cocchiarella 1986). However, provided we bear in mind the integrated nature of complex cognitive structures, it is unnecessary to do anything more than note the use of the terms.

LANGUAGE, THINKING AND CULTURAL ACCRETION

Language is the most complex aspect of our environment, since in normal life we are responding continuously to the abstractions it represents. Some of those abstractions derive from the the accreted learning of past generations. This accreted learning is infused with the values, myths and philosophies of countless cultures. The physical environment itself embodies this accreted learning in an enormous variety of artifacts which necessitate the species' continuous learning of new skills and concepts.

However, whatever new skills and concepts appear or disappear because they are no longer relevant, the skill of inducting the young into human society will persist as long as the species survives. With such a complex organism, this is not a task to take lightly.

The great paradox in teaching is that although language is the instrument that creates the great complexity of human learning and human culture, and, indeed, is the great facilitator in learning and teaching abstractions, it can be the greatest obstacle to such learning and teaching. Teachers who stand and deliver the curriculum are in great danger of mouthing a succession of symbols that amount to nothing more than modulated puffs of air, so far as the students are concerned. The challenge facing teachers and teacher educators is how to structure learners' environments so that they will learn the concepts symbolised by the words, spoken or printed, even if the words are at any one time unsupported by other experience.

Although I have suggested that the psychology of pedagogy is at a primitive stage, I consider that there is information about how people learn that can be used to advantage by teachers. There is a body of empirically-based knowledge about concept learning, problem-solving and the learning of physical skills which is of potentially great importance in teaching. What is lacking is systematic attempts to relate practical teaching to this body of knowledge. The same could be said about information relating to the affective side of learning. The effects of punishment and encouragement on learning, on motivation and on classroom behaviour are little understood by teachers, and yet they can influence student learning most profoundly.

What is sorely needed, however, is much more work that relates this knowledge to practical teaching – not to 'apply' it in a positivistic one-way process, but to use the theory to guide the practice and to use the practice to refine the theory. As I suggested earlier, this approach is a mutually refining dialectic that is truly open ended. Such a process is essential since every teaching-learning encounter differs from all other such encounters in very complex ways. Teachers and teacher educators attempting to implement such an approach in their teaching could reasonably be conceived of as researchers investigating, even if in small ways, the efficacy of particular exemplifications of a pedagogy of more general significance. The cumulation and evaluation of records of teaching encounters of this type could contribute to our understanding of teaching in general (Stones 1986a).

THEORY AND PRACTICE IN QUALITY TEACHING

In my earlier discussions of human learning and thinking and of teachers as inquirers, I projected a view of teachers as very different people from the stereotypical deliverers of the curriculum or dispensers of facts. I depicted them as active explorers and problem solvers. I suggested that their attempts to solve their pedagogical problems could add to our own knowledge about teaching. I am proposing, that is, a view of teaching as potentially a form of action research in a similar tradition to that described by Liston and Zeichner (1990) in their work with students at the University of Wisconsin. Teachers working in this way are fulfilling the dual function of teacher and researcher.

Unlike some researchers I do not think the roles are intrinsically incompatible. However, I accept that current approaches to teacher training and teacher development are unlikely to equip teachers for such a role. This takes me back to the points made earlier about teacher inquirers and their need for a grasp of theoretical principles about human learning. However, given this grounding in theoretical principles, the basis exists for what I have referred to as *systemic research* (Stones 1986a).

Systemic research is research that is part of a pedagogical system. It is not dependent on outside funding, nor does it have to conform to guidelines set by external agencies. Since it is part and parcel of a teacher's professional activity, its duration can be the length of a teacher's professional life.

I am aware of the formidable problems of putting such work into operation. It demands a considerable shift in the way teacher training is conceived at both pre-service and in-service stages. Apart from institutional inertia, there are also many logistical and political problems. Perhaps the most difficult of these are conceptual and pedagogical. Teacher training courses the world over sell student teachers short on the systematic pedagogical knowledge they provide, and their alumni are not equipped to engage in the inquiry I advocate.

The problems, however, are not insuperable. Perhaps the most promising way forward currently is through in-service teacher development courses, but pre-service work is possible given institutional acceptance, as subsequent discussion will show.

How, then, shall we approach the question of theory and practice in teaching in relation to the subject of this book? Since it is my wish to integrate the two as far as I possibly can, I shall try to explain what seem to me some of the key questions in pedagogical theory, and at the same time to analyse examples of actual teaching by a variety of teachers in a variety of subjects, endeavouring to make use of pedagogical principles.

Thus the examination of actual teaching encounters is in the context of the discussion of principles of human learning and is intended to help readers to acquire insights into how they themselves might be able to explore the relevance of the principles in their own teaching. But it does not reject teachers' experience; and I hope the fact that the examples given are drawn from various subjects and age ranges will be of particular help.

The work I shall describe is a practical manifestation of approaches to the exploration of teaching and teacher education being called for by many researchers and writers in the field. It reports investigations by teachers into teaching over many years. Among its most salient aspects are the following:

- The reported investigations comprise accounts of teaching by student teachers and experienced teachers of topics in their fields of interest and within the existing curriculum of the schools they were working in.
- Within the operating structure of the investigations was a course of training for experienced teachers (Masters and Ph. D. candidates) in the supervision of student teaching or in collegial staff development.

This arrangement made possible the pairing of student teachers with non-judgmental mentors, which seems, in the words of Clark (1988), 'to breathe new life into their teaching'.

- The minimum length of time spent on the project by the student teachers was one academic year; for the experienced teachers the time was longer and sometimes several years. The cases reported in this book are samples of the work done by both groups of teachers.

- Teaching was taken to include the preactive, interactive and postactive phases. Its overall aim was to teach meaningful concepts and to foster problem-solving ability in the pupils.

- The preactive phase included a search of the literature for information on the pedagogy of the subjects being taught, the analyses of teaching objectives and pedagogical analysis. Pedagogical analysis included conceptual analyses of the content to be taught in order to identify the key concepts and principles. It also included analyses to identify the key pedagogical actions to be taken to enable pupils to learn those concepts and principles.

- The interactive phase of teaching was routinely video-recorded by unattended cameras providing views of the teacher and the class using split screen techniques. The cameras were unattended once they had been set up in order to avoid undue distortion of what was being recorded into a 'production' by aspirant professional producers or camera operators.

- The postactive phase routinely involved group reflection using the video recordings made by student teachers and experienced teachers. Typical group size for this purpose was around fifteen. The group reflection often assumed the form of mutual counselling. This phase also included the writing by each teacher of an account of a criterion piece of teaching in the form of a journal article reporting a piece of research. The extent of this criterion teaching varied from one lesson with student teachers to several weeks or months work with the experienced teachers. This work was facilitated by having an account on videotape available for viewing and re-viewing, but a written record was also employed. The criterion teaching chosen by the teachers for appraisal was assessed formally as a major element in their course requirements.

- A crucial element in all the work was the possession of a common realm of discourse. Empty jargon, however, would have been useless; the teachers needed the intellectual tools to analyse, plan, execute and evaluate teaching, the aim of which was to help pupils to learn meaningfully and with enjoyment. Since the main studies into human learning and instruction have been in the field of psychology, this was the field from which the main pedagogical constructs were drawn – not, as I have mentioned before, to attempt to *apply* them, but to *test* them in practice (Stones 1986a). This is where the experienced teacher's craft knowledge interacted with a body of systematised theory and where the student teachers' concepts of teaching as merely 'telling' were first challenged.

- The above activities helped to ensure that despite the work being located in the case study/action research paradigm, it would avoid the problem of being 'methodogically radical, but . . . bereft of theoretical rigour and reflection' (Hartley 1990).
- All the pre-service students also took courses with subject specialists and in other fields of educational studies.

Readers will recognise from the above many of the proposals for work in the field of pedagogy, teaching and teacher education currently to be found in the literature (for example: Clark 1988, Cochran-Smith and Lytle 1990). The studies reported here were totally integrated with courses in a university with responsibility for teaching and research in teaching and teacher training. They provided a corpus of investigations that served as the basis for parallel and sequential replications. The work of the student teachers was part of their teaching practice experience during their one year's teacher training course. The work of the trainee M. Ed. supervisors of student teachers was part of their assessed work for the degree.

The theoretical base of the investigations is principles of learning that seem of general utility in teaching. The specific investigations explore the way in which those principles work out in actual teaching. The reflection of teachers and researchers on the process and outcomes of the investigations adds to the research base developmentally and incrementally. The fact that teachers engaging in this form of exploration teach different subjects leads to variety in subject content of the explorations. This variety is a great strength of the approach. It ensures not only the teachers' personal commitment to the investigations but also the variation of the non-criterial attributes of the pedagogy, which is essential for testing the validity of the underlying theoretical principles in educational settings.

The sample of cases that I discuss later address, I believe, the concerns of many researchers, for example Cochran-Smith and Lytle (1990), that teachers are virtually invisible in most reports of research and that their voices are seldom heard. While it is true that the account of the work in this book and the glosses on it are being written by an academic, it is the teachers' work that is being described, and frequently their own voices are heard through direct quotation.

The spread of subjects studied is important for identifying generalisable findings. An attempt is made to evaluate the perceived pedagogical utility of the individual studies and identify general trends. As I suggested earlier, the studies I referred to are based on general principles of learning and, therefore, embrace two main elements, the principles themselves which are common to all studies, and the subject-specific concepts and skills that are unique to the individual studies.

A method of conceptualising the appproach used here is comparable to that of the study of law. The comparable features of individual cases can be systematised into research convention and, as in law, can be cumulative and move to ever more precise definition of cases. Descriptive case-study data cumulates into substantive theory (Tripp 1985). Thus we adopt a number of steps:

1 collect a number of cases of principles in action,
2 discern patterns and regularities that form the basis for generalisation,
3 relate the theories to what is already known about society, teaching, pedagogy and psychology,
4 the nexus of theory then informs our understanding of educational situations, so that unique studies contribute to a general understanding of teaching.

In all these steps analytical rigour must be brought to bear in the examination of the data.

THE STRUCTURE OF THE BOOK

The salient features of the work I report are as follows. Each chapter deals with a particular aspect of teaching and learning. From Chapter 2 onwards I report on and analyse a number of case studies of teaching by experienced and beginning teachers. All the examples are of real teaching, mostly within actual curricula. The teachers were not specially chosen but differed from most teachers in that they were to some extent familiar with the principles of psychopedagogy through their work in the university and were involved in using them in connection with the practical teaching reported in the case studies. Some of the studies report one lesson, some a series of lessons. Some are done by student teachers, some by experienced and senior teachers of many years' standing. A few are in tertiary education, teaching more mature students. The ages of pupils range from five to eighteen in primary and secondary schools, and there are also adult students.

The teaching groups ranged from individual tutoring to normal classroom work. Most the work was done in small groups of six to ten. Smaller groups are necessary for explorations into the relationships between pedagogical theory and practice. In larger groups it is very difficult, if not impossible, to get the fine focus on the pedagogical processes taking place and to identify the nature of any problems that arise. Statistical analysis of many hundreds of teaching experiments (meta-analysis) suggests that working with groups larger than twenty changes the nature of the teacher-class interaction so that teacher effects fall away (Glass and Smith 1978 and 1979). The education of the privileged everywhere has always assumed this and made provision of individual instruction or very small groups its hallmark.

It is possible to draw one of two main conclusions from the comparison between clinical and large group teaching. One is that clinical teaching is not relevant to 'real' teaching. The other is that clinical teaching reveals processes involved in teaching and learning that could lead to improvement in 'normal' teaching practices. I believe, however, that one of the key points to emerge from studies of clinical teaching is the complex nature of human learning and teaching. The lesson I am increasingly drawing from these studies is that 'normal' teaching in large groups is not really teaching at all. Studies of animal learning (the results of which have sometimes been unjustifiably applied to human learning) rarely involve large groups. I have never heard of an investigation of animal learning that used groups of forty rats or apes. Skinner produced generalisations about animal learning through many studies of individual rats. Pavlov did the same for dogs and apes (Pavlov 1941, Skinner 1962). When it comes to the study of human learning, the main approach for many years was based on one used in agriculture, in which plots of one crop are compared with others. Instead of studying individuals, we study hundreds or thousands using agro-botanical techniques. Pavlov and Skinner manipulated learning conditions in a clinical way; our techniques have normally been global and non-analytical. The trend to more clinical work in pedagogy is to my mind, an encouraging trend, and I see no reason why useful generalisable findings should not result.

However, the important thing is that the experience of working with a systematic and analytical theory and practice equips teachers with a knowledge of general pedagogical principles capable of being deployed in a variety of circumstances. Faced with very large classes, they would still know how they should ideally proceed. Just how they would arrange things to maximise their impact on events would be a matter of individual judgment based on their experience.

The studies reported in this book include a number of subjects taught in most schools in the English-speaking world. They were selected not for their experimental potential but because they entailed real teaching problems and were the subjects the teachers were actually grappling with. They are not all 'core' subjects in the British National Curriculum, but this is immaterial. The core of the work is the investigation of pedagogy and all the teachers were drawing on a common body of principles. The different topics they addressed provided essential variants in the investigations. The more heterogeneous the range of subjects, the more information the investigations will yield and the more robust will be the findings.

Not all the the accounts of teaching in this book are success stories. They are real-life accounts recorded in detail of actual lessons. The important thing about them is that they provide cases of teachers grappling with problems of teaching meaningfully and inspirationally and with insight into their efforts. They are not to be held up as models of good practice but should be regarded as material to examine and analyse as the teachers themselves did. This is a process I shall consider in detail later when examining the use of protocols in teaching and learning to teach.

Another point should be made in connection with the work reported here. It is what might be referred to as the 'Nothing new' or 'We're doing it already' syndrome. A teacher might make such a comment after simply noting that practice is integrated with theory. The mismatch between what such a teacher might understand by 'theory' and the notions promulgated in the book, are, however, likely to be very different indeed. The same can be said about other aspects of the work that resemble conventional teaching. It is necessary to look closer at the pedagogy involved before coming to the conclusion that there is nothing different.

Such a conclusion may be inspired by teachers' observing, in some of the case studies, methods and approaches with which they are familiar from their own experience. To conclude that therefore there is nothing new in what is being advocated would be to misunderstand an essential feature of it. The work of all the teachers described is a fusion of basic pedagogical theory, the teachers' knowledge of the field of study and the methods of working they have developed in the course of their previous teaching. Clearly, many of the latter techniques will be common practice in schools and will feature in the teachers' reports of their teaching, but the techniques are not the essential factor. The underlying theoretical principles are.

One final point that bears on my last remarks needs to be stressed. Learning of the kind I am advocating cannot be taught entirely by exposition, either oral or printed. I am under no illusions, therefore, about the effectiveness of lectures or books to teach a complex skill such as teaching. Mindful of this limitation in the use of books to influence learning, I shall, in subsequent chapters, suggest ways of adding the crucial practical element to our exploration of teaching.

2 Aiming for quality

AIMS AND OBJECTIVES

Few teachers are likely to enter their classrooms conscious of the awesome nature of the task I proposed in the last chapter. Their eyes will be on more immediate and more 'down-to-earth' issues. I suggest, however, that an informed realisation of their complexity will help them to achieve the tasks of practical teaching. Teachers hoping to help children to learn even the most mundane things must have some idea of what they hope to achieve and how they hope to achieve it. Their aims and aspirations bespeak some view of pedagogical principles. The more extensive their knowledge of principles and practice in a field, the better equipped they will be to identify their aims and the means of achieving them. Thus the knowledge they have gained in their own teaching interacts with other knowledge to enrich both. Undoubtedly some teachers enter classrooms for reasons other than to help children to learn. They will have their own aims which I do not propose to address here.

It is possible to envisage a teacher walking into a classroom without having the faintest idea of what he or she is hoping to achieve. In reality, however, few people are likely to work in this way. Most teachers will have some aim in mind for their teaching, even though it may be vague and unexplicated. Probably the main activity for teachers who see teaching as delivery of the curriculum will be deciding on the sequence in which information is to be presented. Methods of highlighting specific sections by methods of presentation may be considered. The old teaching adage may also be invoked: 'First I tell 'em what I'm going to tell 'em. Then I tell 'em. Then I tell 'em what I've told 'em.' Even methods that involve more complex teacher activity, such as role play or project activity by younger children, may still boil down to little more than complicated ways of telling.

There is ample evidence from research studies to indicate that teachers do plan their lessons (Clark 1988). There is less available information as to the degree or type of assistance in planning provided by training institutions for their students. The research seems to suggest, however, that little help of a systematic nature is provided. The focus in the planning reported seems largely to be on the subject matter, with preparation ranging from notes and *aides-mémoire* to almost complete scripts of what the teacher intends *to tell* the pupils.

Aims do not seem to figure highly in teacher planning. This fact may well be a consequence of taking a view of teaching as verbal exposition. The aims are given in the syllabus. The teacher's job is to deliver. Experienced teachers take a similar approach but take more account of the pupils' needs. Although, two taxonomies of educational objectives have been available for many years (Bloom 1956, Krathwohl *et al.* 1964), and many other texts have devoted substantial attention to objectives, it seems that they have had little impact on practical teaching. It seems likely that similar factors account for this lack of impact as those I discussed earlier in connection with the neglect of educational studies. Reading, or being told, about objectives is unlikely to convince student teachers, who will accept it as something to learn *about* rather than learning to *do* something about. And once the student teachers graduate there is little chance the subject will be encountered again. Their preoccupation will be to 'cover the syllabus', or to 'do' various elements in it: for example, quadratic equations or French irregular verbs or the American Civil War.

Inquirer teachers will have a different approach. They will still be interested in the curriculum topics, but they will think of their aims in terms of what they hope to enable their pupils to do, for example, to identify novel exemplars of a class of plant they have been learning about, or to solve novel equations of the same type as the ones they have been taught, or to plane a piece of wood to a set standard of squareness. Teachers who see their aims as 'covering the syllabus' or 'delivering the curriculum' will, almost inevitably, have their attention focused on the language in which the topics are couched. The subsequent teaching based on aims of this type will most likely attempt to achieve success by concentrating on methods of presenting the information.

By contrast, teachers adopting an approach to teaching based on notions from learning theory will realise that stating syllabus content is insufficient. They will understand that the presentation of a stimulus (teacher talk) to learners is only one of the elements that lead to effective learning. They will also realise that they could be quite misled as to the learners' final competence if the methods of assessing it are as limited as the teaching. This follows from their realisation that language is a double-edged instrument. On the one hand it is the most powerful aid to human learning. On the other hand, if used without insight, it can lead to the non-conceptual learning discussed in the last chapter. They will understand that 'presenting the information' may have practically no effect on the learners if the teacher has no pedagogical understanding. This is why teachers who do have an understanding of pedagogy will express their aims with reference to student activity.

In working with experienced teachers being introduced to a systematic approach to pedagogy I have commonly found a tension between their traditionally felt need to 'cover the syllabus' and the proposed focus on what the *pupils are able to do* as a result of their teaching. Teachers taking the latter approach may sometimes realise that a syllabus is far too ambitious if their aim is for pupils to acquire the competencies set out in the aims of the teaching. The approach to identifying and clarifying aims of teaching discussed here has frequently been found to reveal similar problems even in the teaching of single lessons. I shall consider some examples of this problem shortly.

The teaching flowing from the adoption of aims expressed in terms of learners' competencies must, of necessity, consider factors in human learning in addition to the presentation of the stimuli. I shall discuss these factors in detail later; just now I should like to introduce some examples of teachers', and student teachers', grappling with their teaching aims in different fields of teaching.

An approach to teaching that combines a grasp of learning theory and an analytical approach to teaching aims is essential to the notion of teacher as inquirer and to the unity of theory and practice discussed earlier. This follows from the view of teachers as people with a shrewd idea of where they want to go, a notion of how to get there, and a commitment to checking whether they got where they wanted to go and trying to decide what factors led to their arriving where they did. They are then in a position to examine the discrepancy between their original aims and the final results. With a knowledge of learning theory and practical experience of teaching, they will be in an informed position to take action that will help to remedy deficiencies and improve their teaching. In the process they will be 'proving' in the sense of 'testing', the pedagogical principles by which they were operating. The proof of the theory is in the teaching.

The word 'aims' is normally used for the very general and often less explicitly defined statements of intent in teaching. The more specific and explicated intentions are usually referred to as 'objectives'. The student teacher whose work I now consider was defining his objectives for a piece of teaching intended to introduce to twelve-year-old children the concepts of 'wage' and 'salary'. Here, I will set out his objectives as he did. I will then discuss them and explain and comment on what seem to be their important aspects.

Teacher: economics graduate in a humanities group on a postgraduate teacher training course.
Objectives for teaching the concepts of 'wage' and 'salary' to twelve-year-old pupils.

Affective

To stimulate an interest in, and a liking for economics/commerce as a new subject

Cognitive

Type A1

The pupils will be able to construct an example of a wage and a salary

Type B1

The pupils will be able to distinguish between a wage and a salary

Type B2

The pupils will be able to distinguish between payment for work done and other forms of payment

Type C3

The pupils remember that a wage is calculated hourly and payment is made weekly

Type C3

The pupils will remember that a salary is calculated yearly and paid monthly

It is interesting that this student teacher placed his overall affective objective first. Objectives relating to the way learners feel about their learning are rarely explicitly referred to in conventional statements of aims of teaching. And yet they are probably the most important of all (see Chapter 10). If pupils do not have positive attitudes and emotions towards particular learning situations, even the most careful planning of teaching can come to nothing. The affective objective in the example explicitly states a commitment to teaching so that pupils will enjoy learning. However, note how this objective differs from the others. The affective objective is expressed in terms of the *teacher's* aspirations, whereas the others state what the teacher hopes the *pupils* will be able to *do* at the end of the teaching. The difference is a symptom of a difficulty with affective objectives. It is far more difficult to envisage an end state to teaching that can be interpreted as evidence that the pupils *feel* positively towards it than to evaluate the success in attaining other types of objective.

Methods are available for the measurement of attitudes, and it would be possible to make use of them. The most common are pencil and paper attitude scales. They need careful construction if they are to provide meaningful information, and many 'research' investigations draw doubtful conclusions from the use of unsatisfactory scales. It is an interesting comment on education that while an immense amount of resources and effort has been made to test the cognitive states of pupils to assess their level of achievement or for selection purposes, relatively little effort has gone into ways of establishing their attitudes to specific programmes of teaching. In the case we are considering, the teacher's affective objective would have been more useful if he had expressed it in terms of the kind of pupil activity that would give evidence of its achievement.

It is, of course, impossible to separate affective and cognitive effects. Objectives that involve pupils in active learning with problem solving as an intended outcome are more likely to induce positive attitudes towards the learning than would be the case if the objectives were restricted to passive rote learning. The cognitive objectives of the teacher whose work we are considering certainly go beyond rote learning and augured well for the attainment of his affective objective. The final outcome, naturally, depends on the teaching by which the teacher seeks to achieve his objectives, but it is a promising start.

The categories of the cognitive objectives referred to are a variation on those developed by Stones and Anderson (1972) and Stones (1979, 1984b). Here, type A objectives demand that learners demonstrate *in action* that they have acquired new competence as a result of teaching. Type B require that the learner *recognise* novel exemplars of newly learned concepts. Type C require that learners should be able to recall information verbally. Type C objectives most closely resemble delivery teaching. However, I must stress that, in the case of type C objectives, it is crucial to ensure that concepts and not just words are learned, so that the learning is meaningful. This point is hardly ever considered in syllabuses or textbooks, or by people who refer to teaching as 'delivering the curriculum'. Thus type C objectives, although bottom of the hierarchy in the method of arriving at teaching objectives being discussed here, assume a much more complex approach to pupil learning than is spelled out in most curricula and syllabuses.

In Figure 2.1 I set out the student's objectives in the form of a matrix to illustrate their relationship. Please note that throughout this book the word 'general', when used to qualify 'skills' or 'concepts', implies 'of general application'. That is, the most general skills and concepts are considered to be the most versatile and comprehensive. The subordinate skills are more specific in their application.

The type A1 objective, '[The pupils will be able to] construct an example of a wage and a salary,' asks that the learners *demonstrate in action* that they know what a wage and what a salary are. It is classified A1 since the student teacher considers that it deals with learning related to his declared overall

Figure 2.1 Types of skills (a)

Level of generality of skills and concepts to be learned 1=very general 3=very specific	Type A Doing	Type B Identifying	Type C Remembering
1	Construct an example of a wage and a salary	Distinguish between a wage and a salary	
2		Distinguish between examples of pay for work done and examples of other forms of payment	
3			Remember that a wage is calculated hourly and paid weekly. A salary is calculated yearly and paid monthly
X		This level is given to indicate that there is no reason to regard level 3 as the most specific level. Nor is it necessary to go as far as 3. The number of levels depends on the nature of the objectives and the teacher's judgment.*	

* Added by the author to the student teacher's matrix

After: Stones 1979, 1984a

This student teacher has set out his view of the relationship between different types of skills involved in learning the concepts of 'wage' and 'salary'. At the bottom right-hand corner (cell C3) is the least complex skill. This is the level at which most current teaching is aimed. However, 'remembering' could be quite meaningless to pupils who knew nothing at all about payment for time spent on work, even if they could recite a definition. 'Distinguishing' (cell B2) is a skill that would be impossible for such pupils since it involves deciding from among novel examples which are salaries and which are wages. 'Constructing' (A1) is the most demanding skill of all – one of which even the pupils who could distinguish at level B2 might not be capable.

aim in this piece of teaching. The 'type C3' objectives require the pupils to remember some very specific information. They thus relate to much simpler learning than the A1 objective. In addition, there will almost certainly be several of the lower-level objectives, since generalisable learning is built on a foundation of many specific experiences. Of course, the actual label is not really important. What matters is that the relationship between different levels of generality of objectives be accurately perceived, since decisions about the way the teaching is structured will depend upon it.

The categories A, B and C, that I suggested above, seem to me appropriate to planning teaching but I do not claim they are exhaustive. The student teachers' attempt to construct a pedagogical matrix for his own purposes may provide an example for readers to evaluate the relevance of the categories. The first point to be observed is that the overall skill to be acquired by the pupil is the one in cell A1 of the matrix. In cell B1 one finds the type of skill that is prerequisite to that in cell A1. Similarly, the skill in cell C1 is the type of skill prerequisite to that in B1, that is, remembering the difference between a wage and a salary in the case being considered. Looking down the matrix we see in cell B2 a constituent element of the entry in cell B1. Skill at alerting pupils to the criterial attributes of the two concepts is a prerequisite to being competent in teaching the concepts. Cell C3 is the most specific skill in the matrix and involves the pupils recalling the defining attributes of the concepts. The actual analysis is unlikely to be agreed by all teachers and would benefit from the completion of the empty cells, but the approach provides a sound foundation for the teaching. Just how far one takes the conceptual analysis is a matter of judgment. It is worth bearing in mind, however, that identifying very specific objectives takes one very close to the translation of the objectives into actual teaching. One can, of course, track in any direction to examine the relationship of the various objectives and to identify any gaps. The bottom right-hand objective will be the simplest type of learning related to the most specific concepts or principles. This objective could well provide a point of departure for the teaching to be undertaken. In brief, one could start with cell A1 and work along the rows and columns to make decisions about the subordinate objectives, and one might work from the bottom right-hand cell and work in the opposite direction when making decisions about the planning of teaching.

An example from the teaching of English to a remedial group of twelve-year-olds with learning difficulties makes the point that pupils' ability to provide definitions is no guarantee that they have learned the concepts the teacher has been trying to teach. The student teacher, an English graduate in teacher training, suggests that an objective for the teaching she intends might be set out as: 'The pupils will be able to state the criterial attributes of a compound word'. She goes on to say that there is an implicit aim in this statement, namely that at the end of the teaching 'the pupils will be able to identify some compound words in the course of the lesson'. She therefore proposes as the objective for the lesson: 'At the end of the teaching the pupils will be able to identify compound words'.

This teacher goes on to analyse her objective according to the scheme adopted by the student in Figure 2.1. The point of this step was to guide her thinking about the nature of the teaching that might be appropriate for her objective. Her scheme is presented in Figure 2.2.

Figure 2.2 Types of skills (b)

Level of generality of skills and concepts to be learned 1=very general 3=very specific	Type A Doing	Type B Identifying	Type C Remembering
1	Identify compound words		
2		Distinguish between positive and negative exemplars	
3			Remember the criterial attributes of a compound word

NB There is no reason to regard level 3 as the most specific level. The number of levels depends on the nature of the objectives and the teacher's judgment.

After: Stones 1979, 1984

This apparently simple lesson was part of a scheme of work in the school in which this student teacher worked. It was intended for remedial readers aged twelve years. Whether this topic should be taught as a separate topic is, perhaps, open to question. Recall that the student teacher's objective was that the pupils should *identify* compound words in their reading. On the face of it there seems very little difference between her *A1* and her *B2* skills. Comments on the *C3* skills are much the same a those made in Figure 2.1. It would probably have been more interesting and a more stringent test to have asked the pupils to make their own compound words and to have discussed how many such words come into being in much the same way. This would probably have been a better 'doing' activity that 'identifying'. It would also have cleared up the confusion between her *A1* activity, which is categorized as an 'identifying' action, and her *B* heading, which is also 'identifying'.

This figure, like the previous example, is a specific case of the general approach to classifying objectives. The layout is simple. The general case is seen when one disregards the specific examples and contemplates empty cells. The last section, which would contain the most specific objectives a teacher would identify, should exemplify the very important point, frequently overlooked, that objectives set for one piece of teaching depend on the prior achievement of earlier objectives. The most specific objectives teachers decide upon constitute the borderline between the objectives they have in mind for the current teaching and the assumptions they make about learners' existing competence in the subject.

In the compound words objective, one could analyse the C3 objective to yield more specific ones that relate to reading skills learned earlier, perhaps, for example, remembering what a word is. There is no reason why we should stop at level 3 rather than level 2 or 5. The number of levels depends upon the nature of the objectives and the teaching. Individual teachers' experience and pedagogical understanding will be the deciding factors in making a judgment about the appropriate level of objectives to take as a cut-off point.

A STEAM HAMMER TO CRACK A WALNUT?

Some readers might wonder what all the fuss is about. Why go through these odd activities to teach a simple thing such as compound words? And what's all this about 'criterial attributes' and so forth? The comments of the student teacher planning the teaching of compound words to backward readers may suggest an answer.

> Although the objective states that the pupils should be able to identify compound words, it does not make explicit the subordinate skills which are needed to achieve this. For example, in the achieving of the ability to identify compound words the pupils must have acquired as a prerequisite the skill of reading, also to understand the concept of a compound word they must first understand the concept of 'word'. Yet another subordinate skill is the understanding of the concept of 'joining' if they are to understand the criterial attributes of a 'compound' word, that is; a compound word is made by joining two words together. Of course, it is possible to find other subordinate skills necessary to achieve the stated objective. However, it seems clear that the pupil learning objective is not as simple as at first it might seem and illustrates that the task of identifying compound words is complex in nature.

But the point of clarifying to oneself the objectives of one's teaching is not to induce paralysis when the unsuspected complexity of apparently simple teaching tasks is revealed. The simple matrix in figure 2.2 is a guide to action, a reminder of the things to bear in mind when planning a piece of teaching. It is also useful in monitoring one's teaching. Here is a comment from another student teacher who had been teaching the concept of 'democracy' to fourteen-year-olds.

She had set out her objectives prior to teaching as follows:

1 to be able to describe both orally and in writing the concept of democracy
2 to be able to identify and classify societies in terms of their systems of government
3 to be able to communicate and discuss information and ideas orally
4 to understand how our own form of government is organised and ordered
5 to be able to compare and contrast different forms of government
6 to be able to appraise information

After she had taught the lesson she considered each objective in turn to determine whether or not she had achieved what she set out to achieve. She then made the general comment:

> I have reconsidered my six objectives and realise now that I was too ambitious. Two of the objectives were not directly related to the concept I was teaching and I, therefore, could not hope to achieve them during the lesson. They are ongoing aims which can only be met . . . over a period of time. These were: to be able to communicate and discuss information and ideas orally and to be able to appraise information.
>
> I really only needed three objectives, each one related to the development of the three skills, A, B and C. My objective for the type C skill would be: 'To be able to describe, both orally and in writing, the concept of democracy'. This objective asks only that the pupils be able to recall or remember information.
>
> The second objective, related to the type B skill, would be: 'To be able to identify societies in terms of their system of government.' Here the pupil is asked to analyse and evaluate specific examples of the body of principles related to the concept of democracy.
>
> The third objective, the type A skill, would be to be able to classify societies (by comparing and contrasting them) in terms of their system of government. This would require the pupils to translate and use the information they have in new situations.
>
> My objectives, therefore, needed to be more clearly stated.
>
> My second major criticism of my own teaching is directly related to the above. I aimed only at achieving the type B skill and should have been aiming at a type A skill. I could have achieved this either by asking thought-provoking questions during the teaching, or by using the worksheet. Here I could have listed societies and examples of systems of government the same, similar or different, from our own and asked the pupils to classify the groups, saying how they differ or are the same as a democratic society.

Here we see a teacher using the framework of objectives as an aid to guide her reflection on her own teaching. Naturally, the matrix on its own would not have been sufficient. If she had been ignorant of the way in which concepts and skills are learned, she would have been unable to construct the objectives she did, even though she might have been able to fill the cells on the matrix.

If we also consider the comments of the teacher who was teaching compound words, we can see two teachers focusing their attention on basic pedagogical questions connected with the planning of their teaching. In the course of appraising their teaching after they have taught, they have come to realise that their assumptions about the relationships among the concepts and skills they had hoped to teach were to some degree inaccurate. Without an understanding of those basic pedagogical principles they would have not been able to analyse their teaching in this way, and in any post-mortem would probably have considered matters related to presentation or delivery.

The first teacher realises that she was unclear about the subordinate skills and concepts essential for the satisfactory learning of compound words. The second also realises that she had been unclear and had included in her objectives items that were not directly related to the teaching of the concept of democracy. Both realise that their teaching had been impeded by this lack of clarity. But the most important point to emerge from these examples, is that both teachers, as a direct result of deciding their objectives before teaching, were able to look ahead to future teaching that would remedy the deficiencies they had identified. The second teacher's insight into the fact that her teaching was aimed at level B skills is particularly significant. Although this level of learning is complex and demands that the learners go beyond the simplest level of concept learning, it does not demand that they demonstrate their competence *in their own activity*. She proposes an objective appropriate to that type of learning and suggests ways of achieving it. Her ideas chime with the other teacher's in that they consider the criterial attributes of the concept she is attempting to teach.

The fact that these teachers appraised the objectives they had set for a piece of teaching after they had taught is not idle retrospection. It is also forward looking. Even if the teachers never attempt to teach the same subjects again, they have tested in their own experience some basic and general pedagogical principles that will stand them in good stead in any teaching situation. I hope that this point is demonstrated by the fact that these teachers were planning objectives for the teaching of very different topics.

Getting things clear

Clarity is not achieved easily, as the work of the teachers outlined above demonstrates. Teachers, therefore, need all the help they can get to achieve it in arriving at useful objectives. The teacher whose work I now describe refers in her report to several important aspects of the planning of teaching that are likely to be useful in achieving clarity.

I have already referred briefly to the first point. Syllabuses and prospectuses are often set out in very general and imprecise terms which offer no real guide to teachers as to what is expected. This imprecision may be regarded as a positive feature by teachers looking for room to manoeuvre in planning and executing their lessons. However, it could be a handicap if their pupils have to take examinations or tests set by outside agencies.

This was the problem of the teacher whose work I am discussing. She is a teacher of biological science of many years' experience. Her pupils are aged sixteen–seventeen. She illustrates the nature of syllabuses in her field by an example from a British science-teaching scheme to which she had to work. The aims of the course were as follows: 'To develop an understanding of man as a living organism and his place in nature: as instanced in the usefulness and social implications of biology in relation to man's everyday needs, such as food and public health.' In her view this was not helpful. 'The enormous scope of the subject matter is daunting to say the least. Nor does it make clear how the pupil who has had the benefit of this teaching differs from one who has not. There is a need to formulate such an objective as a precise description of what the teacher hopes the pupil will be able to do at the end of the teaching.'

In order to translate the vague aims expressed in the syllabus the teacher rewrote them in more precise terms. She also expressed them in relation to their level of complexity. Her approach is based more closely on that of Stones and Anderson than earlier examples.

The teacher makes a systematic analysis of these very general objectives along the lines described earlier. Achieving the type A objective depends on the prior achievement of B, which depends in turn on type C. Achieving the level 1 objectives set out in Figure 2.3 depends on subordinate objectives implicit in each of the three objectives suggested.

Figure 2.3 The general aims written in terms of different types of skills.

Type A	Type B	Type C
Construct practical methods of controlling the organisms which compete with man	Make critical appraisals of the methods used by man to control the competitors within his environment	Recall the the nature of the biotic relationships which exist between man and other organisms

This is an excellent example of linking the objectives of a teaching task to the type of skills they imply. The *A* type objective asks that the learners take action that would *in practice* control organisms hostile to man. In practice, in a school setting, this could be realised in methods of weed or pest control. However, in order to be able to achieve that, the pupils would need to be able to evaluate different methods of control. And in order to do that they would need to know about relationships between human and non-human organisms. It is obvious that 'knowing' in this case would have to be more than memorising what had been 'delivered' earlier.

Note that these objectives are at the highest level of generality. Each one could be examined to identify objectives of the same kind but related to more specific actions. For example, a more specific *A* skill would be deciding upon a method of control appropriate for a specific organism.

The teacher illustrates her approach by taking the type B skill and deriving its subordinate objectives. She considers that, among others, it involves identifying a vector-carried disease. She analyses this objective to clarify the teaching task further, as is set out in Figure 2.4.

Figure 2.4 Analysis of sub-skills and subordinate concepts related to the identification of a vector-carried disease.

	Type A	*Type B*	*Type C*
Level 1	Suggest methods of controlling vector-carried disease	Identify a vector-carried disease	Recall the characteristics of a vector-carried disease
Level 2		Identify an infectious disease	Recall the cause of infectious disease
Level 3		Identify a parasitic relationship	Recall the nature of the parasite

This analysis takes the process started in Figure 2.3 a step further towards increased specificity. The teacher is now addressing a specific noxious relationship between human and non-human organisms. In this case the pupils have to recommend ways of tackling a disease in humans carried by other organisms. In order to do that, they would need to be able to do all the things mentioned in the other cells. This analysis is then a guide to the teaching. One could start at the C3 cell and work upwards or horizontally or, possibly, diagonally. Each sub-skill would be essential learning for the ones higher in the analysis. Note, again, that the simplest skill is one that is most common in conventional teaching and the examinations that test it.

The teacher comments: 'This [analysis] illustrates clearly that the same method of analysis can be applied to the aim of a single lesson. The analysis reveals the hierarchical relationships between the subordinate skills and concepts'.

Readers not familiar with the field will probably be interested in another aspect of the analysis. Although the phrase 'Vector-carried disease' may at first be quite mysterious to them, very quickly the analysis provides clues to its meaning. It also indicates that if the analysis were continued it would reveal quite specific skills and concepts that pupils would need to learn for them to be able to achieve the objective stated in cell A1 of the matrix. Thus the analysis further clarifies the aims of the teaching and also provides strong indications of the nature of the teaching needed to achieve the aims.

The teacher involved in the vector-carried disease teaching made a further interesting analysis of objectives. This time she prepared a matrix of objectives related to her own teaching. This is set out in figure 2.5.

Some of the terms in the matrix may be unfamiliar, and we shall be discussing them later, but I think the general idea it exemplifies should be clear. The teacher concerned stresses the value of the analysis as follows:

The establishment of the teaching objectives in this manner enables the teacher to produce a task analysis in which the overall teaching skill is broken down into its dependent sub-skills. The identification of the teaching competency demanded by each of these sub-skills is then clarified. The task analysis becomes a skeletal framework of type

A skills beginning with level 1 and descending through level 2, level 3 and so on. Analysis of this kind makes the teacher aware of the type B and C skills on which she must draw to operationalise her lesson effectively. Additionally it ensures that some measurement is possible so that the quality and effectiveness of the teaching can be determined.

Figure 2.5 Matrix of skills involved in the teaching of the concept of vector-carried disease

	Type A	*Type B*	*Type C*
Level 1	Shows competence in teaching concept of vector-carried disease	Can appraise a protocol of concept teaching in the light of psychopedagogical principles	Recalls the psychopedagogical principles of concept learning
Level 2	Shows competence in drawing pupils' attention to attributes of vector-carried disease	Can appraise a teaching schedule or protocol whose aim is to emphasise the criterial attributes of the vector-carried disease	Recalls the importance of recognising the criterial attributes in concept formation
Level 3	Shows competence in presenting a series of exemplars to illustrate the concept of vector-carried disease	Can appraise critically a series of exemplars constructed to assist concept formation	Recalls the role of exemplars in concept formation

This analysis shows the biology teacher's application of the skills matrix to her own teaching about vector-carried disease. The highest level skill, A1, a 'doing' skill, demands that the teacher teach the relevant concept *competently*. I have discussed the pitfalls in the use of terms such as 'competence' in relation to teaching, and the teacher could have improved the analysis by being specific about the nature of 'competence' in the matrix. In her report and her teaching she makes it clear that teaching competence is a function of pupils' learning concepts and not just remembering words. If one works back from the A1 objective in any direction through the matrix this soon becomes obvious. Her reminders about producing exemplars and about drawing attention to criterial attributes and the use of protocols all bespeak a grasp of the need to go far beyond 'delivery' methods in a search for useful, meaningful learning.

Assessing the effectiveness of teaching is of particular importance. It is a key element in the theme of this book, which aims to offer guidance to teachers wishing to develop skills of self-reflection that go to the pedagogical heart of their teaching and thus lay the foundation for informed self-improvement. In the next chapter I shall discuss the step, to which this teacher referred, that follows logically from the identification and analysis of objectives. However, before doing that I will attempt to summarise the main features of objectives that seem to me to be useful in planning teaching. I will also provide more examples from various types of teaching to illustrate the range of application of the general approach.

THE KEY QUALITIES OF OBJECTIVES

As is the case with all concepts, the qualities of objectives that I take to be 'key' are my own. However, many other writers in the field would subscribe to them, although few explicitly echo my emphasis on the need for them to be related to theory as well as practice. I suggest the following characteristics:

- Teaching objectives should relate to theory and to practice.
- They should be stated in precise terms.
- The most specific objectives should be stated in terms of what the learner should be able to *do* at the end of teaching rather than in statements of syllabus content.
- Objectives should make explicit how the teacher will be able to ascertain that the objectives have been achieved. How does one discriminate between a pupil who has not been taught and one who has been taught?
- Objectives should be amenable to analysis to make explicit the connections between general pedagogical principles and quite specific teaching activities.
- Objectives are commonly classified as cognitive, affective and psychomotor. This classification is to some extent arbitrary and misleading. However, it is probably useful to bear it in mind as a reminder of the different aspects in learning and teaching.

The theory referred to above, of course, is pedagogical theory, not the theory relating to physics or language, or geography or any other field of study. Teaching that takes an approach of this type is not common. And yet it is crucial if teaching is to consist of more than teacher talk or 'explanation'. The biology teacher's analysis of *her own learning objectives* made these concerns particularly explicit.

An example from a different field of study of a similar type of objectives, relates to courses for art teachers. The tutor is planning to teach pedagogy to art teachers. This is the same process as that adopted by the biology teacher who was essentially planning teaching aimed at improving her teaching. Among the objectives this teacher set himself are that the teachers involved should be able to do the following:

1 conduct a small-scale lesson to teach concepts
2 demonstrate A, B and C skills
3 evaluate the outcome of their teaching
4 discuss and evaluate the outcomes of other teachers' teaching

The first two objectives demand a grasp of pedagogical principles; the second two imply such an understanding, although it is true that they could both be theory free. They are not sufficiently explicit. An additional phrase such as 'in the light of theory of concept learning' could have sharpened them.

The objectives set by the art teachers on the course in relation to their pupils' learning illustrate the application of general pedagogical principles to the teaching of a specific subject. The main objective, which is a type A objective, demands that the learner *do* something as a result of teaching. It should be noted that it is an objective that can be achieved consistently only by learners with an understanding of theoretical principles.

> The learner will be able to arrange a complete [colour] tonal scale from the necessary values presented at random.
> From this may be derived the lower order, type B objective.
> The learner will be able to discriminate between exemplars and non-exemplars of a tonal scale
> Which, itself, necessitates the following type C objective.
> The learner will recall that the value of a given tone is perceived in relation to other tonal values.

It is true that a person could achieve the B and C objectives by rote-learning. Objective C could be achieved parrot fashion by a learner who did not know what 'tone' meant, and the same learner could discriminate between two exemplars encountered previously. Teachers need to ensure that learners would not be able to give the impression of having attained the objectives merely by rote-learning. I shall discuss ways of doing this later. For the moment let me suggest that rote learning to achieve the C objective can be guarded against by ensuring that the learner has acquired the concepts of 'tone' and 'value' before the teaching starts. The B objective can be achieved by ensuring that the learner is presented with discriminations not previously encountered.

The next example comes from the work of a teacher teaching mathematics to fourteen–fifteen-year old pupils. His specific task was teaching the use of graphs in the representation of speed. He specifies objectives for three lessons.

1 The pupils will be able to construct a line graph by plotting values of two quantities which relate to one coordinate point on a graph.
2 The pupils will be able to understand the direct relationship of speed with the combination of distance and time.
3 The pupils will be able to construct a graphical line representing a specific speed. The pupils will be able to read from the speed line related values for time in hours and distance in miles, both to notation of two decimal places.

There is a clear progression here that demands of pupils that they demonstrate newly acquired abilities in action. Objective 2 is the least satisfactory. It would have been of much more use had he made explicit how he would establish that the understanding he refers to had been achieved. As it stands it needs interpreting.

Let us now consider another example from the field of mathematics, this time with pupils aged seven years. The teacher is teaching tessellation, that is, the understanding that certain regular plane shapes will fit together without leaving any spaces. The topic was taken from a national project related to the teaching of mathematics to children aged 5–7. The objectives set by the teacher were as follows. Each objective assumes a prefatory clause such as 'After teaching the pupils will be able to . . .':

1 Discriminate between regular and irregular shapes from a given selection.
2 Identify by name a variety of regular plane shapes: triangle, square, rectangle, circle and hexagon.
3 Identify how many edges each of the shapes has.
4 Identify the shapes in a variety of situations.
5 Sort the shapes into sets according to the attribute 'has the same shape as'.
6 Recognise plane shapes found in the environment.
7 Fit together plane shapes of the same type.
8 Fit together a variety of the regular plane shapes which will tessellate.
9 Sort shapes according to the attributes 'have straight edges', 'have curved edges', 'have straight and curved edges' by means of inter-section of sets.
10 Sort shapes according to the attribute 'will tessellate/will not tessellate'.

Here we see another example of a logical progression of teaching objectives framed in terms of pupil activity that will be readily recognisable and not dependent upon interpretation by individual teachers. Whether all teachers would accept the objectives is another matter. The important point is that they are sufficiently precise for people to be able to judge whether they are, in their eyes, suitable objectives for the teaching intended. If the aims had been stated in generalities this would not have been possible.

The following objectives are taken from the work of a teacher aiming to correct reversals in reading. They are both seen as type A objectives.

1 After looking at any graphic symbol for 'b', 'd', 'p' or 'q' the pupil will read the correct aural/oral letter sound and use that skill when new words containing any of these letters are encountered.
2 After hearing the correct oral letter sound the pupil will write the correct letter symbols for words that begin with a 'b', 'd', 'p' or 'q'.

As with most examples of objectives, one might have reservations about the way in which they are couched. I would prefer a less minatory and more tentative tone: perhaps, 'the pupil should be able to'. In the first objective the words 'use that skill' are redundant and misleading. But these are relatively minor points. The important thing is that the objectives pin the teacher down to clearly identified pupil activity that he has to develop.

The teacher identified several subordinate objectives that he considered his pupils must achieve for them to be able to satisfy his overall objectives. Two examples show the relationship between them:

1 Identify pictures and symbols with a right-facing orientation from similar items with different orientations.
2 Identify the initial explosive sound 'b' in a group of four or five words

This teacher also comments on the importance of affective objectives. He agrees with the view that they are more important than cognitive ones and that the two are really inseparable. He goes on to consider ways in which they may be expressed, with particular reference to the taxonomy of affective objectives produced by Krathwol and Bloom (1964). He does not find that approach particularly helpful; however, he does not produce any specific objectives himself. Instead he refers to aspects of work on psychology of motivation that seem to be relevant to classroom conditions.

Pupil feelings to be aimed for would include the knowledge and acceptance of the purpose and objectives of the work; enjoyment of the work; satisfaction in a job well done and a positive self image in relation to the work. The Krathwohl and Bloom taxonomy includes feelings of this kind and moves hierarchically towards more abstract and complex feelings such as would be attained after a lifetime of education. For example, an objective at the highest level reads: 'Develops a consistent philosophy of life.' Another reads: 'Develops a conscience' (p. 171). These are pretty abstract notions and almost impossible to express in terms that all would accept. At the other end of this hierarchy is the following example: 'Interest in voluntary reading' (p. 110). This objective takes us nearer the type of task that faces teachers in specific teaching situations that typically are much shorter-term than that implied in the higher level objectives. Naturally, I do not suggest that the higher level objectives are to be disregarded in the more specific teaching tasks (The affective aspects of teaching and learning are discussed further in Chapter 10).

The further we pursue the analysis of objectives to identify their constituent parts, the closer we approach the concerns of individual teachers grappling with specific teaching tasks. In the process we are likely to increase the amount of genuine agreement among different teachers about the nature and appropriateness of the objectives. Level 1 of Krathwol and Bloom's taxonomy gives the following objectives among others as illustrations of the category: 'Controlled or selected attention', 'Listens for rhythm in poetry or prose read aloud' and 'Listens to music with some discrimination as to its mood and meaning and with some recognition of the contributions of various musical elements and instruments to the total effect'.

These objectives clearly imply close links with cognitive objectives. Indeed, they illustrate the point made earlier, that any separation of the two is arbitrary and could be misleading. Perhaps the best way of looking at objectives and learning in general is to conceive of them as unities with affective and cognitive aspects. Sometimes the emotional element in a given learning situation will be dominant, sometimes the cognitive; neither can exist without the other. In most approaches to planning teaching the affective aspect is less likely to be explicitly stated than the cognitive, as many of the objectives discussed earlier indicate. Generally they are implicit and of the kind suggested in our first example, which aimed to stimulate an interest in and liking for a particular field of study. It is reasonable to assume that such an objective would be a given in any teaching; nevertheless there is much to be said for making such objectives explicit.

INTEGRATED LEARNING

Objectives from a field that combines several kinds of learning illustrate the usefulness of an analytical approach. The field is orienteering, a sport that combines the physical activity of running with map-reading and route-finding skills. In the case we are considering, the teacher's overall aim was to teach the pupils to participate in competitive orienteering. He set, as his overall, type A, objective: 'At the end of instruction the pupils will be able to participate in orienteering competitions'. His overall type B and type C objectives were as follows: type B, 'At the end of instruction the pupils will be able to identify novel examples of orienteering and classify the examples according to a coherent scheme of classification'; type C, 'Recall the key principles relating to competitive orienteering'. Note how the word 'novel' in the B objective guards against rote learning.

The teacher considers what is involved in achieving the A objective and derives the following second level A objectives, that pupils should be able to

- apply basic navigational skills
- apply navigational skills and techniques peculiar to orienteering
- outline the appropriate procedures for entry and participation in orienteering events of various kinds

These objectives are analysed in turn and their subordinate elements identified. The teacher continues this hierarchical analysis until he reaches level A5, by which time he has identified a set of very specific objectives. To illustrate the process I will take one objective at the remaining levels.

From the first level 2 objective above he derives two level 3 objectives. One requires the learner to travel from a known position to a given point using a map. This, in turn, yields four level 4 objectives, one of which is that the learner be able to 'select and interpret a map appropriate to the particular journey'. This objective is analysed and yields the following two objectives: 'Distinguish the essential features of an orienteering map' and 'Distinguish between a map, plan, chart, diagram and topographic map'. At this stage we are considering very specific objectives that would form part of the aims of individual lessons.

Figure 2.6 Orienteering: Level 5 objectives derived from level 4 objectives.

Level 4 objective	*Level 5 objectives*
1 Select and interpret a map appropriate to a particular journey	1 Distinguish the essential feature of an orienteering map
	2 Distinguish between a map, plan, chart, diagram and topographic map
2 Demonstrate the locational relationship of features	
	1 Identify features in the terrain and on the map
	2 Describe the way in which a feature stands or is related to another by reference to distance
	3 Describe the way in which a feature stands or is related to another by reference to direction
3 Demonstrate understanding of the principle of scale	
	1 Judge distance on a map and relate by means of ratio the distance represented on the ground and vice versa
	2 Explain the principle of representative fraction used in cartography
4 Demonstrate the purpose and function of a compass as an aid to map understanding	
	1 Orient or set the map so that the direction on the map corresponds to the ground
	2 Travel on a bearing
	3 Develop the facility for relocation using resection techniques

The level of objectives here has been reached by proceeding from the very general goal of teaching pupils to orienteer to a given level of competence and identifying the constituent subordinate elements of the skill. From the unitary general goal several less general constituent objectives were identified. Each of these second-level objectives was examined to reveal still more specific objectives which were themselves analysed to produce the level 4 objectives given in the figure. The four level 4 objectives each produced the level 5 objectives shown.

The process of analysis that produced the objectives in figure 2.6 is as follows:

Level 1   This is the general aim that pupils should become competent orienteers.
Level 2   The general aim is examined and a number of sub-objectives are identified. One example: '[The pupils should be able] to apply basic navigational skills'.
Level 3   This objective yields two subordinate (level 3) objectives one of which is 'Travel from a known position to a given point using a map'.
Level 4   The level 3 objective yields four level 4 objectives, one of which is 'Select and interpret a map appropriate to a particular journey.'
Level 5   The level 4 objective produces the objectives in figure 2.6.

Proceeding hierarchically from the top down is a useful way of proceeding, since at every level a decision has to be made about which of the sub-objectives are relevant and crucial. At the same time one is safeguarded against cluttering up the planning with unrelated matter that may have accreted without its being realized. To those who object to this approach on the grounds that it reduces spontaneity, I would suggest that no-one is bound by one's analysis. It is a tool to ensure that one covers the ground. If one wishes to introduce clutter one can do so at any time.

I think most people would agree that the objectives in figure 2.6 provide a serious and valuable guide to lesson planning. The overall analysis produced a complex network of objectives for a course of many lessons. Throughout the teaching this analysis provided the teacher with a map of the pedagogical terrain through which he and his pupils were travelling.

This teacher made a very detailed and thorough analysis of his overall objectives and at level A5 produced around fifty highly specific type A objectives (see figure 2.6). He did a similar analysis of the B and C objectives but did not go beyond level 3. An example of a level 3 objective is 'Recall the processes involved in relating a map to ground with and without a compass'.

Clearly a lot of thought went into making this analysis. At the end of the process, however, the teacher had a network of interrelated and precisely specified activities which clearly connect, on the one hand, with theoretical principles relating to such things as map-reading and the use of a compass and, on the other, to the practical activity of running an orienteering course through a forest. Was the exercise worthwhile, or was it a real case of steam hammer and walnut? Let us now consider the teacher's own appraisal of the process. The teacher is talking about himself in the third person.

How beneficial was the approach to his [the teacher's own] teaching task? He considers there are two main benefits. One is that it enabled him to identify the essential prerequisites for learning to orienteer by revealing the simpler rules and concepts which must be learned and incorporated into the more complex skills. He also found that the analysis enabled him to plan the sequence of tasks in an order in which the concepts and subordinate tasks are taught according to their hierarchical relationship. Overall he considered the exercise of great value in producing a learning hierarchy for the teaching of orienteering.

OBJECTIONS TO OBJECTIVES

Some people think that attempting to specify objectives for teaching in the way I have been discussing spells the death of inspired and interesting teaching. It is also argued that it trivialises teaching and reduces it to teaching for rote learning. (See McNamara [1988] for an extreme example of this viewpoint.) In reality, of course, it is probably impossible for a teacher to operate without any aims or hypotheses in mind. Unless teacher activity is totally random it must be based on some notion of its likely effects. Teachers with some understanding of the way people learn and the human dynamics of classrooms are likely to be better able to reduce randomness and devise aims that focus on action most likely to achieve them. I believe that the work of the teachers reported above and the teaching which followed avoid the pitfalls predicted by the critics of objectives. We shall look more closely at that teaching in subsequent chapters.

Few people would argue the case for the completely 'aimless' teacher or expect such a person to achieve satisfactory pupil learning. At the other extreme to aimlessness one can envisage a set of aims that are so precise and specific that they can be explicated only by spelling them out in enormous detail and in enormous numbers. Aims of this sort are in danger of becoming trivial. They are also likely to overwhelm teachers with a mass of detail. Teachers who set out aims for themselves should use their professional judgment, based on their pedagogical understanding and experience, to strike the balance between total aimlessness and total submersion in extremely specific aims. Critics of objectives who make points such as these, however, seem to overlook the fact that teachers are autonomous people who can exercise judgment to use the general ideas of the definition and analysis of objectives while avoiding the pitfalls.

However, the critics undoubtedly have a case when teacher autonomy is eroded by political and administrative constraints. In the 1970s, when objectives became very fashionable in many English-speaking countries, public bodies concerned with education used objectives to set out goals they expected teachers to achieve. In a swing from the extremely vaguely expressed items on syllabuses, they prescribed objectives for teachers that were so precise and specific that they left virtually no room at all for teachers to exercise any initiative. Many such prescriptions were also pedagogically trivial and emphasised rote learning. To reject the idea of educational objectives because of such distortions, however, is to throw the baby out with the bath water. A more helpful activity would be to attempt to persuade bodies external to actual teaching to confine their activities to delineating fairly general aims and leaving it to the teachers themselves to decide their own objectives.

The present situation in the education systems of most English-speaking countries is one in which both teacher independence in setting objectives and external prescription co-exist. The exact proportion of the two varies and is probably impossible to quantify. However, many teachers who are committed to using objectives are themselves unclear about economical ways of producing objectives that fulfilling their professional needs. I hope that the issues raised in this chapter will provide useful guidance to facilitate achieving their own goal of quality learning.

3 Analyses of quality 1: conceptual analysis

ANALYSES OF CONTENT

Clarifying for oneself the objectives of one's teaching is the first step in getting an insight into ways of tackling an extremely complex task. As I have argued before, teaching is not as simple an operation as most people think. My experience with teachers in all stages in their careers suggests to me that they, too, underestimate its complexity. This is not surprising since they have all spent a lifetime in a society that equates teaching with telling, and teachers are unlikely to have discussed such matters or to have addressed in their training the problems caused by this assumption. In recent years political pressures in many countries have reinforced this view of teaching and have promulgated with increased stridency an image of teaching as a low-level a-theoretical activity.

However, when teachers take an analytical approach to teaching and actually take time to examine the nature of teaching/learning interactions they get a glimpse of its complexity. In this chapter I hope to make a start in analysing the nature of teaching and to discuss approaches based on principles that have been used by teachers to gain insight into their own teaching tasks and ideas about how best to tackle them.

Every end of school year the British educational press publishes 'howlers' collected by examiners marking examination scripts. The howlers are intended to entertain, and, indeed, they are often very funny. However, the universal reaction of amusement is oblivious to the fact that the howler is almost invariably based on the pupils' misconstruing what the teacher had *said* at some time. The teachers had *told* the pupils. The pupils, with their very different and more limited experience, had not learned the meanings of the teachers' words but in their answer to a question had made an attempt to reconstruct the language the teacher had used when 'delivering' the message. In later chapters we will examine exchanges between pupils and teachers that exemplify this problem.

Howlers are mistakes pupils make which are comical because of bizarre and incongruous juxtapositions of words or ideas. They are only a tiny fraction of errors based on similar misunderstandings. But some misunderstandings are caused by mistakes made by the teachers themselves. Mistakes may spring from ignorance of some aspect of the subject they are teaching. They may also result from a poor appreciation of the interrelationships of its constituent concepts and principles. The following remarks by a teacher teaching seven-and eight-year-olds the use of thermometers exemplify the former. In the course of the lesson she said that if the temperature dropped below freezing 'they would all be blocks of ice' (Stones 1979, 1984b). I said this *may* be a case of teacher ignorance of subject matter, since, in the absence of any follow-up discussion, one can only conjecture. It is quite possible that in the flow of her exposition, the teacher made the remark without realising what she was saying or that she was using the expression figuratively. Whatever the case the children were undoubtedly being misled.

An example of teacher error that *was* examined after teaching is provided by a student teacher whose work I report and who used photographs as examples of scaled-down representations of objects in a lesson on scale. In discussion she realised that there were misleading examples because of the distorting effects of photographs connected with such things as camera angle and lens characteristics. In the same subject of teaching of scale, another student teacher misled her pupils not because of a misunderstanding of the subject, but because she confused the idea of 'scale' with the idea and act of 'drawing to scale'. In the course of the lesson the pupils' learning of the concept of scale was hampered by their having to cope with activities connected with drawing. In discussion after the lesson, this teacher realised the nature of the pupils' difficulties and decided that a future lesson would distinguish clearly between 'scale' and 'drawing to scale' and that she would probably teach them in distinct sessions.

These examples of pupil and teacher misunderstanding are not isolated examples. Any teacher can quickly obtain evidence of pupil error through careful questioning about taken-for-granted terms in common usage. Teachers in group discussion trying to arrive at an understanding of what is implied in a particular teaching task frequently discover quite wide differences in perceptions of the concepts involved. Indeed, the same can be said about any group of individuals engaged in this kind of activity.

Normally such errors and inconsistencies are not apparent. Discussion on these matters after teaching is rare, even in teacher training courses, where discussion tends to focus on other things. But although identification of error and success after teaching is clearly of great value in improving teaching, prior activity aimed at reducing error and enhancing success is of at least equal importance. Effective activity prior to teaching should not only improve the teaching itself but also facilitate appraisal after teaching.

It is possible for teachers to ensure effective prior activity of this type through the procedures of pedagogical analysis. These procedures start from the premise of teaching's being a highly complex skill demanding a high-level of problem-solving ability by teachers. Since an important approach to solving complex problems is to break them down into less complex problems, this approach is adopted.

Pedagogical analysis involves making a systematic examination of a teaching task so as to reveal its essential elements. The outcome of this analysis is a plan for the teaching of the lesson or lessons. It is very important to note that the plan resulting from a pedagogical analysis is not a conventional lesson plan. Lesson plans typically resemble scripts or directions detailing lines to be delivered or steps to be taken. Pedagogical analyses produce guides to action in a specific piece of teaching that will take into account such things as the conceptual structure of what is to be taught, what we know about human learning that might enhance the learning and the experiences teachers have had in past teaching. 'Guides' is the operative word, and I use the word 'heuristics' to describe them rather than the more common 'schedules' since the former term implies suggestions whereas the latter implies directions.

In this chapter and the next I try to explain the nature of pedagogical analyses and discuss ways of making such analyses. I also provide examples of pedagogical analyses made by teachers in relation to specific pieces of teaching they were engaged in. These analyses deal with a variety of subject matter and with pupils of different ages; all employ the approach discussed in *Psychology of Education: A Pedagogical Approach* (Stones 1984b). Briefly, this approach examines two main aspects of teaching tasks: those elements relating to the content, that is the concepts or skills being taught, and those elements relating to the pedagogical aspects of the teaching. In making a pedagogical analysis, these two main aspects are considered together and interconnections sought between them and between the subordinate elements identified by the analysis. However, for purposes of presentation in continuous text, I deal with the general approach to pedagogical analysis and the analysis of content in this chapter and discuss approaches to the identification of the appropriate activities linking that analysis to practical teaching in the next.

The analysis of content, that is, conceptual analysis, seeks to identify the essential elements of what is to be taught. In the case of concept learning we are concerned to establish the essential attributes of the concepts we hope to teach. In the case of physical skills we try to identify the simpler actions that combine to constitute the skill we are trying to teach. I recognise that the term 'physical skills' may seem out of place under my rubric 'conceptual analysis'. However, as we shall see, it is hardly ever possible to separate the two. In fact, in psychology the more accurate term, 'psychomotor skills', is normally used, with 'motor skills' as a short form.

The aspects of pedagogical analysis more directly related to practical teaching draw on principles from several fields of study. Psychology of human learning is the most important and underpins the other subjects. It provides guidance to help us to identify the nature of the learning involved. Theories of instruction link theory of learning and practical teaching by proposing teaching activities such as the presentation of learning material and the arranging of feedback in ways most likely to bring about the learning intended. Theories of assessment indicate ways of evaluating learning accurately.

In my approach to the relationship between the theoretical elements and the practical activities of teaching I have taken a pluralistic approach to theory. I have drawn on those principles from learning theory that seem to me to be of value in enhancing classroom learning, without espousing the position of any specific psychological 'school'. However, the principles I draw on are very generally accepted by psychologists of most persuasions. I recognise that only a limited amount of work relating *practical* teaching learning theory has been done. Thus our knowledge about the nature of this relationship is somewhat rudimentary. So it is premature to suggest that we can 'apply' psychological principles to school teaching. It would be more accurate to conceive of work of this kind as 'trying out' the principles and possibly modifying our understanding of them in the light of practical experience. Indeed, it is undesirable to conceive of 'applying' theory to teaching. The dialectical interaction between theory and practice is open ended, and the idea of an end-state where all is known misconceives that relationship and is contrary to the way human knowledge develops.

The general case

There is an important difference between pedagogical analyses for teaching and other job analyses. Analyses for teaching need to embody analyses of the learner's task within the analyses of the teacher's task. The point is that success in teaching is entirely dependent upon an understanding of the factors that make for successful pupil learning. Thus, for example, the analysis needs to identify the type(s) of learning the pupils are expected to engage in, since that will determine the type of teacher action necessary for success.

If the pupils are to learn something by rote, the teacher needs to arrange activities very different from those that would be appropriate if the learning is to be meaningful. For example, learning vocabulary in a foreign language resembles rote learning, since in general the connection between words and their referents is arbitrary, whereas other aspects of language, such as its grammar, are usually rule-governed. The most economical and effective way of learning vocabulary is, therefore, by methods appropriate to simple learning of paired stimuli. Learning rules and principles demands methods appropriate to concept learning, which is more complex and which I discuss in detail later. There would also be considerable differences between teacher action aimed at teaching particular motor skills and action aimed at teaching approaches to problem-solving.

The process of identifying the type(s) of learning involved in the learners' task will suggest to a teacher a number of sub-tasks related to the overall learning problem. The teacher would need to make decisions about the best way to structure the learning environment to cater best for the different kinds of learning. These decisions would demand further decisions about such things as the way in which stimuli should be presented, the type and nature of cues, and feedback.

During the process of analysis, one attempts to keep in mind the idea of the interrelated nature of the various elements. Sub-tasks of a pedagogical analysis are not simple and linear, but complex, elaborate and interconnected. Because of this it is useful, when analysing the conceptual content of the teaching, to have in mind, as far as possible, all related aspects of the teaching task. Thus, while focusing on the concepts to be taught and trying to decide on what are the key elements, one considers the most likely way of teaching them and of evaluating the pupils' learning. It is also helpful to have in mind other aspects of teaching, so that in the process a teaching plan begins to unfold.

This approach to pedagogical analysis is presented in the form of a matrix with the key aspects of the teaching task as columns and the analyses of the constituent elements of the column headings as rows. This presentation enables one to see connections between the various aspects of the task by scanning the rows and to explicate the subordinate elements of the general content by moving down the columns. The matrix provides a framework within which one can move in any direction, when one is analysing a teaching task, as ideas are triggered off by related notions or by the matrix headings.

The approach was developed in work with many groups of experienced and student teachers and exemplifies a form of developmental action research in teaching involving interaction between theoretical notions and practical teaching in the way I have discussed. Teachers used the general approach as a guide to their teaching. Their practical experience in using the approach helped them gain insight into the nature and usefulness of the theory in their specific circumstances. Some of them modified the general approach to suit their particular circumstances, but by and large the general line was found to have general utility. A hierarchical approach was adopted in the belief that it would help ensure rigorous analysis. However, linkages between the different strands in the hierarchy are made explicit, so that the unity of the teaching being analysed is maintained. To illustrate the nature of the analytical approach, figure 3.1 presents an analysis I devised for my own use in introducing teachers to this method of analysing teaching tasks.

Clearly the usefulness of a teacher's analysis aimed at promoting pupil learning will depend greatly on a knowledge of the relevant principles of the psychology of human learning. This knowledge is particularly important since it will enable a teacher to tackle teaching tasks with a flexible approach. Although some school learning is amendable to rigidly

Figure 3.1 Analysis to illustrate the approach to making a pedagogical analysis

Objectives: the learners should be able to make a pedagogical analysis on paper in a subject of their own choosing. The analysis should cover the key aspects of a teaching task suggested in the appropriate heuristic guide.

General Content: The analysis of teaching tasks provides heuristic guides that identify the key pedagogical elements in teaching activities likely to enhance student learning.

Subordinate concepts	Specific examples	Type(s) of learning
1 The general statement of content should be analysed to identify its subordinate concepts/ skills (conceptual analysis)	Pedagogical analyses in different fields. Some ideas: author's own analysis of teaching pedagogical analysis, analysis of aspects of musical composition, analysis of aspects of teaching orienteering.	Concept learning mainly. Problem solving/protocol analysis in the workshop phase.
2 Specific examples of the concepts or skills should be decided on. These will be used in teaching.		
3 A decision should be made on the types of learning involved. This decision is essential in deciding on the appropriate pedagogical activities.		
4 A decision on the method of presentation of stimulus material (concrete or abstract) should be made.		
5 The nature of the learners' responses should be planned for and any materials provided.		
6 The nature of the feedback to the learners should be planned having mind the decisions made in items 1–5.		
7 The nature of the evaluation should be decided on based on the analysis.		

This is my attempt to devise a pedagogical analysis of the task of making a pedagogical analysis. I hope it will serve a double purpose: as an example, and as an exposition and reminder about what seem to me the key elements in such analyses. It is intended to be used in a workshop of people learning the skills of making these analyses.

Method of stimulus presentation	Learners' responses	Feedback	Evaluation
Oral exposition by the author. Handouts of analyses on paper. Reference to appropriate section in the text.	Oral to tutor. Oral to other learners. Written. Elements of analysis in fields of their choice. In workshop sessions produce complete analyses with author consultation.	Oral. Tutor individual and group. Peer comment.	Preparation of analyses in workshop session. These must be new productions. Evaluation will be by tutor and comments from peers.

prescribed activities, for example the mechanical learning of the four rules in arithmetic, most learning is more problematic and demands a flexible approach by the teacher. The point is that it is unlikely that there will be only one correct method of tackling a teaching task even though the various methods are bound to have many common features. Thus, the approach I suggest, and which provides the general line followed by most of the studies reported here, should by no means be taken as a blueprint to be followed rigidly. Rather it should be seen as a heuristic device or guide to action when planning teaching.

ANALYSES IN ACTION

Having outlined the general approach that has guided the work reported here and given an illustrative example, I now consider a variety of analyses produced by teachers with different backgrounds and interests. I hope that the varied nature of the analyses will indicate the flexibility and potential of the general approach and deepen the reader's grasp of its characteristics. This controlled variability is an example of a general theme in the way this book is constructed. It derives from principles of concept learning which I discuss later.

In my discussion of the analyses, I shall be using them, as I mentioned in Chapter 1, as *protocols*. That is, I shall be using them to examine the working out of the general principles I shall be discussing in particular circumstances through the actual work of teachers grappling with genuine teaching problems. In the case of the experienced teachers, the analyses relate, in general, to teaching that they thought particularly challenging. The student teachers were tackling teaching tasks which were part of their work in schools during courses of initial teacher training.

All the teachers adapted the general approach discussed above for their own purposes. The process of drawing on theoretical principles to carry out their analyses, at the same time as they confronted a real classroom problem, produced a creative tension between theory and practice and challenged both. The outcomes were very different from conventional lesson plans and, I believe, constituted genuine pedagogical explorations that would interest teachers other than those who produced the analyses. I shall try to draw attention to aspects of the analyses that illustrate interesting adaptations of the general approach.

There is a problem of presentation in discussing pedagogical analysis using the format presented above. The adoption of the matrix suggested is valuable when carrying out an analysis, but is awkward in a book format. It is also impossible to simulate the thought processes that led to the production of particular analyses. Therefore, I shall examine a number of pedagogical analyses column by column and later discuss the way in which the columns interrelate in individual examples.

General content

First I consider the identification of the key elements in the substance of the teaching. Under the heading 'General Content' the teacher spells out as precisely as possible what principles, concepts and skills are implicit in the lesson objectives. In practice this section of the matrix has raised interesting questions about the nature of the conceptual material being taught. The most important finding to emerge from the work reported here is that experienced teachers and graduate teachers in training, all of whom are specialists in specific fields of study, have very vague ideas about the conceptual structure of the subjects they profess. The pedagogical analysis they engaged in taught them things about their subjects that were quite novel to them.

It is interesting to compare this finding with those from studies of teacher thinking about planning (Clark and Yinger 1987). I suggest that some hard thinking is needed to carry out conceptual analyses such as I have outlined. It seems very likely that this is why teachers find them difficult. The type of thinking commonly found by investigators of teaching as it is now is very different. Planning is found to be related to time allocation, such as the day or the week or the year. It is concerned with the presentation of the material, and one study indicated that the contents of the stock cupboard were influential in determining the nature of the teachers' planning. In their distillation of the outcomes of the research they reviewed, Clark and Yinger drew attention to several points they considered important. Among them are such things as what teachers think about 'students, subject matter, teaching environments, *and the teaching process itself*' (my italics). Other formulations of a similar nature describe the complexity of teaching but with no more analytical detail. The picture that emerges is that managerial concerns predominate in teachers' thinking at the planning stage and that there is little, if any, pedagogical analysis.

It should be noted that conceptual analysis as presented here is not the same as listing topics in a syllabus. Listing topics does not necessarily guarantee that the topics are interrelated. Nor does it give one any logical means of ensuring that all important aspects of the subject have been included or offer guidance on optimum teaching sequences. The approach adopted here is hierarchical and attempts to identify the logical and psychological relationships among the constituent elements of the overall theme of the content being taught and to ensure that nothing important is overlooked. Without some such analytical approach to the content to be taught, any hope of identifying generally useful 'pedagogical content knowledge' from teacher action is likely to be unfulfilled.

Uncertainty about the conceptual structure of the content may have contributed to another aspect of this part of the analysis. This section produced some divergences from the basic design set out in the general case. The most common difference was that, whereas in the general approach the sub-sections arising from the analysis are couched in words resembling definitions, some teachers' versions were stated more in the terms one might find in syllabuses, merely bald titles. For example, in an analysis of vector-carried disease in biology, the teacher merely entered 'disease' rather than explicating the term. The teacher may well have had a clear idea in her own mind about the word, but spelling out the meaning in terms such as, for example, 'a pathological change leading to impairment of an organism's normal physiological functioning, especially when caused by infection or stress' would have added precision and brought to mind several important concepts related to the teaching task. Note that this definition is not intended for the pupils but for the teacher and her peers working in the field.

Divergences from the general approach relate to learning other than concept learning. For example, some analyses produced by teachers working on the learning of motor activities not unreasonably produced constituent motor activities rather than sub-concepts. In some problem-solving analyses, the subordinate skills the teachers thought necessary for success took the place of an analysis of conceptual content. Any modifications or extension of the general approach intended to cater for these cases would exemplify the interactive development of a theoretical approach and actual practice. As I suggested earlier, teachers' own plans and specific teaching tasks interacted with the heuristics to produce different pedagogical analyses appropriate to specific teaching conditions. The heuristics *remind* teachers of things to bear in mind and do not dictate the course they should follow. We shall see examples of variant analyses later. For the moment I will concentrate on the more general problem of analyses related to teaching of conceptual material, usually referred to as the 'content', which is the staple of most lessons.

1 Social studies

As an example of the tendency to set out the subordinate elements of general content in terms of syllabus headings, here is the analysis of the general content of the concept of 'an election' which was to be taught by a student teacher to a group of 13–14-year-old pupils as part of a humanities course dealing with the more general topic of 'democracy'. The overall concept in the specific lesson was 'election', and as constituent elements the teacher derived three sub-concepts: 'choice', 'vote' and 'representative'. In his analysis he merely listed the sub-concepts and did not attempt to provide a definition or statement of principles in the form 'Choice is/implies/involves'. It might be thought that spelling out these seemingly simple concepts would be redundant, or possibly that the pupils would already understand them. The teacher does not presume the latter, since, in the analysis, he goes on to provide examples of the various concepts that he would use in the teaching. There is little doubt that the student teacher is merely doing what he has so often seen in syllabuses, which are often no more than lists of topics with no explication of how pupils are expected to 'learn' them. Presumably this is in part because it is assumed that delivery teaching will be employed, but it also seems to assume that the rubrics are unproblematic and that everyone will agree on their meaning. The experience of the teachers who looked more closely than usual at their teaching testifies to the fact that these rubrics are, in fact, more often than not, extremely problematic.

In the event, the teacher had problems with his teaching of the sub-concepts. Not having got clarity on the criterial attributes of the concepts, he was unclear about the nature of the attributes and confused the pupils. He realised he had a problem and referred to it in his evaluation of his teaching. In his critique of his teaching, which he had video-recorded, he reported pupils' difficulty in identifying an exemplar of the concept of vote. At one stage in the lesson he declared that 'we have a vote because we want to make our choices known to other people'. This confused the pupils, who construed the statement as implying open voting, i.e. excluding secret ballots. His critique suggested another more precise definition, but this was *post hoc*. More thought prior to teaching could well have prevented this confusion.

2 Social studies

Another example from the work of a student teacher, this time teaching the concepts of exports and imports to eleven–twelve-year-old pupils, illustrates the same point. The general content of this teaching task was the concepts of exports and imports. The subordinate concepts were stated as 'transport', 'immigration', 'agriculture', 'industry', 'local history', 'map work'. Leaving to one side the question as to whether the sub-concepts are really criterial to the main concepts, let us consider the teacher's self-appraisal after teaching. Direct quotation in this case makes the point effectively.

> I think the most glaring criticism of my teaching would be that I had not got clear in my own head the criterial attributes involved in teaching the concepts of imports and exports. This was evident when the children became confused about, for example, whether coal brought to London from South Wales was in fact an import. I must confess it floored me completely! I felt the best way out of that awkward situation was not to say that this *was* a positive exemplar or *was not*, but to leave the question open and hope the children would come up with some ideas, which fortunately they did.'

She goes on to wonder what the criterial attributes are and finally hypothesises: 'trade between two economically independent countries' as a 'reasonable explanation'.

Elsewhere in her report, the teacher comments on her inclusion of such things as 'immigration', 'transport', 'local history', 'mapwork' as subordinate elements in the concepts of 'import' and 'export'. In fact she used them in the actual teaching, not as constituent sub-concepts, but as non-exemplars for pupils to identify, or as vehicles for her teaching. The confusion of the analysis of the concepts contributed to her lack of clarity about their attributes.

This student teacher's difficulty with the conceptual analysis of the subject she aimed to teach was not caused by a low level of education. She had recently graduated with honours after a three-year course of academic study. Most people find this type of analysis difficult when they first encounter it. Whether this difficulty is intrinsic or a consequence of the fact that it is not to be found in conventional courses is difficult to determine. There is little doubt, however, that all the teachers in these studies who attempted such analysis found that it added an interesting and important dimension to their understanding of their field of study which suggests to me that there is a case for including this kind of activity in conventional courses.

As in the previous example, the analysis came *post hoc*. However, it was not fruitless. The self-appraisal provided invaluable feedback to guide future action. It is worth noting that the feedback related to principles of concept learning, and not merely to aspects of one particular lesson that would probably not have been generalisable to other situations.

3 Conventions in drawing

An example of an analysis by an experienced teacher teaching eight-and nine-year-old pupils the concept of 'plan' illustrates the way in which sub-concepts may be derived from the overall content. Her analysis sets out the sub-concepts as follows:

1 A drawing represents an object.
2 A plan is a special kind of representation with its own conventions.
3 A plan shows objects from above and in outline.
4 There are conventional ways of representing doors, windows and stairs.

In her appraisal of the lesson the teacher considers that she was probably too narrow in her construing of 'plan'. Sub-concept 4 illustrates this point. While the statement is true, it is only partial, in that it relates to one sub-set of plans and does not cover plans of objects other than buildings. Her discussion of the teaching makes it clear that she also had other kinds of plans in mind, for example maps and plans in engineering. Acknowledging the incompleteness of coverage of the subject, she raises the question of how one should approach the task. In her view, her teaching of the concept of a plan of a building was the first step in teaching the more comprehensive concept of plans in general. One has to start somewhere.

The issue she raises is crucial to all teaching. Should one attempt to teach the overall general idea in complex material, or is it better to deal with it piece by piece? It is a question that is raised in some form or other in most attempts at pedagogical analysis. The content analysis of the teaching of 'plan' in part takes the second approach. In so doing it seems to me to be prone to the problem that the pupils' learning will be erroneous, in that sub-concept 4 may lead them to believe that plans of buildings constitute the whole class of 'plans' rather than just one sub-set of plans in general. This comment does not imply that one should not start teaching particular aspects of general complex concepts, but that one should try to ensure that pupils understand the embeddedness of the specific in the general. In the case of 'plans', an alternative approach might have been to concentrate on the general idea of conventional representation, as the teacher has in her sub-concepts 1–3, but in 4 she could have taken up the idea of conventions in the representation of hidden features in plans in general instead of concentrating entirely on plans of buildings. In fact, the analysis seems to confuse the general (1–3) with the particular (4).

4 Music

We now consider an example of the overall application of the general approach provided by the work of a specialist music teacher teaching musical composition to thirteen-year-old pupils. It is particularly interesting since the idea of taking systematic approaches to subjects of this kind is sometimes anathematised by musicians and teachers of music on the grounds that composition is a personal creative gift liable to destruction by systematic teaching. In fact, some British examination boards now include composition in some of their examinations, a fact which this teacher welcomes, with comments that I report later.

The teacher of the analysis we now consider effectively demolishes the position of those who think composition should not be taught, through both argument and practical teaching. He found that pupils taught using the approach discussed here produced melodies of originality and individuality. Other pupils with musical qualifications, having passed public examination at about sixteen years of age taught by different methods, produced melodies that were more dependent upon models they had encountered before, and showed uncertainty about the nature of the concept of 'melody' by including haphazard rhythms and pitch in their melodies.

Figure 3.2 Teaching the concept of 'melody': pedagogical analysis

General Concept	Specific Examples	Type of Learning
The concept of melody consists in a pattern of notes constructed to have a beginning, a middle and an end. *Subordinate concepts.* *Pitch* 1) The beginning of a melody is established by using the 1st and/or 3rd notes of the major scale.	*Pitch* 1) a) going stepwise or by leaps of 3rd, 5th, and octave from 1st, 3rd notes of the scale. b) going stepwise or by leap of 3rd, 5th and octave from other notes.	The learning is concept learning achieved by dividing the overall concept of melody into three sub-concepts, dictated by the unique form of melody as more than a mere progression of notes in temporal sequence. Much of this learning depends on pre-requisite learning especially in the ability to notate musical symbols and count in 2 or 3 time. There is provision for a programme of positive and negative exemplars necessary to bring out the criterial attributes of the concept of melody.
Rhythm and Form (Announcing Phrase) 2) The melody progresses by the use of stepwise movement and/or by leaps of 1st, 3rd 5th and octave in crotchet time (♩) to arrive at Bar Four (midway) on the fifth note of the scale as a minim (♩) or dotted minim. (♩.) This establishes the middle of the melody.	*Rhythm and Form* (Announcing Phrase) 2) a) going stepwise or by leap of 3rd, 5th and octave to finish on the 5th note of the scale. b) going stepwise or by leap of 3rd, 5th and octave to finish on any other note.	
Rhythm and Form (Responding phrase) 3) The melody progresses by use of stepwise movement and/or by leaps of 1st, 3rd and 5th and octave in crotchet time (♩) to end the melody. The end is established by using the first note of the major scale as a minim (♩) or dotted minim (♩.).	*Rhythm and Form* (Responding phrase) 3) a) going stepwise or by leap of 3rd, 5th and octave to finish on the 1st note of the scale. b) going stepwise or by leap of 3rd, 5th and octave to finish on any other note.	

Method of Stimulus Presentation	Pupils' Response	Feedback	Evaluation
In each area: a) Teacher telling b) Demonstrating by singing or playing e.g. Xylophone/Casio electronic instrument. c) Drawing notation on blackboard stave. d) Tape recording and playback. Each of the above would be in regard of positive and negative exemplars.	In each area: a) Pupil spoken answer b) Demonstrates by singing or playing xylophone. c) Writes melodies on manuscript paper.	In each area: This could be achieved by the teacher testing the successful identification of melodies by the pupil. That is, the melody had a beginning, a middle and an end. The pupil demonstrates this successfully to the teacher.	The best way to check that the concept of melody has been learned is for the pupil to produce new examplars of melodies based on those in the learning sequence. That is, Pupils produce melodies with a beginning, a middle and an end, according to the criteria of the subordinate concepts.

This pedagogical analysis of the teaching of the concept of 'melody' is an excellent example of the specific application of the general principles of analysis. Note particularly the conceptual analysis in column 1, which is followed through the other columns, and the method of evaluation. The teacher has produced a powerful guide to teaching of a high quality. If he failed to produce high-level learning, he would know that he had and would have had a good idea where he failed. However, the nature of the analysis is such that his chances of success were high and his teaching vindicated his view that the analysis was a crucial aspect of his teaching.

I should like make one further point of clarification of the entries in columns 1 and 2. The teacher has spelled out in such detail the subordinate concepts in column 1 that they closely resemble the specific examples in column 2. There is nothing wrong in this, of course. The difference between entries in the columns is that those in column 2 are details of teacher *action*, whereas those in column 1 are entries to clarify the nature of the overall content.

Taking melody as a crucial element in composition, he states his general content as follows:

Melody consists in a pattern of notes constructed to have a beginning, a middle and an end

Subordinate elements are as follows:

Pitch

The beginning of a melody is established by using the 1st and/or 3rd notes of the major scale.

Rhythm and Form (Announcing phase)

The melody progresses by the use of stepwise movement and/or by leaps of 1st, 3rd, 5th and octave in crochet time to arrive at Bar Four (midway) on the 5th note of the scale as a minim or dotted minim. This establishes the middle of the melody.

Rhythm and Form (Responding phase)

The melody progresses by the use of stepwise movement and/or by leaps of 1st, 3rd, 5th and octave in crochet time to end the melody. The end is established by using the first note of the major scale as a minim or dotted minim.

One does not have to be a musical expert to observe that here the teacher has quite carefully spelled out the constituent elements of his main theme and thereby rendered it more precise. In addition to clarifying the nature of the overall content, the specifying of the constituent sub-concepts makes it easier to identify specific teaching action to help pupils learn the concepts. Thus the teacher decided on the specific examples he would use to clarify the nature of the concepts for the pupils: the nature of the learning involved, type of feedback and mode of evaluation of learning. Note that the breaking down of the overall content into subordinate elements did not fragment the pupils' learning, since the teacher related the individual sub-concepts to the overall content in his teaching. In addition, in the evaluation phase he demanded that the pupils respond to the overall concept satisfactorily, not to its subordinate elements separately (See Figure 3.2).

There is one other very important aspect of this approach to teaching. Although the teacher's evaluation of his teaching seemed to be satisfactory, he was able to pinpoint weaknesses in his pedagogical analysis and his teaching that needed modification to improve the pupils' learning. I will consider this further in a later chapter.

5 Art

Another example from an artistic field suggesting that a systematic approach has much to offer comes from a visual art. The teaching in this case was for pupils to learn the concept of 'pattern'. The teacher confronts the commonly held view that artistic skills and abilities spring from within the individual unaided. A crucial consequence of this view is that little consideration is given to the nature of artistic concepts. This neglect deprives learners of important areas of experience and affects their performance and appreciation of artistic phenomena.

The teacher addressed the problem of teaching an understanding of the nature of pattern by preparing a pedagogical analysis, the first part of which is an analysis of the general content of a lesson. His analysis produced the following sub-concepts:

Repetition	The recurrence of a theme, line, shape or colour
Balance	The distribution of weight in a seemingly even manner
Symmetry	The equal proportion of space
Asymmetry	The counterbalance of disproportionate weights in order to achieve harmonious illusion of balance
Abstraction	To take from or simplify, e.g. to derive from a complex form.

In the process of analysis the teacher concluded that the aim was too ambitious and could not be achieved in one lesson. He came to realise that the concept of pattern was 'vast' and could not be covered as economically as he had thought. He therefore decided to concentrate on a few of the more essential attributes of the concept to form a basis for expansion later. His major decision was to remove the subordinate concept of abstraction from the plan. In the process of his analysis he concluded that this concept demanded a lesson in its own right, and he later devised and taught such a lesson. He also realised that his first approach to the analysis had missed an important element, 'texture'. He made other, less important, modifications to his plan. He comments that the actual checking on his intended actions 'would be more difficult to follow through in the absence of a structured plan or schedule. Further, it could be argued that the need for such an examination might not even become apparent'.

I suggest that his decision to exclude the concept of 'abstraction' from his plan was a wise one. One might go further. It could be argued that the idea of abstraction is so important for human learning that there is a good case for giving it a place of its own in the curriculum. I am not now talking about abstraction solely in the field of art, but about its all-pervasive nature in human affairs, perhaps especially in language. Questions such as this are frequently raised in the process of pedagogical analysis. This is intriguing since the process of analysis is often criticised for fragmenting learning and teaching, whereas the analysis of usually 'taken for granted' concepts often reveals unifying connections among very different 'subjects'.

6 Biology

The teacher of biology whose work we considered in Chapter 2 provides an example of an analysis from a rather different field. On this occasion she made her analysis more explicit. She was teaching the concept of 'cell' to pupils about thirteen years old. She set out the elements of the general content in the form of a definition with three elements: 'A cell is a unit of living material bounded by a membrane or wall and controlled by a nucleus'. This simple and straightforward statement focused her attention on the basic concepts she needed to teach in order for the pupils to learn what cells are. In fact she took the ability to distinguish between living and non-living things as part of the pupils' existing competence, so that her teaching concentrated on providing exemplars and non-exemplars of cell wall and nucleus.

The simplicity of a definition of this kind does not imply that making it is a redundant activity. Omitting to make things explicit because they are 'obvious' can be very misleading and bring about the mis-matches between pupil and teacher understandings I referred to earlier. Making things explicit, having in mind the nature of the concepts involved and not merely the words, reminds the teacher and indicates the nature of the teaching that has to be done. It also hints at the nature of any pre-test designed to establish necessary prior learning and any final test of learning at the end of teaching.

7 Map reading

This point is well illustrated in an account of teaching the concept of a 'bearing' in map reading. The general content was as follows:

A bearing is a horizontal angle fixing a point in respect of North and is measured in degrees in a clockwise direction from North.

Sub-concepts were:

Turning is to give rotary motion to [something].
Clockwise means moving in a curve from left to right, right to left as seen from the centre.
Direction is stated in relation to magnetic North.
The amount of turn to a new direction is called an angle.
Angles are measured in degrees.
Direction is expressed in degrees.
Bearings are measured in the horizontal plane.

The teacher devised a test based on these sub-concepts to be given prior to teaching. The aim of the test was to assess the pupils' levels of understanding to indicate the most appropriate point to start instruction. In the event, he was surprised to find that although he knew the pupils well, he had overestimated their level of understanding of the sub-concepts. He was particularly surprised at their inability to estimate angles and to measure them accurately. Remedial teaching was imperative to prepare the pupils for learning the concept of bearing. Without the breakdown of the overall content he would not have discovered this discrepancy between his appraisal of the pupils' abilities and their actual competence.

8 The problem of route choice in orienteering

Teaching the concept of bearing was a subordinate element in a more complex teaching task. The ultimate aim of the teaching was to equip pupils with the skills necessary to follow a complicated course through a forest using map and compass. However, there are intermediate steps between learning this general skill and learning the concept of bearing. One of them is the ability to solve orienteering route choice problems of easy and medium difficulty. The teacher who analysed the concept of bearing continued by making an analysis of the problem of making a route choice. This analysis provides an example of the point I made earlier, that the analysis of the task of teaching problem solving may involve some modification in the analysis.

The main content of the analysis, as in other analyses, identified the key subordinate principles necessary for competent performance. They comprised the following:

Map reading skills
Concept of an attack point
Concept of a handrail
Concept of a collector
Aiming off
Concept of bearing
Travelling on a bearing

These items do not explicate the nature of the concepts involved and, in fact, in the analysis the explication has been transferred to the specific examples column, leaving the specific examples used unexplicated in this analysis. (They are made explicit elsewhere in the teacher's report.) 'Map-reading skills' and 'Aiming off' are less explicit still. In fact the teacher explains in his report that the individual items refer to skills and concepts the pupils should already possess if they are to solve a route-finding problem successfully. They clarify for him the necessary elements to be taken into account in his teaching the pupils how to tackle problems of route choice. The interactive part of teaching draws on another guide.

This example is another instance of my general point about the interactive nature of theory and practice. The general principles do not dictate to the teacher. The teacher uses them as a guide to address a specific pedagogical problem. Another teacher might not agree with the detail of his procedure or his implementation of the principles, but there would be little disagreement about the general line.

9 Language teaching

We now consider an example of a content analysis in language teaching. This example indicates the way in which a teacher uses his knowledge of French to identify the key sub-elements in the general content of a fairly specific piece of teaching. His task was to teach that 'when communicating in French we use meaningful structures equivalent to the English "What is it/this? It is a . . ." and "Is this a . . .? Yes/No, it is a . . .".'

He listed the following as subordinate concepts:

1 The student will learn the French equivalents for 'a pen', 'a pencil', 'a note book', 'a text book', 'a pupil's desk'.
2 The correct pronunciation of 'un', 'on', 'r', and 'u' are . . . [Here he gives the phonetic symbols of the International Phonetic Association].
3 The French equivalent of 'What is it/this?' elicits the French equivalent of the reply 'It is . . .'.
4 A question in French has a rising intonation with the last syllable high. A statement has a rising intonation but falls on the last syllable.
5 The statement 'It is . . .' can be completed with a noun in French as in English.
6 The statement 'It is . . .' can be turned into a question eliciting the answer 'Yes/No, it is . . .' in French as in English.

We might note here that the first item is at odds with the others in the list. Item 1 is expressed in the form of an aim or objective of teaching, whereas the other items actually spell out the characteristics of the subordinate principles or concepts to be learned. The reason for this discrepancy could well be that the type of learning involved in vocabulary learning is non-conceptual, or rote, so that conceptual analysis of this type is inappropriate.

There is evidence, from the rest of this teacher's analysis, that he was unclear about the nature of the constituent elements of the task. He considered that most of them involved rote learning, whereas they are clearly statements of principles. Rote learning implies total specificity of the material being memorised. Thus in item 1 the implicit statement 'pen = stylo' is a specific piece of learning that applies only to the linkage of two sounds. Drill methods appropriate to stimulus–response learning are all that is needed here. I should stress that I am talking only about the learning of vocabulary. The learning of *meaning* in relation to the two words, the native and the foreign, must be taught using methods appropriate to concept learning.

I discuss this point at greater length in a discussion of concept learning. For the moment the point might be briefly summarised by saying that drill methods can teach vocabulary but not how to make use of grammatical principles. It is, of course, possible to teach grammatical principles by drill methods, but it is unlikely that pupils will be able to *use* the 'knowledge' any more than a parrot could.

Statement 4 above, 'A question in French has a rising intonation with the last syllable high,' does not imply rote learning but the learning of concepts or principles of general utility – unless, of course, the teacher merely teaches the pupils to recite the statement. To teach so that the pupils will be able to *use* the new learning and not just parrot the rule demands teaching that makes use of an understanding of the way concepts and principles are learned and taught, and that kind of teaching is very different from teaching leading to rote learning. A similar lack of clarity is to be seen elsewhere in the analysis, and the teaching of the characteristics of questions and statements in French is rather specific because of that. This is a matter to which we shall return later. The important point here is that the confusion implicit in the content analysis misled the teacher in his subsequent teaching, making it less effective than it might have been.

10 Reading comprehension

In this section, I should like to discuss a pedagogical analysis for the teaching of group oral clozure in English comprehension. This technique is used to improve comprehension skills in reading. It consists of readers having to supply key words blanked out of passages of text to enhance their word attack skills through contextual cuing. In this case the teacher seems to have been unclear about the nature of his content analysis. He used the first column to state his objectives and shifted the general content analysis one column to the right under the 'Specific examples' heading. Thus one of the key entries under 'General content' was

Pupils to use syntactic and semantic cues in order to make appropriate substitutions for words deleted from a passage, which is at or below their instructional level.

This may hint at the elements in an analysis, but it is little guidance to the teacher in his planning for action to achieve the aim, which is the purpose of pedagogical analysis. His column headed 'Specific examples', in fact, provides the guidance. Under this heading we find the following:

An order of difficulty can be created by:
a Deleting nouns and/or verbs only and by supplying two choices, one of which is syntactically or semantically inappropriate.
b Increasing the number of choices and narrowing their range.
c Offering no choice, but giving structural prompts such as initial letter of blend, configuration, word length, etc.
d Leaving just a blank.
e Deleting of adjectives and/or adverbs.
f Deleting of prepositions and other function words.

These are clearly principles of general application to the use of cloze procedures in teaching. However, these principles do not derive from an analysis of the pupils' learning task, but are a guide to the teachers' classroom activity that might be based on such an analysis. It may be that the teacher could give guidance to pupils in dealing with cloze exercises, but the guidance would be *ad hoc* since it could not be based on the type of analysis he had made.

An appropriate analysis of general content in this case would have taken the statement of intent given above, perhaps restated it in terms of a principle such as 'Syntactic and semantic cues can be used to suggest appropriate substitutions for missing words in cloze exercises', and then examined it to determine what its important sub-elements were. These sub-elements would have been indicators of the principles the pupils needed to learn to achieve competence in cloze exercises. In view of the lack of explicit analysis, the teacher would have had to decide what the subordinate concepts were at the same time as actually teaching. They are, of course, quite inaccessible to others, and we have no means of assessing the appropriateness of the constituent elements to the overall content.

11 Geology

An experienced teacher and teacher trainer produced the following analysis of a concept in geology which exemplifies very well the process of identifying the key sub-concepts in general content. The sub-concepts are stated clearly and simply, providing a firm basis for the development of the interactive stage of teaching. The overall content was the concept of 'strike lines', which are used in contoured geological maps involving uniformly dipping rock series. The overall concept was presented as follows: 'Strike lines are structured contours'. This yielded the following sub-concepts:

1 A strike line is a construct (an imaginary line).
2 A strike line joins places of equal height on the bedding plane.
3 A strike line is drawn horizontally on the bedding plane.

The fact that this analysis may not be too meaningful to the non-geologist, or may seem rather simple, illustrates the two key points mentioned earlier. The analysis is an *aide memoire* to the teacher and not an explanation to the pupils. The simplicity and precision of the statement is an aid to clarifying the nature of the sub-concepts, which are all too often unexplicated and unclarified in the teacher's mind. They would be more meaningful to his peers than the bald rubric 'strike line' in a statement of content of a piece of teaching. In this particular case, because of his past experience, the teacher firmly believed that the concept was a difficult one for beginners and certainly worthy of careful consideration. His appraisal of his subsequent teaching of the concept stressed the crucial importance of the analysis preceding teaching. I shall consider later the way in which this analysis guided the teaching and how the appraisal of the teaching by the teacher reflected back upon the analysis and brought home to him the fundamental importance of the analysis of general content. As I said earlier, this is a universal reaction by teachers who attempt a systematic psychological and pedagogical analysis of a teaching task.

4 Analyses of quality 2: pedagogical analysis

The discussion so far has focused on the crucial element in pedagogical analysis of clarifying the conceptual structure of content to be taught. This clarification aims to help ensure that the essential features (criterial attributes) of the content are clearly distinguished from the non-essential (non-criterial attributes).

This is not always a simple task, as many of the teachers whose work I discuss in this book came to realise. For example, while it is fairly clear that the colour of a chair is not essential to its being a chair, it is less clear whether the number of legs is a criterial attribute. Whether it must have a back is probably more problematic, and the consideration of this question raises a further question as to whether a stool is a form of chair. Etymologically speaking the word 'chair' originally referred to a seat for one person; the back was non-criterial. Later, as the language changed, the back became criterial, so that most dictionaries now define 'chair' as a seat with a back for one person. The Cobuild Dictionary which records the way English speakers throughout the world use the language, confirms that current usage corresponds to conventional dictionary definitions (Sinclair 1987).

This is a relatively simple concept. How much more problematic must be some of the concepts that teachers routinely aspire to teach. Some concepts that appeared straightforward to the teachers whose work I consider in this book, such as 'imports' and 'tourist', were found to be less simple than they appeared at first sight. Significantly, this complexity appeared only when the teachers, taking a systematic approach, attempted to teach the concepts to pupils and were later able to appraise their performance analytically. This refinement of teacher understanding is another example of one of the most important aspects of the work I report: the interaction between theoretical understanding and the actual practice of teaching.

When one considers more abstract concepts in the same way, the complexity of the teacher's task becomes even more obvious. Concepts such as 'deviance', 'evidence' and 'reneging' were all tackled by the teachers. The inherently problematic nature of many such concepts needs also to be considered, as the work of the teacher attempting to teach 'deviance' makes clear. This work reminds us that concepts are categories of abstractions that develop, change and decay to the extent that a social group finds them useful. The implications of this for teachers are that one needs to be sensitive to the fact that many concepts one attempts to teach are more problematic than is often realised. Thus, the exact determination of the criterial attributes of many concepts is often a matter for judgment by the teacher, taking into account social attitudes, the objectives of the lesson and the current level of pupils' understanding.

The identification of the essential features of the concepts one is trying to teach has two main purposes. The first is that it assists teachers more effectively to focus their attention on those aspects of content that pupils *must* learn if they are to accomplish the learning task. The alternative, which is much less likely to be effective, is to start teaching with diffuse ideas and try to sort things out during the actual teaching. The second advantage of identifying the key aspects of the concepts being taught, is that they guide teachers in their planning of pedagogical actions likely to ensure that pupils actually learn the concepts efficiently and comprehensively. I now consider ways in which teachers can take a systematic approach to the identification of these other crucial aspects of effective teaching in their planning.

TYPE OF LEARNING

The careful examination of the 'content' of a proposed piece of teaching is the essential preliminary to identifying the kind of learning involved. If teacher action is to produce effective pupil learning it is crucial for the action to be based on processes relevant to that learning. To take an obvious example, teaching physical (motor) skills such as sawing a piece of wood will demand the use of different pedagogical actions from those likely to produce satisfactory learning of conceptual material such as systems of classification used in libraries. Unfortunately this is not always clearly understood, and very similar approaches are used whatever the kind of learning; most commonly, of course, just 'telling'.

In the example just given, the difference between the two tasks is clear. However, it is quite common for differences to be less obvious. The example of the teacher of French referred to earlier (see p. 76) is a case in point. In that case there was a lack of clarity in distinguishing between rote and conceptual learning in the teaching of vocabulary (rote) and grammatical structures (conceptual). Lack of clarity in making such distinctions can lead to quite inappropriate teaching.

In general teachers do not consider the type of learning implicit in specific episodes of teaching. As I have already suggested, any lesson plans they may make are likely to focus on the sequence of activities within the lesson, without any consideration of the underlying rationale for the activities themselves, or for their sequence. This is not surprising, of course, since they are most unlikely to have been introduced *in any practical way* to the underlying psychological principles during the course of their initial teacher training. However, the effectiveness of a teacher's classroom activity is dependent upon an understanding of the way those principles interact with practical teaching. I do not deny that some teachers make use of teaching approaches that follow similar lines to those they might have derived from an explicit use of pedagogical principles. However, if they do, their practice is likely to be intuitive, difficult to systematise and virtually inaccessible to others.

The studies reported here are accounts of attempts by teachers to decide explicitly what kind of learning is involved in specific lessons or sequences of lessons. Broad categories of learning are employed. They comprise rote learning, concept learning, problem-solving and the learning of motor skills. I recognise that many psychologists might wish to subdivide these categories and some might wish to focus on one of them particularly. However, I believe that the types of learning considered meet with wide recognition.

Rote learning

Some kinds of learning do not demand the abstraction that constitutes concept learning. The memorising of links between two visual or verbal stimuli, as in learning tables or number bonds, is an example of such learning. Another is learning the alphabet. Learning of this type is the 'rote learning' referred to earlier. It is entirely specific to the conditions in which it is learned. Learning to respond orally when the letter 'a' is presented, is the learning of nothing more than a simple pairing of a stimulus with a response. The learning applies only to that sight–sound connection and cannot be transferred to other situations. On the other hand, the idea of 'alphabet' is a concept. It is an abstraction from a variety of exemplars of alphabet. One finds alphabets in a wide variety of languages. The alphabets are composed of different letters or signs, but they have the same criterial attributes, they are all sets of signs or letters that represent one or occasionally more than one phoneme. The word 'alphabet', therefore, has meaning beyond the linking of the sight of the word with the sound and would be useful in circumstances other than the 'learning the alphabet' lesson. It is true that in some circumstances, such as the early stages of learning to read, the alphabet may be learned by rote recitation, but as children experience the use of the alphabet in a variety of situations they will gradually acquire a concept of 'alphabet'. The concept will change and become more complex with the child's experience (especially if the pupil grows up to become a professor of linguistics). The skill of the teacher making a pedagogical analysis will be to take such factors into account when deciding on the type of learning involved in achieving the aims of the teaching.

Concept learning

The teaching of concepts is the activity with which most teachers are concerned. The general category of concept learning embraces concepts at every level of abstraction, ranging from simple concepts, sometimes referred to as 'concrete concepts', such as 'tree' or 'man', to the highly abstract bodies of concepts that constitute a field of academic study such as laws of physics that determine planetary motion or the principles of genetics that determine the transmission of hereditary characteristics. However, there are certain fundamental processes that seem to be relevant at all levels of concept learning. A knowledge of those processes is indispensable to the systematic and consistently effective teaching of concepts. It is, therefore, important to be able to decide when a teaching task involves pupils in conceptual learning. Pedagogical analysis offers a guide to teachers to make those decisions more effectively.

Psychomotor learning

The teaching of physical skills, usually referred to as *psychomotor skills* is one other major category of learning with which teachers are likely to be involved. It is also a field in which one may observe a great lack of clarity as to the nature of the most appropriate teacher action. It is very common to find the teaching of such skills consisting in great part of 'show and tell' activity. The teacher demonstrates and explains what to do and how to do it. In the learning of most psychomotor skills this approach is unlikely to be particularly effective. This is because show and tell methods ignore some of the basic psychological aspects of psychomotor learning.

I shall consider the problems of show and tell approaches in a later chapter. The main point that bears on pedagogical analysis is the need to identify those aspects of the skill that are entirely *motor*, that is, concerned with physical activity of some sort, and which aspects may be considered *psychological*, in that they involve some element of concept learning, or perhaps rote verbal learning. In fact most psychomotor skills involve some element of concept learning, but this is often overlooked or not understood in teaching and coaching of these skills. Conversely, some attempts to teach concepts may founder because the teacher has not understood that lack of a particular motor skill may impede the pupils' learning.

Problem solving

Learning of problem-solving skills is one of the most important kinds of learning. It has been suggested that solving problems is a variant of concept learning involving the learning of particularly complex concepts with less information than is usually available in learning new concepts.

Undoubtedly some of the aspects of concept learning apply to problem solving. However, learning to tackle problems effectively necessitates giving particular attention to activities that are less emphasised in concept learning, since concept learning has the active support of the teacher. In teaching, problem-solving activities are often seen as the end point in learning when the teacher's support is removed.

Given the crucial nature of problem solving in school learning, it is reasonable to do one's best to help pupils tackle problems as effectively as possible. At the planning stage of teaching, therefore, it is useful to build into the teaching some discussion and activities that offer opportunities for pupils to acquire and practise activities that will enhance their ability to attack problems with good chances of success. By doing this a teacher not only helps pupils with new learning, but at the same time increases motivation considerably – success being a powerful reinforcement, especially in the case of problem solving. It should not be overlooked, either, that raising systematically and explicitly the idea that one can learn ways of tackling problems can connect particularly clearly with the world outside school.

SOME ANALYSES OF LEARNING

Let us now consider some of the ways in which teachers of various subjects have managed to identify the type of learning involved in reaching the goals they set for their pupils. The first example refers to concept learning, which is the most common type of learning teachers aspire to.

It concerns the work of the music teacher referred to earlier (see p. 69). He was teaching melody. On the face of it, the learning of melody would seem to consist essentially of psychomotor activity, such as listening and discriminating among sequences of notes. In fact, the teacher's analysis revealed that the key to learning melody was learning concepts. His analysis does not discount other types of learning, but the type of learning that equips a person to acquire the ability to compose simple melodies is essentially concept learning.

In his analysis he sets out the key elements of the learning as follows:

The learning is concept learning achieved by dividing the overall concept of melody into the three sub-concepts dictated by the unique form of melody as more than a mere progression of notes in a temporal sequence.

Much of this learning depends on prerequisite learning, especially in the ability to notate musical symbols and count in 2 or 3 time.

There is provision for a programme of positive and negative exemplars necessary to bring out the criterial attributes of the concept of melody.

Note that there is clear acceptance of the dependence of this learning on earlier and simpler forms of learning. There is also a reference to essential aspects of the teaching for satisfactory concept learning (provision of positive and negative exemplars).

A simpler type of learning is exemplified by the following analysis of part of a teacher's report into teaching children to avoid reversal errors in reading. The problem is the propensity for beginning readers to confuse such letters as 'b' and 'd', and 'p' and 'q', and to read 'on' as 'no'.

The objectives on which his analysis was based imply a variety of types of learning. He states his objectives as: 'The pupil will, at the 80 per cent success level, coordinate kinesthetic, visual and auditory stimuli in order to read, write or sound, as appropriate, the letter "b" when used at the beginning of simple words'.

The first type of learning he identified was concept learning. He considered it crucial for the children to understand the direction 'right'. This relates to the word-attack skills of reading from left to right. Note that he does not, at this stage, introduce the word 'left', but concentrates on the pupils' being able to distinguish between 'right' and 'not right'.

The next entry in his analysis takes the learning a stage further. He now has in his 'General Content' column: 'Correctly identify pictures with a right-facing orientation from similar pictures with a different orientation'. He considers that achieving this objective involves 'Stimulus–response learning and visual discrimination by reference to an object's position in space'. The implication here is that the ability to respond accurately to the discrimination problem is a low-level type of learning akin to the rote learning I have discussed earlier. An animal in an experimental laboratory could be taught to make such discriminations.

The teacher's view of the type of learning involved here is not wholly satisfactory. The intended pupils' learning before they were asked to make the discrimination was their learning the concept of 'right'. If the pupils learn the concept satisfactorily any *subsequent* identification of right-facing pictures would entail their identifying new exemplars of the concept 'right' which they had just learned. It would, therefore, be more a demonstration of satisfactory concept learning than the more simple kind of responding implied in the 'stimulus–response' classification the teacher suggested. On the other hand, it is true that before one can identify new exemplars of the concept 'right' in this context one has to be able to discriminate physically between pictures facing left and right. The weakness of the analysis is more a case of lack of clarity than of error.

The second point we might question follows from the teacher's proposal for the pupils' responses: 'Identify with a marker the matching picture. Give an explanation of the similarity'. The second sentence indicates unequivocally that the learning involved is conceptual. Simple response learning and simple visual discrimination involve automatic reactions. *Explaining* the basis for the responses involves the pupil in the use of language, which, if meaningful (i.e. not merely repeating by rote what the teacher had previously said) by definition involves the use of concepts. This is not to suggest that the act of making the discriminations and responses does not involve lower levels of learning. Unless one can discriminate *physically* between two stimuli, one will not be able to tell which of the given stimuli are in the same category. In the case we are considering the stimuli are the pictures with different orientations.

Distinguishing between different types of learning, as in this example, is not a trivial exercise or psychological hair splitting. In the case we are discussing the teacher would not be able to decide with any certainty the reason for failure of any learners who had not been able to match pictures with the same orientation. A faulty assessment of the type of learning involved could well lead to his approaching remedial teaching with inappropriate methods.

The teacher set out a statement of the abilities he considered essential for the pupils to have before he started the teaching. He says they should be capable of 'gross visual discrimination'. It is not clear if this covers the discriminations the children are being asked to make in the task we are considering. If it does *not* then his classification of the learning involved as stimulus–response learning is correct, since this will be new learning and he needs to teach the pupils to discriminate at the visual level using methods appropriate to that type of learning. If, however, he expects them already to be able to tell that the pictures are different at the beginning of teaching, he would be concerned with teaching the pupils the concept of 'right', and the appropriate teaching would be that related to the teaching of concepts.

In fact, the teacher indicates in a subsequent appraisal of the lesson that he regards the ability to discriminate on the basis of the *physical* characteristics of verbal or non-verbal stimuli (words, pictures, objects) as contributory to concept learning, a point he leaves unclear in his analysis.

Error in deciding what kind of learning is involved in order to reach a given teaching objective could lead to a teacher's using an approach to teaching that was quite inappropriate for the learning involved. In some cases this might result in the pupils' not learning. In others the teacher might waste a lot of time using methods more sophisticated than the teaching task demands.

The case of the teacher of orienteering discussed in the last chapter is a clear example of concept learning. The concept of 'bearing' is subordinate to that of making a route choice. The teacher's list of sub-concepts (see p. 74) illustrates the nature of this type of analysis.

The teacher considers that 'all [the listed sub-concepts] involve concept learning by definition – therefore a sequential and graduated programme of positive and negative exemplars will be used to bring out the criterial attributes of the concept'. (Concepts 'by definition' are concepts that relate to such things as definitions and rules that are entirely socially constructed as distinct from concepts that relate to objects occurring in the natural world.)

The case of the teaching of elements of French discussed earlier (see p. 76) is, as I suggested, an example of faulty analysis of the type of learning involved in a particular teaching task. The teacher considered that most of the elements of the teaching task involved rote learning, whereas most are clearly statements of principles. The underlying distinction between the two types of learning is that in rote learning and drill approaches there is no abstraction. The learner is learning to respond to specific stimuli that are practically the same every time they are encountered. Conceptual learning, by definition, involves abstraction. The best way of teaching for the one kind of learning differs considerably from the best way of teaching for the other kind. These are questions we shall consider in detail later.

The examples of analyses I have just discussed illustrate one of the most prevalent problems I have encountered in the study of teachers' analyses of teaching tasks. Learning that seems to involve simple rote learning more often than not turns out to be far more complex than it first appears. Indeed, very little school learning after the very early stages of learning to read involves only rote learning. Some examples of learning that involves mainly rote methods are learning to identify digits, to learn new symbols, as in learning the Cyrillic alphabet, or to learn vocabulary in a foreign language. Even in learning that is basically paired associate learning in instances such as these, teachers and learners often try to bring some sort of meaning into the task, and thus make it easier by using mnemonics or related techniques.

The analysis by the teacher I referred to earlier, in the field of map-reading skills, may serve as an illustration of the complexity inherent in apparently simple learning tasks. A sub-skill derived from the main task of identifying the symbols on maps was taken to involve multiple discrimination. Learning of this type, as it is normally understood by learning psychologists, is learning without abstraction. In the first place one learns to respond to a particular stimulus. In the case of map reading, this would involve, initially, being able to pick out specific stimuli (the signs on the map used to stand for the features on the terrain). Later one would be expected to discriminate among many different signs. This is the multiple discrimination the teacher identified. This classification of student learning is accurate since no abstraction is necessary for a person to be able to tell one sign from another.

Map signs tend to be a mixture of pictograms, which attempt to depict the features they signal, for example stylised drawings of windmills, and other conventional signs which bear no resemblance to the appearance of the actual feature they stand for, for example, the British Ordnance Survey sign for bus or railway station. The particular signs, however, are always the same on maps of all scales. However, responding to the sign for unmetalled road on maps of different scale and with different colours does not *necessarily* involve abstraction. It could be the same kind of learning as may be found in lower animals, such as pigeons, which can be trained to respond in similar ways to sights and sounds that resemble each other even if they are not identical. This is called 'stimulus generalisation'.

But human learning is more complex than pigeon learning. Pigeons almost certainly progress no further than responding automatically to a sign, for example, by pecking. Humans learning map-reading skills are doing much more than that. The first step is learning to distinguish one sign from another. But note: once people are able to tell one sign from another they enter a different world of learning. They are now able to connect the sign on the map with the words we normally use to symbolise the concepts the signs signify. Thus, the line $- + - + - +$ indicates 'national boundary' on a British Ordnance Survey map, and the line. . . . indicates 'parish boundary'. Humans learn that the lines stand for the words, either spoken or written. The words, themselves, stand for, or symbolise concepts we have already learned. One cannot learn what a national boundary is by learning to read a map. One has to have learned both concepts before the signs on the map can be interpreted meaningfully. Thus, knowing what 'national' and 'boundary' mean is a prerequisite to learning to read the map effectively. The same, of course, applies to all the conventional signs used on the map. Any learner who has not acquired the concept the signs signify might well be able to discriminate at the 'pigeon level' between the sign for 'bracken', 'heath' and 'rough grassland' and the sign for 'dunes'. However the learning will be of little use in working from the map to the terrain it represents. It will be rote learning only, since the learner has no idea what dunes or bracken, etc., are.

Thus, the classification of the *identification* of the symbols as multiple discrimination is correct and will be useful in guiding the teacher to take the most appropriate action when he takes the first step in teaching his students to tell one sign from another. Learners who are familiar with the features the pictographic signs represent will have nothing new to learn when they see them on a map. In the case of features that are not near-pictograms, teaching appropriate to rote learning would suffice to teach the pupils to discriminate among the conventions. A teacher wishing to teach map-reading skills might, therefore, wish to check the learners' knowledge of the pictographic signs for reassurance that they do, in fact, understand them, but then concentrate on teaching the significance of the arbitrary signs that bear no resemblance to the appearance of the features themselves.

The teacher analysing the task of teaching children to avoid reversal errors in beginning reading identified another type of learning. He considered one of the subordinate skills necessary for achieving this aim to be that the learners develop the appropriate kinesthetic 'feel' during the process of writing words. This he identified as psychomotor skill learning with cognitive relationships. The appropriate teaching would therefore draw on knowledge about the teaching of such skills. In this particular example the teacher thought it suitable to break the skill into a chain of very specific movements and teach it by 'backward chaining'. In this approach learners start to learn the task by adding the last link (the last movement) in a chain complete except for the last element and gradually have to supply more and more links until they can complete the whole chain. In the case in point, the learners would start by adding the final small piece of an otherwise correctly written word or letter. Thus the first word or letter would be almost complete. The pupil would have to add just one part of a stroke to a letter or one letter to a word. The following word or letter would be a little less complete so that the learner would have to add a little more. Then the pupil would be asked to write increasing amounts to complete the letter or word in a gradual series of less and less complete examples. Eventually all support is withdrawn and the learner has to carry out the task without help and write the complete word or letter from scratch.

An example from the teaching of six- to seven-year-olds provides an interesting angle on the relationship between different kinds of learning. This teacher was concerned to teach the children the concept of 'solid' shape in the context of teaching about 'shape' in general.

She considered that in addition to the obvious category of concept learning, an element of psychomotor learning was (or should be) involved. As part of the teaching she used an approach common in British infant schools involving children handling solid objects hidden from sight in a bag. The first thing the children had to learn was to discriminate among a variety of solid objects by their feel, not unlike the children learning left to right orientation that we discussed earlier. But even at this early stage the children were laying the foundations for the concept learning. They learned that solid objects could be any shape, any size, any texture and weight, all through this experience. The two invariants in the learning situation were the three-dimensionality of the objects and the teacher's speech. One of the invariants, three-dimensionality, is a criterial attribute of 'solid' in the sense it is used here. All the other aspects are non-criterial attributes. Changing shape or weight or texture makes no difference. Change the number of dimensions, however, and the objects are no longer solid objects. (I acknowledge that the teacher would find it difficult to introduce objects with fewer dimensions.)

The other invariant in the teaching, language, is not *by nature* an attribute of the concept at all. However, the teacher's speech is a very powerful influence on the learning. Telling the children that all the objects, heterogeneous as they may be, are all classified by adults as 'solids', acts as a criterial attribute and a cue to their learning. It is not that language merely labels the concept when the children have learned it. It helps and guides the learners in the process of learning the concept. Note: it is one thing to use language in this way as a guide and an invariant to help children experience the concepts being learned, and another just giving children a definition of 'solid'. The former helps them towards meaningful learning, the latter encourages learning without meaning.

The teacher could probably have taught 'solid' without providing the kinesthetic experiences she did. This illustrates an interesting and important aspect of concept learning. The richness of one's concepts depends entirely upon one's experiences of a variety of occurrences of the concepts. Children who learned 'solid' without handling the variety of objects will have less rich concepts than those who had. In the extreme case, attempts at learning with no experience of exemplars of the concept(s) being taught can only result in rote learning. Children taught the words that define a solid with no practical experience would be learning without meaning. 'Meaning' depends on experience. Learning without experience of the realities words symbolise is doomed to be rote. 'Experiential learning', which is currently a fashionable phrase in some educational circles, is grappling with this point but misses it. The expression is tautological. All learning is experiential. The trouble with rote learning is that the experience is restricted to learning arbitrary sounds: words bereft of the experience that gives them substance and enables one to develop concepts and invest the sounds with meaning. The trouble with teaching that merely provides unguided experience is that intentions to teach concepts often pave the way to rote learning.

The very important and interesting thing that becomes clear when one does a serious systematic analysis of the types of learning implied in plans for teaching is the way in which the teaching of different 'subjects' makes use of common psychopedagogical principles. This finding is not a consequence of the forcing of teaching into a Procrustean mould. It has been observed in practice by many teachers working on real teaching problems. All the work reported in these pages is based on the work of groups of teachers and student teachers heterogeneous as to subject and age of pupil. The heterogeneity was a strength, not a problem, in the work for reasons that are entirely consistent with the learning theories we are discussing. If one is to acquire a comprehensive conceptual grasp of the psychological underpinnings of human learning and teaching, it is essential that one experience a wide variety of exemplars of teaching and learning. By focusing on the *pedagogical* bases of teaching and learning one can regard the 'subject' being studied and the age of the children as non-criterial attributes of the teaching. This by no means implies that these are unimportant factors, far from it. The conceptual analysis takes these questions very seriously, and the analysis of the types of learning, draws heavily on information related to human development, as do other elements of pedagogical analysis.

SPECIFIC EXAMPLES

Considering the nature of the learning involved in relation to the analysis of conceptual content is integral with the planning of the type of examples to present to the learner. Having the category in the pedagogical analysis helps to remind one of the fact that learning is, in the last analysis, entirely dependent upon the learner's experience of the world. This does not preclude the use of the teacher's speech in concept learning. Indeed, adult speech is one of the most potent aids to concept learning and is, in fact, a crucial part of the learner's experience. But conceptual learning will be difficult and in some cases impossible if the teacher's talk is the learner's *sole* experience in new learning. Speech and experience must be integrated. Teacher talk on its own may be effective in *some* new learning, provided that the teaching builds upon already existing concepts that in turn have been learned through experience with concrete reality. However, even in such circumstances it should be recognised that the concepts learned by pupils will be less extensive, and therefore less amenable to transfer to new situations, than if they had been learned with the additional benefit of action in the real world. For example, a teacher's explanation of the way a car engine works may be followed quite well by students of automobile engineering. Their learning could also be enhanced by the use of charts, diagrams and films. But the complexity of their concepts about engine functioning will be immeasurably increased through experience of a variety of engines in different states of repair, and in different vehicles, of different shapes, colours and smells.

This argument applies not only to teaching in fields such as engineering. Aesthetic subjects such as music are subject to the same principles. Explanation on its own may be valuable, for example in the teaching of composition. It would also be greatly enriched by recordings to illustrate the teacher's argument. However, a wide variety of examples drawn from people composing music in different societies at different times would develop the learners' concepts very much more.

In the case of learning psychomotor skills the same general principles apply. Explaining and demonstrating may provide some basic information *if the learners are familiar with the concepts used in the explanation.* Demonstrating may be of assistance to the learners if the skills demonstrated are not overly complex. Introducing a wide variety of examples of the skills involved through the use of different media, such as diagrams, pictures and film, and by observing a variety of people practising the skills, not just experts, would be more effective than one expert showing and telling.

The nature of the examples to be presented will be determined in part by the teacher's previous experience of working in similar fields, in part by the elements revealed by the conceptual analysis, and in part by the teacher's understanding of the nature of the learning involved. As an overall guide, the emphasis should be on systematic variation of the examples in whatever kind of learning in order to make learning more flexible and transferable across different situations.

However, in all the above examples, the key point is that although the learners' concepts of the various phenomena may be enhanced, their ability in any related activity is not necessarily assured. This point is probably quite evident in the case of psychomotor skills such as have just been discussed. (Having a good grasp of the principles of serving at tennis does not by any means guarantee skilled performance.) But it almost certainly applies in other less obvious ways to the learning of new concepts. This follows since, although it is often argued that learning is valuable 'for its own sake', there are almost invariably implicit, perhaps more fundamental, aims underlying any attempt to teach anyone anything. 'Learning for its own sake' probably implies an underlying hope that the learners will be better able to cope with some aspect(s) of their lives more effectively. This hope might well be cherished even in fields that may have little obvious relationship to practical activity, such as the study of literature or music, and even though the teacher may not make this aspiration explicit.

Cases of examples

A few cases may help to illustrate the approach to deciding on specific examples and at the same time indicate some of the difficulties. Here are two analyses by different teachers teaching different subjects to different ages of pupils but each with a similar specific task in mind.

The first is taken from the pedagogical analysis of a teacher of engineering subjects in a technical college. His task was to teach the angle of inclination of a flat cold chisel. This angle varies according to the rake and point angles of the chisel. The angle also governs the direction of the cutting forces. The teacher classified the learning of this statement as stimulus–response learning, since it was new information to his students, as it may well be to most readers. However, he went on to fill out the definition and build up some conceptual content by presenting the students with diagrams to illustrate the nature of the relationship between the angles and by cuing the students orally.

This approach is in line with commonly observed methods in the teaching of subjects of this type. However, there is probably an important difference in that this teacher recognises that the presentation of a definition involves nothing more than S–R or rote learning. It is not useful learning on its own. This is really quite an important point in view of the common stereotype of teaching as merely 'telling'.

A teacher working with younger children (about ten years old) teaching the concept of 'rectangle' was also concerned with the teaching of angles. In this case the concept of 'right angle' was deemed to be a subordinate concept to the idea of 'rectangle'. Attempting to teach that rectangles contain four right angles, she presented diagrams of different geometrical figures, some with right angles and some without. She also pointed out the angles in different figures and explained that angles can be of different sizes.

This teacher's approach resembles the one we have just considered and is fairly familiar to practising teachers. The teacher's speech provides the invariant that draws attention to the criterial attributes of the concept.

In this example the teacher decided, after analysing the way the lesson had gone and assessing the pupils' learning, that the presentation of exemplars of 'right angle' had not been entirely satisfactory and that she should have presented more positive exemplars. This is a point of some importance generally. Learning is just not possible if no positive exemplars are provided. If very few are provided learning may not be ruled out, but it cannot be assured.

An example from the work of a student teacher teaching the concept of 'deviance' provides an illustration from another field. The conceptual analysis identified several subordinate concepts and the teacher prepared examples to illustrate each of them. To illustrate the idea of deviance as non-conformity the teacher gave examples of school rules and of behaviour that would be deviant in respect of them: unpunctuality, wearing proscribed dress. The two examples would be a very limited selection to build up the concept. However, the teacher also introduces the idea of relativeness of the concept of deviance and presents further examples to make that point. Thus school rules vary from school to school and from time to time. Killing is deviant in normal times and acceptable in wartime. Injecting morphine is acceptable if done by a nurse but deviant if self-injected by a drug addict. Drinking alcohol is deviant in strict Muslim communities but perfectly acceptable in most contemporary societies. A woman who smoked and drank in public would have been considered deviant 100 years ago but such behaviour is commonplace now. The presentation of these examples in discussion with the pupils was very useful in helping the pupils to acquire the two key aspects of deviance so far presented. The fact that deviance is observed in widely different contexts such as the observation of school rules, drug injection and murder focuses the learners' attention on the criterial attributes of the concept which remain inherent in the examples given.

STIMULUS PRESENTATION

As I have suggested, it is not possible to consider aspects of pedagogical planning in isolation. Thus while I have been considering such things as the nature of the learning involved and the examples to be presented, I have willy-nilly been raising implicitly questions about the way in which the students' learning environment is to be structured. How are the examples to be presented? Using what media? In what contexts? In what sequence?

The teacher's talk is the most pervasive medium for presenting examples. We need to consider most carefully whether this pervasiveness is likely to be beneficial to a given teaching task.

In view of the essentiality of practical experience in many new learning situations, it is almost certain that the ubiquitous use of teacher talk is counterproductive. Finding alternatives is a challenging task that demands imaginative approaches.

The consideration of the nature of learning involved in specific teaching situations will guide a teacher in identifying modes of structuring the learning environment so that it contains more than just a teacher talking. This consideration should also guide a teacher to spot when sophisticated hardware is being extolled as a breakthrough in teaching when its main use is actually little more than an alternative to teacher talk. In the 1960s teaching machines were thought to herald a pedagogical revolution. In fact they did little more than present teacher talk in writing by turning pages electrically or electronically. In the 1990s the technology is much more sophisticated, using computers, lasers and video-disks. But, like teaching machines, very often it does little more than present teacher talk. Video-disks and computers *can* be valuable for the presentation of stimuli, especially visual material. But *in themselves* they are inert. Successful pedagogy depends upon teacher thought not teacher talk on disk, even illustrated by pictures. Structuring the learner's environment by careful organisation of stimuli would fit such aids into the framework of the teaching, not replace them.

The examples I gave earlier from various fields indicate some possible ways of presenting stimuli. Imaginative teachers have made many contributions in this field. Field work, out-of-school visits, bringing reality into the classroom, involving pupils in discussions are just a few examples. I discuss others below. The marriage of these contributions with systematic pedagogical methods of structuring the pupils' experience is essential to fruitful outcomes.

PUPILS' RESPONSES

Having the category of pupils' responses in the analysis forces an important activity on the teacher's attention. Any teachers worth their salt will have cause to reflect if they find, when considering this section, that the type of pupil response envisaged in their teaching is nearly always 'to listen'. For *any* type of learning to take place there must be a response from the learner to a particular event or series of events in the environment. Students in a 'listening posture' may or not be responding. Experienced teachers may be able to detect from non-verbal cues whether or not any inner activity is taking place while they are addressing their pupils. Whether any activity detected is related to the learning intended is, one might say, problematic.

Even if the inner activity detected is related to the subject of the teacher talk, the nature of what is happening is still problematic. In view of the great difference between pupil and teacher experiences the chances are extremely high that there are considerable discrepancies between pupil thought and teacher thought. Forcing one to think about the nature of the pupils' responses helps to remind one of these discrepancies. It is also the first step in providing for the pupil experiences that are indispensable for learning to take place.

Any type of activity pupils may engage in related to the new learning is likely to be a form of simple problem solving. The teacher may be very active in support of their activity by structuring the learning environment, as has been discussed above. But even with very simple learning such as learning number bonds or vocabulary, the pupil is faced with a problem, that of moving from a state of incompetence (not 'knowing') to a state of competence ('knowing'). With learning such as concept learning the required responses may be more complex but the same general point applies. The pupil's response is essential to the pupil and to the teacher. It is a vital part of the learning for the pupil and it provides feedback to the teacher about the effects of the way the teaching has been structured.

Expository teaching comprising talk by the teacher and questions to the pupils does not preclude worthwhile learning since it does involve pupil responses. However, the range of possible responses is limited in question-and-answer sessions. When the most salient feature of the learning milieu is the teacher's speech there is always the danger that any learning will be detached from reality and pupil replies to questions will lack any conceptual content.

Teacher talk is not necessarily confined to asking questions demanding verbal replies. It may be suggesting courses of action or prompting and guiding pupil activities that could help to solve the learning problem the pupils are grappling with at any one time. Pupil responses here could well involve many different types of activity. For example, to continue with previous illustrations, the student learning about motor vehicles might be learning about methods of carburation. An appropriate response here might well be to demonstrate a grasp of principles by discriminating between different approaches to carburation, either in actual engines or in drawings or descriptions of engines. A student learning intervals in music might be asked to distinguish between exemplars and non-exemplars of various intervals. It might be that the response is communicated to the teacher verbally. But this is vastly different from answering a teacher's questions in the course of an expository lesson. Answering questions is then the *end point* of the activity, not the *only* type of activity. The response that matters is the act of discriminating among different things or the recognising of instances of newly learned concepts, or deploying elements in new motor skill learning.

FEEDBACK

As I intimated in Chapter 1, feedback is the process by which information about the results of activity is reflected back to the originator of the activity. This is a very general statement that covers all kinds of systems; those found in nature and those constructed by humans in such fields as engineering. Feedback is essential for effective human learning. Unless one knows the effect of a given activity one cannot adjust the activity to increase its effectiveness. I instanced, earlier, the case of a person aiming at a target who would have little hope of scoring a hit without feedback providing information about where the missile struck. Thus it is quite crucial that teachers arrange suitable feedback to their pupils about the results of their activity. Without feedback learning is guaranteed *not* to take place.

Feedback does not necessarily have to be provided by the teacher personally. It is possible to arrange the learners' environment so that they get automatic feedback. This was the basis of the programmed learning movement of the 1960s. There was, however, another aspect to programmed learning frequently confused with feedback that merits our attention. Programmed learning *aficionados* stressed the beneficial effects of *reinforcement* in learning. A reinforcer is an event that increases the likelihood of the activity that immediately preceded it being repeated. Thus, the teaching programs were constructed so as to ensure a high level of success in answering the questions posed as part of the structure of the program. The idea that frequent success would ensure that the learners would maintain their activity of working at the program.

There is general agreement that high levels of success are important in enhancing learner motivation, and I shall discuss this question later. The point I am making here is that reinforcement is not the same as feedback, and feedback is very important for effective learning for a different reason. Not because feedback *necessarily* increases motivation, but because it provides knowledge of results of one's activity.

This is not merely an academic distinction or hairsplitting. There are times when a teacher might consider it advisable to restrict or filter feedback to a learner. Should a pupil fail totally to cope with a learning task, it could be disastrous to give chapter and verse about the nature of the failure, since it could be so punishing that motivation to continue working would be destroyed. And yet it is necessary to provide learners with information about their efforts. There can be no general prescription for resolving this dilemma. Probably the most useful approach is to encourage the effort while pointing out the key deficiencies in the pupils' responses and suggesting ways of overcoming them. It should be said, however, that if pupils are in this position frequently there is likely to be something wrong with the teaching.

At the stage of pedagogical analysis, however, the main point to consider is how best to provide feedback giving knowledge of results. Teachers' oral comment is tremendously flexible and can be very effective. The way in which it is used, however, is a crucial consideration. It should not merely be related to the pupils' activity of answering questions about what teacher has told them. It should be related to active pupil learning and, in general, it should provide more information than whether the pupil's solution to the learning problem posed is correct. More analytical information, the 'why' and the 'how', for example, will help more.

Methods of arranging feedback other than teacher talk are important and should be considered at this stage of the pedagogical analysis while considering such things as the conceptual nature of the new learning and the type of learning involved. The methods decided upon will be the product of teacher imagination and experience and a consideration of psychological principles related to human learning. Making effective connections between the two is rarely a simple matter, although it may sometimes appear to be.

Teacher talk as a method of providing feedback is another general category. Its effectiveness depends entirely upon the specific nature of the pupil activity and the teacher comment. Another general channel for providing feedback is the provision of self-checking devices for learners to consult at the end of a specific piece of work. Peer consultation also offers possibilities for providing feedback in certain circumstances. Teacher action in all these categories could be of an almost infinite variety to suit specific situations. The key point is that learners should be provided with precise information about the results of their actions so as to enable them to adjust their next responses if necessary to solve the problem they are currently tackling.

EVALUATION

The best method of evaluating new learning is to see if it is of use in circumstances other than those in which it took place. In the case of conceptual learning it is the main way of determining if the learning really does involve the learning of new concepts or if the learners have merely memorised the language that goes with the concepts, the process I have referred to as 'rote learning'. Learning of this type is particularly likely to occur when teaching is largely by oral exposition and assessment is by conventional verbal methods, whether of the short answer or essay-type of questions.

To evaluate pupils' learning of concepts it is best to avoid asking them just to state the general principles they embody, as in a dictionary definition. Presenting novel problems which depend on having learned the concept is the best way of making certain that conceptual learning has taken place. It should also be possible for a person who has learned a concept to discriminate between exemplars and non-exemplars of the concept with a very high level of accuracy.

Similar comments can be made about other forms of learning. Even the learning of simple stimulus–response connections such as learning tables in arithmetic or foreign language vocabulary may be more accurately assessed if the conditions of assessment are systematically varied so as to reduce the cuing effects of the context in which the original learning took place, for example in the chanting of a list where one thing cues the next. Methods used by teachers to accomplish this involve such things as the random presentation of stimuli for the pupil to respond to, and switching the order of presentation if it is possible, so that the stimulus on one occasion becomes the response on another occasion. These techniques are often used by teachers, and it would be useful if we could systematise our knowledge of how they are employed and how the methods of employment square with knowledge of rote learning in psychology. Of course, in the teaching phase, the cuing effect of context can be used by teachers to assist this type of learning, for example, by the use of mnemonics.

In the case of psychomotor skills a good test of competence is for the learner to execute the activity in various conditions. Being able to demonstrate ability in exactly the same conditions as those in which the learning took place is very limited evidence of effective learning. In some circumstances such an assessment could be very misleading, since even in the case of physical skills the learning being demonstrated could very well resemble rote learning. The performer may go through a rigidly defined set of actions that could be disrupted at the slightest deviation from the usual conditions. Learning of this type would not survive a test which asked the performer to demonstrate competence in novel conditions.

Thus if we were interested in evaluating the learning of skill in tennis playing we should obtain a more accurate picture by asking the learner to play in a variety of conditions, not merely those in which the skill had been learned. We might try to test using various playing surfaces, in different wind and sun conditions, and perhaps we might vary the weight of the racket. If we assessed the learning solely on an indoor court we would get a very limited view of the competence of the learner.

Of course, our approach to the evaluation of learning reflects back on those items of our analysis in which we considered the type of learning involved, the nature of the stimulus and provision of feedback, and the learner's response. In the teaching flowing from that analysis we would be alive to the need for varying the key aspects of the learning so that it would be versatile and applicable to varied conditions. Then, at the assessment stage, although the *specific* exemplification of the skill might be different from those encountered in the previous learning conditions, the *general* underlying features of the learned skill would be the same. The general point at work here is, that the more varied the learning conditions, the more flexible the performance. Our methods of evaluation should take this into account.

DELIVERANCE FROM DELIVERY

In concluding my consideration of pedagogical analysis, I should like to consider briefly those aspects that bear particularly on methods of developing teaching that escape from the 'delivery teaching trap'. I shall do this by looking at a few examples of experienced teachers working from a base of pedagogical analyses while at the same time drawing on their practical teaching experiences. The first case is taken from an analysis for a series of lessons by a teacher of six-year-olds. The complete analysis is to be seen in figure 6.3, 160. The teacher wished to teach 2 and 3 time rhythmic patterns. There were several subordinate concepts: long/short, accent, two and three beats, tempo, and rhythmic patterns in 2 or 3 time. To teach long/short she used the following examples and methods of presentation: different lengths of straws, ribbons, spills, centimetre rods and dowelling; pendulum; sand-timer; beads; pegs; interlocking cubes; plastic coins; pencil; paper. To illustrate sound she used pre-recorded audio-tape (fog horn, scream and others), various musical instruments (chime bars, tambourines, wooden blocks, whistles, beads, crumpled paper). She also used most of these as well as electronic devices, in teaching the other subordinate concepts. Later, she introduced general discussion.

There is, undoubtedly, a tradition of using 'practical' approaches such as these in the teaching of younger children. The varied and systematic relating of the presentations to the concepts they exemplify is somewhat less observed. Note, also, the introduction of discussion at the later stage. When the concepts are becoming clearer, genuine discussion as opposed to straightforward teacher talk can be very useful in clarifying understanding. Obviously, with such young children 'discussion' is likely to be rather different from that in which adults might engage; nevertheless, the teacher did find it helpful in guiding the children's learning, even though it was difficult to involve some children.

The analysis of the task of remedying reversal/inversion confusion in learning to read and write illustrates the close interrelationship between stimulus presentation and pupil response. The teacher involved set out to use kinesthetic, visual and auditory stimuli in coordination, in the first place, to teach the pupil to read, write and sound the letter 'b' when used at the beginning of words.

Teacher talk involved introducing the idea 'right' and then asking the pupils themselves to demonstrate by touching parts of the body as requested, and then asking them to point out the object on the right of a group of objects. This activity was to be followed by the presentation of an array of objects with distinctive features oriented in different directions from among which the pupils had to discriminate those objects facing right and to explain the nature of the common attribute. This was followed by the presentation of a variety of printed and written forms of 'b' in lower case for the pupils to discriminate. Similarly, auditory discrimination was to be developed by the teacher presenting a short series of words for the pupils to identify those beginning with 'b'. Pupil verbal commentary on the action in train was to be encouraged. This procedure is discussed further in Chapter 6.

When it came to writing, kinesthetic cues were to be introduced by presenting letter 'b's' overlaid with sandpaper for the pupils to trace. The teacher's speech explained the task and guided the learners at first and asked them to say the letter when it was complete. The tactile stimulus was to be phased out first, and then the teacher's guidance. The pupils' task was to write a series of 'b's' correctly.

Finally, the stimulus presentation took the form of pictures of objects with the names below, but with the initial letter missing. The response requested was for the learner to add the letter 'b' correctly written to those words that begin with 'b'.

The salient things about this planned teacher presentation and pupil response seem to be the following: the teacher drew on her own experience and her knowledge of the work of others in the field of teaching reading to identify the key aspects of the learning task; the approach to pedagogical analysis provided a pedagogical framework for planning teaching that took account of factors involved in the pupils' learning that would not otherwise have been realised; stimulus presentation, specifically, went beyond 'telling' and demonstrating, and pupil response was varied and explicit and took up the major part of the lesson time. The intimate relationship between stimulus presentation and pupil response reminds us of the artificiality of considering different aspects of pedagogical analyses one at a time; all the other aspects of the analysis bear on the two we have considered.

Let us now consider the case of the types of presentation used by the teacher I mentioned before who was teaching rather older pupils the principles of orienteering. Conventional teaching in this subject commonly makes use of traditional show and tell methods. Teacher tells and demonstrates and then exhorts the learners to do the same. In the case we are considering, a much more flexible and imaginative approach was adopted that made use of psychopedagogical principles.

This teacher considered in some detail the nature of the sport of orienteering and the way it is usually taught. He considered that the conventional approach (show and tell) is unlikely to teach at all effectively and adopted an objectives-oriented approach. The identification and analysis of the objectives and subordinate objectives of the teaching of orienteering produced a complex array of concepts and skills to be taught and integrated in teaching the sport. In the course of the teaching the teacher employed an impressive range of modes of presentation. These included pictures, solid objects, the learner's own body orientation, clock faces, diagrams, charts, models, overhead projections, Silva compasses (for orienteering), chess pieces and many other devices. These methods of presentation were not merely random applications of a 'more the merrier' approach. Each one was carefully related to the analysis of the concepts to be learned and was devised to present a controlled sequence of exemplars of the concepts. The criterial attributes were the constant elements in the examples presented and the variety of modes of presentation enabled the teacher more effectively to help the learners to discriminate between criterial and non-criterial attributes.

Orienteering is an interesting *mélange* of physical and intellectual skills. The overall aim is to find your way through forest using orienteering map and compass. Presentation of examples, thus, to be comprehensive, demanded that the students work on the terrain. Therefore, the teacher gradually progressed from work in the classroom, presenting material in the ways described above, into the school grounds and finally into the forest, where the various features discussed earlier could be observed and used to build up concepts previously introduced to a level of complexity more appropriate to the task of following a route with facility.

One further example which picks up the earlier discussion in Chapter 3 of the case of the adult student being introduced for the first time to a concept in elementary geology, which was a totally new field to him. The teacher, an experienced college lecturer, hoped to teach the concept in the space of one hour. His pedagogical analysis identified seven subordinate concepts and decided on specific methods of presentation for each one. The first sub-concept was that a strike line is a construct, i.e. a defined concept in the sense mentioned above (see p. 86–7). Specifically it is an imaginary line. Clearly, it is not possible to present exemplars of imaginary lines, and in his introduction he very reasonably chose to start his teaching by discussing the idea with the student. This opening presented the student with a preliminary idea of the learning task and oriented him to it. From there the teacher moved to using a Plasticine model which enabled him to present an *analogue* of a strike line. This stage was intended to teach that a strike line joins places of equal height on the bedding plane. The next step was to teach that a strike line is drawn horizontally on the bedding plane. This was presented through the use of a cardboard model in discussion with the student of the disposition of strike lines on the model. Further methods of presentation related to other sub-concepts used explanatory diagrams and projections of strike lines from the cardboard model onto plastic sheet and different geological maps.

I have tried, here, to provide a sample of ways of presenting stimuli for learning. I could have produced more from the work of other teachers. However, in a one-way communication such as a book, this might have been counterproductive. The proliferation of detail might have swamped the reader, who would not have been able to see the wood for the trees. The main points flowing from the examples that I would like to stress are these.

The key point is to escape from the conventional 'delivery' mode. 'Delivering the curriculum' is currently a vogue synonym for 'teaching'. The use of such expressions, it seems to me, betrays an appallingly trivial view of teaching and is one of the greatest obstacles to the development of an effective pedagogy. Presenting the stimuli for learning is just one element in a complex operation aimed to structure the learner's environment so as to lead to meaningful and transferable learning and is completely different from 'delivering the curriculum'.

Abandoning the delivery mode of just telling the learners, presents teachers with challenges. The main challenge is to provide imaginative and effective ways of structuring the learners' experiences by introducing interesting and relevant material and situations into the learning environment. The examples discussed give an indication of how one might proceed. But really, all is grist to the teacher's mill, provided it is controlled and logically and psychologically relevant to the nature of the learning desired.

5 Concepts of quality

CONCEPT TEACHING: KEY TO QUALITY

The drift of the argument so far has been that the hallmark of quality teaching is that it fosters understanding and equips learners to apply their learning in new circumstances. To support this argument I have drawn on the work of a number of teachers grappling with the problems of planning and analysis of teaching to help them decide the appropriate action to achieve learning with understanding. I now turn to a discussion of the nature of 'appropriate' action with illustrations from the work of several teachers.

This action may reasonably be considered as involving the deployment of a body of skills related to practical teaching. In the work reported here, these skills are derived from a systematic consideration of the objectives and an analysis of specific teaching tasks in the light of pedagogical principles. They differ from those often derived from other analyses of teaching that do not have this basis. Some common examples of the latter are: beginning a lesson, asking questions, writing on the chalkboard or ending a lesson. Not that such skills are not relevant; they may or they may not be. They are probably not *criterial* attributes of quality teaching. To illustrate: skilful questioning is desirable because it enables a teacher to stimulate and enhance pupils' thinking in such a way as to develop complex bodies of concepts. But it is no good asking questions that demand no cognitive effort. Such questions may produce the right answers without the pupils' having learned the concept. Even 'probing' questions, which require pupils to think deeper, are likely to be of limited effect unless they are based on an understanding of the use of language to highlight criterial attributes and distinguish them from non-criterial attributes.

The same could be said about 'wait time' which has received a good deal of attention in recent years in the study of teaching (Rowe 1974). Wait time refers to the widely observed phenomenon that teachers commonly give pupils very little time to respond to a question they have posed. By giving them a little more time (waiting a bit longer for the answer), one is likely to obtain better responses. Nevertheless, unless the teacher posing the question has consciously structured the questioning with some knowledge of the way concepts are learned, waiting might just provide the pupils with a little more guessing time.

As I have argued throughout, the skills aimed at teaching for learning that will lead to understanding and transfer to new situations are themselves of general application. That is they do not relate to the teaching of this or that subject, but to learning and teaching in general. However, it is hardly likely that useful approaches of general application will be identified by an unsystematic, *ad hoc* collection of teaching skills. A coherent, interlocking body of skills can be devised only on the basis of a coherent body of theoretical principles.

Figure 5.1 The relationship between general skills and phases of teaching

Type of skill	Phase of Teaching		
	Preactive	*Interactive*	*Evaluative*
A	Analyses task Ascertains pupil entry competence	Teaches employing pedagogical principles	Evaluates pupils' learning
B	Appraises an example of pedagogical analysis and pupils' entry competence	Appraises an example of teaching in light of pedagogical principles	Appraises an example of the assessment of pupils' learning
C	Explains how the principles of pedagogical analysis and entry competence apply to a specific teaching task	Explains how principles of pedagogy relate to a specific teaching task	Explains how the principles of assessing pupils' learning may be applied to a specific teaching task

Source: After Stones 1979, 1984

This schematic view of teaching skills depicts the activities that may be considered amenable to application in all teaching situations. It serves as a reminder of the relationship between the different types of skill requisite for planning, executing and evaluating a teaching task. Type A skills are the 'doing' skills, which are sustained by those learned earlier, types B and C. In this figure the three types of skill are deployed in the three stages. The hierarchical relationship applies only to the columns.

In order to elucidate the way the principles I have suggested relate to actual teaching, I have set out in Figure 5.1 a general view of the planning, execution and evaluation of a teaching task. These three phases of teaching are commonly referred to as the pre-active, interactive and evaluative phases. As before, the key skill is a type A skill. The appropriate type A skill in the case of teaching is, therefore, the planning, execution and evaluation of a piece of teaching. The other skills are contributory to this skill and do not involve the teacher in actually teaching but in activities closely related to teaching. Type C skills are likely to be familiar to most readers, since the ability to explain something is often taken as evidence of competence. Type B skills, as I suggested earlier, provide a vital connection between theoretical principles and practice – in the case of teaching, between the principles of psychopedagogy and practical teaching.

In the specific case of concept teaching the links are between principles relating to concept learning and teaching and the actual teaching in all three phases. Thus a teacher should be able to appraise an example of a pedagogical analysis and assessment of current competence relating to the teaching of a specific concept or body of concepts. Similarly, the teacher should be able to appraise an example of concept teaching and the related assessment of learner post-teaching competence in the light of principles relating to concept learning and teaching.

BASES OF TEACHING FOR CONCEPTUAL LEARNING

I have already discussed the way concepts are learned and often not learned despite teacher intentions. I have argued that language plays a crucial part in learning concepts and warned that it can also hinder concept teaching, as when a teacher does not realise that the pupils' ability to use a word does not necessarily imply that the concept the word symbolises has been learned. I have also made the point that no two persons' concepts are identical even though they may use the same word to refer to them. I have further suggested that teachers need to be particularly sensitive to mismatches of this type. I shall now attempt to bring together the key aspects of effective concept teaching as they are presently understood.

Clearly, ensuring learners' existing competence is of vital importance. In the work of some of the teachers discussed in this book, several examples occur of teachers over-estimating the understanding of their students at the beginning of teaching. They were surprised because their intuitive feelings were different, and they discovered the discrepancy only when they systematically reflected on their teaching and students' reactions, usually using recordings of the teaching. The teacher teaching orienteering found that his pupils had difficulty in estimating the size of angles. Another teacher, whose work I shall discuss later, used the size of a football pitch to illustrate scale and found that some pupils had bizarre notions and thought it would be less than 10 metres in length. Almost invariably the teachers encountering problems of this type ascribed them to their inadequate task analyses before teaching.

One of the elements in the pedagogical analysis is the identification of the criterial attributes of the concepts being taught. The criterial attributes are likely, themselves, to be concepts with their own criterial attributes and so on down a hierarchical structure to more and more specific concepts. Working down the hierarchy of concepts from the very general to the very particular reminds the teacher of the key elements in the teaching. The test of the teacher's professional judgment is in identifying the level of specificity at which the learners may be considered sufficiently competent to cope with proposed new learning. If there is any doubt that they are competent, it is desirable to take steps to establish the actual state of understanding of the learners.

Some form of diagnostic action is needed. This action could take the form of a short written or oral test prior to starting the main teaching task. Should lack of clarity be revealed, a short teaching sequence to prepare the learners for the main task should be introduced. A thorough pedagogical analysis is likely to identify the concepts subordinate to the main learning and guide the teacher in identifying lack of understanding and its remediation. A less satisfactory analysis will produce effects such as those encountered by the teachers just mentioned.

Whether the pedagogical analysis was satisfactory or not, preparing one prior to teaching enables a teacher to identify with some precision where problems arise in the course of teaching. Post-teaching analysis may point to deficiencies in the pedagogical analysis or in the interactive phase of teaching. Teachers thus get an insight into their work that they could not otherwise obtain.

At the interactive phase of teaching it is important to ensure that new learning can be related to bodies of concepts the learners already possess. Knowledge of the learners' existing competence will help, but care will be needed to ensure that any explanations used in the teaching are already understood by the learners. This can be done by introducing to the pupils the key terms to be used in talking about new concepts or their attributes and by checking that the learners are acquainted with the words and their meanings.

The relationship of new learning to existing levels of understanding will vary considerably in different lessons. Teaching which extends the existing knowledge in a particular field will take a different tack from that which introduces pupils to a new field of study. In the former the teacher will be able to make use of existing bodies of higher-level concepts to which pupils can relate new comparable concepts by direct verbal teaching. In the latter it will be necessary to arrange for direct sense experience if the field of study is completely novel. If it is not possible to arrange for direct sense experience, for example in teaching about the nature of stars, it is important to provide vicarious experience that resembles as closely as possible the actual phenomena. Recourse will have to be made to aids such as film, slides, pictures and diagrams. Even with these aids the concepts learned are bound to be limited, but far less so than if the teacher uses only verbal instruction.

Extending knowledge in a given field may often be accomplished verbally by giving a definition. For example, most adults will extend their knowledge of ichthyology, even if only by an infinitesimal amount, on being informed that 'a "powan" is a fish of British lakes similar to a trout'. Some people will have their knowledge of psychology extended if they read or are informed that 'a "construct" is a bipolar concept as defined in construct theory'. Obviously 'facts' such as these are at different levels of abstraction and esotericism. The first is generally accessible, the second accessible to a few workers in a particular field. Telling adult learners what a powan is will relate to an existing body of concepts and could be regarded as meaningful learning. Telling people what a construct is would be meaningless to most people and their learning of the definition would be rote learning. Thus the value of teaching 'facts' depends entirely upon the teachers' competence in analysing the teaching task and teaching in a way that takes into account the learners' existing levels of understanding.

The procedures for teaching concepts in a new field necessitating direct sensory experience or its close approximation resemble those for teaching by exposition. Both need to connect new learning with existing understanding. Often, of course, teaching will be an amalgam of the two: exposition and arranging direct sensory experience for the learners. Among the key aspects of such teaching will be the need to call to mind the prerequisite understanding for the new learning, the need to give the learners a preliminary idea of the learning task and the need to explain any new terms using concepts the learners already possess. Finally, through careful presentation of exemplars of the new concept, the teacher should be able to lead the learners, by gradually reducing cuing, to an independent grasp of the concept.

A key element in developing this independence is the sensitive guidance of learners in the identification of the criterial attributes of the new concepts. The trout-like nature of a powan is a criterial attribute, for example, but its weight is not. The action of a galloping horse is criterial but not the length of the stride. Teachers can assist learners to distinguish criterial from non-criterial attributes by emphasising them in some way. This procedure is often referred to as 'increasing their salience' or the amount they stand out. Attention may be drawn to the criterial attributes by verbal means such as the teacher's explanation or by information in a book. Teachers using learners' direct sensory experience may draw attention to the criterial attributes orally or through such devices as staining the important features of microscope specimens or exaggerating the vertical scale in diagrams of rock strata to emphasise geological features.

However, there is a danger in such practices that is often not appreciated. Great care needs to be exercised by the teacher to ensure that the pupils do not get the impression that the staining on the slide or the exaggerated vertical scale is integral with the criterial attributes. In the case of stained slides it would be necessary gradually to fade out the different colours until the slides were untouched but the pupils could make the necessary discriminations. Their ideas about the relation between horizontal and vertical scale would need to be refined, once particular points had been made, by using such things as pictures and diagrams where the scales were the same. This is a challenging problem for any teacher. Experience in the field would be of great help, but even that could not really bring home the relationship of the two dimensions, if only because of the difficulty of encompassing a large enough vista.

Teachers can speed up concept learning by careful programming of the exemplars the learners encounter. This activity is really one of the main functions of formal schooling although it is rarely made explicit or fully understood by teachers and other educators. In many learning situations outside formal schooling learners may well encounter exemplars of unfamiliar concepts quite randomly and in undifferentiated confusion. In these conditions learners are likely to have difficulty in actually *identifying* the criterial attributes, let alone recognising that they are, in fact, criterial. A teacher drawing on an understanding of the way humans learn concepts is in a position to reduce the randomness and confusion to facilitate new learning. However, I should like to stress that although a teacher may reduce the complexity of the learners' environment to enable them to learn effectively and more quickly, the ultimate aim of the teaching is to equip learners to use their new learning to cope more effectively with the complexity and randomness of the world outside formal schooling.

A teacher who arranges a systematic program of exemplars that embody the criterial attributes of the new concept or concepts will ensure that all the criterial attributes are experienced by the learner. In an unstructured environment there is no guarantee that this would occur. It is even more unlikely that the criterial attributes will be highlighted in the unstructured environment. Teachers who understand this will arrange the learners' environment so as to increase the salience of the criterial attributes of the new concept(s) in ways I have already suggested.

Teachers wishing to help learners distinguish between criterial and non-criterial attributes might find the procedure of counterpositioning useful (Fleshner 1963). This procedure involves presenting exemplars and non-exemplars of concepts in juxtaposition and drawing attention to the factors that make one an exemplar and the other a non-exemplar. Juxtaposing pictures of, and information about, a whale and a fish of comparable size (say a shark) and drawing attention to the key characteristics that distinguish the two, helps the development of accurate concepts.

The example of fish and whale is a useful example of an important phenomenon. It is the problem that the perceptual, usually the visual, aspects of concrete phenomena can be dominant in concept learning. Whales and sharks are animals of different biological types that have adapted to life in water naturally by developing similar outward forms. Since most animals living in the sea that young children encounter are fish, and since the outward form of the whale is like that of most fish, the whale tends to be classified as a fish. Juxtaposing whale and shark would draw attention to the whale's criterial mammalian features, perhaps through illustrations of suckling young, the need for protection against cold and the need for air, and would contrast these features with the shark's cold blood, its gills and the non-suckling young. The shape and size would then be seen as non-criterial and the natural consequence of different animals, adapting to life in the same environment. The learners' concepts of 'fish' and 'mammal' and probably 'animal' would be more in line with informed adult thinking. The concept of 'animal' is, in fact, an interesting example of a concept that is usually learned without the benefit of a teacher. Many adults equate 'animal' with 'mammal' and go through life using the terms 'fish', 'bird' and 'animal' as if they were equivalent categories.

In all concept teaching, language has a powerful influence. Its uses may be summed up as the providing of cues and feedback to the learner and especially in providing the invariant 'artificial' criterial attribute. But as I suggested earlier, the aim should be to reduce the help provided the learners as soon as possible. This might be done by passing through a phase where the learners use their own speech to themselves or sometimes to their peers to guide their actions eventually to dispense with the need for speech altogether. Oral feedback from the teacher should also be faded out eventually, but only after ample opportunity to test the grasp of the concept(s) with the benefit of feedback has been arranged. Successful later use of the concept in other activity will act as continuing confirmatory feedback.

Feedback confirming that teaching has been successful will be provided by the learners' successful use of the new learning in novel situations; for example, when after learning the concept of 'spinnaker' the learners are able to identify spinnakers on types of yacht they have not seen before, or if they successfully identify novel examples of 'erratics' in a landscape after instruction on glacial action.

A HEURISTIC GUIDE FOR CONCEPT TEACHING

I should now like to bring together the aspects of human learning and their implications for teaching that seem particularly important to ensure true conceptual learning. Given our current state of knowledge about human learning it is impossible to construct an algorithm that would infallibly lead to the results required. The best we can do at present, and quite likely the best we shall ever be able to do, is to develop *heuristic* guides. Such a guide takes us beyond raw trial and error into guided inquiry or exploration. Guidance is provided by principles induced from previous experience and research in related fields. In our case those principles are the ones I have considered in my discussion of human learning and teaching. Teachers following a heuristic guide derived from these principles will, in their actions, be testing the relevance of those principles to their own teaching. The outcome of these explorations in practical teaching will modify their views of the way the theory relates to the practice and probably modify their understanding of the theory itself. In effect, the teachers will be extending their own concepts of the nature of teaching through a complex dialectical process in which theoretical principles and practical teaching interact with and influence each other.

The heuristic guide I now consider focuses on the most complex skills of teaching, those I referred to earlier as type A skills. I have attempted to present a synoptic guide to the activities it would be useful for a teacher to consider when attempting to teach for conceptual learning. It is not a prescription to be followed slavishly but more an *aide memoire* to remind a teacher of the kind of actions that are likely to result in fruitful concept learning. I should also like to stress that although the guide may somewhat resemble the many schedules for describing what takes place in a classroom it does not fall into the same category. Such schedules, of which the Flanders system (1970) is the most widely known, *describe* what the teacher *did* during teaching. There is no necessary contact with theory. The heuristic I describe here and those I consider later look forward, not back, not to what the teacher did, but to what the teacher might do to ensure successful teaching.

Heuristic for the teaching of concepts

A   Preactive

1 Make a pedagogical analysis of the teaching objectives to identify the key concepts involved, the subordinate concepts, specific examples, methods of presentation, learner activities and methods of evaluation of learning.
2 Ascertain learners' prior knowledge. If this is not possible, plan for diagnosis at the interactive phase.

B   Interactive

3 Give a preliminary idea of the nature of the new learning.
4 Explain terms to be used in labelling the new concepts and their attributes and call to mind existing concepts relevant to the new learning.
5 First provide a series of simplified exemplars with few attributes to facilitate identification of the criterial attributes.
6 Increase the salience of the criterial attributes to enable learners to discriminate readily between criterial and non-criterial attributes. Decrease the salience as learning develops.

7 Provide a series of exemplars organised to provide a complete range of criterial attributes as economically as possible.

8 Provide non-exemplars in juxtaposition to exemplars to enhance discrimination between criterial and non-criterial attributes.

9 Provide new exemplars and non-exemplars and ask learners to identify the exemplars. Provide feedback for each discrimination.

10 Encourage learners to use their own language in explaining the nature of the concepts.

11 Provide suitable cuing throughout to ensure that pupils gradually become independent in their ability to identify novel exemplars of the concepts.

C   *Evaluative (This process is naturally much the same procedure as would be used in diagnosing prior level of ability)*

12 Present novel exemplars of the concepts for the pupils to identify and/or discriminate from non-exemplars.

Item 12 is the acid test of the understanding of concepts. It would be perfectly reasonable to ask a learner to give a definition or explain a concept. The thing to watch for, of course, is the response that has been rote-learned. Skilful questioning could reveal if this were the case and enable a teacher to take necessary action. However, the ability to identify novel exemplars would be the only real guarantee that the words the learner was using were based on a real grasp of the concept and were not mere verbalising.

I should like to stress, here, that these remarks do not apply merely to the learning of concepts relating to concrete objects. The learning of abstract qualities is also subject to the same procedures. 'Colour' is one example of such an abstraction, as is 'blue'. 'Irony' is a different kind of example, much more abstract and complex, normally to be observed only in language. Nevertheless, the teaching of all these concepts can be approached along similar lines. The case of relatively simple concepts is worth noting. With young learners and people with learning difficulties care needs to be taken to ensure that abstraction has taken place even when teaching relatively primitive concepts such as 'yellow' or 'triangularity'. Learners may be able to recognise that phenomena belong together purely as a result of the visual similarities and not because they have learned the concepts of 'yellow' or 'triangular'. This point is sometimes difficult for adults to grasp since they have usually been operating at a conceptual level with such phenomena for many years. The way to establish what the real situation is, as I said earlier, to ask the learners to identify exemplars of the concepts in totally new situations. For example: ask children who have been learning 'yellow' and 'triangle' in the classroom to identify exemplars outside school in objects in the streets or countryside or in stars or constellations in the night sky.

GUIDED ACTION

I have already considered examples of the first element in the guide, pedagogical analysis. To be consistent with my suggestions about concept teaching I now consider examples of the work of teachers who have planned and taught lessons taking this type of approach. The fact that the teachers were all drawing on the suggestions in the heuristic in their teaching did not result in uniformity. All the teachers brought their own experience and understanding to bear in a unique situation, so naturally the various examples of practical teaching differed and were personal to the teachers concerned.

Reading comprehension

My first example illustrates the way in which teachers may use the heuristic to guide their planning and execution of a lesson with a personal approach. After a discussion of other work in the field and a consideration of suggested methods of teaching the subject, the teacher proposed the following approach.

> Putting together these viewpoints a teacher could devise a schedule for their application in subject areas incorporating the pedagogic principles enunciated by Stones (1979). An example of such a schedule for a teacher-led group discussion, following the reading of text is set out below.

  Schedule for the use of higher-order comprehension questions

A   Preactive

  1 Select textual material at the pupils' readability level which can be utilised for analysis or synthesis or evaluating of important concepts in the particular subject area being studied.
  2 Ascertain pupils' prior knowledge in the subject area.
  3 Make a pedagogical analysis of the teaching objectives identifying these [in 1] important concepts, stating the target level of cognitive functioning to be aimed at in each concept area in the form of key questions, decide what questions at lower cognitive levels in the hierarchy need to be answered in order for the pupils to be able to satisfactorily tackle the key questions (these subordinate questions should be related at the lowest level to literal comprehension of the text).

B Interactive

4 State clearly the key headings of the discussion planned to follow reading of the text.

5 Ask the pupils to read the text carefully making short notes (if they have been trained to do this and wish to do so).

6 Select an appropriate concept for beginning the discussion, state clearly what the concept is and ask questions at the literal level to ascertain if pupils have correctly identified relevant parts of the text.

7 Lead the pupils to consider the key questions for this concept area through a chaining of questions leading from the literal through the reorganisation and so on to the target cognitive level, utilising pupils' experience and knowledge outside the text.

8 Where appropriate, remind the pupils of previously learned strategies which can be used in accomplishing this particular cognitive task.

9 Require the pupils to summarise their conclusions in their own words.

10 Repeat 5, 6, 7, 8 for other concept areas.

11 Throughout the question–response sections above:

a Listen carefully to individual pupil responses and respond in such a way as to show the pupil response has been understood correctly and accurately.

b Ask pupils to elaborate and extend incomplete or initially 'weak' answers.

c Show approval for pupil responses which are appropriate and demonstrate the ability to reply at the cognitive level the questions require.

d Avoid approving irrelevant comments or following up interesting 'red herrings'.

C Evaluation

12 Repeat the key questions, rephrased or requiring application in another form, at the end of the discussion period.

13 Provide opportunities for recitation of key concepts, whether orally or in writing, subsequently.

The teacher goes on to suggest that as a result of his using the guide he considers that it should be used flexibly rather than followed systematically as he did at first. He also suggests that it should stress pupils' own activity more overtly, since he thought the guide assumed learner passivity and he had been too directive in his approach.

I concur with these sentiments. The essence of a heuristic device is that it is, as I have already stated, a *guide* to action, not a *prescription* for action. The second point is clearly very important, since the whole point of the teaching discussed in this book is to help learners to become independent in their learning,

The guide and the teacher's reflection on its use illustrate two of the most important aspects of the approach to teaching developed in this book. I have already alluded to one: the flexible use by the teacher of the heuristic for the teaching of concepts. The other relates to the way in which teaching that draws on theoretical principles may be integrated with principles drawn from other fields, in this case from the literature on the teaching of reading comprehension. Both interact with the teacher's practical experience to refine his understanding and practice of teaching. His reflection on the interaction among the different elements of the teaching provides a springboard for the improvement of his practice and the deepening of his understanding of theory.

Musical composition

I now consider a very different teaching problem. In my consideration of pedagogical analysis I discussed the work of the teacher of musical composition. His teaching was based on that analysis, and he very carefully and systematically developed a lesson strategy to ensure satisfactory learning of the concept of melody. In his pedagogical analysis he considered that successful learning would be achieved if the pupils were able to compose simple but novel melodies.

It is worth considering part of the background for this work. The teacher draws attention to the neglect of the teaching of composition in British schools. In public examinations, until recently, little weight was given to composition. Performance, listening and appreciation probably still receive the main attention. He considers that music teachers and others perpetuate the myth of the inaccessibility of composition and that composers and their compositions are accorded a spurious mystique. As a result many music teachers shy away from composition, and it continues to be seen as a complex and mysterious phenomenon imbued with an 'inspirational' aura beyond their reach.

He found it extraordinary, at a time when creative pursuits were being encouraged in and out of school, that creating one's own music was so badly neglected. He examines the creative musical activity that does take place in schools and questions whether this is really composition. He was, therefore, pleasantly surprised to find an emphasis on composition in the aims of the new British public examination in music for secondary schools. Stress was placed on composition, and other musical skills were to be seen as subserving composition.

In view of the previous neglect of the teaching of composition and in view of the mystique still attaching to it, the teacher thought it essential to take urgent action to prepare plans for the teaching of composition. These plans should transcend the dominant haphazard way of approaching the subject. He was encouraged by the fact that the aims of the new examination referred to conceptual understanding related to musical composition (GCE/CSE 1981). This is a significant element in the new examination that helps change attitudes from awe in the face of the mysteries of creativity in composing to the more encouraging view that there are skills and understandings within the reach of most people, even though few will achieve the accomplishments of a Mozart or a Beethoven. I suggest that this teacher's refusal to accept mystery as a constituent of composition and to adopt a systematic and analytical approach is relevant beyond the field of music teaching.

I have already discussed aspects of his analysis. I should now like to consider that part of the analysis that bears on my current theme. The ultimate aim was for pupils to be able to compose original melodies. He considered it essential to teach the concepts related to melody. Thus, the route to creativity is to be found by a structured approach to helping pupils learn the theory related to composition.

To check pupils' readiness for the task he asked them to demonstrate various musical skills. For example: Could they discriminate between high and low sounds? Could they recognise the keynote (e.g. C as the first note of the scale)? Could they recognise and perform crotchet, minim and dotted minim? He also ascertained that they could recognise and understand the significance of the necessary musical symbols such as the treble clef, bar lines and so on. Apart from these tests of readiness, the teacher thought it worthwhile to see if the learners actually needed the teaching. This is a point rather particular to music since many children take music lessons out of school and might already have reached the stage the teacher was aiming for. He therefore questioned them about 'melody' and asked them to write eight-bar melodies. The pupils' compositions were analysed, and he found that they were not melodies, nor did they demonstrate any understanding of the concept of melody. The teacher therefore concluded that all the children possessed the necessary skills for starting to learn about and compose melodies and that all needed the teaching.

Although I suggested that the case of music was a particular one, in view of the possibility that the pupils might already have the concepts to be taught, it is a possibility that teachers of all subjects need to consider. So many influences other than school could bear on young peoples' learning that it is unwise to assume ignorance before starting new teaching. The action a teacher takes as a result of ascertaining the two levels of competence – the essential prior ability and the previous achievement or non-achievement of the projected new level – is a matter for individual judgment. Both measures are diagnostic. A learner lacking the necessary prerequisite abilities will be unable to cope with the new learning and must have the deficiencies remedied before new teaching starts. If, on the other hand, full mastery of the new learning is demonstrated, the proposed new teaching is redundant and the teacher would be better occupied in other activities. In the intermediate case where learners do not have full competence in the new learning but demonstrate some knowledge, a comparison of their competence with the pedagogical analysis will indicate those aspects of the proposed teaching that may be dropped and those that need attention.

The precise diagnosis implied in these procedures is, of course, the ideal case. Given classroom, school and outside societal influences, especially ideological and financial, compromise is inevitable. However, the important point is the one that pervades all the discussion in this book; it is teachers' understanding of and sensitivity to the relationship between the theoretical insights and practical realities that is important, not the mechanical implementation of steps prescribed by outside agents, whatever their origins.

The teacher whose work I am discussing adapted the concept teaching heuristic to his own purposes under the heading 'Schedule for the teaching of musical composition'. In fact this guide went beyond concept teaching to the actual production of melodies by the pupils. Although this is the logical and obvious reason for teaching about melody, I shall confine my comments at this stage to discussing the way in which the concept of melody was taught.

On the basis of his pedagogical analysis he identified three concepts subordinate to the overall concept of 'melody'. These comprised pitch, rhythm and form (announcing phrase) and pitch, rhythm and form (responding phrase). He decided on the most appropriate sequence in which to introduce the sub-concepts. He taught the sub-concepts by explaining and by providing a sequence of exemplars on a keyboard and writing on a chalkboard. He also provided non-exemplars of the sub-concepts. The non-exemplars were introduced in order for the students to discriminate between them and exemplars, so as to establish that the learning was not mechanical or rote.

In his guide he set out the nature of the teacher's action in presenting the exemplars down the left half of the page and paired them with the pupils' actions on the right half of the page. At the end of each phase he checked that the learners had learned the sub-concept by asking them to demonstrate the aspect of the concept being taught. This is built-in formative evaluation of his teaching, and I discuss this in greater detail in Chapter 9. When the pupils have demonstrated competence in all the units, they should have learned the overall concept and be ready to attempt their own compositions. However, before moving on to composing, the teacher checked that the pupils had, in fact, learned the overall concept.

The test used included oral questioning by the teacher using printed examples and examples of simple melodies, performed first by pupils and teacher together and then by the pupils alone. This is the summative evaluation of the pupils' learning of the concept of 'melody' and this is also discussed in detail in Chapter 9. It may also act as one of the prerequisites for learning to compose melodies. This is an excellent example of the never-ending process of cumulative learning supported by teacher analysis and action.

Map reading: concept of a bearing

My next example, although drawn from a very different field, has, pedagogically, a great deal in common with the previous one. Both teachers involved had a very clear idea of the reason for teaching the concept, namely to provide a basis for the teaching of a problem-solving skill, in the previous example, the ability to compose simple melodies; in the current example, the ability to follow a bearing on the terrain using a particular type of compass. They both interpreted the heuristic for teaching concepts in their own way according to their individual circumstances.

We have already met this teacher deciding his objectives and making an analysis of the task of teaching the concept of 'bearing'. He discovered, when he embarked on the analysis, that the concept was far more difficult than he had imagined. The complexity of the task became apparent when he identified the subordinate concepts of 'bearing'. He reduced the complexity somewhat by excluding from consideration the sub-concept 'bearings are measured in a horizontal plane', since all the work would be in that plane. This decision illustrates two very important points about theory and practice of teaching. One is that concepts are not discrete and circumscribed things that one has or has not. They are fluid abstractions born of and nurtured by one's experience, never 'complete' and always personal and idiosyncratic. Thus, the teacher's concept of a bearing includes the sub-concept of 'in the horizontal plane' as a criterial attribute of 'bearing'. His decision not to include it in his teaching inevitably implied that the concepts the students learned would be different from and less complex than his. The act of making the decision illustrates the second important point about pedagogical theory and practice. It is that teachers are constantly faced with such problems of decision making since all their tasks involve taking learners from a state of conceptual naiveté to a state as closely resembling their own as possible. It is rarely possible to make the transition in one leap, so teachers have to decide which aspects of new concepts are sufficient for the current teaching task and which can be addressed at a later stage. The analysis the teacher made in the case we are considering enabled him to make a logical decision he might not otherwise have made.

The Interactive phase

The analysis also clarified his ideas about the way he would ascertain the pupils' beginning competence. On the basis of the analysis he prepared a pre-test to assess the pupils' knowledge of the essential prerequisite abilities. The test covered such things as their knowledge of right-angle turns and clockwise direction, their understanding of 'an angle', knowledge of 45 degrees and 90 degrees rotation including anti-clockwise movement. The test items were arranged in ascending order of difficulty. The last item in the test aimed to check whether they already knew what a 'bearing' was. As a result of the test he discovered that the pupils did not know what a bearing was. He also pin pointed one or two weak spots in the pupils' grasp of the necessary prior knowledge. For example, many pupils were unable to measure angles accurately given a margin of error of 4 degrees, and more than half were unable to estimate angles with a tolerance of 10 degrees.

Apart from the feedback to the teacher indicating that he needed to be aware of the gaps in the pupils' knowledge, the test had an interesting effect on pupils' attitudes. The gradual increase in difficulty of the items and the fact that most were aimed at their current level of competence proved highly motivating and stimulated their interest. The item relating to the concept to be taught, 'bearing', and a related one, 'course', linked their current competence with new learning so that the pupils saw the rationale for the test and the need to establish baseline competence. In fact, they were learning something about pedagogy as well as about 'bearing'.

At the interactive stage the teacher spent much of the time explaining and labelling subordinate concepts. He also tried to help the pupils remedy their deficiencies in the estimating of angles. After the lesson he concluded that this had been an error and had wasted time during the lesson. He used a variety of concrete exemplars and graded their sequencing. Thus, he went from angles such as 45 degrees and 90 degrees before introducing 135 degrees or 315 degrees and introduced N, S, E, and W before NE, SW, etc. Models and diagrams were used as vehicles to present the exemplars. He enhanced the salience of the criterial attributes and provided feedback to the pupils by the use of coloured labels, signs and arrows, and gradually faded these out. In the course of the lesson he monitored the development of pupil learning by asking them to discriminate between exemplars and non-exemplars of the concept. Diagrams showing angles which were not bearings were juxtaposed with those that were. Possible areas of confusion were introduced in order of complexity to add rigour to the evaluation. For example: bearings not measured from North, bearings not measured from North showing unequal presentation of legs, clockwise/anti-clockwise confusion, presentation of North other than 'at the top'. In the process of this formative evaluation the pupils were asked to explain the reasons for their decisions. All the pupils were fully successful at this stage.

Evaluation after the teaching aimed to test the pupils' ability to apply their new learning to novel situations. All showed virtually total mastery. Analysis of the pupils' errors suggested that the main problems were errors of measurement. These, in turn, had several constituent elements. One was that some pupils were not very familiar with the circular protractor. Another was caused by the small diagrams which made accurate measurement difficult. However, this problem was overcome when the pupils realised that they could extend the arms of bearings, thus making them easy to measure. Other problems were attributable to poor design of questions by the teacher and mistakes in arithmetic by the pupils. Pupil reaction to the final test was very positive. The teacher reported that they enjoyed the test, and some of the pupils devised questions of their own for the group to answer.

The reflections of the teacher on the problem of teaching the concept of a bearing provide an illuminating account of the way in which pedagogical analysis, substantive knowledge in a field of study, the teacher's past experience and his practical teaching interact to produce a novel approach to teaching conceptual material explicitly aimed at forming the basis for a practical skill. After discussing the way in which the lessons had been devised and conducted and the evaluation of student learning, the teacher considers the question of concept teaching.

> Though I achieved the objectives I set, this does not mean that I would not wish to change certain aspects should I teach the lesson again. On the contrary, I would probably change the involved introduction to the concept lesson by including discussion and examples of situations in which a bearing is used rather than stressing the component parts of a bearing. Secondly, I would not become sidetracked with work on estimation during the teaching of a specific concept but teach the concept and skills of estimation as a separate entity and thirdly, I would change those situations which, *while appearing to be satisfactory at the theoretical stage, needed refinement in practice.* I refer to the instances of evaluating the compass skill and the attempt to provide realistic, competitive problem-solving activities. I realise that this came about because my planning was incomplete, *but it took the actual teaching to bring home the difficulties and inadequacies to me.* [my italics]
>
> However, none of the alterations and refinements detract from, invalidate or provide evidence of the impracticability of the approach and the schedules [heuristics], rather, because of them I was able to evaluate my teaching to become more efficient and effective. Further, through my daily work in mathematics, science and geography, I have become more aware of the interrelatedness and comprehensiveness of the schedules for different contexts.

Biology: the concept of vector-carried disease

I discussed the work of the teacher teaching this concept earlier when I described her approach to deciding on her objectives. Let us now consider how she set about achieving them. As she explained, she drew on the objectives she had decided on as the basis for an analysis of the teaching task. This analysis led her close to a plan for her teaching. Implementing the plan at the interactive phase was facilitated by the analysis, as was the procedure for evaluating the effectiveness of teaching.

She did not have first-hand knowledge of the pupils' existing level of understanding, so she introduced into the early stages of her lesson questioning to assess their knowledge of the subordinate concepts of the one she is trying to teach. She also explained the nature of the topic they were to study and the new terms she would be using to label the new concept. Specifically, she ascertained the prior knowledge of the causal agents of infectious disease. By referring to two different vectors, the malarial mosquito and the dog, she cued the pupils on one of the criterial attributes of a vector, that is, that it bites the host. To ensure that 'insect' was not considered a criterial attribute, the teacher referred to dogs carrying rabies. She later juxtaposed an exemplar of non-vector-caused disease, a non-disease-bearing insect bite, with an example of a vector-carried disease. Lest the pupils get the idea that only humans are susceptible to vector-carried diseases, she instanced myxomatosis in rabbits. By this sequencing of exemplars and non-exemplars the teacher systematically focused attention on the essential aspects of the concept and de-emphasised the non-essential. She used illustrative material to enrich the pupils' concepts as far as possible. However, since the constituent elements in the concept of vector-caused disease, such as host, parasite and disease, were part of the pupils' beginning competence, the teacher's main task was to establish relationships among existing understandings. Thus most of the cuing and enhancing of the criterial attributes was accomplished by the teacher's language.

The teacher finally assessed the pupils' learning by presenting information about diseases they had not discussed and asked them to decide whether or not they were vector-carried diseases. For example:

> Parrot disease is caught from sick parrots or budgies. When their droppings are allowed to remain a long time at the bottom of the cage they turn to dust. This germ-laden dust is carried in air currents and if inhaled by humans may cause parrot disease in them.

She also reproduced part of the log of a slave ship from 1731 which recorded the loading of 200 healthy slaves, many of whom died from yellow fever during the voyage. The ship's monkey also died from yellow fever, and the log records:

> Mr Leech [the surgeon] and I are mystified by this, as he [the monkey] has been tethered by a chain in his cage since we left Liverpool. The poor creature had suffered grievously from the bites of the mosquitoes.

In her appraisal of the lesson the teacher considered that this item was unsatisfactory. Although neither the situation in which the case was presented nor the disease had been mentioned before, she thought it possible that the pupils might have responded to the use of the same vector as had been used earlier, mosquito, and reached the right conclusion for the wrong reason. They might have believed that mosquitoes always carry diseases. On the strength of a correct response to the yellow fever question, however, she had no means of knowing one way or the other. She might have ensured a more accurate assessment by introducing an example in which a non-vector-induced disease, such as measles, was contracted by a person who had been bitten by mosquitoes. Better still, she could have introduced examples of this type in her teaching as well as examples of people or other animals being bitten by mosquitoes or fleas or other vectors without contracting any disease.

My point here is to stress the importance of identifying the criterial attributes of the concept one is trying to teach and of ensuring that these attributes are held constant while all the important non-criterial attributes are varied. If this is done the learner comes to understand what attributes must always be present and what, in particular exemplars, are not essential. In the case of yellow fever, transmission by vector is essential and proximity to a person carrying the disease is not essential. The teacher in our current example drew attention to the essential element in vector-transmitted disease by ringing the changes on infected organisms and vectors while keeping the nature of transmission of the disease constant, using examples of rabbits, humans and cattle as sufferers and mosquitoes, rats and vampire bats as vectors.

Other comments by the teacher on this example of concept teaching were that in a future lesson on the same subject she would attempt to provide more varied forms of feedback to the pupils during the course of the lesson and that she would attempt to build in more reinforcement. She said this on the basis of having looked at a video recording of the lesson. As I mentioned earlier, the teacher's speech was the main cuing agent in the lesson since it was used as an invariant in the early stages of concept learning. The teacher would present exemplars of the concept and tell the pupils that this is an example of vector-borne disease for these reasons. Her feedback was predominantly oral. She might have provided other types of feedback by using methods by which the pupils could check for themselves whether or not their classifications were correct. This would have developed their ability to make independent judgments. It would also have enhanced the reinforcing effect of competent performance *provided that the teacher had arranged learning experiences graded to ensure successful learning*. This is a question we shall consider in a later chapter.

Social studies: the concept of election

The examples of concept teaching we have discussed so far were taken from the work of experienced teachers. I now turn to some examples from the work of students in initial teacher training. My first case continues the discussion started earlier of the teaching of the concept of 'election'. The teacher based his teaching on the pedagogical analysis mentioned in Chapter 3 in which he had identified three criterial attributes of 'election': 'choice', 'vote' and 'representative'.

He first introduced the topic orally to give the pupils a preliminary idea of the learning. He then went on to explain the sub-concept of 'choice' and in a question-and-answer session with the class he presented exemplars and non-exemplars such as: 'If you were told you had to draw a picture in a lesson would you have a choice?' 'If [I asked you to pick one sweet] and I had three in my hand, would you have a choice?' He followed the same procedure with the other sub-concepts and summed up by stating the three defining attributes. He followed this up with an evaluation phase comprising ten questions embodying exemplars and non-exemplars of 'election' for the pupils to classify.

His appraisal of his teaching provides some points of interest. One of the questions he asked in teaching the sub-concept of choice was: 'If the three sweets I offered you were all caramels, would you have a choice?' The words: 'If I asked you to pick one sweet from my hand' were omitted, the teacher clearly expecting the pupils to realise that they were implied. In fact the pupils had great difficulty in accepting that this question implied a choice. He cued heavily for a time until the pupils gave the 'right' answer. The teacher had anticipated the difficulty and said, in his appraisal of his lesson, that he had introduced the exemplar to stress that the criterial attribute is availability of choice and not the nature of the choice. However, in the absence of the prefatory request to choose one sweet it is not surprising that the pupils were confused. I do not think this is a trivial matter pedagogically speaking. It is an example of a good idea for emphasising a criterial attribute being unconsciously sabotaged by a subtle nuance in the teacher's use of language. If this kind of thing can occur when a teacher has thought carefully and systematically about the teaching task, it seems highly likely that the incidence of such occurrences will be much higher in 'normal' teaching.

He also caused some confusion in his teaching of the sub-concept of vote. As was mentioned earlier, he told the class that a vote was a way of making our choices known to other people. This caused confusion because it seemed to conflict with pupils' ideas based on their observations of political elections which are secret, whereas the teachers' explanation implied that they were open. The teacher commented that he should have defined a vote as 'the means by which our choices can be counted'. This is another example of the care needed in the use of language in teaching. In this case the teacher's diagnosis of the problem did not explicate the important aspect of the pupils' confusion, namely that they were taking the secret ballot as a criterial attribute of 'election' whereas it is not.

Sociology: historical materialism

This apparently bizarre topic for a student teacher to deal with in one lesson is presented here since it exemplifies in particularly acute form some of the real-life problems student teachers face when they go to schools for teaching practice. It also illustrates a problem that some students occasionally experience when recording their teaching.

The student teacher whose work we now consider is an honours graduate in sociology. She was working with a teacher who was not a sociologist and who felt diffident about teaching the subject. Historical materialism, which is a central aspect of Marxist theory, was in the syllabus in the sociological studies of a group of seventeen-year-old pupils as part of their work for a national examination (Advanced level General Certificate of Education [GCE]). From the syllabus she selected this topic, since it seemed to be central to the course and because it would not be covered by the cooperating teacher. She comments that her own experience of studying the subject at school had left her in a state of ignorance. She thought it was taught unsystematically as a collection of categories for the students to memorise and regurgitate later in examinations. She wished to avoid this kind of teaching and learning with her students. She wished to teach so that her students would be able to use the knowledge and apply it elsewhere, since she felt that it had widespread application in most aspects of the study of society.

In preparation for the teaching she revisited reading she had done in the past and consulted new sources. She produced a pedagogical analysis and identified the following as criterial attributes: 1 the idea of internal conflict; 2 the idea of surplus labour/non-producers; 3 class struggle over the means of production; 4 domination and subordination; 5 the idea of change from one society to another by social revolution.

One does not need to be an honours graduate in sociology to realise that these sub-topics are highly complex concepts in themselves. The teacher, herself, realised this and also the fact that they were controversial. Her pedagogical analysis was very sketchy and provided just one or two examples and no non-exemplars, since she averred that it was not possible to provide non-exemplars. Her pedagogical analysis proposed teaching by verbal exposition with the pupils responding orally to her questions. She did expand somewhat on her pedagogical analysis as set out by saying that she would draw on Marx's writings for specific examples but did not give details.

Then a problem arose that I have often encountered in discussing with teachers questions relating to teaching that diverges from conventional delivery. The student teacher wrote: 'Since I had been given a specific area to be covered which would not be touched on again I felt my inexperience of using these [psychopedagogical] principles may result in my not completing the amount of work I had been scheduled to do'. She too, therefore, felt that she 'could not deviate from the norm' on her teaching practice although she said she would bear in mind the language she was using. Hence she decided to teach by traditional delivery methods.

The lesson was to be videotaped. Although she had worked with video in her seminar groups the recording seems to have caused a severe problem. However, it is difficult to disentangle its effects from those resulting from the complexity of concepts she was dealing with and her limited analysis of the teaching task.

In the event she reacted very badly emotionally. She felt she wanted to walk out of the room, and she turned her back to the camera (which was unobtrusive and without an operator) for the bulk of the lesson. She faced the chalkboard and wrote and spoke to it for most of the time, as she thought later, to hide from the pupils that her hands and legs were trembling almost uncontrollably. She overcame this to some extent but still continued talking and writing.

She later wrote that at this stage she seemed to have totally abandoned her lesson plan and that 'it was difficult to find many points where I was following any plan at all'. Significantly, she added that she gave up all hope of teaching using ideas from psychopedagogy and 'resorted to the traditional tactics of "telling" the pupils and hoping they could retrieve something out of the mine of information I was bombarding them with'.

Despite the trauma which my account can only hint at, the student viewed the recording of the lesson and wrote a critique of her performance which indicates that the experience had not been entirely negative. She wrote: 'With hindsight I have to accept that this lesson could never have been successful regardless of my personal reaction. The enormous range of symbols that had to be presented require a much longer period of time than I allowed. This, I feel, was the major lesson I learned'.

She went on to suggest ways in which she would deal with the same topic were she to teach it again. She would take each sub-concept and teach it separately, probably taking six or seven lessons. She suggests non-exemplars that she could use, which implies that her earlier comment about it not being possible to provide any related, not to a conceptual problem, but to the fact that she did not have time in view of her need to 'cover the syllabus'. She goes on to say that she would involve students in discussions of the sub-concepts with the aims of bringing about genuine understanding that would contribute to the understanding of the overall concept and equip the students to use their understanding in new situations. This is crucial since, as she says: 'It is a pointless exercise, I have found to my cost, to attempt an understanding [of the criterial attributes] until all the other categories [sub-concepts] are firmly understood'.

Her final words were: 'I have to say that although [the experience] had negative results for me, all was not lost. For out of failure I have learned one important lesson. It is one thing to have an understanding of psychopedagogy and another putting it into practice'.

What lessons are there in this student teacher's experience for other teachers? To take the last point first. Unless there is some confusion in her account, her final comment seems at odds with the earlier statement that she did not attempt to implement psychopedagogical principles. It is highly unlikely that she could have implemented them if she did not try. Apart from that, the point needs to be made that in any approach to teaching and learning 'understanding' actually involves practice. In fact, of course, she demonstrates this by the way she modifies her analysis of the overall concepts and realises that the sub-concepts are far more complex than she had thought and cannot be taught solely by exposition.

The 'covering the syllabus' problem was dramatically revealed in this lesson as the snare and delusion it is. Teachers all over the world are reciting vast amounts of text to 'cover syllabuses'. One might imagine that the fastest talkers would be the best teachers since they can recite more of the syllabus within the time allotted for lessons than those with a more deliberate delivery. The interesting thing about this student's experience is that she commented on the lessons using concepts from pedagogy. These ideas helped her to see the cause of her failure and to plan with a hope of future success.

Another aspect of chalking and talking was revealed by this account. The student teacher used it as a defence mechanism. In her nervousness she talked and talked and chalked and chalked, so much so that she said she would have covered three chalkboards if there had been three. Is she the only one to have used this ploy?

In conclusion, I should like to suggest that the fact that the student teacher was able to reflect on her teaching with sufficient insight and grasp of pedagogy to perceive ways of resolving the problems that had arisen is an augury of improvement of the quality of her teaching.

History: the nature of evidence

The next example is also of a student teacher. This time the topic was the use of evidence in the English Schools Council History 13–16 project: *A New Look at History*. The lesson was about half an hour in length and the pupils were aged thirteen–fourteen. The teacher hoped to encourage the pupils to discriminate between different types of primary and secondary source material and 'to be more critical in general of what they see and read in history books and hear from teachers hitherto taken as the last word on anything historical'. Her objective was that at the end of teaching the pupils would be able to distinguish between primary and secondary sources of historical evidence.

Her pedagogical analysis reminded her of subordinate concepts such as 'primary', 'secondary', 'evidence', 'time', 'authenticity', 'fact' and 'fiction'. She did not record any thoughts she might have had about further analysis of the subordinate concepts. In order to provide exemplars of these concepts she produced photographs and pictures of the following: pottery from Ancient Greece including remains of an Athenian temple, a statue of Pericles, maps, a coin, Roman farmland, Roman towns, the story of the alphabet, an original historical essay, an Athenian wine jar and jewelry, a painting of Henry VIII, Thracian treasure and a history book. An imitation coin was also used.

I will not describe the interactive stage of the lesson in detail. In outline the student teacher started by attempting to give the pupils a preliminary idea of the learning. She then moved systematically through the lesson using her material as exemplars of the concepts she was trying to teach. She discussed the nature of evidence and presented positive and negative exemplars for the pupils to discriminate and provide evidence of their level of comprehension.

A few points from the record of the lesson merit consideration. The first is that, in her introduction, she 'explained' that 'evidence is split into two sorts called primary and secondary'. She does not take any steps to ensure that the idea of 'evidence' itself is familiar to the pupils. The next point illustrates only too well the ease with which confusion can arise and the care needed by teachers to avoid it. The problem started to become apparent after she had explained the nature of primary evidence and then moved on to teach secondary evidence. The main difficulty was that she confused the pupils by introducing photographs of primary evidence as if it were the primary evidence itself. The pupils' incipient concepts must have been in a turmoil. Grasping for the criterial attributes they clutched at 'photograph' as criterial and 'drawing' or 'painting' as attributes of secondary evidence.

The nature of the confusion is quite subtle. When presented with a photograph of Thracian treasures in a history book the pupils said it was secondary evidence. The teacher considered this response to be a consequence of her earlier statement that secondary evidence was information depicted at a later date than the existence of the subject of study. She had alluded to history books earlier and clearly they were regarded as important sources of secondary evidence. When informed by the teacher that the objects illustrated were real objects that had been evacuated by archaeologists, the pupils agreed that they were primary evidence. The teacher was astute enough, however, to realise that the pupils were giving her what they thought she wanted and not necessarily demonstrating genuine understanding. Shortly afterward, one of the pupils said that a print of a painting of Henry VIII was secondary evidence 'because they did not have cameras in those days'. The problem is that the teacher had not thought to make quite clear that when she used photographs of objects as illustrations or material for the pupils to appraise, her explanations and questions *related to the objects themselves* and not to the photographs. The pupils, on the other hand, were making judgments on the photographs and not on the objects photographed. This is an entirely reasonable way of proceeding since none of the other objects were used in this way. Thus, it is very likely that the pupils were still confused even after they had agreed with her that the photo of the

Thracian treasures was primary evidence. The teacher concluded with the thought that the pupils were probably confused about the difference between photographs, drawings, books and prints in the context of historical evidence.

PROTOCOLS AND REFLECTION

Although this teacher's experience was very different from that of the previous one, they had one important similarity. Both were able to use the video-recording to reinstate their lessons and appraise them in relative calm after the event. In the case we are now considering, the teacher's analysis of her performance illustrates beautifully the use by a teacher of a record of her own teaching as *protocol* material for self-development. In particular, it highlights the advantages of using recorded material in conjunction with a consistent theory-based method to analyse the material.

Protocols, in the sense I am using here, derive from the work of B. O. Smith (1969), who argued for their use in fostering complex learning. They comprise any material taken from life that embodies concepts or activities that one is attempting to learn. One scrutinises the material and appraises it in the light of the concepts and principles one is learning. Thus one is bringing to bear the new learning to analyse and appraise phenomena. The more skilled in the learning one is, the more likely one will be able to appraise with facility and accuracy. However, more important for learners, the very act of analysing and appraising helps to clarify and consolidate one's grasp of the new learning.

I mentioned this process when I discussed objectives. The B type objectives are virtually the same as the use of protocols. In the case of the teacher we are discussing, she was practising and developing type B skills related to teaching; that is, the skills of appraising a piece of teaching in the light of principles and relating the nature of the interactions between teacher and pupils to those principles. In the process the teacher clarifies and enriches her understanding of effective teaching. The practice and the theory work together for teacher self-improvement. (See also Verloop 1989.)

The opening comments of the teacher's self-appraisal are particularly interesting in view of currently fashionable and rather naive calls for teacher reflection. If this teacher had merely sat down and reflected after the lesson without benefit of recording or theory she would have thought it had been a reasonable performance and would have learned practically nothing. She would have been trying to unlock a door without a key. Her initial appraisal attests to this:

> I felt the lesson had gone according to plan and the pupils seemed to be giving reasonably correct responses and to be grasping the meaning of the concepts of primary and secondary evidence.

She continues:

> However, having critically scrutinised the video at a later date, I found
> the faults both in my preparation and in the use of examples to be
> glaringly obvious. I had thoughtlessly assumed that the pupils had
> an understanding of the concept of 'evidence' in the wider sense,
> e.g. the use of evidence in police work, and I merely tested them
> on their knowledge of historical evidence without asking them what
> they knew of primary and secondary evidence. Understandably, the
> pupils were unclear of the terms 'primary evidence' and 'secondary
> evidence' although a few knew that archaeologists play an important
> part in the provision of historical remains, information, etc. This lack
> of careful preparatory testing had repercussions later in the teaching
> with the confusion over the photographs of primary evidence and
> primary evidence itself.

She goes on to suggest in some detail the way she would ensure in any future
teaching that this problem was addressed. She then continues:

> The most glaring and major fault with the whole lesson was my
> thoughtless blunder in not explaining fully that when I showed a
> photograph of an Athenian temple, it is the temple itself that is
> primary evidence and not the photograph of the temple. Again,
> although I was aware of the essential difference, I assumed the pupils
> were also aware of it and they were not. This major error produced
> further problems when I moved on to explain secondary evidence,
> saying that history books and artists' impressions were second-hand
> for purposes of historical evidence. This led the pupils to believe that
> anything *not a photograph*, e.g. a print, was not primary evidence. This
> became clear in the use of the example of Henry VIII and the fact that
> it was in a history book, itself secondary evidence. Pupils, here, made
> intelligent remarks like Paul's 'They didn't have cameras in those days'
> and Graham's 'But it's been printed on the page . . .'. At this point it
> was clear that through my clumsy use of language and the similarity
> of many of these examples, the boys were genuinely confused. Yet,
> throughout the video, the explanations of Jimmy seemed to reassure
> me at the time, that after a brief explanation from me as to why the
> print of Henry VIII was primary evidence, the pupils really understood
> the concepts. This was probably due to my wanting only to hear and
> latch on to a correct answer, which Jimmy often gave, and his peers,
> soon realising that he had grasped the concepts, decided that to follow
> his lead was a safe policy. Consequently questions such as 'Do you all
> agree with Jimmy?' were fairly worthless in retrospect. With regard to
> any further teaching on this topic, more preparation in the choice of
> different examples would be of great help, together with more individual
> questioning of the pupils that say little and may be confused.

She goes on to point out that all her examples were on paper and that it would been easy to have produced real primary evidence such as the previous day's newspaper or old coins. She ascribes these errors also to inadequate preparation and points out that the photograph problem could have been avoided by producing real primary evidence instead of photographs. She was confident that she now had many ideas for examples of evidence to be used in any future lessons on the subject.

The teacher was not entirely negative about her lesson. Although she decided that she had not achieved her objectives, she considered that the failings were not in the approach to the teaching of concepts but in the way the procedures were implemented. She had no doubt that the systematic use of exemplars was the key to teaching concepts. She continues: 'Perhaps the most important lesson that I have learned is the need for a clear objective in any proposed piece of teaching and then careful planning of exactly what is needed in the way of materials and examples to achieve that objective. The schedule for the teaching of concepts [heuristic guide] that I used to plan the lesson was certainly helpful and it is as useful to have a handy check list, much as in my plan, to refer to during the actual teaching'. She concludes her self-appraisal with the comment 'The exercise has been a useful, although slightly painful eye-opener as to just what is involved in the seemingly straightforward tasks of teaching concepts like primary and secondary evidence'.

The realism and resilience in this student teacher's analysis is a good example of reactions of most teachers and student teachers I have observed to experiences of this nature. I find this most encouraging in its clear espousal of the need for change and the need to employ systematic theory-based methods of seeking to bring it about. The realisation that 'seemingly straightforward tasks' are in fact very complex would not have occurred without the recording and the critical tools to make the analysis. The vast majority of teachers in training do not experience this type of activity, even if they are exhorted to 'reflect'. Many practising teachers and virtually the whole of the non-teaching population have no idea at all of the nature of these complexities. To continue my earlier metaphor: not only do they not have a key to unlock the door leading to the understanding of the processes of teaching and learning, they do not even know that there is a door and that they are on the outside.

CONCLUSION

What can we gain from the experience of these teachers and student teachers? First I must emphasise one point very strongly. None of the lessons we have considered is proposed as a model to be emulated. Nor should they be taken to be examples of the teaching of particular subjects. They are examples of a variety of approaches to a pedagogy based on the systematic use of principles of human learning. Teaching in all fields from arithmetic to zoology depends for its efficacy on the use of procedures resembling those considered in this chapter. Sometimes concepts are taught effectively by teachers who have little or no theoretical understanding of the underlying processes but who have learned from experience how to do so. All too frequently, however, teaching fails to produce conceptual learning, producing instead, the rote learning I discussed earlier. Adventitious conceptual learning may be welcome but cannot be regarded as sufficient by anyone seriously interested in the systematic development of pedagogy. To effect such development it is essential for teachers to develop their own concepts of conceptual learning to gain insights into how pupils learn concepts and how teachers might enhance the process.

Some of the cases I have discussed in this chapter illustrate another difficult problem that is endemic in teaching but often not perceived by teachers. It is the problem of cross-purposes. A teacher understands one thing when using a particular word and the pupils understand another. Teachers with no knowledge about the way concepts are learned will have difficulty detecting such mismatches. Those who do know are not guaranteed success, but their understanding in conjunction with their practice equips them to become more adept at identifying mismatches and in taking steps to remove misunderstandings so as to ensure that they do not recur.

The cases I have presented exemplify this process. The teachers involved are grappling with real pedagogical problems, and the discussion has reflected this process. However, the emphasis is on the *process*, and I have not considered the outcomes in detail. In most cases reported, the pupils achieved satisfactory learning. In some, the learning could be described as 'excellent' by conventional standards. Naturally, this is gratifying and important, but also important is the analysis to ascertain whether the learning is satisfactory using standards based on teaching aimed at high-level concept learning. The positive and negative aspects of the teaching revealed by the analysis provide information with the potential for improving future teaching.

Wordsworth described poetry as emotion recollected in tranquility. A recent article by Kagan discusses teaching as an aesthetic experience (Kagan 1989). She refers to the elevated state sometimes experienced by teachers. We have considered a strongly contrasted state in the example of the teacher teaching historical materialism. No doubt most teachers experience an emotional state somewhere between the two when they are teaching. However, that state itself, for most teachers, is vastly different from that which characterises their lives outside the classroom. Thus, apart from the enormous problems of information processing involved in monitoring the events in a busy classroom, the emotional involvement when one is interacting with pupils makes it very difficult to monitor and appraise the way one's teaching is going while one is engaged in the act itself. As Wordsworth implies, one cannot distill emotional experience while one is in its throes. We observe this truth in a pedagogical context in all our case studies.

But Wordsworth did not merely recollect. His recollections were focused by the lenses of his sensitivity to language, his wide knowledge of other literature and his contact with other poets and writers. His raw recollections would not have moved his readers in the way his finished verses do. Similarly, teachers need to do more than relive their classroom experience if their teaching is to achieve its aims. Currently, it is doubtful that many teachers attempt even to recollect. Given the way in which teaching has been conceived by politicians and administrators, it is difficult not to sympathise with teachers. They might reasonably claim that they do not have time to 'recollect', let alone 'reflect'. Their time is devoted to much more 'important' things connected with administration and management. And, of course, they have to contend with the stereotypical notion that unless they are actually confronting a class of pupils they are not really 'teaching'.

In teacher training institutions, while much attention may be given to the preparation for teaching by student teachers, much less is given to retrospective analysis. And yet we have seen, from the studies reported above, that this is one of the most important aspects of the teaching cycle. The self-appraisal guided by knowledge about the processes of concept learning enabled the teachers to detect critical incidents in their teaching where their plans went astray and they misled their pupils. The outcomes of their self-appraisals fed back into the teaching system to be incorporated in future planning.

Problems of planning were frequently referred to in the remarks made by teachers in their self-appraisals. A general comment was that the importance of pedagogical analysis had been underestimated. Pedagogical analyses can be made in a tranquil period before teaching. They enable one to plan the presentation of exemplars to the best effect. Many of the problems encountered by the teachers whose work we have discussed may be attributable to inadequate conceptual analysis at this stage. The most dramatic example of this problem was the lesson on historical materialism. Each of the sub-concepts merited an analysis of its own and further, almost certainly, more detailed analysis down the conceptual hierarchy along the lines suggested in the chapters on pedagogical analysis.

By contrast, the teacher teaching the concept of 'melody' identified essential prerequisites that the pupils would need to have before embarking on the new learning, even such 'simple' things as being able to distinguish between the higher and lower of two notes and knowing the notation for minim, crochet and so on. In the course of his teaching he presented exemplars of melodies in musical notation and on a keyboard, carefully varying the criterial attributes and juxtaposing them with non-exemplars for the pupils to discriminate to ensure that their learning was truly conceptual and not rote. By using different modes of presentation such as chalkboard, keyboard and an electronic instrument for producing simple melodies, he was able to produce melodies in a variety of forms. He thus ensured that the pupils were in a position to develop richer concepts than if he had used only one medium of presentation.

The principle of systematic variation is of great importance in the presentation of exemplars. The pedagogic art is to provide interesting exemplars that introduce all the criterial attributes with maximum efficiency and maximum economy. The structure of the heuristic provides a framework and a reminder of things to bear in mind. Teachers' imaginations provide the way in which the pedagogic principles and their own knowledge of the field of study come together to provide elegant solutions to teaching problems.

6 Skills of quality

PSYCHOMOTOR SKILLS

Psychomotor skills are skills that include a significant element of physical activity. These skills are often neglected both by teachers and by writers on teaching and educational psychology. It is a field in which the gap between theory and practice is particularly wide inside and outside formal education. This could be in part a consequence of the low status of physical skills teaching and also because of a distrust of theory by the practitioners of the skills (Sparkes *et al.* 1990). Whatever the fundamental reason, few teachers will have considered the question in their teacher training and are unlikely to be aware that motor skill learning could be problematic for many children.

I am not now referring only to psychomotor skills in relation to those under the rubric of 'physical education' or similar terms. Competence in certain psychomotor skills has an important influence on all children's learning, including concept learning. This is because certain basic skills are prerequisite to learning in many subjects of the curriculum. This is, perhaps, particularly the case in the learning of younger children. The key subjects of reading and writing present very young learners with problems of psychomotor learning in addition to the very considerable problems of conceptual learning. Older pupils may have problems with handling apparatus in scientific experiments or in using simple equipment in geography. It is not unknown for teachers to demonstrate experiments themselves because of their fear that pupils might damage expensive equipment.

Problems of motor learning are often overlooked by teachers. As adults they have had many years of practice in manipulative skills such as holding a pencil and skills involving hand–eye coordination such as sketching or writing letters of the alphabet. It is, therefore, difficult for them to understand the problems of very young learners. They might get some insight into the problems by considering the difficulty many adults have in learning a new motor skill. Many teachers find themselves in such situations when they wish to use audio-visual aids in their teaching. A knowledge of some principles of motor skill learning would enable them to help their pupils learn new psychomotor skills and help themselves to handle new equipment more effectively.

Unlike the learning of concepts and principles, which, in the main, tends to be open-ended, in the sense that one never reaches a full and final level of understanding, psychomotor skills can be conceived of as having optimum end states of competence. This is not to imply that perfection is reached by all learners but that it is possible to analyse the task and make a description of a response pattern optimally suited (in the light of current knowledge) to carrying out the activity in question.

Motor skills and cognitive learning also differ in that, after reaching a satisfactory level of competence in a motor skill, learners can 'polish' it by repeated practice, or 'overlearning', so that it eventually becomes habitual and automatic in performance. There is a potential problem, however. Unless the initial training is satisfactory, it is quite possible for a learner to acquire unsatisfactory response patterns in the learning stage and practise these responses in an overlearning stage so that the bad habits become habitual and difficult to alter if they are detected. A child who does not learn to hold a pen satisfactorily will continue to practise the wrong actions so much that any later attempt to correct the wrong action is likely to prove very difficult. It is, therefore, important to ensure that the early stages of learning a new motor skill embody satisfactory actions and give adequate practice to establish them permanently. Note, I am not suggesting that all learners conform to identical actions, but that they be given what might be referred to as ergonomic guidance to what is currently conceived to be the optimum approach.

This chapter will therefore be concerned with ways in which a teacher can help pupils to acquire the kind of perceptual-motor skills that are instrumental to other learning. It will also attempt to show how to guard against the learning of unsatisfactory actions that may interfere with efficient operation of these skills. In fact much of the approach would be relevant to skill learning in fields more centrally involved motor skills, such as crafts and physical education.

SHOW AND TELL

Most adults will, at some time, have tried to teach a child a motor skill. The chances are high that the approach adopted will be a 'show and tell' approach. The teacher demonstrates the skill and tells the learner to imitate the movements involved. Some familiar examples are catching a ball, riding a bicycle and handwriting. The teacher demonstrating is likely to have had many years of overlearning through continuous practice and could have a very hazy idea about just how the action is performed and little recollection of the problems encountered when first learning the skill. It may well be that the learners will also be hazy in their understanding of what the skill entails.

A mismatch between teachers' understanding and learners' understanding similar to those I discussed in concept teaching would thus ensue.

Show and tell teaching of motor skills resembles delivery teaching. Both are likely to lead to rote learning. The idea of rote learning a motor skill might seem strange. But the mechanical performance of a series of actions under another person's direction and without an understanding of what is going on could lead to a kind of non-transferable learning similar to that which I discussed in connection with concept teaching. Apart from that difficulty, the skills being demonstrated are frequently more complex than the demonstrator realises. There may be elements in an action that just cannot be observed. For example, an expert demonstrating how to plane a piece of wood using a hand plane will find it difficult, if not impossible, to demonstrate in action how to avoid a downward slope at the forward end of the wood. Telling may help but cannot be relied on, since the relevant aspect of the skill is likely to be 'remembered in the muscles' and difficult to verbalise. It is possible that the teacher also does not realise what are the key constituent elements in the skill, so that the explanation may not refer to them. In addition, it is possible that the learners may lack motor skills that are prerequisite for the new learning. If the teacher assumes, mistakenly, that the learners have these skills, they may simply not understand the explanation.

The teaching of handwriting to young children provides a common example of several of the problems just mentioned. A teacher teaching writing by show and tell methods is likely to write on a chalkboard and tell the pupils how to form letters and, later, how to join them together. This approach to teaching the skill could well be creating difficulties for the pupils. Writing on the chalkboard involves different actions from writing on paper. The chalk is held differently, the arm moves differently, the whole body posture is different. Apart from this, the performance will probably be a smooth and unified whole, and it will be very difficult for the learners to discern elements in the activity that lead to its smooth implementation.

Thus a very perplexing problem faces young learners in this situation. They are expected to observe a combination of the teacher's explanation and demonstration of one skill and translate them into another. There will be some common elements. The direction of movement of the hand will be similar, but the elements that differ are unlikely to be remarked upon by the teacher. Thus the pupils will have to sort out the elements to imitate from those not to imitate. Given these problematic learning conditions, it is a fair assumption that such demonstrations are of little value and that most learning will take place when the teacher is giving individual guidance at the pupils' desks.

PEDAGOGICAL ANALYSIS

The efficacy of that guidance will be enhanced if a teacher is aware of the pitfalls in show and tell methods and has an idea of the nature of the skill being taught. To get an insight into what teaching a skill involves, a similar approach to that suggested for other types of learning will prove useful. The key operation, as with other types of learning, is ascertaining, through pedagogical analysis, what is involved in the learning. This analysis will reveal what the necessary competence for beginning learning is and will provide guidance to the teacher as to how the teaching should be approached.

To illustrate how such an analysis might be made, I have set out a suggested approach to analysing the task of teaching handwriting in figure 6.1. I present this analysis at this stage since the matrix is somewhat different from those discussed earlier, particularly in the 'General Content' column, which lists sub-skills rather than sub-concepts. One needs to take care, however, not to overlook the fact that, for some children, some concept learning may well be involved in acquiring a sub-skill in motor learning. 'Slope' and 'lightly' are two examples that may present problems for very young learners.

The way in which a teacher might approach the interactive stage of teaching the skill is implicit in the analysis. As with all teaching, the actual working out will, naturally, be an amalgam of the teachers' interpretation of the analysis, their past experience, the number and educational level of the pupils and many other factors. Thus every implementation will be different and personal to the teacher involved. So will the analysis itself. My example uses the general approach for a specific implementation which draws on analyses of work in the field of skills training and the specific skill of handwriting.

This is my attempt at an analysis of the skill of teaching handwriting. It is based on my experience as a teacher, my reading of research on the motor skills involved in handwriting and my understanding of psychology and pedagogy. It is, thus, a product of personal experience and is not proposed as a model to be followed unquestioningly. For example, another teacher might consider it desirable to break down the constituent skills further. This decision would be based on that teacher's different experience and knowledge. Neither the latter analysis nor my own would be the right one. This follows because of the often-overlooked fact that differences between teachers, like differences between pupils, are important even when the same subject and the same pupils are involved. Thus, it might be necessary for one teacher to identify very fine sub-skills because of lack of experience or understanding, whereas another with a different life story would conclude that it was not. This proposition could be inverted. It could be the more experienced and knowledgeable teacher with greater awareness of the problems involved who considered deeper analysis necessary.

Figure 6.1 Illustrative analysis of the task of teaching handwriting*

General content	Method of stimulus presentation	Pupils' responses	Feedback	Evaluation
Writing (This is the overall skill)	Pictures Blackboard Films	Pupil *explains* how to carry out the sub-skills and the overall skill. (This is a type C skill)	Teachers's comments (Can be used with skills A, B and C)	Teacher assessment of sample of handwriting
Subordinate skills† The instrument rests between the thumb and index finger and is grasped lightly by the thumb and middle and index finger.	Teacher explains Teachers explains Teacher demonstrates Teacher guides Teacher cues Video recordings Other pupils	Pupil points out or sorts positive and negative exemplars of correct methods in overall skill and subordinate skills. (This is a type B skill.)	Comparison with 'model' examples Comparison with product of own earlier attempts It would be possible to devise some instrumentation of feedback.	Pupil's own evaluation on criteria established in teaching phase
The hand slopes so that it rests on the third and fourth fingers		Pupil demonstrates writing himself. (Type A skill.)	Kinesthetic; 'feel' in muscles	
The hand slides across the working surface as as the letters are formed				
The arm, hand and fingers are all used in forming letters.				

Source: Stones 1979, 1984

* In comparison with an analysis for conceptual learning, specific examples are not given, because the general principles are the same throughout. No category of learning type is given, since the learning of motor skills in formal education almost always involves multiple discrimination.

† See *Encyclopedia of Educational Research* ed. R. L. Ebel, Collier-Macmillan, 1969, pp.571–9.

N.B. This analysis could be continued by examining the finer grain of the movements involved. Only the first column would be affected by the additional entries.

Although different teachers taking an analytical theory-based approach to teaching may produce different analyses and hence different lessons, they will be implementing common basic principles. As I have suggested earlier, different ways of working out theoretical principles in practice test the theory, perhaps to enrich it, perhaps to call it into question. Should any aspect of the general approach to pedagogical analysis, or the process itself, prove regularly not to be useful in enhancing teaching, then it should be dropped or refined. Even if it is useful, it is still open to constant trial and improvement. Thus a diversity of teaching approaches is very useful for the development of theory and practice in teaching.

A thorough pedagogical analysis by a teacher is an effective indicator of the optimum route for a teacher to take to attain the goal in mind. In the case of motor learning, it will help to avoid the pitfalls associated with show and tell methods. It could be regarded as a map to guide the teacher on the road to pupil competence.

However, it is one thing to read a map and another to transfer the information to the terrain and actually follow the route successfully. This demands expertise in working out a bearing and following it on the ground. Identifying a feature on the terrain from its symbolic representation on the map is also a necessary skill. Similarly, successful translation of the guidance provided by the pedagogical analysis demands other actions by the teacher. The categories in the analysis need spelling out and the learning principles involved need explicating. I therefore now consider the way in which the guidance afforded by the pedagogical analysis can be translated into action on the ground, the classroom.

GUIDING AND CUING

As with most teaching, the first thing to do is to give the learners an idea of what the finished performance involves. In motor learning, the relation of the subordinate skills to the overall skill should be clarified. Teacher talk can be augmented by examples in pictures, films and drawings on the chalkboard and by the teacher demonstrating the individual subordinate skills. By these means the pupils will start to build up simple concepts about the correct movements and their interrelationships. To strengthen their understanding and give an indication of its current state, the pupils could be asked to explain to the teacher or discriminate between examples of correct and incorrect activities.

The way a teacher teaching soldering introduced the subject provides an example of the process of giving learners a preliminary idea of the learning being aimed at. He had established that the pupils could not wire an electric plug and knew nothing about soldering. Both are useful skills of general application. The teacher started by demonstrating two simple working electrical circuits. Both switched a lamp on and off, but one had soldered joints and the other had joints made by twisted leads.

A more complicated piece of electrical circuitry was also shown in order to demonstrate the large number of soldered joints needed. The teacher was deliberately trying to connect the new learning to their existing knowledge of lights and switches.

The next stage shades into the first. Using much the same methods of presenting the task, the teacher now involves the learners. The general idea is that the learners shadow the teacher's actions in the first instance and gradually assume more independence so that they eventually are able to perform satisfactorily on their own.

The constituent elements of the skill should be tackled first. This simplifies the activity and helps accuracy. In the case of handwriting, if a beginner has to attempt to cope with all four of the subordinate skills at the same time, he or she might well grip the pencil properly but get into difficulties by bearing down too heavily on the working surface. Concentrating on one thing at a time at the beginning helps avoid problems like this.

Once the sub-skills are acquired they are linked together. Completion of the first element becomes the stimulus for the second. Taking the correct grip of the pen becomes the stimulus for resting the hand lightly on the writing surface as described, which in turn leads to the forming of the letter and then to the sliding motion across the surface. Throughout the teacher prompts and guides. This guidance is likely to be mainly oral but could be by actually guiding the learner's activity physically. In the case of handwriting the teacher might actually *guide* pupils' hand and fingers as lightly as possible so that they experience something like correct muscular tensions.

A variation on this approach developed by Galperin (1954) has proved effective. After demonstrating and explaining the activity the teacher carries out the activity under the directions of the learner. The great advantage of this approach in the first stage of motor learning is that the learner is getting an insight into the nature of the skill without the difficulty of carrying out the activity at the same time. Having guided the teacher the learner is better equipped for self-guidance. This self-guidance could be the learner's speech at first, gradually to be replaced by sub-vocal guidance, which eventually itself decays and the activity becomes 'automatic'. I touched on this approach in Chapter 4 and shall return to it later.

FEEDBACK

Carefully planned feedback is one of the key elements in guiding learning. In motor skill learning the teacher's voice is a versatile and effective medium of feedback for the reasons I have discussed earlier. It can be used to help learners detect subtle differences in technique that would be difficult to convey otherwise. It is particularly important to provide prompt and frequent feedback in the early stages of learning. If it is not provided, learners will be unsure about their performance and could go astray in their learning.

A teacher teaching a skill such as handwriting to a class of pupils and providing feedback has a difficult task. Show and tell to the whole class precludes satisfactory feedback to individual learners and is thus deleterious to learning. While show and tell is a natural enough approach, given an impossible situation, it will almost certainly result in less satisfactory and slower learning than would focusing on a few children using methods based on teacher-guided pupil action such as suggested above.

In my pedagogical analysis of teaching handwriting I suggested that it might be possible to devise instrumentation to provide feedback. Although the suggestion was made in the context of teaching handwriting, it is a suggestion that applies to all skill learning. How best to provide feedback in psychomotor skills can present teachers with some of the most interesting and challenging pedagogical problems. While the teacher's voice may be a very powerful and flexible channel for feedback, it has its limitations. The most obvious one is that its effectiveness is limited in formal schooling by the size of classes. Another limitation is that it cannot provide perceptual or kinesthetic feedback.

In the soldering lesson referred to earlier the teacher provided verbal feedback at crucial stages of the pupils' attempts at soldering. He also tried to arrange for the outcome of their activity to provide feedback. He points out that psychomotor activities, by their nature, generate their own feedback. If you miss the target the missing provides feedback. If the wires in a joint fall apart you get feedback that your soldering has been unsuccessful. A teacher's guidance can augment this kind of feedback by making suggestions as to the reasons for failure, especially when no obvious remedial action presents itself to the learner. In the case of the soldering lesson the pupils got excellent feedback, since if they succeeded the lamp in the circuit lit up. The light indicates success and almost certainly provided reinforcement as well as feedback. The pupils were pleased at having acquired a new skill and having it demonstrated.

It should be noted, however, that the successful lighting of the bulb could be achieved by a very untidy joint. The teacher in this instance had aimed no further than soldering that completed a circuit. Later work would have led to more refined results. If he had set out to have the pupils produce more elegant joints he would have had to augment the appearance of the light with guidance and cuing that influenced the tidiness of the joints they were making. He did try to provide this type of feedback in the lesson, but when he analysed the recording he had made he found that he was being less informative than he should have been and that his guidance could have been more detailed. This finding is related to the common finding when teachers view their teaching that they provide much less reinforcement than they think they do. The general point, of course, is one that pervades the discussion in this book: the complexities of teaching are unsuspected by most people and often unexpected by experienced teachers when they take an analytical look at their own teaching.

In some athletic activities and in dance, very large mirrors, sometimes taking up a whole wall of the room are used so that learners can see their actions. They are thus in a position to observe the nature of the movement associated with particular muscular activity. There is an obvious problem with this type of feedback, useful though it may be. It is that the reflection is a mirror image with left-right reversal.

Recent developments in electronics and related technology have made possible new methods of providing feedback. *Made possible* are the operative words. The use of such technology to provide appropriate feedback will not be devised by the manufacturers, who are sublimely naive about pedagogy. Nor will it be devised by AVA experts seeking ways of using their equipment in teaching. They can be devised only by teachers using their knowledge of pedagogy and their native ingenuity and creativity to solve problems of providing effective feedback to their pupils. The problem comes first. The use of the appropriate equipment follows. Sometimes simple equipment will be preferred to sophisticated equipment. The point is that, contrary to some claims, the use of the equipment *in itself* will not suffice. It is the way it is deployed that counts, and that depends on pedagogical expertise and not expertise in the use of AVA equipment. I have been at pains to stress this point because it is a widely held fallacy that the mere use of newfangled gadgetry will solve problems of teaching.

With the caveat that hardware is no substitute for thought, let us now consider some of the ways in which feedback might be instrumented. Closed circuit television (CCTV) has great potential for providing feedback in motor skill learning. Dancers can overcome the reversal problems created by mirrors by using CCTV. Moreover, they can see themselves not only the right way round, but in slow motion, frozen in a particular posture and even moving backwards! Above all, they can go through the same sequence of actions time and again by merely replaying the recording. Through the use of large screen techniques learners can see themselves from different angles while they are actually practising the activity. I mentioned dancers, but these techniques can be used in virtually any skill one can think of that involves physical activity. Virtually all learners of ball games can benefit from such feedback. So can athletes seeking to improve their action. It would certainly be possible to use CCTV to provide feedback for pupils learning to write.

Visual feedback can also be provided for non-visual activity. Deaf people can *see* to what extent the sound they make when pronouncing a word resembles the sound made by a hearing person by comparing the wave pattern made by the two sounds on an oscilloscope screen. Similar techniques can also be used to provide feedback in singing.

Some years ago I devised a technique that I find particularly useful. It provides feedback for teachers that is totally unobtainable in any other way. Using split screen techniques in CCTV it is possible to present simultaneously on a TV screen a picture showing the teacher more or less from the pupils' viewpoint and one showing the pupils as they appear to the teacher. The teachers viewing recordings of this type are able to see how the pupils react to every move they make and every word they say and how they, the teachers, react to pupil actions. Thus they get an insight into the very complex interplay of feedback from pupil to teacher and teacher to pupil, while the act of viewing the recording provides global feedback on the way the lesson went.

This approach to feedback raises another aspect of the teacher's role in enhancing learning. While the feedback, in itself, is essential for bringing about learning, its value can be enhanced by the teacher. Video feedback used with teachers in training is more effective when it is 'focused' (Fuller and Manning 1973). Focusing involves the teacher's intervening to reduce the complexity of the learning situation so that learners are better able to perceive the results of their activity. In the case of recordings of teaching in classrooms, the complexity of the situation is so great, involving the learning of some very complex principles, that neophyte teachers need all the help they can get to distinguish the important aspects of feedback provided by the recording. Although the complexity in simpler learning situations, which are predominantly concerned with motor activity, is much less, it is still important to help pupils to get the maximum of benefit from feedback by drawing attention to the key factors leading to error. Better still, teaching should aim to equip them to scrutinise their own performances critically. Careful cuing and guiding can help to foster this ability.

PRACTICE

Achieving an aimed-for level of competence in a skill is a demonstration of learning. However, for a skill to be useful it is necessary for it to become part of one's routine activity. For this to happen it is necessary for the learner to practise the skill, that is, to engage in activity involving the deployment of the newly acquired skill. Repeated practice leads to the overlearning referred to earlier and makes the skill resistant to decay. Repeated practice also develops a more integrated and smoother performance.

Repeated practice on its own, however, may not necessarily lead to improvement. As I suggested earlier, any unsatisfactory elements in the learning could also be practised and gradually lead to a deterioration in the skill. To prevent this deterioration the continuation of feedback after learners reach criterion levels of performance is essential. This is important in the early stages of overlearning, but is also useful even when the skill is habitual to ensure that its effectiveness is fully maintained and to guard against a drift towards sloppy inefficiency.

One need not look far for an example of motor skill learning that is rarely practised sufficiently. Driving a car is a common example of such a skill. Most people have to pay for driving lessons and are, therefore, highly motivated to take a driving test as soon as possible. Once through the test, few people receive feedback on their performance and even if something goes wrong they are unlikely to be able to detect the reasons for the error. If nothing goes wrong, a drift away from the correct exercise of the skill may take place unintentionally.

Many societies with a high level of car ownership seem tacitly to acknowledge the unsatisfactory nature of driving skills by their approach to highway engineering and automobile design. They address the problem that driver error accounts for an extremely high percentage of road casualties by developing road systems and vehicles that demand increasingly lower levels of skills by drivers. A little insight into the learning of psychomotor skills would indicate that a more effective approach would be to allocate resources for the re-testing of drivers at intervals after taking their driving test to provide feedback and prevent the overlearning of bad driving habits.

Better still would be to develop methods of driver training with a pedagogical base. Such a method would aim to teach driving with under-standing of some general principles of car control and road safety instead of rote actions with little conceptual content. A key issue, however, is the evaluation of driver training and the stringency of the testing. Current lax standards in many countries are consequences of wider social attitudes, rather than, or as well as, pedagogical ignorance.

In order for a skill to be maximally useful it should be capable of application in a variety of conditions. Learning to drive one particular car along quiet country lanes in bright sunny weather is a useful but limited skill if the learner is to be faced with driving on a motorway on a dark snowy night or through city traffic in the rush hour. The same applies to other skills. A pupil needs to be able to write using a variety of instruments on different of surfaces at different heights and in different light conditions. The learning involved resembles effective concept learning in that it is transferable to novel conditions. But in order to achieve that level of competence economically and effectively, the pupil needs guided practice in systematically varied conditions. Thus the general approach to teaching motor skills is virtually the same as that for teaching concepts. In introducing the variety of experiences to the learners, in order for them to achieve this flexibility and versatility, a teacher should bear in mind the principles rehearsed earlier: introduce the learners gradually to the more complicated conditions; do not throw them in at the deep end; do not send them onto the motorway on a snowy night the first time they drive; let them practice on canvas on an easel before asking any of them to paint the ceiling of the Sistine Chapel.

In the end, of course, the teacher withdraws. The withdrawal should also be planned carefully. If the teacher withdraws too early the learner will be in danger of practising incorrect sub-skills until they become fixed. The teacher's skill lies in judging the moment that avoids this problem as well as the problem of continuing with support too long. I hope the methods suggested above will help teachers to withdraw their support in a controlled and satisfactory manner. The gradual fading of cuing and prompting at the early stage, the gradual tapering off of feedback at the practice stage, involving the learners in directing their own attempts through verbal commentary at different stages of their learning and linking all these methods of providing feedback through means other than the teacher; all of these will contribute to the learners' being able to monitor their own exercise of their newly learned skill.

NORMS

Teachers need to be particularly sensitive to the question of norms in connection with physical skills. By 'norms' I mean the levels of performance typical of a particular group. Notions that teachers have of normal levels of motor abilities may impede them in their attempts to teach non-motor skills that depend on motor ability. The problem is that these notions lead to expectations that all pupils should be able to cope with the skills at the level teachers observe in almost all pupils of the same age. Some pupils, however, have physiological problems that interfere with their execution of some motor activities. These pupils do not have the gross physical difficulties that some people have, and their problems are often not understood.

Thus minor physiological problems result in these pupils performing below the norm in common physical skills such as running, jumping, hopping, kicking or throwing a ball. The reasons for this failure frequently lie in poor coordination of hand and eye and foot and eye. Such pupils are sometimes referred to as 'clumsy'. Their disabilities are not totally incapacitating and are often overlooked, resulting in lack of sympathy by peers and teachers. The derision of peers and impatience of teachers create a vicious circle from which few escape.

Pupils with problems of coordination may have difficulty in learning conceptual material entirely because of the intrusion of essentially irrelevant motor activities. Pupils are often expected to draw apparatus, maps and graphs when they are learning concepts in the physical sciences, geography and mathematics. Teachers need to be aware of the difficulty pupils with minor motor problems may have with such activities and to make allowances for it in their teaching particularly in their assessment of pupil competence at the end of teaching. The question to ask is whether or not these motor activities are criterial to the learning aimed for. Should the ability to draw accurately and tidily be taken as part of the evidence of conceptual learning in fields such as chemistry, history or geography?

For children with difficulties in motor coordination a lot depends on the answer teachers give.

A HEURISTIC FOR TEACHING MOTOR SKILLS

I now bring together the key elements in a heuristic for the teaching of psychomotor skills. The heuristic provides a check list for teachers attempting to monitor their own teaching skills. It could also be used by a colleague to advise or a supervisor of student teachers to guide and evaluate their learning. It provides an explicit rationale for tutor and student teacher to identify the key elements in teaching which both attempt to monitor. However, I stress that all the caveats I made in connection with the heuristic on concept teaching apply also to this guide to the teaching of motor skills.

Heuristic for the teaching of psychomotor skills

A   *Preactive*

1 Make a pedagogical analysis of teaching objectives to decide on the key subordinate skills, the methods of presentation, the nature of pupil activities, the provision of feedback, the evaluation of performance and the arrangements for monitored practice.
2 Ascertain the pupils' existing levels of competence. Pupils lacking the prerequisite motor abilities to perform the subordinate skills should not be admitted to the main programme of teaching but should be given remedial teaching to bring them up to scratch.

B   *Interactive*

3 Establish a preliminary idea of the task by explaining and demonstrating.
4 Identify for the learners the subordinate skills and show their relationship to the overall task as in (3).
5 Involve the learners in describing the activity, possibly by letting them guide the teacher in performing the activity and in the use of subordinate skills.
6 Prompt and guide the learners in carrying out the subdivisions of the task.
7 Prompt and guide the learners to make a smooth transition from one division of the task to the next. Use counterpositioning in areas of difficulty.
8 Fade the prompts gradually to ensure that the learners assume responsibility for self-prompting.

   9 Provide feedback at all stages and for all responses if possible.

10 Arrange for practice to ensure that learners consolidate their new skills.

11 Monitor the practice from time to time but gradually fade the monitoring.

12 Arrange for practice to take place in varying circumstances.

C   Evaluative

13 Assess the level of success of the learners' performance against the objectives set out in the preactive stage.

14 Encourage the learners to assess their own practice against the criteria established in the interactive stage particularly (3), (4) and (5).

I have discussed what seem to me to be important aspects in the learning of psychomotor skills. My aim is not to produce guidelines for teachers of athletics or craft subjects, although I believe that the principles could be useful for such teachers. My purpose is to draw attention to the need to be aware that problems learners experience in conceptual learning may be caused by difficulties related to physical skills. This is an important point when diagnosing learning difficulties. I also suggested that the learning of motor skills is rarely unconnected with concept learning. Learners need to conceptualise the nature of the skill they are trying to learn. That is, they need to learn the key concepts and principles involved in the exercise of the skill in order to relate the physical activities to an overall conceptual framework. Having a conceptual as well as a motor understanding of the skills is essential to developing transferability and flexibility in motor skill learning. Learners who learn a motor skill as a set routine of mechanical actions could have great difficulty when faced with a situation different from the one in which they learned the skill.

It might be argued that it is possible to learn motor skills without their underlying principles. This may be the case, although whether, in fact, learning of this kind does take place with human learners seems to me more a subject for empirical investigation than an accepted fact. My point here is that even without overt teaching of the concepts and principles related to a physical skill, learners are likely to abstract their own concepts inductively from their experience. Learning principles in this way is unlikely to be the most effective way of learning. A teacher's help should enhance that learning. I suggest that a teacher who does not try to teach the key principles underlying a motor skill is encouraging a type of rote learning which is likely to be useful only in near-identical situations. Conversely, one who does will be encouraging meaningful learning that may offer the possibility of transfer to other non-identical situations. In the case of learning handwriting, for example, understanding that a relaxed grip enhances control of a tool will be useful in other circumstances as well as speeding up the learning of that particular skill.

It is important for teachers to be alert to the close interconnections between conceptual and motor learning and to tease out their nature. This will help to provide insight into the planning, execution and evaluation of the teaching. This elucidation will be helped by an appropriate pedagogical analysis, which should enable them to focus on the key elements of the learning intended. I should now like to consider some examples of teachers teaching psychomotor skills in which these questions are addressed in practice.

MOTOR SKILLS IN PRACTICE

Volleyball

My first example is taken from an account of teaching a skill in playing volleyball. While I am conscious that not all readers are likely to be passionately interested in this sport, I have chosen this example because it illustrates several of the points I have made above in the space of one relatively limited piece of teaching. The teacher was an experienced teacher of secondary pupils of eleven years old and above. He was particularly involved in teaching physical education, and in this example was teaching a boy of eleven one of the sub-skills in playing volleyball.

The skill in question was the 'dig', which is one of the main ways of handling the ball during the course of the game. The teacher's pedagogical analysis gives an indication of its nature. It is presented in figure 6.2.

The teacher had checked the boy's ability and understanding of the skills involved in volleyball and decided that, although he understood the nature of the game, he was unclear about and inexpert in the dig-pass. The pedagogical analysis was intended to identify the nature of the teaching to remedy these deficiencies.

In the report of his teaching the teacher discusses a common problem facing anyone wishing to take a systematic approach to the teaching of physical skills. He finds that there is little in the literature that is much help to teachers. While there is a wealth of books on the playing and teaching of a wide range of sports, it consists almost exclusively of anecdotes and reminiscences of leading players with intricate analyses of specific actions in particular games. There is virtually nothing in the field of volleyball suitable for younger learners.

Thus the teacher's pedagogical analysis was perforce derived solely from his knowledge and experience of the game and his application of pedagogical analysis to the task of teaching young learners. He used the general approach to pedagogical analysis I have discussed in previous chapters and related it to

Figure 6.2 Analysis of the task of teaching the dig pass in volleyball

General content	Method of stimulus presentation
The Dig Pass The ability to intercept the path of the ball after it has passed over the net. Changing a defensive action into that of a possible attacking situation.	Pictures. Watching pupils in a competition match. Watching a pupil perform the Dig. Teacher explains. Teacher demonstrates. Teacher Guides. Teacher Cues.
Subordinate skills 1 Moving into position to intercept the ball. 2 Body position before contact with ball. i) Body in flight path but facing the direction of the intended pass. ii) Handgrip and arm position (arm outstretched and locked at the elbows). iii) Legs apart – one in front of the other. 3 Body position on making contact with the ball. Ball is played on the fleshy part of the forearm. Body is extended smoothly upwards and forwards off the backfoot to give more control to the pass.	

This analysis resembles, in its layout, the one on handwriting. However, note the statements under 'General Content'. The skills and sub-skills are not all explicated. Sub skill one suggests that one should move into position to intercept the ball but does not explain what the position should be. Most of the other statements do give an indication of the action to take; see 2 (i), (ii) and (iii). Note the precision of the evaluative test. One might add that although the focus is on the psychomotor skill, the teacher takes steps to build up the pupil's concepts about the skill. In all the other columns except evaluation the teacher is describing activity aimed at concept teaching. I do not comment on whether it would have been better to have devised a separate anlysis for the concept teaching or to have built it into the existing one more systematically. This is the kind of question that is open to empirical investigation in the actual teaching bearing in mind the inextricability of the two types of learning.

Pupil's responses	Feedback	Evaluation
Pupil explains why a dig pass is used and how to perform it. Pupil on seeing a pass demonstration or his own, points out or recognises positive and negative examples of correct method of overall skill. Pupil demonstrates the Dig Pass.	Teacher comments. Comparison with model examples from game the previous night. Comparison with standard of own earlier attempts (accuracy and quality of pass). Kinesthetic feedback.	The ability to perform the Dig pass intercepting a ball thrown from the opposite side of the net and directing the dig pass to a player standing in a semicircle whose Diameter is 5 metres with an accuracy of 80 per cent. The test of accuracy being that the ball was received by the boy inside the semicircle without its touching the ground, i.e. that he be in a volley position on receiving the pass.

the heuristic guide to teaching motor skills discussed earlier in this chapter. Under the 'General Content' heading he substituted an analysis of the main skill for the analysis of the main concepts. He does not refer to the nature of the learning involved, presumably because he is focusing on the motor aspect of the skill and takes as given that the learning is motor learning. However, in the report of the planning and execution of the teaching he refers to specific types of learning that are implicit in his approach. He sees the motor learning as comprising learning of motor responses. The sub-skills are learned and then linked together in a chain of responses and smoothed by dint of practice, as I have already discussed. He also discusses concept learning, although without using the term explicitly. In fact he took steps to develop the pupil's understanding of the game, and the 'dig' in particular, before starting to teach the motor activity. He did this by taking the pupil to volleyball games and cuing and guiding his observations of the skills involved, particularly the 'dig'. This activity was, in essence, concept teaching and giving the pupil a preliminary idea of the task. The teacher also checked the development of the pupil's concepts relating to the skills involved by asking him to appraise specific examples of the skill in the 'Students' Responses' section of the pedagogical analysis.

After instruction the learner achieved a level of accuracy of 60 per cent, determined by the teacher's assessment of his performance according to the evaluation procedure set out in the pedagogical analysis. The teacher failed to reach his objective of 80 per cent success. He wished to know why. It is instructive that he did not entertain the notion that it was the pupil's fault. Instead he considered three main possibilities: the boy lacked the motor abilities to perform the subordinate skills of the dig; his own evaluation was inaccurate; his teaching was faulty. The teacher ruled out the first possibility since he had strong evidence from his pre-test that the boy had good motor abilities. The second possibility was also discounted since the criteria set out in his pedagogical analysis, although stringent, were appropriate to the requirements of the game. He accepted the third possibility as the reason for the boy's failure to achieve 80 per cent success. One or more of the sub-skills had not been taught satisfactorily. He examined the details of the final test and decided that the problem lay in an unsatisfactory body position on making contact with the ball.

Why had he failed to teach this sub-skill adequately? Since he had videotaped the teaching he was able to examine his teaching closely. His examination in essence revealed the following: feedback and encouragement were inadequate. In the early stages of the lesson he had progressed too quickly, not allowing time to practise the new actions. He spent too much time explaining (telling) instead of involving the boy in activity guided by verbal cuing. He failed to provide feedback and reinforcement on occasions when the pupil had performed actions well. He found that he overlooked newly acquired correct actions and did not provide feedback or reinforcement because he was focusing attention on a still undeveloped action. To remedy the situation it would be necessary to review the sub-skills of the dig pass with the pupil, providing more feedback and reinforcement and to give much more practice. 'Telling' needs to be de-emphasised.

What can we learn about teaching motor skills from this example? First, I suggest, we can see the value of taking an analytical approach to the task. The literature on the sport was either very general and descriptive or devoted to detailed descriptions of expert performance. It offered the teacher no pedagogically useful information. The analysis, on the other hand, clarified the nature of the skill by revealing its main subordinate skills. This clarification provided not only useful guidance for the teacher at the teaching phase but also a tool for identifying pedagogical strengths and weaknesses of his teaching afterwards. I discuss the evaluation of this teaching further in Chapter 9.

The teacher's post-teaching analysis is an example of reflection in action whereby he appraised his own performance in the light of theoretical principles. The principles helped the teacher to understand the nature of the strengths and weaknesses of his teaching and to take action to build up the former and avoid the latter in future. His findings resemble some we have already encountered. His low level of reinforcement and unsatisfactory feedback are very commonly found when analyses such as this are made. Despite his realising the futility of 'showing and telling' he found that he had done quite a bit of this instead of the cuing and guiding he had intended to do. He attributes this failing, in part, to the fact that he attempted to progress too quickly. This, also, is a very common failing. It is an example of the 'covering the ground', or 'getting though the material' approach. The compulsion which drives many teachers to unburden themselves of the lesson they have planned, come what may, exemplifies the fallacy which equates a teacher's having 'got through the material' with the pupils' having learned what the teacher intended.

In the case we are considering, the teacher had an advantage over most teachers. He was able to review his performance on videotape and he had pedagogical knowledge to help him understand what he saw and guide his steps in future teaching. He saw himself explaining instead of guiding and providing practice, and realised that although it might have been quicker to explain, it would have been counterproductive.

This action by the teacher of this relatively straightforward piece of teaching illustrates several very important pedagogical phenomena. Perhaps the most important general point, once again, is that, in teaching, things are much more complex than is generally thought. The complexity is unrealised until one takes an analytical look at the process, such as was taken by the teacher in this example. It is also conceivable that this analysis itself is crude and that more refined ways of examining teaching would reveal further complexity not discovered by the approach we are considering here.

Another important point is in the nature of the learning. The pupil improved his skill *and so did the teacher*. Although the teacher does not manifest an improvement in practice in this account, he has clearly enlarged his understanding of the process of teaching a motor skill and is thus better equipped for his next attempt. Note, I suggest that he has learned something about teaching a motor skill, not merely about teaching the volleyball dig. The points he raises are of general application to motor skills and, some, to teaching.

The way the teacher learned is important. He used his own teaching as protocol material and learned several things about his teaching that I have already mentioned. There is a further point that relates to a more general question than the learning of specific pedagogical skills. It is that theory and practice develop together. His understanding of the use of feedback in teaching and learning is enlarged and made more precise by his analysis of the way he provided feedback to the pupil in the lesson. It is not just a case of learning by experience; it is a case of learning by analysing experience in the light of theoretical perspectives which are, themselves, modified in the process. This is the same process underlying the approach the teacher adopted with the pupil when he was trying to develop his concept of volleyball skills. It is, of course, possible to learn by experience without theoretical understanding. Learning of this type may lead to improvement but, lacking a body of concepts to connect to, is unlikely to be as comprehensive or as quickly developed as learning informed by a theoretical perspective.

Finally, it is instructive to consider that this learning, although clearly predominantly the learning of a physical skill, was much dependent upon conceptual learning. The teacher recognised this, as we see from the steps he took to build up concepts relating to volleyball skills. He does not say whether or not he tried explicitly to teach the theoretical basis for the recommendations in the analysis of subordinate skills, although he mentions some of the reasoning involved. He refers to the faults that led to faulty passing techniques. The ball flies off the arm to one side for several reasons, the majority of them related to the lack of provision of a stable platform for the ball by incorrect posture by the player. One might take this analysis further and go into the physics underlying the movement of the ball in various conditions. This depth of analysis might be appropriate for someone aspiring to a high level of skill but probably not for this teacher's purposes. The teacher's understanding of the theory related to playing the game and his experience as player or teacher is currently the best guide to how far such an analysis should be taken.

Teaching the Green Cross Code

The Green Cross Code is a British guide to road crossing skills prepared by road safety specialists and educationists for the guidance of teachers and young children. The actual use of the code is a matter for local decision either by schools or district education authorities.

The teacher whose work we now consider had considerable misgivings about the very little time usually devoted to the subject and also to the approach to its teaching in primary schools (ages seven–eleven approximately). The teaching of road safety in many schools was left to infrequent visits by road safety organisations or the police, who lack training in teaching. The normal approach to the subject was by talks more in the nature of exhortation than teaching.

The age group of the children concerned is very vulnerable to road accidents, with around 900 pedestrian fatalities and 60,000 injured per year among children up to the age of 15 years. Most casualties occur among children walking home from school or playing after school. Competence in road crossing skills is clearly a subject that should be taken seriously.

Analysis

The teacher considered that the skill of safe road crossing was essentially a motor skill. She accordingly prepared a pedagogical analysis. But she was also conscious of the fact that significant elements of cognitive and perceptual learning were involved. Thus her objectives, which were based on the code, included such things as the pupils' being able to identify on a local street a straight route across the road, a safe place to cross, parked vehicles, road junction, traffic approaching and traffic receding. She also considered affective aspects of learning. Drawing on concepts from the Krathwohl *et al. Taxonomy of Affective Objectives* (1964), she adopted objectives that aimed for the pupils to show that they were aware of the dangers and hazards involved in crossing a road and that they practised the Green Cross Code willingly during lessons. Her overall objectives were that the children would be able to cross a street in the locality in daylight and normal weather conditions using the taught street crossing skills. She set a minimum standard of 90 per cent efficiency.

These examples are just a sample of her objectives. They all involve elements of concept learning. It is impossible to have an attitude towards something of which you have no knowledge. What needs sensitive appraisal is the depth of understanding on which the expressed attitudes are based. Pupil understanding based on exhortations such as the teacher had observed in the past could clearly do little or nothing to establish pupils' concepts, perceptual abilities and attitudes towards real-life road crossing practices. Thus, even if they enjoyed the untutored policeman's exposition, their attitudes would not be related to road crossing skills but to the policeman's performance. Any concepts they learned could be only marginally related to practical activity. Quite likely their learning would be more rote than conceptual. If they did not enjoy the talk, the fact that it would have been introduced as being concerned with road crossing safety could well result in negative attitudes to the real thing.

The idea of a safe place to cross is clearly one of the key concepts to be taught. Subordinate elements include the ones mentioned, such as road junctions and approaching traffic. Words such as 'traffic', 'vehicle', 'kerb' and 'pavement' are commonly used in guides and in talks on pedestrian safety. The teacher cites evidence for the fact that some of these concepts are poorly understood by children of this age. Others, such as 'kerb', are not understood partly because of variant regional usage. 'Traffic', for example, was considered by children aged six to refer to 'where there are signs on the road'. At eight, 'the cars drive one after another in a long row' and at ten 'when there are lots of cars so that there are long queues' (Sandels 1975). The teacher's intention to take a systematic approach to concept teaching and her identification of the key elements in such things as a safe place to cross, would expose the problems inherent in the pupils' misunderstanding. Further, if her teaching were successful, she would clarify these concepts for the children and lay the basis for successful teaching of the target skills.

In the same way that young children's concepts are different from those of adults, so are their perceptual abilities. Visual and auditory perception are less developed and thus less effective in discriminating among stimuli. All these factors are very important in developing effective road crossing skills. None of them could be taught by delivery methods. The fact that such methods are used illustrates the widespread misconception of teaching as involving nothing more than telling and the general lack of knowledge of pedagogy. In our present case, the teacher's pedagogical analysis had brought the problems to the surface. She therefore decided to give the children an idea of, and practice in, listening and visual observation.

She also considered questions of attention and divided attention. When preparing to cross the road one has to concentrate on the important things like approaching traffic. Children playing as they walk along or engaged in conversation are not as able, as adults, to divide their attention and concentrate on the traffic and the conversation at the same time. This does not imply that adults are in general as competent as they really ought to be to cross safely. It is worth remembering that one of the key reasons for teaching children these skills is the fact that the adults driving the cars are mostly trying to attend to more things than they are competent to do. I have no doubt that the same applies to adults crossing roads. In view of this problem the teacher decided to give the children practice in divided attention. She recognises, however, that this is a very difficult task, about which there is little reliable information and no simple solutions.

All these complexities come together in the psychomotor skill of crossing the road safely. Commonly used methods of teaching this subject are sublimely ignorant of these complexities. The teacher attempting to teach this vital skill realised that even in a series of lessons she was unlikely to resolve all the problems. However, she set about her lessons in a systematic way to attempt to cope with the difficulties and help the children become much more competent in the skill.

Teaching

After making a thorough analysis of her objectives and ascertaining the nature of the skills and concepts to be taught, the teacher adopted similar systematic and painstaking methods in her teaching. She drew on work by people in such fields as psychology, child development, instructional design and literature relating to the teaching of road crossing skills, as well as on her own experience as a practising teacher, and applied it to the specific task of teaching the Green Cross Code. It is not possible to give a full account of her teaching in a page or two, but I will try to single out its key elements. I must stress, however, that I can give only an outline and that a great richness of thought and action lies behind the account.

The pre-test to her teaching gives a flavour of her approach. She wished to establish the existing level of road crossing skills before starting. This, in itself, is innovatory in teaching of this type. Her method is even more innovatory. She drew up a check list of actions related to road crossing skills and recorded on video the children's actual behaviour on the way home from school. These observations enabled her to identify the most important failings by the children. They were, in fact, not looking around before crossing and not continuing to look around when crossing. These were the features to give particular attention to.

She prepared the pupils affectively for the teaching and also ascertained their understanding of the need for road safety practices by having a brainstorming session. She used a poster depicting an injured child and the legend 'Teach them how to cross the road'. She found that the pupils gave a few indications of what they should do when crossing the road, but none of them knew all the elements in the Green Cross Code. This lesson also sensitised the pupils to the need to learn the skills involved and gave them a preliminary idea of the task.

Learning this skill presents formidable problems of stimulus presentation. The possibilities range from teaching the children on a busy street to telling them in the classroom, as is customary in current methods. In between these two extremes is an infinite variety of approaches limited only by the teacher's imagination. Most of these approaches are likely to be variants of simulation. Simulation provides a safe environment for the practising of skills which in normal circumstances involve danger. One well-known example is the simulator for training aeroplane pilots. With modern sophisticated equipment the sensation produced by the simulator is virtually identical with that of sitting in a cockpit and flying an aircraft. No such sophistication is available to teach children to survive on today's urban roads. The teacher, wishing to use simulation, had, therefore, to devise her own.

The teacher arranged graded simulations ranging from work with table-top models to outdoor work with simulated traffic. However, there was more to the teaching than simply setting up situations for the children to pretend to be crossing the road. The simulation work was integral with the teacher's theoretical analysis and use of the various heuristic guides.

Using pictures and worksheets she taught the concepts of road, pavement, kerb, vehicles and traffic. She tested the pupils' grasp of the concepts by showing them videotapes of streets in their locality and asking them to identify exemplars of the concepts on the tapes. She asked them to demonstrate their understanding of going straight across the road by drawing chalk lines across a road painted in the playground.

She used audio-recordings to sharpen up their perceptual and attention skills. Pupils had to identify various vehicles from the recordings, to decide whether a vehicle was approaching or receding and to locate the direction of traffic sounds when blindfolded.

On a table-top model of a road with model vehicles and pedestrians she demonstrated correct road crossing procedures using the model pedestrians and drawing attention orally to the key aspects to be noted. She then adopted Galperin's approach and had the children directing her as she manipulated the model. The pupils then manipulated the model themselves and explained what they were doing. They also appraised each others' and the teacher's efforts at demonstrating correct road crossing procedures on the model. In this way she moved from ignorance by the children to their being able to appraise each others' efforts as protocols (type B skills) and to simulate correct road crossing skills on the model.

From the table top the next step was outdoors into the school playground. Here the children had to demonstrate in their own actions the procedures they had developed in the classroom by crossing marked-out roads. These demonstrations were videotaped, and the children were able to appraise their efforts and get feedback about them.

Taking up the points made earlier about distractions in enacting motor skills, the teacher complicated the operation of crossing the road by making it into a team game in which the children had to hop around skittles before running up to the road and crossing using correct procedures. This exercise was further complicated by three pupils from another class cycling up and down the 'road'. This exercise was also followed by the pupils' viewing the recordings of their crossings as before.

The next step took the children out into the road. They were supervised but unprompted by the teacher while they crossed a road with moderate traffic flow. The children crossed very well, but the fact that such an activity is problematic for young children is graphically illustrated in the recording by the length of time taken by one pupil before he decided it was safe to cross. He missed many 'opportunities', but in his own terms he was acting correctly.

Before the next step the children were asked to point out safe places to cross, road junctions and parked cars on a street not previously used for teaching. The teacher then moved on to the final stage. Effectively this was also a summative evaluation of the teaching. Children were sent in twos on errands that involved their crossing roads out of school. This brought together all the elements planned for by the teacher. All aspects of the code were involved and also the teacher's concern that the distractions should not divert the children from adopting the correct method even outside formal instruction. The pupils were videorecorded without their being aware of it. The recording showed children engrossed in conversation coming to a road and going through the Green Cross routines as they crossed.

Outcomes and evaluation

I shall concentrate on the teacher's evaluation of the children's learning without going into the explicatory detail she does, in order to focus on the essentials relating to the discussion in this chapter. First she reports on the effects of the brainstorming session, especially with regard to the affective outcomes. The pupils contributed anecdotes about themselves and their friends who had unfortunate experiences in crossing the road. They were willing to participate in the programme and practised the skills with enjoyment and were eager to participate. The teacher assessed the value they placed on the skills by observing the children crossing the road when they believed they were unobserved. There was an improvement of pupil behaviour on the skills from a range of 45 to 62 per cent on her pre-teaching rating to a range of 87 to 100 per cent on her post-teaching rating. The fact that the children applied their learning out of school when they thought they were unobserved allows the reasonable conclusion that they valued the taught skills.

The use of the models proved successful in engaging the children's attention. The Galperin approach was particular stimulating. The teacher's prompting and guiding was pronounced at first but was reduced gradually so that eventually the pupils, actions were mainly under their own control in their playground simulation. The practice was varied and gradually increased in difficulty to help the children consolidate the skill and apply it in different circumstances.

The use of video recordings was very useful in providing feedback. One of the children, during the table-top simulation, turned the head of the model pedestrian much too frequently. This error was pointed out and the correct movements demonstrated. However, the child did exactly the same when crossing the playground road. After seeing the recording of herself doing this and discussing with the other pupils, she carried out the action correctly the next time. Showing and telling had failed, but providing guided feedback had succeeded in this case.

The teacher considered that the extensive use of simulation was a success. She confessed to some trepidation when she took the children to cross a relatively busy road at the final stage. But she would not have felt comfortable taking a less experienced group into the same situation. When one views the video recording one understands this only too vividly. The sequence that moves from work in the playground to children standing on a pavement waiting to cross the road has a dramatic impact. The noise of the traffic and the obvious vulnerability of the children brings home to the viewer the importance of the skills being taught and reveals the woeful inadequacy of customary approaches to safety training.

I suggest that the stark contrast between this sequence of lessons and the usual methods of teaching road crossing skills epitomises the gulf between conventional delivery teaching employing show and tell methods and an approach based on analytical techniques and theoretical principles. The complexity of the task of teaching this skill, revealed by the teacher's analysis, teaching and assessment, illustrates the widespread depth of ignorance of the nature of teaching. This ignorance is implicit in the expectation that a brief talk from an unschooled policeman can change practical out-of-school behaviour involving some difficult concepts and complex psychomotor skills.

It might be argued that the amount of time and effort necessary to teach a series of lessons such as those we have been considering is prohibitive. This argument is in a similar category to the one that eschews such methods of teaching because one would not have time to 'cover the syllabus'. Both lead to what might be referred to as 'non-teaching'. The syllabus is covered or the road crossing training is achieved by adults talking, often merely 'reciting' words, about the topic. The words are 'delivered', some may be received. But all too often the words are empty and no skills are learned. The difficult problem of teaching for productive and meaningful learning is resolved by doing something else.

Teaching rhythmic patterns to young children

My next example involves aural discrimination and simple motor activity in the production of rhythmic patterns. This teaching, like the last example (see p. 99), extended over a sequence of lessons and involved a group of ten children from what was referred to at the time as a 'social priority' area in normal classroom conditions. The teacher was an experienced infant (age 5–7) teacher and head teacher but was not a music specialist. She was particularly interested in exploring the possibilities a systematic pedagogical approach might offer to non-specialist staff in teaching aspects of music, since there are normally few specialist staff in schools for younger children.

The ultimate aim of the teaching was for the children to produce their own examples of 2 and 3 time rhythmic patterns. In terms of the types of skills referred to earlier, this ability would be considered a type A skill. However, the teacher envisaged a progression in her teaching, going through simpler skills. In her words: 'The pupils were expected to discriminate between examples and non-examples of the concept to be learned; to identify and name examples of two and three beats; demonstrate conservation of this beat when presented with 2 and 3 time rhythmic patterns and ultimately produce their own examples of them'. It is interesting to note that although the final outcome was to be a form of motor activity, the learning of musical concepts was central to the teaching.

In her teaching the teacher started each lesson by explaining the aims of the lesson and what its content was to be. This introduction was followed by practical activities, so that the pupils would master the various actions through manipulating objects. A variety of percussion instruments was provided, including an electronic musical instrument, and the children's own bodily actions such as clapping, stamping and slapping were used.

As the teacher explained, 'The combination of speech and activity would, it was hoped, ensure that the action would be transferred to the mental plane. A demonstration that this was so was when the pupil could generalise the action . . . and produce further examples of the concept learned. The ability of the child to describe verbally, although important, was not considered reliable since the child might be merely repeating something learned by heart, or . . . his self-initiated language [might fall] short of his conceptual development.'

An excerpt from the teacher's pedagogical analysis is presented in figure 6.3. This gives an idea of the way in which she married physical activities and concept learning. It also illustrates very well the way in which a teacher's practical experience and customary use of materials interact with pedagogical principles. The theoretical principles provide direction and guidance to the way the teacher structures the children's learning environment. The way the principles are realised are influenced by her experience of the activities commonly found in English infant schools.

Figure 6.3 Teaching rhythmic patterns

Contents	Examples	Presentation	Response	Feedback	Evaluation
Subordinate Concept: *ACCENT*					
a Comparisons between loud and soft sounds.	Discriminating between sounds on an audio-tape.	Pre-recorded auto-tape having a selection of loud and soft sounds and some more difficult to determine.	Discriminating between and identifying 'loud' or 'soft' sounds. Pupil/Teacher discussion of non-examples.	Teacher-pupil talk Teacher's response to pupils' actions.	Correct response and identifications made by pupils. Pupils produce own examples.
b Pupils provide examples of 'loud' or 'soft' sounds through physical movements.	Discriminating between sounds made by themselves or others.	Pupils actions such as stamping: tip-toeing; clapping, tapping, shouting whispering.	—— ditto ——	—— ditto ——	—— ditto ——
c —— ditto —— But now divided into groups and pupils making patterns of 'loud' and 'soft' sounds.	—— ditto —— For example: 'clap, slap, slap' or 'stamp, tap, tap, tap'.	—— ditto ——	—— ditto ——	—— ditto ——	—— ditto ——
d As above but now using musical instruments.	Discrimination between 'loud' and 'soft' patterns of sound made by musical instruments; stress placed on first sound.	Pupils actions using musical instruments such as tambour, chime bars, triangles, wooden blocks.	—— ditto ——	—— ditto ——	—— ditto ——

Contents	Examples	Presentation	Response	Feedback	Evaluation
e Pupils produce own examples of 'accent'.	—— ditto —— Non-examples are if no clear pattern emerges because first, louder sound is not perceptible.	—— ditto —— or voice/songs or body-movement.	Pupils produce own examples of 'accent' using a variety of sound patterns.	—— ditto ——	Pupils should now be able to identify and produce examples of accent where the first of a series of sounds is louder than the others.

This analysis is part of the teacher's pedagogical analysis to teach rhythmic patterns in 2 or 3 time. She identified as subordinate concepts: long and short, accent, two and three beats and tempo. She aims to teach the concepts in that order. The part of the analysis presented in figure 6.3 is 'accent'.

I should like to comment on two points in this analysis. One is to remind the reader that the teacher is trying to teach *concepts*, not the use of instruments. Therefore there is no column head 'type of learning'. The second is to draw attention to columns 1 and 2. The teacher heads the column with the title of the subordinate concept but does not explicate it. We cannot decide what she considers to be the criterial attributes of 'accent'. We can infer it from the rest of the matrix, and it seems that her implicit understanding is clear enough to produce a satisfactory analysis. Instead of column 1 setting out the criterial attributes of 'accent' she sets out activities planned for the pupils that would have been more appropriate in other columns.

While I accept the need to avoid rigid formalistic approaches to making pedagogical analyses, I believe it best to be crystal clear about the nature of the elements in an analysis in order to avoid amorphousness. In the case of 'accent' it might have been better to have spelled out the fact that accent is the relative prominence or salience of a syllable. The way the salience is effected might then be presented as specific examples, thus:

Column 1

Accent

Accent is the relative salience of a syllable
Accent can be placed on any syllable in a sequence
In music, accent is usually effected by the relative loudness of a sound.

Column 2

Examples

Stressed sounds on audio-tape, musical instruments, clapping, singing, stressed sounds in different places in a sequence.

It might be worthwhile addressing the general idea of 'accent' by referring to such things as ordinary speech, to underlined words in text, to a dramatic change in the frequency of a sound, to sung sounds or to instrumental sound. All these would used by the teacher as examples of the concept of 'accent' when she is teaching and would remind her of the things to cover, at the same time that the variety of exemplifications would be building up richer concepts in the children.

I have been able to give only a small part of the detailed pedagogical analysis which covered the series of lessons. She also prepared teaching schedules as guidance at the interactive stage of teaching. I produce, below, part of the schedule she prepared for the teaching of tempo:

Pupils [are] asked to clap, tap, or speak going either fast or slow. Other pupils have to decide which. Then asked to produce their own examples and non-examples and discuss them.

Pupils to choose from a selection of instruments those which would be suitable for producing 'slow' or 'fast' sounds. Pupils to decide upon their suitability and discuss.

Two groups of children. One song. One group to sing it slowly while others decide whether it is fast or slow. Then asked to explain.

Two groups of children. One group sing, others play instruments. At teacher's direction one group speeds up and others try to maintain original speed. Groups alternate. Teacher asks them to explain and give opinion on resulting sounds.

Pupils working in twos told they can use any combination of: singing, clapping, tapping, playing instrument or anything else they suggest. They have to decide between them which of two things they are going to do and also which is to go faster or slower or stay the same. Other pupils have to discriminate and discuss. All pupils to have a turn at producing their own examples and non-examples.

In an evaluation of her lesson the teacher discussed a problem encountered by some of the children that raises questions about a commonly used method in music teaching. She reports: 'Some pupils met with difficulty in producing examples of "long£ sounds. They were not aware that a pause after clapping can have the effect of "lengthening" a note. One child, for example, held her hands wide apart and then slowly brought them together, hoping, perhaps that the ensuing sound would be long'. The problem was resolved when the teacher used an electronic tone generator to produce tones of different length.

In fact, of course, the pause following a clap does not lengthen the sound. The use of the pause mentioned by the teacher is a convention. What is lengthened is the silence between claps. The child trying to produce a long sound by bringing her hands slowly together had not learned the convention and was experimenting to try to achieve the impossible. The use of the tone generator solved the problem because it really did produce longer tones and not longer silences.

This is a good example of the mismatch between learner and teacher that can so often occur without the teacher's apprehending the nature of the problem. The teacher's use of conventional teaching techniques was really confusing the child without the teacher's realising. She could probably have overcome the problem by explaining the convention to the children. It would probably be better still to have avoided using the clapping convention altogether in the early stages of learning. In fact the teacher had adequately provided for suitable stimuli of other types and could have managed without clapping quite satisfactorily.

I suggest that the teacher might have got more insight into this problem if she had looked more carefully at the nature of the general content of the teaching in her pedagogical analysis. Note that instead of identifying the subordinate elements in the idea of 'long' and 'short' she provided examples of activities the children might engage in.

A more accurate analysis of the overall concept of rhythmic pattern would have produced a statement such as 'Rhythmic patterns comprise sounds of different length and accent', rather than the unexplicated statement 'long and short' and 'accent', as she had it. This would have led to a statement such as 'Sounds in music last for varying lengths of time'. The learning of the more general concept of 'long' and 'short' might have been considered as part of the prerequisites to the specific task of teaching rhythm. When considering which examples to use to teach the concept, I suggest that the teacher would have had her attention focused more closely on the claims of clapping as an exemplar. One cannot be certain, of course, that she would then have realised the nature of the problem. However, this sharper focus would have increased her sensitivity to it and increased the likelihood of her realising the nature of the children's difficulty in learning the convention of equating sound with silence.

In the actual teaching the teacher used a great variety of exemplars. The use of the tone generator resolved the difficulty caused by the clapping convention. Similarly, throughout the teaching of other concepts subordinate to the general skill, children were introduced to graded examples, presented with a variety of examples and asked to discriminate among them and produce examples themselves. In bringing things together in the overall concept she produced examples of 2 time and 3 time rhythms for pupils to echo while she explained. She then produced non-exemplars and cued them in discriminating between 2 and 3 time. The tone generator was used to produce 2 or 3 time for the pupils to discriminate unaided. Finally they were asked to produce their own 2 or 3 time rhythms and rhythms that did not fit into these categories.

All the teaching was recorded on audio-tape, and transcripts were made later. This facilitated the teacher's appraisal of her teaching. In her evaluation the teacher comments that before attempting it she was sceptical about systematic approaches to teaching music, thinking they would stifle the children's creativity. In the event and after reviewing the tape of her teaching and examining transcripts, she concludes that she would have been intervening anyway, trying to guide the children's learning. Taking an overtly systematic approach enabled her to intervene more insightfully.

One aspect of the teaching that relates particularly to work with young children is the role of speech. The teacher used her own speech for cuing and for reinforcing and providing feedback. She also asked the children to explain and comment on sounds they produced, in the expectation that this would help clarify their thinking and help direct their actions. At the end of each lesson the children were asked to discriminate among and produce sounds and also to explain what they had done. This procedure bears some resemblance to Galperin's approach referred to earlier and draws on the work of Vigotsky (1962) and Luria (1961). The teacher observed during the lessons when the children were attempting to solve the problems the teacher set them, such as discriminating among or producing sounds, that they used speech to enhance their activity. When questioned by the teacher the pupils were often unaware that they had been talking. Speech of this type is functional and not to be discouraged.

One other point relates centrally to the discussion in this chapter. Pupils with less-developed manual dexterity had more difficulty in their learning than the others. This was especially the case when activities making particular demands on motor activities, such as clapping, were involved. Although the teacher's central aim was for children to learn concepts, some of them were hampered by problems related to motor abilities. This difficulty would also have been alleviated by using apparatus that depended less on motor ability in the early stages of learning. It was actually overcome by the teacher's careful structuring of the children's learning experiences. They were engaged in a wide variety of activities which involved overt psychomotor elements, such as discriminating between tones and tapping out rhythms, but which were also deliberately aimed to build up the children's musical concepts. Here, as so often, motor and conceptual learning are difficult to disentangle.

The teacher's assessment of the children's learning indicated that four of them had learned the concept of, and had acquired the ability to produce, 2 and 3 time rhythmic patterns. Three needed further practice and three needed further practice in aspects of the subordinate skills. The teacher considered this outcome very encouraging. The children had had no previous musical instruction and they came from disadvantaged homes with little support for musical interests. Nevertheless most of them had learned a complex concept and developed a complicated motor skill. She was surprised at the level of expertise attained. She comments: 'That the results surprised me is more a reflection on my preconceptions than on the ability of the pupils involved'. She later comments that the systematic approach supported by theoretical insights was a crucial factor in producing the results.

It should be noted that the criteria of successful teaching in these lessons are stringent. The aim was a 100 per cent achievement. By the usual standards of assessment in British schools, the results were very good. Moreover, the teaching of the musical skills and concepts attempted was more complex than would normally be attempted with children of this age and background. The demand that the children transfer their learning to the production of new rhythms is particularly testing.

What can we learn from the work of this teacher? First, I suggest, we have another example of the way motor and conceptual learning are inextricably related. Abstract notions, concepts, interact with motor activity to change the nature of both. The task teachers face is to ensure that the change is benign and ameliorative, leading to economical and transferable learning and avoiding the rigidities of rote learning.

The way in which the teacher guided the learning through her speech in cuing and reinforcing motor activity is also worthy of attention. Young children's own speech is also of use and should be encouraged in the early stages of learning a new motor skill.

The value of a large variety of exemplars that rings the changes on the non-criterial attributes of an activity while holding the criterial attributes constant is seen in this teacher's pedagogical analysis and her teaching. The involvement of children in producing protocol material for analysis by other children not only sharpens their understanding of the concepts and enhances their perceptions and motor abilities, it also enhances group cohesion and enjoyment of the activities. The problem the teacher encountered with the use of clapping as an indication of length of a sound might have been avoided had the conceptual analysis element in her pedagogical analysis been more rigorous. It seems to me that this was an occasion when a universal practice that is clearly misleading to young learners did not get the close scrutiny it needed. The fact that it is so universally employed presumably overwhelmed the teacher's thinking about the question. Since it is unlikely that this is the only erroneous teaching convention, it behoves teachers of quality to keep an open mind to the validity of such conventions.

7 Quality problem solving

TEACHING PROBLEM SOLVING

Our discussion of the aspects of human learning culminates in this chapter. We are now a very long way from the kind of learning implicit in the talk of 'delivering the curriculum'. I have tried to point out how such talk grossly misrepresents the nature of productive human learning and have suggested ways of ensuring that pupils' learning is meaningful rather than rote and meaningless. I have argued that traditional approaches to teaching are unlikely to teach the abstractions and bodies of principles essential to true learning. In the learning of psychomotor skills I have suggested ways in which key influences on human learning might be more systematically employed by teachers to transcend the limitations of demonstration.

Two leitmotifs pervade the discussion. One is the essential unity of the various types of learning. The other is the implicit recognition that the learning discussed has a purpose beyond itself. These two themes come together to inform the key pedagogical skill of teaching problem solving, which depends on both.

WHAT IS PROBLEM SOLVING?

In the context of the theme of this book, problem solving involves bringing to bear concepts and motor skills to deal with complex novel situations. These situations typically have a higher level of ambiguity and uncertainty than one would experience in learning new concepts or using existing concepts in conditions similar to those one has experienced before. The more complex the situation in which one finds oneself, the more problematic will be the nature of the activity necessary to resolve the ambiguity and reduce the complexity.

However, since the perceived degree of complexity in any human activity is a function of the sensitivity and degree of sophistication of the perceiver, the complexity of teaching is almost invariably unrecognised. The widely held view of teaching as 'delivering the curriculum' by teacher talk ignores its complexity and thereby renders teaching apparently less problematic.

This apparent reduction in complexity, however, is possible only by taking an extremely simplistic view of teaching to which the idea of attempting to teach pupils approaches to problem solving would be quite alien. The logic of my argument so far leads me to suggest that the least problematic aspect of a delivery approach to teaching is that the pupils' learning will be limited and likely to be rote. Since I have also argued that this type of learning neglects the type of learning that is quintessentially human, I consider it crucial to examine the available information on problem solving.

The view of teaching I have been presenting is of an extremely complex enterprise that presents teachers constantly with problematic situations demanding the resolution of high levels of ambiguity and uncertainty. Students are also, at times, in similar situations in school and out of school. A particular problem, inherent in any teaching–learning situation, is that both teacher and pupil are trying to reduce complexity and resolve ambiguity. The pupils' problem is learning what the teacher is trying to teach them. The teachers' problem is how best to help their pupils to learn what they are trying to teach them. Both would benefit from an understanding of ways of enhancing problem solving. I therefore now consider aspects of our knowledge about problem solving in relation to practical teaching problems.

Problems are often categorised as 'open' or 'closed'. The latter are of the type one encounters in books of puzzles. An example of a type used in studies of thinking is the water-jar problem. Given jars of 10, 19 and 45 fl oz capacity, how can one obtain exactly 3 fl oz of water? This is usually a pencil and paper problem. In ordinary life, and certainly in teaching, problems are rarely, if ever, of this type. There are so many known and unknown variables in most teaching–learning encounters that it is impossible to take them all into account when trying to work out a solution.

In the case of closed problems there is often a best way to solve the problem. Open problems are very different. Given the enormous complexity of human interactions in a normal classroom, the idea of there being an identifiable optimum way of achieving a specific pedagogical aim can only be described as nonsense.

Closed problems can be tackled using algorithms. Algorithms are set procedures that, if followed, will inevitably lead to a correct solution. An example is the rules for long division in arithmetic. Open problems are more usefully tackled by heuristics or guides to action such as those I have proposed earlier. Heuristics cannot guide one infallibly to a solution, but they help to reduce the complexity and ambiguity in the problematic conditions. They enable one to test, evaluate and refine one's ideas and hypotheses relating to the solution of specific problems. Heuristic approaches are ideally suited to teaching, which should be an activity that involves open-ended exploration and continual refinement of actions and reappraisal of aims. The heuristics I have proposed so far in this book are suggested in the hope that they will help teachers in this pedagogically dynamic activity.

The idea of a 'correct' solution is alien to individual teaching problems if only because of the impossibility of there being identical lessons. Since every teaching problem is unique, every solution must be unique, and the planning and execution of every lesson will differ. It is thus impossible for any author to set out algorithmic methods of teaching, and any proposal that claims to do so is a snare and a delusion. An author wishing to offer helpful guidance to teachers has another problem. Since teaching is a highly complex psychomotor-cum-social skill it cannot be learned solely by reading. The best an author can do is to draw attention to some possibly useful general theoretical principles, illustrate them with examples and offer suggestions for practice. Only by exploring the interaction between these principles and actual teaching practice, either in the appraisal of protocols (type B skills in my classification) or in actual teaching (type A skills) can teachers acquire the depth of understanding necessary to enhance the outcomes of their work.

In the suggestions I have made in earlier chapters for enhancing the effects of teaching on pupil learning. I have drawn on some very general principles relating to the way humans learn and suggested methods by which these principles might be related to teacher action. The examples I gave of teachers exploring these connections indicate the extent to which the actual process involves the teachers' interpretation and adaptation of the principles in real teaching. These are examples of teacher problem solving. But, as I suggested earlier, the essence of pupil learning is solving the problem of learning what the teacher intends them to learn. Teachers' problems will be solved if they are able to help pupils solve their own problems! Helping pupils to acquire some skills relating to problem solving should, thus, be a crucial element in teachers' activity. It is, therefore, doubly important for teachers to have some idea of useful ways of tackling open problems such as one encounters in teaching: first to help themselves and second to help their pupils.

For reasons I have already discussed, it is not possible to give an infallible guide to solving open problems. Nor is it possible for an author to give adequate guidance to problem solving at a distance. This is because complex learning such as this depends on the learner's grappling with specific problems with active guidance and the provision of feedback during the process along the lines I have discussed earlier. What can be done is to draw attention to some of the key factors relating to problem solving that have emerged from research in the field and present them to teachers as heuristics for them to try to evaluate in grappling with their own and their pupils' open problems. I now turn to one of the most important elements in problem solving.

FIRM FOUNDATIONS

When Archimedes leaped out of the bath in elation at having solved a key problem relating to the theory of flotation, his leap was not entirely out of the blue. His mind had for some time been just as immersed in cogitation about the theoretical principles related to the problem as his body had been in water just prior to his historic leap. In other words, people do not solve problems in areas of knowledge they know nothing about. The best qualification for successful problem solving is an extensive knowledge of the appropriate field of study.

But an extensive knowledge of a field cannot be built by rote verbal learning. Students will not be able to resolve ambiguity or reduce complexity in problematic situations by being able to recite words or answers they have learned by heart. Unless, of course, the words happen to be magic spells! In fact, one might conjecture that anyone expecting pupils to be able to tackle complex problems necessitating the transfer of learning of this kind is relying on magic.

Since, in my experience, magic is of doubtful reliability, it seems to me preferable to build on learning of a conceptual nature such as I have considered earlier. Learning of this type is helpful in problem solving because it holds within it seeds of transferability, which is the most potent element in earlier learning that one can bring to bear on current problems.

When I use the word 'problem' I am not implying that every teaching encounter is likely to present great difficulties. But teachers worth their salt will regard each lesson they teach as something of a challenge, even if only a small one. Each lesson will present a different problem from one with the same rubric on last year's timetable. The pupils will be different. There will almost certainly be a different number of them. The teacher will be older (wiser, one hopes) and may well have different ideas about the subject to be taught. In other words, helping this group of pupils at this particular time and in these particular conditions is actually a different problem from the one faced last year in the same lesson.

The challenge, therefore, is how to tackle the teaching in an interesting and effective way. Since each lesson is unique there is no question of using the notes from last year unless the teacher wishes to join the ranks of the partly living and not of the living teachers. Thus in every lesson the teacher will need to apply basic pedagogical principles in novel conditions. Transferable conceptual learning on the part of the teacher is essential in these conditions. Since the teacher is almost certain to be working independently and unguided, the effective application of a body of principles to ensure effective pupil learning in a particular lesson is a pedagogical problem for any teacher with a modicum of vocational zeal.

GUIDES TO THINKING

In earlier chapters I have tried to present ideas that would facilitate teachers' ability to provide pupils with the foundations of skills of successful problem solving. In those chapters I foreshadowed our current discussion when I considered the setting of objectives and the carrying out of pedagogical analyses. These ideas relate to an essential aspect of successful problem solving: the identification of the problem. Knowing what the problem is may seem an obvious and reasonable prerequisite to tackling it, but I believe there are still those on the fringes of discovery learning who are so committed to the ideas of self actualisation and independent discovery that they have difficulty in bringing themselves to reveal what the problem is. I believe we should let pupils into the secret.

I believe this not only because I think it is important to know what one's goal is as accurately as possible when working out a route, but also because it is an important element in one of the strategies one can use in tackling problems. The strategy of means–ends analysis involves the learner's assessing the difference between the current state of knowledge about the problem and the state of knowledge required for the problem's solution. This technique is essentially a sub-section of a pedagogical analysis that a learner can use when in the course of problem-solving activity. One weighs up the current situation and the one aimed for and adopts the course of action that seems to offer the best chance of achieving the goal. Naturally, this technique can be married to the technique of breaking down the overall problem into smaller units if necessary in order to simplify the activity one is currently engaged in.

In the case of problems presented to pupils by the teacher, the nature of the problem might be made clear by the teacher's informing the pupils of the objectives of the lesson. In the case of problems pupils encounter without the benefit of a teacher, they should be introduced to methods of approaching problems analytically. Taking an analytical approach would help them to reveal what sub-problems may be embedded in the overall problem. Identifying the sub-problems reduces complexity and makes it easier to see linkages between concepts and principles that may be relevant to the solution of the sub-problems and thereby to the overall one. Means–ends analysis and many of the techniques discussed in earlier chapters relate to this type of activity.

Algorithms and heuristics are useful devices to facilitate problem solving, but they are not keys to the solution of all problems. In some cases it will be possible and sensible to apply ready-made algorithms or heuristic guides in tackling problems. But the most useful approach to help pupils tackle problems effectively is to introduce them to a variety of problems and guide them in the use of both approaches. The basic principle operating here is the one that underlies all teaching and learning discussed earlier. Varied experience is the key to learning the abstractions and skills that enable learners to cope with novel situations. Experience of grappling with a wide variety of problems is, like a thorough grasp of the concepts and principles in the relevant field, essential for the development of *general* ideas relating to problem solving. These ideas will enhance the ability of pupils to tackle problems they have not previously experienced. It cannot be claimed that they will then be able to solve all problems, but they will be better equipped to tackle problems they do encounter. In the process of teaching pupils the use of algorithms and heuristics in this way we are also teaching them the methods of algorithmic and heuristic thinking (Landa 1976).

One specific and important outcome of this type of teacher action is that it can contribute to the development of semi-automatic sub-routines for tackling problems. Varied experience of problems, explicit identification of the problem in hand, the cultivation of an analytical approach and learning about the use of algorithms and heuristics all contribute to the informed reduction in difficulty of the activity necessary to solve a given problem. This simplification is vastly different from that referred to earlier which simplified by ignoring complexity. Complexity is recognised but the insight into the problem obtained by the analytical procedures and varied experiences discussed above eventually enable one to combine activities that were originally specific and distinct into more general and unified moves that demand little thought. Readers will note the similarity of this process to the actions referred to in the previous chapter, when I discussed the combination of discrete motor activities into a more integrated and 'smoother' performance.

Most teachers seem to develop this type of semi-automatic routine for dealing with the complexity of the classroom. However, in general, this is done without understanding the processes that are at work, and teachers are unable to explain how they actually operate in the classroom (Brown and McIntyre 1988). I suggest that this inability to explain their activity stems from their lack of knowledge of theoretical pedagogical principles. Since they are most unlikely to have been taught such principles in their teacher training, they not only lack the pedagogical expertise systematically to implement these principles, they also lack the understanding that would enable them to explain their actions in pedagogical terms. Teachers with an understanding of the principles also develop semi-automatic routines and have the conceptual and linguistic equipment to explain their nature to others.

Many of the devices mentioned in the heuristics I discussed earlier may be useful in helping pupils to become more proficient in solving problems. In particular, the language that teachers use to cue their moves as they tackle a problem can help them to move from stage to stage and provide the vital feedback to confirm that they are on the right lines. We could consider the knowledge pupils acquire about the nature of problem solving as type C learning in the taxonomy discussed earlier. Type B skills provide a link between that knowledge and developing problem-solving ability.

Type B activity can be mediated by the use of protocols of examples of problem-solving activities by others. Galperin's method of approaching teaching tasks is an interesting variant on this approach which has been little explored but is worth trying. The protocol in this case consists of the teacher's activity in working on the problem while the pupils describe what is going on and then guide the teacher on the action to take. Moving from this type of activity to the exercise of type A skills, grappling with problems oneself, is more likely to succeed than jumping from information gathering to execution in one fell swoop.

Other activities teachers might employ in teaching pupils ways of tackling problems have been raised in earlier discussion. Teaching motor skills and teaching concepts refer to such things as cuing, establishing the nature of the task (i.e. the problem to be solved), involving the learners themselves in the activity, providing feedback, arranging practice and, finally, weaning the learners so that they become independent in the activity. All of these are of potential use in helping pupils to develop useful ways of attacking problems.

The process of weaning is of crucial importance. It is the means *par excellence* whereby pupils become independent learners. The skill of the teacher is deciding on the appropriate moment to withdraw support: a difficult problem that will test teachers' own understanding of approaches to problem solving!

A GUIDE TO TEACHING

I will now endeavour to draw together the main teaching activities that offer means of helping pupils develop effective ways of solving problems. I shall assume, in the discussion, that problem solving is a form of learning. People in the normal course of everyday life do learn to solve particular problems and in the process probably learn something about problem solving in general. Teachers should be particularly interested in helping pupils to go beyond the random learning of everyday life and trying to give pupils an insight into reducing the randomness. Their aim should be not only to help pupils solve particular problems but the methods also to give them of attacking any problem. I now consider the type of thing to have in mind when trying to foster problem-solving ability.

Identify the problem

This is not always done. Sometimes this may because of a teacher's pedagogical conviction that the nature of the problem is something the pupils should discover for themselves. This may be reasonable after the weaning I referred to earlier, but prior to that it is unhelpful. Remember, the teacher is concerned not mainly with helping the pupils to solve particular problems but with helping them to acquire insights into ways of tackling any problems in the same general field of study. The teacher's problem, then, is how best to teach problem solving, and as I suggested before, the pupils should know that this is the objective. Specific problems, when this approach is taken, then become the stuff of the new learning. That is, solving the problems is not the object of the exercise but learning how to tackle problems is. For the teacher the problem is to teach the pupils that they must try to clarify for themselves the nature of problems they encounter. Analytical approaches will help them to do this.

The vital importance of clarifying the nature of the problem is well illustrated by the difficulties that ensue when this clarity is not achieved. Reid reports an investigation into the problems of children learning to read (Reid 1966). Teachers thought the problem facing the children was of distinguishing between words. The problem the children were actually trying to solve was of the nature of what a printed word actually is. This misunderstanding of the nature of the problem arises from taking adult perceptions of the problem as equivalent to those of the children. If, instead, the teachers had approached the task more analytically they would have had a better chance of clarifying the nature of the problem. Pedagogical analysis leading to the assessment of necessary pre-task competence would have raised the chances of successful outcomes considerably.

The case of the children clapping to produce long and short sounds is an example of the pupils' not being sure of the nature of the problem. The adult teacher's long familiarity with the convention of 'silence=sound' had blinded her to the children's difficulty. Here is another example of a misunderstanding that might well have been resolved by a more effective pedagogical analysis.

Bring to mind the relevant concepts and principles

All famous problem solvers from Archimedes to Einstein have been noted for their feats of bringing to bear on difficult problems concepts and principles from apparently disparate fields of knowledge. Their feats are impressive because of the unexpected yoking together of existing ideas into a new synthesis. But, as I have already said, nobody accomplishes this kind of feat from a position of ignorance. One can't solve problems by bringing together ideas from various fields unless one has ideas. As in other kinds of learning, it is necessary in problem solving for the learners to have the prerequisite capabilities, that is, a substantial body of concepts and principles relating to the field.

Once it is established that learners have acquired a sufficient body of concepts and principles in a given field they can be encouraged to bring them to mind and test their relevance to the problem in hand. In addition to knowledge about the field of study, some of these principles may well comprise making use of previously learned routines such as algorithms and heuristics. Bringing together ideas about the substance of the problem and ideas about how problems might be tackled illustrates the power of language. These ideas that have been acquired in different places and at different times are brought together to solve problems in ways that are inaccessible to non-verbal animals, which are willy-nilly compelled to attempt to solve problems they encounter almost entirely by trial and error and conditioning.

A teacher can help pupils remember ideas that might be useful by cuing them about aspects of the problem that might be helpful. Reminding them of the properties of some of the elements of the problem will give them a useful focus rather than lead to a blind alley. It is important, too, to encourage the learners not to be too restrictive in their thought. Encouragement to range wide in thinking about the problem may help them to see connections they might otherwise have missed. Too narrow a focus may get them stuck in cognitive tramlines and make them blind to other routes to the solution (see Luchins 1942). The experience of the teacher teaching volleyball is an example of this problem, and I consider more later.

In the approach to pedagogical analysis I discussed earlier, I recommended that when making the analysis one should let one's mind range over all the aspects involved in the analysis, so as more easily to see links between its different elements. I am referring to such things as the type of principles involved, the method of assessment, specific exemplars of concepts and the type of learning involved. This approach to analysis is, itself, a heuristic and might well be used by pupils as well as teachers.

Analyse the task

The heuristic suggested for pedagogical analysis is very closely linked with the idea of bringing to the fore of one's mind ideas that relate to the problem. It can be used as a help to self-cuing in problem solving. Young pupils may have difficulty in implementing an approach as sophisticated as this, but, of course, it is unlikely that we should be posing problems that needed such a sophisticated approach. However, the general principle is still valid. Explaining to pupils that problems can be analysed, demonstrating how this can be done with a variety of problems and giving them guided exercises in practising this method will equip them to tackle things on their own later. Obviously the heuristic I described above is specifically related to teaching tasks and would be largely inappropriate for young learners. However, the idea of trying to think of principles relating to the problems and of concrete instances of the principles will naturally be useful for any learner.

Give prompted practice

Practice implies rehearsing an acquired skill. Using the term in connection with learning problem-solving skills puts into focus the learning of the skill, rather than solving the specific problem. The prompting may, in fact, help the pupil solve the current problem, but its main point is to draw attention to ways of approaching problem solving that enhance the likelihood of reaching a satisfactory solution. Prompting can take different forms and has been discussed in connection with other aspects of teaching. Suffice it to say that teachers' and pupils' use of language are both key aids to prompting. In particular, the pupils' own use of language will help them towards greater independence in problem solving, since it will encourage them to develop the habit and ability of providing their own cues, probably in relation to thinking about the concepts and principles evoked through calling things to mind and attempting to analyse the problem. This was a particular feature of the children learning rhythmic patterns mentioned in the previous chapter.

Having coped with problems of a particular type with prompting from the teacher, pupils should be given work on other problems of similar types. As in the teaching of psychomotor skills, this form of prompted practice should be faded gradually so that the learners become independent in their approach to new problems of the same type. Careful planning by the teacher with regard to prompted practice and practice with feedback should be aimed at enhancing pupil motivation by ensuring that the learners experience a fair degree of success in solving the problems. This is not to say that they should be given practice by endless repetition of the same kind of problem once they have mastered the method. This question is discussed at greater length in the next chapter.

Develop independent activity

All the preceding items have had the aim of helping pupils to deal with problems independently. Discussing with learners the various elements in problem solving outlined here and elsewhere should help them tackle problems on their own with assurance. This item is the keystone to the operation of helping pupils to solve problems.

My description and suggestions on the subject of problem solving themselves exemplify the concept of heuristic. Clearly they do not provide an algorithm, or anyone who followed the set of instructions would be guaranteed success with every lesson. Nor is the language couched in completely unambiguous terms. All that I have been able to do is propose a plan of action that may help teachers to achieve a greater degree of success than if they did not follow such a plan. Different teachers will interpret the heuristic in their own ways, but the foundations will be of the same type. Naturally, there is no prescription to use the particular heuristic. Teachers may use the one proposed or a modified version of it, or possibly something quite different. My view is, however, that any heuristic likely to be useful would have considerable similarities with the one I have suggested, since it is closely related to our current knowledge about problem solving. If anyone were to reject the approach entirely, the most likely reason would be a fundamental objection to systematic approaches to encouraging pupils in the problem-solving activity. In such a case the whole concept of heuristics would be rejected, not merely the approach suggested here.

A HEURISTIC FOR TEACHING PROBLEM SOLVING

I now bring together what seem to be the key aspects of the teaching of problem solving. As before, the intention is to provide an *aide mémoire* to remind teachers of these key points, not for them to follow step by step, but to adapt them to their own use. It should be used in the context of the discussion in this chapter. Note that the heuristic relates to a specific problem. It, therefore, serves as an exemplar of general problem solving procedures. This point should be made clear to the pupils. Generalisation to other problems will be encouraged by the teacher's explicitly drawing attention to the various aspects of the heuristic in attacking other problems.

Problem solving heuristic

A   *Preactive*

1 Make a pedagogical analysis to clarify the nature of the problem to be solved.
2 Ascertain that the pupils have the prerequisite concepts.

B *Interactive*

3 Explain the nature of the problem to the pupils.
4 Encourage pupils to range widely in their approaches to solving the problem.
5 Remind pupils of elements of the problem that might be useful (concepts, principles, routines, algorithms and anything else that seems appropriate).
6 Encourage the pupils to analyse the problem. The teacher's own analysis could be referred to here as a guide to pupil action.
7 Prompt the pupils judiciously without solving the problem for them. This applies particularly to item 5.
8 Provide feedback at key points, where possible without teacher intervention.
9 Encourage an independent approach to problems solving by explaining methods of tackling problems.

C Evaluation

10 Present pupils with novel problems of the same general type.

In addition to item 10 a teacher might present different *types* of problem to evaluate the pupils' more general approach to problem solving. The object would then be not so much whether the problems were solved but whether the activities likely to enhance problem solving were employed. It would be useless attempting this, however, without having carried out steps 1 and 2 first.

PROBLEM SOLVING IN PRACTICE

Musical composition

My first example of a teacher grappling with helping pupils to solve problems picks up work discussed earlier in the field of musical composition. The work of this teacher illustrates the way 'problem solving' is interpreted in this book and some other sources on systematic approaches to teaching (cf. Shuell 1990). It goes beyond the tendency to consider problems as being essentially like puzzles I referred to earlier. The example also illustrates another point germane to our consideration of problem solving. Our focus is on the pedagogical aspects of the teaching and not primarily on the subject being taught. I suggest that by considering work in a field such as music, we are subjecting the approach to a particularly stringent test. It is often argued that only science- or mathematics-based subjects, which are 'logical' or 'well structured', are amenable to systematic approaches and that the more 'arts oriented' subjects are not. Thus, if adopting a psychopedagogical approach to the teaching of a subject with a less tight conceptual structure can be seen to be successful, there would be a particularly good case for considering the approach to be of general applicability. In the present case, although many readers may not be musically informed, few are likely to be baffled for that reason alone in considering this teacher's work.

At the stage of the teaching we now consider, the teacher had taught all the prerequisite skills and concepts, and the pupils had demonstrated competence in them. Competence had been established by very careful assessment using exemplars and non-exemplars of the prerequisite concepts. This work, done over a series of lessons, laid the foundation for a two-stage approach to sessions aimed at helping the pupils to solve an interesting type of problem, the composition and performance of original melodies. The aim itself is unusual since, as the teacher argues, composition is often invested with the mystique of 'creativity' and, therefore, considered to be not amenable to systematic teaching. Ironically, when it is taught, it is often taught along algorithmic or 'recipe' lines, and this approach may well have fostered the notion of composition being the province of gifted individuals rather than a skill accessible to most people who have learned the necessary foundation concepts.

In an exploration of the British and US literature on teaching composition, the teacher found confusing recommendations. The methods discussed fell into the two categories of those espousing the 'creative' approach and those espousing the 'traditional' approach. As a result, methods of teaching were vague, and often the subject was not taught at all. In view of the stress beginning to be placed in the British public examination system on the importance of composing in music examinations, he considered that a systematic approach to the question that would avoid the confusions and shortcomings of the two approaches was long overdue. The teacher investigated the ability of pupils who had passed examinations in musical composition and found, when he asked them to produce melodies, that they had little ability to produce *original* melodies and that their productions echoed the stereotypical routines they had been taught. His own work was an exploration of a systematic approach based explicitly on theoretical principles and open to scrutiny by others. Its explicit nature and attempt at a grounded theoretical approach also built into it a system of feedback to the teacher for his own self-correcting action.

The first stage of the work on problem solving was to build on the concepts and principles the pupils had learned and provide guided experience of grappling with the problem of producing melodies. A melody, pared down to the basic essentials of beginning, middle and end, was presented in score and recorded form. Pupils were asked specific questions about the melody such as 'What do you see at the beginning of the melody?' and 'What is significant about this bar?' The pupils had no difficulty in coping with this task.

Two melodies rather more complex than the first in 2 and 3 time, including their essential subordinate concepts, were then presented in the same way. The pupils were then asked to perform the first of these two melodies on an electronic instrument, and the teacher also performed the melody. The performances were recorded. The pupils were then asked to identify the way in which the specific melody exemplified general principles. The teacher is thus using the melody as introductory material to sharpen up the pupils' learning.

The questions asked were related to subordinate concepts of the overall concept of 'melody'. For example, knowledge of 'form' was checked by the question 'What is the extent of the announcing phrase?' Pitch was checked by the questions 'What note does the announcing phrase finish on?' and 'Is this the best note to finish the announcing phrase on?'

The second of the two melodies was then performed by the pupils only, and the same questions were asked. The teacher checked that the pupils had succeeded in discriminating the essential subordinate concepts in the two melodies. The teacher's approach at this stage illustrates the way cuing was withdrawn so as to equip the pupils to cope on their own. Reporting one aspect of the teaching in which he writes about himself in the third person, the teacher observes, 'In the melody in 2 time, the teacher offered a specific example of performing the melody. However, he omitted this in the 3 time melody to allow the pupils' performance independence without exemplar cuing before they embarked on production'.

In his subsequent evaluation of the process of gradually withdrawing cuing, the teacher isolated one difficulty experienced by the pupils. He reports:

> They found intervals more difficult to play than stepwise movement. They also had greater difficulty with 3 time melodies than 2 time melodies. This caused a loss of rhythmic drive in the melodies as pupils hesitated, looking for the interval of the next note. However, the conceptual framework certainly did hold together as the pupils correctly counted minim or dotted minim however far off the pulse they had become.

The teacher interprets this as indicating that the pupils needed more cued practice with the instrument. He makes the point that composing does not depend upon performance but that performance adds to the creative aspect and the relevance of the melodies to the pupil and is, therefore, desirable.

A final point his experience brought home to the teacher is the way in which the cued introduction to problem solving acted as a link between his pedagogical analysis and teaching heuristics and the problem of producing original melodies. In part the operation looked back and evaluated the teaching up to that point and in part it looked ahead, orienting the pupils to the next challenge.

The challenge came when the pupils were asked to compose their own melodies. Each pupil composed four or five melodies with no assistance from the teacher. They then performed a sample of their compositions which were evaluated by the teacher.

I will not discuss in detail the method of evaluation adopted but will return to it when I discuss methods of evaluation in general. However, in brief, the pupils all produced melodies of their own without the teacher's help. The melodies were not flawless but were personal to the pupils. They had been produced by ordinary pupils, not particularly 'gifted' in musical ability. The fact that they were melodies personal to themselves while still conforming to the principles of melody construction without being 'mechanical patterns of a model melody', as the teacher put it, was a clear demonstration of successful problem solving by the pupils (See p. 237–9).

However, the other pupils whose work was evaluated but who had had traditional teaching, produced melodies that echoed the two approaches (algorithmic and creative) discussed earlier. The one method produced melodies with a free, undisciplined air but produced odd rhythms and errors of pitch. The other method produced melodies that looked so similar as to be almost mechanical copies of a model melody. Pupils taught by this method can produce only one kind of melody and cannot vary the pattern. Such pupils are not problem solving. They are virtually following an algorithm rather than using their understanding of musical composition to create novel melodies. In fact, the teacher thought it possible that the pupils might not really have learned the concept of melody at all.

Before leaving our consideration of the work of this teacher, I should like to return to the argument with which I started this section. I suggested that although, or possibly because, the subject the teacher was teaching was not one of the 'core' subjects and was on the unstructured end of the pedagogical continuum, it could be a particularly potent test of the efficacy of a systematic psychopedagogical approach to teaching. In the light of the discussion, to what extent can this view be supported? Let us consider the way in which key pedagogical principles are exemplified in the teacher's report.

First, however, it is worth noting the dearth of helpful information in the literature on music teaching (cf. May 1990). This is a very common problem encountered by teachers who look for bodies of pedagogical principles that might be helpful to them. Some authors would comment on this point that those principles do not exist. However, many texts do recommend teaching practices with very little foundation in theory and often automatically assume nothing more than delivery methods and concentrate on the subject content. As suggested earlier, the hegemony of delivery teaching persists by default of action by theorists and practitioners aimed at developing stringent pedagogical procedures that hold promise of leading to meaningful, complex and transferable learning. The present case exemplifies the work of one theorist/practitioner who takes a sceptical view of conventional approaches and tries to take action to improve on them. This is, surely, a model to all teachers at whatever age, stage and subject.

The key points to emerge from this work seem to be as follows:

1 *The careful attention given to checking that the pupils had learned the concepts prerequisite to the next stage of learning.* This was not a perfunctory pencil and paper pre-test but a stringent practical assessment.
2 *The thorough pedagogical analysis.* In the phase of the teaching prior to the presentation of the final problem-solving task, the teacher gradually phased out his cuing and support of the pupils' efforts so as to prepare them for independence. Throughout, the pupils were actively involved in work related to composition and not acting in a passive mode.
3 *Feedback to the teacher.* As a result of the systematic and detailed planning of the teaching, which I have only been able to hint at here, the teacher was able to analyse the pupils' performance to learn about his

own performance and the efficacy of the approach. He himself made the point that this kind of *post-hoc* analysis is incumbent on all teachers who decide to take the analytical pedagogical road. There is a great advantage in doing this which the teacher also recognises. Although it takes time in the beginning, this is a passing phase since one can learn from the lessons one teaches in a cumulative, self-correcting spiral of improvement. It is vastly different from the practice of keeping one's notes and repeating the same litany from year to year with different groups of pupils. This type of development is an exemplar of a self-correcting pedagogical system of teaching and of research into teaching. I discuss this point further in Chapter 11.

4 *Flexibility and the testing of the heuristic.* A final point is particularly important. The teacher himself alludes to one aspect of it. He stresses that his approach is in no way prescriptive and that other teachers will work things out in their own way even if they follow the same general guidelines. His method is based on the heuristics set out in this book, but he uses them flexibly in his own way as a basis for the development of his teaching. If he had found any aspects of the guidelines not to be useful he would have discarded them. If a large number of teachers using the approach encounter the same type of deficiency, it will be necessary to re-examine the heuristics. A regular pattern of deficiencies in the heuristics emerging from the work of many teachers may well reveal errors in theoretical elements of the heuristics. Alternatively, analysis may reveal that there is ambiguity or error in the actual teaching that could be resolved by amendment to theory and practice. Of course, these possibilities are only two of many that could be considered when this kind of problem occurs. If, however, only one or two teachers have difficulty and most do not, then the teachers with difficulties would need to examine their practice to see if the problem lies there rather than with the principles they are trying to employ.

Reading comprehension

The teacher whose work we now discuss investigated the teaching of reading comprehension. As in the case of musical composition, it is sometimes argued that this subject is not amenable to systematic teaching. The teacher does not accept this view and considered that reading comprehension involved mainly problem-solving activity that could be taught using an approach such as I have been discussing. However, he thought that the heuristic on problem solving discussed above needed amplification to suit his purposes. In particular he needed to take into account work on reading techniques such as SQ3R (Robinson 1946). (SURVEY the material; pose QUESTIONS that need to be answered; READ the passage and take notes related to the questions; REVIEW the material with the questions in mind, trying to answer them without consulting the notes; REVISE the material within forty-eight hours of first studying it and thereafter at regular intervals).

He discusses in detail the way in which he proposed to adapt SQ3R for use in group learning conditions and considered other approaches to learning comprehension and study skills. He proposes to use the heuristic referred to earlier (Stones 1979) as a guide to teaching reading comprehension, which he sees as a problem-solving activity. He makes the point that 'the specific reading schedules already discussed could be combined to produce an effective and worthwhile programme for junior school children. It would appear that integrating SQ3R, which stresses the need to establish a clear reading purpose, and linking that to the formulation of a set of related questions with the Directed Reading Activity, where the emphasis is on concept and vocabulary development, plus blending with both those approaches a thoughtful use of study skills ought to produce a method that would be hard to better. So why look at a general problem-solving approach?'

The main point made in answer to this question was that the heuristic is based on principles of pedagogy and learning theory. Two key specific points are also adduced. The first is the stress in the heuristic on the detailed analysis of the learning task coupled with the identification of the nature of the learning involved. The second is the ascertaining of the pupil's present level of competence to ensure that it matches the prerequisite skills for the work being set.

He considers the rigorous approach to these two points to be the crucial transforming elements in his work on teaching reading comprehension. He also goes back to the heuristic related to concept teaching, specifically the suggestion 'Plan for diagnosis at the interactive stage'. He considered that using the problem-solving heuristic would clarify the function and purpose of the group oral discussion work he planned as part of his teaching. While other authors have considered group discussion in work of this kind (he refers particularly to Walker's (1974) work in this connection) the role of the teacher in the activity had not been considered. Nor had the pedagogical theory, whereas both are central in the Stones heuristic. The widely used reading strategies he mentioned do not consider analysis, prompting or feedback, all of which are crucial to effective teaching.

This was the reasoning that led the teacher to adopt the heuristic on problem solving and adapt it to his specific needs. The psychopedagogical theory provided the grounding for his work while the specific suggestions within the problem-solving heuristic provided guidance for their use. His experience of using other approaches such as SQ3R in the field of reading and study skills provided further guidance related to the specific field of reading comprehension. He aimed to integrate these elements into a series of lessons that would be suitable for a group of pupils aged ten–eleven all rather above average in reading ability. He took the problem-solving heuristic and expanded it to include most of the direct guidance a teacher might need. He also adapted it to incorporate contextual cuing through the use of clozure (a method that makes use of controlled completion of incomplete text), to develop prediction skills in reading, and to incorporate group discussion activities. He considered that a group for this purpose should be between six and eight, and his group had six children. For the material of the problem-solving activity the teacher took a passage from a book of comprehension exercises, Rosemary Sutcliffes's 'Terror of the Soul' which is an extract from her novel *Warrior Scarlet*. The second passage was a factual account produced by the teacher 'How was our earth made?' The overall aim was for the pupils to be able to use a reading strategy, to develop a reading purpose, to work together cooperatively until the purpose is achieved and to produce a written or oral summary of their findings if asked.

A selection of elements taken from the interactive section of the teacher's version of the heuristic will give an idea of his approach. These elements follow a preactive stage concerned with pedagogical analysis and establishing the level of the pupils' current abilities in reading comprehension. The reader will note a combination of material from the pedagogical heuristic and guides to comprehension. In addition the teacher incorporates some of the points from the heuristic on enhancing motivation which I shall discuss later. The first item mentioned below is an example. The emphases throughout are the teacher's.

Arouse pupils' *interest* in the task.

Teach any *essential vocabulary* that might present difficulties.

Teach the *concepts* identified as a potential source of difficulty for the reader.

Introduce, explain or revise the *reading strategy* to be used.

Carry out *a survey* of the passage by:

i)   analysing the title

ii) studying illustrations, maps, charts, diagrams

iii) using typographical aids as a means of understanding the author's organisation of his material

iv) reading the first and last paragraph or the conclusion if one is given

Pupils *read* the passage independently *and answer* the agreed *questions* in note form.

Afterwards the questions and answers are *reviewed in group oral discussion*.

Pupils *analyse and evaluate* their own and each other's *answers* justifying responses by the internal and external evidence.

The teacher *judiciously prompts* without supplying definite answers.

These items illustrate the marrying of the SQ3R system and pedagogical principles. The teacher suggests other items relating to the use of clozure techniques.

> Commencing at the second paragraph, make deletions in the passage using one or more of the following methods
> i)   every n'th word, with or without structural prompts
> ii)   adjectives and adverbs
> iii) nouns and/or verbs
> iv) function words in particular prepositions
> v)   a combination of one or more of the above

The teacher used the general pedagogical analysis I have discussed earlier as a guide to implementing this heuristic of interactive activities. Within the framework of the analysis, procedures such as the SQ3R were identified as subordinate elements contributing to the development of reading comprehension. Once having located them in the field of 'general content' in the pedagogical analysis, the teacher was able to follow through the steps in the analysis to identify such things as the type of learning involved, how he would present the learning task and how he would provide feedback. In other words, the pedagogical action indicated by the pedagogical analysis was to be deployed to teach the procedures relating to the task of reading with understanding.

This process makes clear the aptness of the teacher's contention that a systematic pedagogical approach is essential in teaching this particular problem-solving activity. The SQ3R and similar devices are specific procedures to facilitate the learning of problem solving in the field of reading comprehension, but their effectiveness is dependent upon an effective pedagogy. Pedagogically sound teacher action could lead to the solving of reading comprehension problems without, for example, SQ3R. But SQ3R could never lead to the same outcome without pedagogically sound teacher action.

The other key aspect of preparation is ascertaining that the pupils' current level of competence is equal to the task they are to tackle. In the case of comprehension, this implies that they should be able to cope with the language in which the material to be used in the comprehension exercise was couched. As I have said, the teacher knew the reading ages of the pupils. To ensure that the two passages to be used were suitable, the teacher calculated a readability score for both, using the Mugford readability test (Mugford 1972). He found that they were both about the right level for his pupils and were thus suitable for his purposes, although one of the passages presented some problems of vocabulary that needed to be cleared up.

The teacher makes the point that he could not have used either passage as an introductory lesson for SQ3R since the demands of the passages themselves left no room for mastering the technique. This point reflects back on my comment that the pedagogical analysis indicated that the

SQ3R technique had to be approached as a topic to be taught within the framework of the pedagogical heuristic.

Let us now return to the interactive stage of the teaching. As you will see from the excerpts presented above, the teacher spends the first part of his teaching preparing the pupils for the problem-solving task. He uses the guidelines from the basic heuristic to teach the use of devices such as the SQ3R. He is giving the pupils the tools to do the job. He is also clearing up possible obstacles such as difficulties with vocabulary, so that when they are confronted with the new learning they will be able to cope with minimal help from the teacher, which is one of the distinguishing features of problem solving.

Exploring and reflecting

It is worth prefacing our consideration of the teacher's experience in working with his schedule with the quotation he himself uses to introduce his report. He says that his schedule is based on Stones's (1979) work and refers to the following paragraph.

> Each venture into teaching is an experiment even if only in a very small way. . . . Your personal attempts to apply the [psychopedagogical] principles to your own lessons with an experimental cast of mind is likely to be the most effective way of clarifying and consolidating your understanding of the theory and practice of teaching. . . . Putting interesting hypotheses to the test in your own way may help to provide some of the evidence.

The teacher made recordings of two lessons and prepared transcripts. He then analysed the transcripts and discussed the lessons with recourse to the analysis.

He attempted to take an accepting approach to the pupils in the conviction that this would enhance motivation. Apart from being receptive to pupils' contributions, he aimed to resist imposing himself on them, taking his cue from Montessori's idea that help and guidance should be given only when requested or when it is clearly necessary (Montessori 1964). As is so often found when teaching is analysed, the teacher's intentions were unrealised in the event. Although the transcript of the recordings showed that the teacher was receptive of pupils' contributions, he foisted help and guidance on them as he saw fit, and in fact his interventions in the lessons were about two-fifths of those of the pupils but invariably longer so that they almost certainly exceeded the pupils' contributions in time. Nor were the teacher's interventions always apt. He was aiming for the pupils to answer questions that necessitated reflection on the passages being studied, rather than merely ascertaining facts directly from the text. Nevertheless exchanges such as the following demonstrate that the aim was not always achieved.

Teacher: Right. Now what questions are going to be asked?
Paul: What change.
Teacher: Yes, what change came over the forest.

The teacher considers that this exchange is unsatisfactory because, while encouraging active learning up to a point, it needs to be developed more effectively. He considers that he should not have allowed the pupil to offer an incomplete statement, which suggests that the pupil is on the right lines but does not demonstrate that he 'will arrive at the right destination'.

Several things might be said about the exchange that illustrate the complexity of teaching and makes totally comprehensible and excusable the fact that teachers do not pick up every nuance in their interactions with pupils and take the best course of action. After the pupil's answer the teacher picked up his point and associated himself with it. From the affective point of view this was fine and probably encouraging to the pupil. However, the teacher transgressed against his own intentions and jumped in before it was necessary. He therefore probably pre-empted a further remark from the pupil that would have given evidence of reflection and could well have produced the full statement the teacher gave. Given time the pupil would have had chance to think further. His answer could have been more complete, and the outcome could well have been a gain in the cognitive effort by the pupil. Its consequent affective impact would also have been enhanced since it would have been his own contribution and not the teacher's.

The teacher examines his use of reinforcement during his teaching. He discusses the suggestion in the schedule on reinforcement taken from *Psychopedagogy* (Stones 1979) that a conscious attempt should be made to provide reinforcement extrinsically by commendation and encouragement, and intrinsically by arranging a learning gradient designed for success. In one lesson he deliberately planned to reinforce all one pupil's responses and reinforced twenty-three out of forty responses. In a subsequent lesson he did not take such a conscious decision. This time the pupil's responses dropped dramatically from forty to fifteen, only six of which were reinforced. As the teacher comments: 'Reinforcement is a crucial factor'.

The teacher continues in this vein with a detailed analysis of the transcript of his lesson. A general theme emerges. He identifies the way in which his attempts to follow the heuristic guide for the teaching of problem solving fall short of his aim and considers the reasons for the failure and the course of action that could have led to success. The nature of his comments is important. They relate to theoretical pedagogical factors and illustrate most effectively the reflection in action and on action that holds the seeds for improvement in teaching. An excerpt from an early part of the first lesson gives the flavour. He had been trying to teach the concept of 'particle' and had spent a fair amount of time trying to coax a definition from the pupils. In response, the pupils engaged in a guessing game to produce what the teacher wanted. After reviewing the transcript he comments as follows:

> There was total failure to label the criterial attributes of a new concept, apart from identifying 'part'. No sequence of exemplars was provided, no counter-positioning was used, cuing techniques that were used were inappropriate and non-productive. . . . It would have been much more sensible to have given pupils a different dictionary or a thesaurus . . . to get them to identify the criterial attributes of the term.

This part of the lesson was the least satisfactory, and clearly the teacher is very self-critical. But the teaching was by no means all negative. He followed the schedule to teach the use of the SQ3R, and the pupils learned to use it satisfactorily. He provided feedback throughout the lesson and stresses in his report his concern with formative evaluation. He also comments on the difficulties of providing this formative feedback economically and illustrates the tension between the desire on the part of the teacher to do this and his years of experience in the archetypal role of teacher as dispenser of information. He quotes from the transcript of the last lesson. He is trying to encourage the pupils to explore the meaning of a phrase in the passage about the formation of the earth. Things go well until the teacher responds to the pupils' suggestions by expanding their replies into a ten-line discourse (on the transcript) followed by several more lengthy interjections that give the pupils little chance of replying. As a consequence the pupils' responses died away, and as the teacher remarked, 'Active learning has ceased here.' Fortunately things picked up later and the pupils started to participate again.

Evaluation of the learning took two forms. The first required the pupils to answer questions about the 'Terror of the Soul' passage for homework. The second took the form of group activity. The pupils worked in a room without the teacher and were asked as a group to produce a summary based on a selection of key sentences. This was a different activity from what had been asked of them in other sessions. It was another way of assessing their understanding of a passage than those used previously. It tested their ability to apply their learning of the techniques of textual analysis such as SQ3R in new circumstances. The resulting summary was not perfect but was better than the teacher had thought possible.

The teacher's assessment of the outcome of the teaching makes modest claims. The teaching did lead to the satisfactory achievement of clearly identified teaching objectives. There were weaknesses, as we have already discovered. He itemizes these in four categories. His cuing and guiding was too heavy handed, and he dominated the group and undermined its motivation. His feedback was poorly timed on occasion and provided less information than he had intended. He sometimes undermined motivation and participation by misjudging the learning gradient. I shall return to this question later in a discussion of motivation. His teaching of the preparatory concepts was unsatisfactory in that he attempted to rely too much on the pupils' prior knowledge as he (mis-)perceived it.

A further comment is that success in the teaching occurred when he followed the guidelines of the schedule. Despite his best efforts he too frequently diverted from these guidelines. He makes the point that this teacher-variability may well be a crucial factor in the failure to identify a single best reading method, which has been a 'Holy Grail' sought by teachers of reading over the years. This fruitless search may well be the reason for the resurgence of interest in a psychologically based approach to the study of reading. He considers that the overall success of his work with the modified form of the heuristic for problem solving supports this view and confirms the validity of the underlying theory.

The teacher himself has identified the main significant points arising from this study, as I have reported. One or two additional observations might be in order. One is to make the point that some of the key pedagogical moves in teaching problem solving are common to the concept-teaching heuristic. This is not surprising since both build on existing concepts to form higher-order abstractions, and, indeed, some people view problem solving as concept learning in particularly complex conditions. One key feature of the heuristic is the suggestion that learners be encouraged to range widely in their search for ways of tackling problems. The teacher's difficulty in restraining himself and so allowing the pupils to explore possibilities themselves was unfortunate but all too common. It is probably the point most worthy of note by any teacher attempting to help pupils to become proficient in tackling problems.

The use of evidence

My next example comes from work done by a student teacher in the field of social studies. She had worked with the pupils over several months in the course of her extended teaching practice. During that time she had been teaching various concepts and skills in connection with the teaching of history, such as the organisation of evidence, extrapolation from evidence, and synthesis. She took the problem-solving lesson as a good opportunity to test the effectiveness of her teaching.

Her approach was rather different from others we have considered. Her pedagogical point of departure was suggestions in the books on educational objectives by Stones and Anderson (1972) and on educational objectives in the study of history (Coltham and Fines 1971). She also drew on the ideas in the problem-solving schedule in Stones (1979). Using these sources she devised a short schedule of her own as a guide to her teaching. She chose as the material to test the pupils' skills, a dispute between the British train drivers' union and the management of the British railway system, British Rail. Her sources were two national British newspapers, *The Times* and

The Guardian. The problem the pupils were posed was for them to come to a conclusion on the basis of the evidence provided as to who was to blame for the dispute and how it might be resolved. She fully appreciates that there is no right answer, but aspires to help her pupils come to a reasoned judgment on the controversy. She is also sensitive to the fact that she may be making rather ambitious demands on her thirteen-year-old pupils.

Her objectives for the pupils correspond roughly to the A, B, C types I have discussed earlier. She aims for them to:

1 Show understanding of the concepts and abbreviations within the material selected on the rail dispute [type C].
2 Use previously learned skills on evidence in a novel context, the rail dispute. The skills are: comprehension, analysis, identification of bias, interpretation, synthesis and reasoned judgment [type B].
3 Put forward reasoned solutions to the problems posed based on knowledge gained from using skills mentioned above [type A].

She discusses two views on approaches to problem solving in teaching. On the one hand there is the argument that one should not interfere in the pupils' attempts to solve problems but let them find their own solutions. On the other hand is the view that pupils should be helped and guided in acquiring problem-solving skills. She espouses the latter view, in line with the argument in this book and stresses that guiding pupils in ways of tackling problems does not imply that one is solving problems for them. She comments:

> I believe it would be asking a great deal for children . . . thirteen years old to tackle problems of this [size] without some method of attack. Although they have the individual skills to attack the problem and perhaps to come to a conclusion in a haphazard way, it is my aim to give them a way that will help them cope efficiently and put their skills to maximum use.

Her analysis of the objectives of her teaching resembled the pedagogical analysis I have considered earlier and, in fact, went into a fair amount of detail. One of the first points she adduces is the need to look carefully at the pre-entry competence of the pupils. The newspapers and TV at the time were full of references to such things as 'flexible rostering', 'arbitration', 'productivity', 'reneging' and 'commitment'. The pupils would need to have some idea of the meaning of these terms before they could hope to tackle the problem set. She knew the pupils well, and from her own work with them she felt they would not be totally ignorant of the expressions. However, she could not be sure and decided that the discussion and elucidation of these terms should occupy the first section of the lesson. She thought the key concept to be considered was 'bias' and decided to give this particular attention.

In the realisation that the problem is open ended, the teacher drew up a list of principles she thought the pupils should be familiar with when tackling such problems. The suggestions bear some resemblance to those of the teacher teaching comprehension skills, which is not surprising really, since before one can possibly make a reasoned judgment one must understand what is involved. She suggests:

1 Have as much information on the problem as possible.   ORGANIZATION

2 Examine the information and select the most important parts that are relevant to the problems.   ANALYSIS

3 Evaluate the material by examining for bias.   IDENTIFY BIAS

4 Make tenable propositions after examination.   INTERPRET

5 Search for a reasonable synthesis which takes account of point of view.   SYNTHESIS

6 Argue a conclusion based on the above.   REASONED JUDGMENT

The teacher refers to the crucial role of language in this particular learning task. She makes the point that since she is dealing with abstractions there is little that visual aids could contribute to the learning. The nature of the discourse is the thing on which all else hangs.

Her guide for the interactive stage of the teaching is a variation on the themes I have discussed earlier.

1 Explain the nature of the task.
2 Encourage the pupils to make a preliminary reading of all the available evidence and to sort out the major issues.
3 Encourage them to analyse the evidence for bias and make interpretations from their analysis.
4 Encourage them to synthesize what they have interpreted.
5 Prompt children without solving the problem.
6 Provide feedback and reinforcement.
7 Encourage the children to make a judgment of the problem.
8 Encourage an independent approach to solving problems of a similar kind by giving them novel problems to solve.

The difference between this scheme and most of the ones we have seen earlier is that it is less precise and specific. In a way it is little more than a rewrite of the general heuristic I described earlier and, therefore, of limited use in particular circumstances. However the teacher made it more specific by writing out a lesson plan of the type commonly required in teacher training institutions. This plan is an interesting conjunction of the two approaches referred to, giving the pupils an idea of the objectives of the lesson, the skills they will need in order to solve the problems posed, and the relationship between the problems. Giving the pupils an idea of the learning task is related to motivation. Concern for the necessary prior knowledge is expressed, as I mentioned above. She charts the way in which she proposes to develop the lesson in terms of the demands she intends to make on the pupils. She gives the pupils a handout of suggested questions and goes through the evidence with them 'prompting them to use their skills of comprehension, analysis, interpretation, etc'. She then asks the pupils to identify the different viewpoints of the contenders in the dispute and finally sets up a discussion of the pupils' conclusions. She attaches great importance to the discussion since 'it helps the children improve their thinking'. She makes a specific reference to Piaget's views on the value of discussion among peers for clarifying thinking, but she could have also cited many other psychologists.

This scheme chartered the route she proposed to follow. Let us now consider how she fared on the ground. The lesson was recorded on CCTV, and she worked through the recording to assess the extent to which her execution accorded with her intentions. The main point she makes in her evaluation is that she focused so much on one objective, the pupils' use of the skills of comprehension, analysis, interpretation, synthesis and reasoned judgment, that she paid insufficient attention to the problems these activities were intended to solve. She considers that the reason for this was that she stuck too rigidly to her schedule but is somewhat equivocal about this since she finds that the pupils did seem to produce some commendable reasoning about the dispute. She gives examples from the recording of the lesson of exchanges that illustrate the pupils' deployment of the various skills. One showing a pupil's interpretation of the evidence is as follows:

Teacher: Who do you think this is aimed at then? BR (British Rail) are saying we are standing for something that will make for a better railway in the future.

Pupil: The people. The people who use the railways.

Teacher: What is he trying to say then? What's he saying there?

Pupil: He's trying to get the people on his side and show ASLEF (the union) is wrong

Teacher: What . . .?

Pupil: Do it so the people will think ASLEF's wrong.

The student teacher makes one further observation on the basis of her viewing of this section of the recording. She notes that when the pupils took different views about the causes of the dispute, she missed an opportunity of encouraging a discussion between them asking them to justify their positions by sticking too rigidly to her lesson plan. She thinks the session would have benefitted from taking this line by being less teacher directed: 'It would have encouraged peer group socialisation which Piaget recognises as so important for the improvement of thinking'. One might comment that Piaget is not alone in supporting group discussion as holding potential for stimulating thinking, especially when contenders have to justify the positions they take. Nor is the teacher alone in her being trapped in the tramlines of her lesson plan. It seems that the majority of teachers diverge little from the line they set for themselves at the beginning of lessons.

There is one further point to make in connection with the above. It concerns the difference between a conventional lesson plan and heuristic guides such as I have discussed in this book and elsewhere. Lesson plans tend to be reminders about specific teacher actions and frequently about what the teacher is going to tell the students. In other words the delivery mode of teaching is taken as given. Lesson plans related to teaching of this kind resemble notes for a speech and are thus relatively inflexible. A heuristic guide such as the one discussed above is much less prone to this lack of flexibility. This follows because of its emphasis on general principles of learning rather than on teacher talk; in order to learn, the pupils have to be active and senses other than hearing have to be engaged. The teacher is a facilitator of productive student activity; and, while always bearing in mind the general principles involved, the specific working out of those principles is dependent upon how the students react to particular learning situations. Flexibility, I suggest, is indispensable to the implementation of the heuristic but inimical to the conventional 'lesson plan'.

The student teacher invited a colleague to evaluate the teaching. He suggested that it was too ambitious in view of the complexity of the material. The teacher defended herself in some respects but agreed that 'on reflection there is (*sic*) perhaps too many difficult abstract concepts and relationships involved in the exercise which made it at times too difficult and over confusing'. She also pointed out, however, that the pupils had analysed and interpreted quite well the relationships among the key ideas related to the dispute. She quotes from the answer given by one of the pupils to the question of who was blame for the strike: 'When ASLEF striked (*sic*) it meant that the NUS [the general railway workers's union] were losing working time, so this shows ASLEF as being selfish.' The teacher comments: 'This also illustrates an interpretive point as the idea of ASLEF being selfish was never overtly mentioned. In fact throughout Iain's written work there is a myriad of related concepts all put and used correctly in context'.

The teacher makes further detailed comments on her teaching based on the recording. An idea of the approach is provided by an exchange taken from her appraisal of her skill in explaining.

Teacher: Do you know what a union is? What does a union represent? Jacqueline, do you know what a union represents?
Pupil: People who work.
Teacher: Who are BR? Who will they be?
Pupil: The leaders.

Teacher: The leaders. The word begins with an M.
Pupil: The managers.

She comments: 'A pupil listening to this may have got the idea that managers do not work and that BR is just the managers when it is much more of a "blanket term"'. We might also consider the nature of her last remark in the quoted exchange. She does not add a question mark to her 'The leaders', but there almost certainly is one in her voice. This point illustrates the caution one needs to exercise when reading transcripts and the power inherent in video recording, which is so much richer in its ability to provide nuances of intonation as well as non-verbal cues that are totally absent from transcripts. We might also consider the nature of the cuing in the statement 'The word begins with an "m"'. This is an example of 'formal cuing'. The cue has no relationship to the concept of 'managers'. It may be referred to as a 'formal prompt', since the only connection it has with the concept of 'management' is in the form of the word that labels it, the letter 'm'. It is no real help to stimulating the pupils' thinking. The opposite, in fact. It could reduce their activity to a guessing game and thus inculcate counterproductive methods of tackling problems.

The teacher says that there were other examples of unsatisfactory explanations but thought that overall her explanation had improved on her previous (recorded) efforts, and she now explains things more slowly to avoid confusing the pupils.

One other comment from among many illustrates the student teacher's self-appraisal. She is commenting on her use of questions, specifically in relation to a discussion on binding arbitration.

Teacher: Why do you think ASLEF do not want to go to binding arbitration Trudy?
Pupil: They might think the outcome is going against them.
Teacher: That could be one thing. Yes that's a good point, Trudy. You might think that ASLEF don't want to go to binding arbitration because they're scared. What else might ASLEF think about the whole thing, about going to arbitration?
Pupil: They're right. They don't think they should have anybody else's point of view.
Teacher: Good girl. They think why should we go to binding arbitration. We're right. We won our three per cent.

She examines other aspects of the teaching in the same way, illustrating her points by referring to episodes in the recording. She concludes her report with a number of 'recommendations'.

1 I must give much greater thought to the planning of teaching episodes so that my teaching skills are used to maximum effect to give pupils greater understanding and knowledge.

2 I must reappraise the schedules I devised in the light of this evaluation and see what changes could be made. (Some suggestions have already been made in the evaluation.)

3 I should try to use a less teacher directed methodology in a further problem-solving episode to give me knowledge of its strengths and weaknesses and to see what use it would be in history. This would give me a much more balanced view on problem solving.

4 I should take more care when selecting material so that it is not too complex or difficult. This necessarily entails a study of children's abilities and levels of thinking. . . . If the material is not appropriate the children will not learn at all or learn maladaptively.

5 I should ensure in problem solving episodes that the problem is kept in mind.

There is much in these recommendations that we have met before, for example, in the perennial plea for more careful prior analysis of the teaching proposed. Her recommendation that she go back to the schedule to examine it in the light of her teaching is a classic example of a dialectical approach to theory and practice. In the implementation of the recommendation, however, it would be important to ensure that both the theory and the practice were appraised. Furthermore, I would consider it important to look carefully at the schedule she had devised to see to what extent it really embodied pedagogical constructs as distinct from notes of procedure for her to follow in her teaching.

Overall, I suggest, this student teacher's appraisal of her attempt to employ pedagogical principles to help pupils to solve problems is exemplary. She planned and carried out her teaching drawing on psychological and pedagogical principles related to the teaching of a specific subject, history. She adapted the general principles to her specific teaching task. She analysed the task, drawing on a systematic analysis of her teaching objectives. She taught the topic doing her best to implement ideas from her knowledge of pedagogy and psychology. Finally, and crucially, she used the recording to scrutinise her teaching systematically and in detail, appraising it in the light of principles relating to human learning and ideas relating to the teaching of history. There is no suggestion that she has taught a superlative lesson, as she recognises well herself. But she has taken an approach to teaching that will give her the basis for a professional life of continuous self development, a not unimportant aspect of initial teacher training.

Crossing the road

I do not wish to go into the example of the teaching of the Green Cross Code in detail since I have already discussed it at some length. However, I think it merits consideration since it illustrates the interrelatedness of most human learning.

In the case of the children learning the Green Cross Code, the teacher's main concern was to enable them to cross the road safely. Her pedagogical analysis and her teaching stressed, particularly, learning with understanding. She adopted an approach that made use of knowledge about concept learning and the learning of psychomotor skills. She thought it important to go beyond teaching drills and help the children to acquire an understanding of the factors involved in crossing a busy road so that they would be able to exercise their judgment in solving a very real problem in their daily lives.

Thus, although she makes particular use in her teaching of the heuristics relating to concept teaching and the teaching of motor skills, in fact these combine to cover most aspects of the guide to problem solving. Contrast her teaching with that commonly observed in the teaching of road safety in junior schools. Instead of a talk that takes it for granted that the children understand the terms used in the Green Cross Code such as 'vehicle' and 'traffic', she makes a systematic attempt to *ensure* that they learn the concepts involved. Instead of 'showing and telling' psychomotor skills, she arranges graded practice with carefully arranged feedback which is tailed off gradually as the pupils improve their performance.

In any viewing of the part of the recording of the teaching where the pupils are asked to use their new skills to cross a busy road, few would doubt that they are in a problem-solving situation in the sense proposed at the beginning of this chapter. This is clearly evidenced by the way in which different children approach the task. Each one brings to bear their individual understanding and personality to make judgments about just when and how to cross. The pupil who takes such a long time to cross seems to the viewer unlikely ever to take the plunge. He does eventually, but clearly he has less confidence or understanding than the others. His hesitancy brings home to the adult and active viewer the extremely problematic nature of this operation to the young and less active. In this case the video recording provides feedback to the teacher that would be difficult to obtain otherwise. It is fulfilling a diagnostic purpose. Should the teacher take action to help the boy build up his confidence and judgment so that he will not linger so long? Or is it better to leave things as they are? This is not a trivial question in learning this particular skill.

The one thing that might be suggested to this teacher is that she explicitly introduce ideas about problem solving and suggestions how to approach problems. This would not have been easy in view of the fact that her group of pupils were underachievers about ten years old. However, her follow-up lessons could focus particularly on questions relating to road crossing in a wide variety of conditions and aim for flexibility of deployment of the skills she had taught. My next example illustrates this process of building upon earlier learning to encourage versatility in coping with new challenges.

Orienteering

This example of the teaching of problem solving builds on the work of the teacher discussed earlier. Although a somewhat unusual subject in school syllabuses, it is an extremely interesting and useful activity that draws on many complex concepts and skills that are conventional in school curricula. In the case I wish to consider now, the teacher set out his objectives as follows:

At the end of the instruction the pupils will be able to generate, implement and evaluate solutions to orienteering problems of easy and medium difficulty, some of which involve bearings.

He used the heuristic for pedagogical analysis to identify the subordinate concepts and skills involved in this overall objective. The following were identified: map reading, route choice, handrail features, attack points, collecting features, aiming off and bearings. In planning the lesson he followed the problem-solving heuristic described above.

It should be recalled that the teacher had taught the pupils earlier, in a series of lessons, the constituent concepts and motor skills related to the problems they would be tackling. He had ensured that they had, indeed, learned the concepts and skills by the use of carefully designed assessment procedures. The pupils were therefore prepared for the next stage of learning to use their new abilities in conditions with little or no support from the teacher.

The teacher decided to place the pupils in the conditions they would encounter in actual competitive orienteering rather than produce a graded set of problems for them to attempt. Although this decision made more stringent demands on the pupils, solving actual problems was clearly the object of the whole exercise and would probably be more motivating. The added pressures in such conditions are crucial to the problems to be solved so that problems solved without those pressures would be of a different kind. One could, however, have used a graded set of problems as an intermediate stage between the learning of concepts and motor skills and the final involvement in competitive orienteering.

The problems posed for the pupils were of various kinds. Some could be solved without a knowledge of bearings, some with a partial knowledge and some with only an extensive knowledge of bearings. Thus the pupils had to make judgments as to when to use their knowledge of bearings and when to use other methods to solve the problem. The teacher had to ensure that he provided a wide variety of problems so that the pupils would be prepared for genuine competitive conditions. There was no point in concentrating on one or two types of problem. The guideline for practically all learning applies again: variety in the learning conditions is essential for flexibility and transfer in the subsequent use of the new knowledge.

In his preparatory work the teacher considered particularly that he should ensure that the pupils had an accurate understanding of the concepts of handrail (a feature on the terrain such as a path or road that can be followed without recourse to following a bearing), attack points, collecting features and the skill of aiming off.

At the interactive stage he spent the first part of the lesson revising these prerequisites using a display of courses. He then moved on to discuss the generation of solutions to problems. Using an overhead projection of an orienteering map, he encouraged the pupils to note all the information on the first leg of the route. They were prompted to decide whether the use of a bearing would provide an effective solution, and he encouraged them to generate more than one solution. The solutions were discussed in order to find the optimum one, and finally the pupils were asked if they could identify the problem the course planner had chosen that would delay the hesitant and careless orienteer.

A similar pattern of activity was used with legs two, three and four, which were graded in difficulty but did not necessitate the following of a bearing. The video recording shows the teacher prompting the pupils and reminding them of elements of the problem that might be useful while continuing to encourage them to discover the obstacles devised by the planner. Although he consciously tried to encourage the pupils to provide responses and to reinforce all suggestions, when he viewed the recording of the lesson he realised, like many other teachers whose work we have discussed, that intentions are not always fulfilled. He found that he had, in his own mind, a fixed answer to a solution to leg four and dismissed a solution proposed by one of the pupils. He makes the point: 'Since the solution was proposed in seriousness, I should have paid attention to it even if I could see that it was rather cumbersome. Through discussion the pupils, themselves, will see that one solution may be better than another but that it is useful to have more than one solution to discuss'.

The teacher suggests that these activities fall under headings 3–7 in the problem-solving heuristic (see p. 176). His experience leads him to see the way in which it differs from the guides to concept and motor skill teaching. In particular, he refers to the way in which it provides a check list of a variety of approaches available to the teacher should the pupils centre on one course of action, whereas the others provide a pattern of steps to guide teaching.

In attempting to implement the next step in the heuristic, the teacher moved rather too quickly. Wanting to encourage the pupils to take an independent approach, he decided to explain different methods of tackling problems. He tried to do this by introducing the idea of working backwards from the control (checkpoint), via the approach line to the start. The pupils did, in fact, generate four solutions, but the teacher thought he was in danger of confusing them and postponed this approach for a future lesson.

The next step was to introduce a device to provide independent practice while still providing cues and prompts. This was a chart for the analysis of route choices for the pupils to use in appraising their solutions. This device enabled them to progress to individual work while still having some support. They were, thus, more nearly in the situation of an individual orienteer trying to find the best route without support from others.

The teacher then drew all the elements of the lesson together, but later he considered that it would have been better to have asked the pupils to summarize the activities they had engaged in to solve orienteering problems.

Reflecting on his teaching after viewing the videotape, the teacher felt dissatisfied. He thought he had tried to accomplish too much. In his words he thought that he 'fell between the stools of trying to teach a set approach to solve problems and introducing different types of problems to get a general approach'.

Later practice by the pupils reassured him that the pupils had a firm grasp of how to solve orienteering problems in theory, and he ascribed this competence to the use of the route analysis chart. The next step was to go into the forest and tackle real orienteering problems.

This stage corresponded to the evaluative phase of the heuristic. The results showed that the pupils were able to generate, implement and evaluate solutions to orienteering problems of the yellow/orange range of difficulty, which was the level of the British Orienteering Federation's grades he had set in his objectives.

Every stage in the test was achieved in times rated as 'good' by the teacher and an expert orienteering assessor. On every occasion but one, all the pupils solved the problems either by the optimum routes or by readily acceptable alternatives routes.

The teacher's comments on the nature of the problems facing the pupils is interesting and very relevant to many problematic situations. He observes:

> The competitiveness of the activity requires that decisions be made and implemented as quickly as possible. Thus, while one knows what to do and how to do it, circumstances force an element of risk taking. Also a momentary loss of concentration, perhaps due to sighting an opponent, is often severely punished. The ability to concentrate and to make use of all information to analyse a problem in the heat of competition and when fatigued are the hallmarks of a good orienteer.

In many situations other than those occasioned by competition, judgments have to be made about courses of action such as he describes.

The teacher held a debriefing session with the pupils after they had run the courses using the sheet for analysing route choices. This was found very productive. In fact this was an example of using the learner's own performance as material for analysis and reflection, in the same way that the teacher used the recording of the lessons to analyse and reflect on his teaching.

One aspect of the teacher's work with these pupils is particularly interesting. Inherent in the evaluation of the work in the forest is the notion of different degrees of elegance of solution to problems. At one stage in his teaching the teacher addresses this question with the pupils and they appraise different solutions to particular problems. This approach flows naturally from the general line of the heuristic, which recognises that there is not always one 'right' answer to a problem. The heuristic suggests that pupils be encouraged to range widely in their consideration of possible ways of tackling problems. The 'debriefing' element in the teaching that considers the elegance of solutions seems to me to be a powerful tool for engendering self-development in learning after the pupils have left the teacher.

WHAT WAS ACHIEVED?

As a preamble to this section, I think it important to remind readers that, in all the cases reported, extensive recording, mainly video but some audio, took place. In addition, transcripts were made. Further, all the preliminary work of pedagogical analysis and preparation of material and adaptation of heuristic devices was available for use by the teachers or others for the study of the teaching we are discussing. What follows, therefore, is based on a considerable body of evidence, and the reports, analyses and comments by the teachers are based on repeated viewing and re-viewing of the recording and the written material.

Thinking?

Using this material I have attempted to consider what seem to me to be key aspects of teacher action that offer possibilities of improving pupils' abilities to solve problems. In the process I have considered the work of teachers who are themselves trying to solve the problem of how best to accomplish their tasks. Both groups of learners, teachers and pupils, are likely to be working at the margins of their cognitive competence. This activity is what I had in mind when I referred to guides to thinking at the beginning of the chapter. In the case of the pupils, they were stimulated to think because the teachers were deliberately attempting to arrange the learning conditions to make such demands on them. The teachers had to think hard partly because they were grappling with approaches to teaching that were different from conventional delivery teaching but also because pedagogical problem solving is part and parcel of that type of teaching.

Whether operating at the margins of one's cognitive competence is an activity that one should or could or would wish to engage in all the time is questionable. However, I believe that most teachers would prefer to live professional lives with a fair proportion of such activity rather than pass their time in the state of pedagogical torpor characteristic of delivery teaching. Perhaps I should say that I have no difficulty in envisaging states of 'pedagogical torpor' co-existing with states of frantic and exhausting classroom activity, or even vast amounts of burning the midnight oil to prepare lectures, or 'presentations', in the jargon of the deliverers of the curriculum.

I also believe that most pupils would prefer their time in school to include a fair proportion of problem solving and the learning activities that lead up to it. The work of the teachers I have discussed in this chapter treated the pupils as active explorers of their world rather than sponges to soak up the teacher's oral spillage, to be squeezed out later in recitation or written answers. Success in learning ways of solving problems is more likely to appeal to pupils and encourage them in their learning activities than is success in yielding up the last drop of the teacher's verbalisings they had managed to absorb. I think there is supporting evidence for this belief in the reports of these teachers. I also suggest that evidence indicates that considerable productive teacher and pupil thinking occurred.

Kagan (1988), discussing the teaching of problem solving in teaching and referring to theoretical and empirical studies in cognitive psychology and problem solving, draws attention to some useful mechanisms for cognitive growth. She concludes that the refinement of knowledge 'appears to require the violation of expectations: the learner must perceive the discrepancy between expected and achieved results, must correctly analyse the cause and then must repair the faulty element embedded in the faulty problem solving strategy [i.e. the teaching being considered]. For more radical cognitive restructuring to occur, . . . learners must be more dramatically confronted with the anomalies and inconsistencies in their existing strategies' (p. 499).

In the process of re-viewing their teaching on video, discussing it with their colleagues and, in the case of the student teachers, with their mentors, and writing an analytical appraisal, these teachers were working very much along those lines.

Success?

To a great extent the answer to the last question provides the answer to this. However, it is necessary to consider the nature and extent of the success of the teachers in achieving their aims if we are to benefit from their experience, which is the aim of this book.

After making due allowance for their vested interest in reporting successful outcomes, I consider that the teachers were, indeed, successful. I do not suggest, any more than did the teachers themselves, that they achieved unqualified success. Indeed, it might be considered that such implied perfection is impossible and may be an undesirable conception. The teachers' assessments of the pupils' achievement all had an element of analytical self-appraisal that, while reporting pupil success, identified shortcomings that could improve future teaching. The idea of complete success is inimical to this kind of in-built ameliorative mechanism. As I have suggested throughout, teaching as investigative pedagogy is totally open ended with a perspective of continuous improvement to which the idea of a perfect end state would be alien.

The teachers were successful in achieving their aims in that their pupils were able to solve problems after their teaching that they could not solve at the beginning. The tasks set the pupils were not trivial, and their achievement was a genuine addition to the pupils' overall competence. In all the cases we considered the teachers had earlier laid the ground for the complicated tasks they reported by teaching the prerequisite concepts and psychomotor skills. They also introduced pupils to some of the ideas about problem solving to equip them to tackle new problems in the same general field of study. The pupils, in the main, were able to accomplish this transfer task. Whether their new skill would be helpful in vastly different fields was not tested by any one teacher. However, the teachers' collective experience suggests that the approach travels effectively from one field of study to another.

This is an important outcome but one that I find unsurprising in view of the nature of the heuristic guides, based as they were on general principles relating to human learning and not on specific subject fields. This is the point behind the teacher's comment about the teaching of reading that I mentioned earlier. The search for the 'Holy Grail' of the best method got nowhere, mainly because the methods tried rarely took into account knowledge of pedagogy and questions relating to human learning, or, indeed, of work in instructional analysis exemplified in the teachers' pedagogical analyses.

The diversity of the specific learning outcomes of the teaching we have just considered is interesting in itself. Also interesting, however, is the unifying factor that the pupils acquire skills and, in some cases, produce material that is essentially their own. The pupils are not simply giving back teachers what they had been given earlier. Pupils produced melodies that were original and personal to them. At the end of the teaching they could go away and write more melodies, and the chances are that these would be original and not rote reproductions of earlier teaching. Other pupils developed the skill of using the various devices to aid reading comprehension so that they were able to work as a group to arrive at a satisfactory summary of a piece of prose. The pupils learning to analyse contemporary accounts of topical social issues were developing very useful abilities to help them appraise complex questions affecting their everyday lives. The clash of ideas in their discussions sharpened their understanding of the issues involved and helped them to understand the difficulty of deciding what is 'right' in complex social phenomena.

The quality of the discourse and the written products provided the evidence for the success of the learning and teaching in the last two examples. The orienteering teaching produced tangible outcomes, demonstrated in the routes chosen by the pupils and their appraisals of the elegance of various solutions to problems of route choice. This group of pupils also demonstrated their understanding of the problem in a rather amusing way. An expert in the sport explained and demonstrated aspects of choice and implementation of route choice to the group. As he set off into the forest the pupils appraised his performance. He did not get full marks! Two longer-term outcomes resulted from this exploration into teaching this subject. The pupils became interested in the sport, and the teacher went on to become a leading world authority on its teaching.

8 Assessment of quality 1: problems of testing

THE TROUBLE WITH TESTING

The vicar's wife in a mid-nineteenth-century country school is demonstrating the children's abilities to a visitor, Margaret.

> 'First class stand up for a parsing lesson' . . . one of the girls was stumbling over the apparently simple word 'a', uncertain what to call it.
> '"A", an indefinite article', said Margaret mildly.
> 'I beg your pardon', said the Vicar's wife, all eyes and ears; 'but we were taught by Mr Milsome to call "a" an – who can remember?'
> 'An adjective absolute,' said half a dozen voices at once. And Margaret sate abashed. The children knew more than she did.
>
> (Elizabeth Gaskell, *North and South* 1855)

Thus a nineteenth-century novelist sharply and sensitively depicting a typical school scene of the period. The irony in this exchange is a reminder that our current troubles have deep roots. Troubles? I am referring to the influence of methods of testing on teaching which the Gaskell quotation encapsulates so well and which are alive and well a century and a half later.

In this chapter I examine these troubles and discuss problems in the assessment of learning. However, I shall not attempt to discuss the administrative minutiae of examining as it exists in public examination systems in anglophone countries such as the UK or the USA. To do that would be to accept an agenda for discussion as deeply flawed in its views on the assessment of learning as it is in its conception of teaching, and there are quite enough other books around that do this. Instead my concern will be with some more general questions that examine what seem to me to be fundamental issues about how we should try to assess pupils' learning. Thus, although I am not unaware of the *angst* currently being experienced by large numbers of teachers in many countries trying to implement schemes imposed upon them by politicians and administrators, I shall focus on ways in which teachers can develop an autonomous approach to testing that genuinely taps meaningful pupil learning. I hope that taking this line will help relieve the *angst* and enhance teachers' confidence in their own approaches to assessment and enable them to seek out the flaws in methods handed down from above. I also hope that it may enable them to come to a realisation that many current problems besetting teaching have no roots, are likely to be transitory and are amenable to subversion.

Should this aim seem somewhat immodest, I suggest that readers consider the baseline of knowledge possessed by the overwhelming majority of teachers and their overseers about theories and methods relating to testing. Few teachers are initiated into the mysteries of test construction in their training. The same can be said about inspectors, advisers and supervisors, many of whom are 'promoted' from the ranks of the pedagogical proletariat in the classrooms. Legislators and administrators holding the purse strings are even less well informed. Thus professional testing agencies have, until recently, had a clear field to promulgate their own nostrums for the relief of the itch to assess.

Given this state of affairs perhaps the aim of this chapter is not too ambitious. I hope not, and I also hope that the examples I provide will encourage teachers to try, themselves, methods of evaluating their pupils' learning in ways that tap meaningful, transferable learning with an emphasis on problem solving and enjoyment.

Readers might raise their eyebrows at the immoderate tone of my introductory comments. Let me, therefore, consider in a little more detail the nature of the problems in current approaches to testing as they appear to me.

Some of my earlier remarks have foreshadowed the main difficulties. Given a view of teaching as verbal delivery it is no surprise to find that the most prevalent approaches to assessment are to seek evidence that the words have been delivered. How best to do this? Clearly by asking the recipient to show the goods. In many countries this is accomplished by asking pupils to reproduce the words of the teacher or lecturer. If a pupil can repeat a teacher's message verbatim how can anyone fail to award less than full marks? Dickens gave the answer to that in his book *Hard Times*, when Bitzer, a child of the nineteenth-century London slums, responds to the schoolmaster's question by describing a horse thus:

> 'Quadruped. Graminivorous. Forty teeth, namely twenty-four grinders, four eye-teeth, and twelve incisive. Sheds coat in the spring; in marshy countries sheds hooves too. Hooves hard requiring to be shod with iron. Age known by marks in mouth.'
>
> (Charles Dickens, *Hard Times* 1845)

Bitzer was a model pupil. He had produced evidence that the message had been received. He has satisfied the examiner. He has passed the test. But what does his proficiency demonstrate about his knowledge of horses? I suggest to you that there was unlikely to be any conceptual link between his response and the concepts he had learned from seeing, smelling, hearing, avoiding, holding, grooming and a hundred other activities connected with the animal in the teeming urban environment of London of that time. And which was the 'right' definition of a horse? The one Bitzer might have tried to articulate had he had the opportunity, or the one his teacher, Mr Gradgrind, had decreed and 'delivered'?

By the same token, we might muse on the end of year rituals in schools around the world in which pupils, although possibly in more benign circumstances than Mr Gradgrind's school, are following in Bitzer's footsteps. Meaningless messages delivered over the previous year are reconstituted as accurately as possible, all too frequently virtually un-processed. And if you are the assessor, how can you not award good marks to the pupils who parrot your quotidian words of wisdom in their end of year test. The Soviet psychologist L.S. Vigotsky put it in an expression I have yet to see bettered when he described verbalising, such as Bitzer's reply and the reconstituted lectures or lessons in the end of year scripts, as words that 'cover a conceptual vacuum'. (Vigotsky 1962)

Conceptual vacuums are created when words themselves are taken by testers as actually equivalent to the concepts they symbolize. I discussed this question when considering the learning of concepts. All too often test questions, whether of the essay type or the short multiple answer type, test pupils' recall of words that have little or no conceptual content. Instead of being symbols charged with meaning they are merely empty noises. Language, which transforms human learning, is double edged and many current approaches to testing misuse it so that it cuts learners off from an understanding of what they are trying to learn.

Mr Gradgrind is immortalized for insisting: 'Now what I want is Facts. . . . Facts alone are wanted in life'. In Britain the current demands from many politicians and their administrators repeat Gradgrind's and call for the abolition of the kind of teaching and learning for understanding and problem solving I have discussed at length in previous chapters. See, for example, the debate in the British House of Commons on 29 March 1990 where Sir John Stoke, M.P., called for a return to the 'good old days' in the teaching of history when 'we learnt dates by heart and the names of the kings and queens of England' (Hansard 29 March 1990). Similar problems beset other anglophone countries, with the USA particularly blighted by its tradition of highly structured multiple choice tests designed to be used ubiquitously. The problem with these tests is not necessarily their multiple choice format but the fact that the criteria determining their construction are so often administrative rather than pedagogical. They have to be widely used, easily administered and easily and unambiguously scored. (Nickerson 1989) Mr Gradgrind would have heartily approved.

But he couldn't have taught them how to test for the kind of learning I have discussed in this book. Open problems, such as I referred to in the previous chapter, are unlikely ever to be amenable to the large-scale testing that has dominated assessment in education for decades in many parts of the world. An argument of this type is bad news to many vested interests, and until administrative and commercial interests are replaced by pedagogical considerations I think it unlikely that we shall see the official introduction of such tests. I also suspect that this refocusing of attention is unlikely until teachers themselves acquire an understanding of the nature of testing and are able to deploy it within their own pedagogy instead of having it imposed from without.

Testing from without could not cater for the kind of evaluation of learning exemplified by the work of teachers discussed in this book. All of them were attempting to teach for understanding and transfer of learning and some were explicitly trying to teach their pupils the elements of problem solving. Currently, there is much discussion among educational researchers as to whether or how testing of such 'higher-level skills' can be accomplished. Such discussions will need to move into the classroom to find an answer. The examples I report here of teachers grappling with the problem using psychopedagogical guidelines are worthy of their study.

THE POINT OF TESTING

It is a moot point whether Mr Gradgrind was intent on teaching Bitzer what a horse really was. More likely his aim was the strengthening of a form of social control, not merely over Bitzer, who was a model pupil when it came to rote repetition, but over the other children. Children with imagination, such as Bitzer's classmate Sissy Jupe, were unsatisfactory receptacles for Gradgrind's facts and had to be remade in a mould uncongenial to imagination and unquestioning of authority no matter how inept, trivial, useless or unjust it might be. Any kind of learning other than rote-learning of *ex cathedra* assertions would undermine authority and was not to be tolerated. Attitudes of this type are well documented in the history of the nineteenth-century in the anglophone countries and there was no attempt to hide them. Consciously or unconsciously, explicitly or implicitly, many of those attitudes linger on, although they may not be expressed so forthrightly. Anyone interested in using methods of evaluation of learning needs to be sensitive to these attitudes and their accompanying assumptions when considering how to evaluate learning. It is, therefore, important to clarify the reasons for testing before setting about it.

DIAGNOSTIC TESTING

I begin with what I consider to be the most important type of testing. Diagnostic testing, in the sense I am using it, has several aspects. In general we might consider its purpose to be to identify the strengths and weaknesses of pupil learning and to pinpoint specific problems as precisely as possible. In order to be able to do this we must take an analytical approach. Global reportage of a pupil's accomplishment reveals none of the details that go towards making up the pupil's performance, nor can it help one to identify the mistakes that lead to imperfect performance or the nature of the action that led to success.

Does this matter? Clearly not, if you are in Mr Gradgrind's camp. Nor if you are mainly interested in testing in order to sort out the sheep from the goats, as is done in many school systems which select pupils for different types of school. If, on the other hand, your aim is to equip pupils to solve problems, to learn conceptually rather than by rote and to enjoy learning, it is of crucial importance that you are able to chart the routes they follow in the course of their learning.

It is important for many reasons. Perhaps most important is that without the analytical diagnosis of what went on in the teaching, teachers have no means of knowing what kind of action might enhance future learning by their pupils. It may be that their teaching has been faulty and all the class have failed to learn in some particular. It may be that one or two pupils have failed for reasons peculiar to themselves, rather than because of flawed teaching. Another important use of testing that fits very uneasily into conventional methods but which has great potential for diagnostic purposes is the feedback it can provide pupils. In much testing nothing is revealed to the pupil about the reasons for failure or success. Diagnostic testing can be a powerful aid to pupil learning through the information it provides learners and teachers.

The virtue of diagnostic testing, then, is that it can be a great aid to reflection on action. This is currently a very fashionable concept. But it almost invariably refers solely to teacher reflection. Diagnostic testing can also be used as an aid to pupil reflection, which seems to me to be equally as important. The work reported in the last chapter by the teachers who had debriefing sessions following their teaching was developing a powerful technique in which pupils and teachers engaged in joint reflection. This approach, when used in a spirit of openness and trust between teacher and pupils, could enhance the performance of both. As I have implied throughout this book, a teaching encounter should involve at least two learners, even if one teacher and one pupil are the only people present. The only tests that can help produce this kind of interaction are diagnostic tests.

I can illustrate the process by reference to the way in which a programmed text was produced. While it does not have all the features of the approach to assessment discussed in the work of the teachers considered in this book, it employs techniques that are useful in designing diagnostic tests.

The text was one produced to introduce student teachers to the elements of educational psychology as it applies to teaching (Stones 1968b and c). It is a self-instructional program in book form which attempts to simulate a discussion between a tutor and a student. It is presented in a series of learning sessions, each of which is divided into a number of subsections referred to as 'frames'. A series of teaching frames discusses and attempts to teach concepts or several related concepts. Each frame has a teaching element and asks for a student response. The response is evaluated in the following frame to help a student who has misunderstood or to confirm the correct answers. At the end of each section are several review frames which provide no teaching but aim to assess the students' learning of the material presented in the preceding teaching frames. Each review frame is linked to the instructional frames, which discuss the concepts being assessed by a reference to the numbers of the appropriate frames as shown in the example.

Frame 9.57

Question

Here are a few items from a test designed to evaluate the results of teaching an aspect of botany. Pick out the two items which are technically poor. Say why they are poor.

A From the collection of leaves given, pick out the oak leaf, the chestnut leaf and the beech leaf.

B What is an ovary?

C What is the difference between the root and the stem of a plant?

D Sketch the flower provided and on your sketch label the following parts. (parts specified)

Answer

B and C are poor because the answers could well have been memorized by the pupil as a verbal chain. This would be rote-learning. (Frames 4–19)

Thus, students working through the test, by looking back to the frames given in the linking reference, are able to locate the source of any error they may have made on the review frames, to read the teaching frames again and, thereby, to remedy their misunderstanding. At the end of the program, the students can take a short answer test, the items of which are also linked to specific teaching frames in the program. The tutor can thus inform each student precisely where in the program the source of any error might be and thus give them the opportunity of revising the necessary concepts.

Although the program was entirely in the form of a book, all the review frames and the final test attempted to test transfer of learning. In no case was an example used more than once to illustrate a principle and in no case were students asked for definitions or statements of principles. Always they were asked to use principles to make decisions about specific cases.

The program review sections and the final test were examples of diagnostic testing. They were intended to provide feedback to enhance student learning. I tried out the program with several groups of students, and after each trial I analysed every frame to check how the students had reacted to it. In all, over 1,000 students worked through the program. If all the students' answers to the question asked in a specific frame were wrong, I looked back to the frame to see what was wrong with it. If it were a review frame or an item in the final test, I would go back to the corresponding teaching frames to see if they were deficient in any way and try to rectify them. I was thus learning, as a teacher, from the results of my efforts. In the development of the teaching program the students' responses provided crucial diagnostic information about the way the teaching was operating. After several revisions of the program, student performance on the final test reached between 70 and 80 per cent, and its effectiveness was confirmed independently in a large-scale test comparing it to other methods of instruction (Leytham, 1970).

There is an aspect of this diagnostic test that is rarely encountered in tests of substantive material. Students could start with the final test and see if they were able to answer the questions. If they were able to answer all the questions they would not need to read the program. If they were able to answer some of the questions, the option would be open for them to use the key to go the frames where the material teaching the concepts they were unsure about was discussed. They could even go back to the review frames to each section for a more detailed indication of their level of competence before reading the program.

The principles used to develop this self-instructional program are undoubtedly appropriate to interactive teaching. The procedure described is a method of systematizing the development of diagnostic testing and teaching. Teaching and testing are integrated, and this integration is essential for the development of productive teaching and any associated testing.

FORMATIVE TESTING

Formative tests are, or should be, diagnostic tests. They are tests used in the process of teaching to monitor pupil learning and guide the teaching. The term is used to distinguish this type of test from summative tests, which are given at the end of instruction. The test I mentioned in connection with the self-instructional program was a summative test as well as being diagnostic. The continuous self-monitoring of pupil learning might also qualify it as formative assessment. Diagnostic tests, in fact, can be used for different purposes, whereas tests designed for other purposes are rarely useful diagnostically.

SUMMATIVE TESTS

These are the tests that are probably most familiar to readers. They are tests taken at the end of a course of study. Their aim is to assess the learning that has taken place. I have already drawn attention to some of the problems related to the most prevalent methods of summative testing. The problems are not caused by the tests' being summative but by the methods used to make the assessment. I discuss these methods below, but first I should like to consider some general points that are independent of the methods used.

I shall not dwell on the problem I have raised above in the discussion of Gradgrind and Bitzer, except to say that the problem of taking learners' verbalisings as evidence of conceptual learning is endemic in most testing but, perhaps, most prevalent in the end of course assessment. The reason it is so prevalent is, as I have already argued, that the practitioners and the administrators know little about the way humans learn or the role of language in that learning. Clearly, any test of this type cannot assess quality learning and is to be avoided.

Even when test constructors are alive to the problems of rote-learning and seek to avoid it, the nature of their testing bespeaks a view of teaching very close to a delivery mode. Most tests attempt to assess no more than what the teacher has already worked through with the pupils. Even if the pupils learn the concepts, they are not called upon to demonstrate their ability to make use of them. In the classification I used earlier of A, B and C type skills, they are operating at the lowest level, C. True, this is better than operating purely at the level of rote, i.e. non-conceptual, learning, but tests of worthwhile learning should, in my view, seek out evidence of more complex abilities than remembering what the teacher has previously expounded. The first step towards the construction of such tests is to aim to assess the ability of pupils to use the new learning in different conditions from those in which learning took place. Here we are considering the question of transfer, the apex of which is expressed in the ability of pupils to solve problems in the field they have been studying. I do not mean that pupils should be able to use routines, previously taught, as algorithms to be applied, but that they should be able to use principles, concepts and methods in combinations they have not previously experienced to solve problems in ways personal to themselves.

Psychomotor skills may be assessed along similar lines. The ability to imitate aspects of an expert's performance exactly (were it possible), with no understanding of the principles underlying the action, would be rote-learning and would be very situation-specific. The greater the understanding of the principles, the more able the pupil would be to take into account personal factors, such as eyesight, reaction time and physique, that indicate an optimum action divergent from the expert's. Thus tests of psychomotor skills should aim to test for the versatile deployment of learned abilities in ways appropriate to the learner and to the particular conditions existing at the time of testing. An attempt at a carbon copy of an expert's action would be unlikely to demonstrate competence as effectively.

In a sense the division between formative and summative testing is artificial. If one takes an approach to teaching such as that proposed in this book, the overall final assessment in any teaching is preceded by more specific assessments of its subordinate elements. The question naturally arises: 'When is the end state reached?' The formative assessments are summative for the subordinate elements, and the summative test will probably be a formative assessment for future learning.

All the teachers whose work I discussed above made use of summative assessment, and they all attempted to avoid the pitfalls I have mentioned. There is, however, a most important difference between the tests they produced and those most frequently used to test learning at the end of a course of teaching. The difference is that the tests produced by the teachers were integrated with the teaching. The bulk of summative tests are produced outside the classroom.

Tests imposed on teaching from without can never be integrated with the teaching since the test constructors can have no idea of the conditions existing within the teaching milieu in which the tests are to be used. Not knowing, for example, the conditions in which concepts were taught, they can never be sure that the items they produce genuinely test conceptual learning or whether the pupils' answers comprise preprepared rote responses, responses with some understanding but of the same type they have previously encountered, or whether they indicate the application of previous learning in different circumstances. Merely looking at the test will not reveal its nature. Only in the work of individual teachers working over an extended period can a test be integrated with the teaching by one teacher in one school.

IPSATIVE TESTS

Ipsative questionnaires have a long history in the assessment of individual attitudes. (Allport *et al*. 1960) They are called 'ipsative' (from the Latin *ipse* (self)) because they refer solely to individuals and do not compare them to others. An ipsative scale of values is intended to discover which aspects of an individual's personality are most salient. Thus, for example, one individual's attitudes may be more inclined towards religion than towards commerce and towards physical activities more than musical interests. This is not to say that individual A's interest in one thing is greater than B's. A really apathetic person may have a low level of interest in most things, so that even strong preferences would be at a lower level of intensity than those of a person with a lively interest in many things.

I have taken the idea of ipsative testing and applied it in fields other than personality testing. Basically, a test of this type is a form of diagnostic test. However, it incorporates elements of baseline tests and summative tests. The approach was originally devised for use in teacher education where external bodies demanded that student teachers be judged and declared competent (Stones 1984a). Although I am sceptical about the possibility of making such a declaration that would be valid, the idea of competence was incorporated in the testing. However, over and above this level of minimum competence I introduced elements based on the heuristics I have described earlier. Thus a teacher might be more skilled at arranging feedback than presenting a variety of exemplars of a concept. A profile could be drawn for each teacher where the base was minimum competence and the peaks and troughs above the baseline would indicate the teacher's pedagogical strong and weaker points. Teachers are not compared with each other, and any difference of heights between peaks on the profiles of two teachers is of no significance.

Tests of this type resemble any other diagnostic test; differences arise from the way they are used and the assimilation to them of the baseline. Where they were used as tests of beginning competence for a new course of learning, the baseline would constitute the minimum entry level and the profile above the line would provide teacher and pupils with information relevant to the teaching and learning they were about to embark upon. Used at the end of a course, they would give an assurance of minimum competence with the same kind of information in the profile as that provided by the entry test.

One or two points may be made in favour of tests of this type. They provide diagnostic information to teacher and learner. They also provide feedback that is less likely to be perceived negatively by learners, since, assuming they are secure on the baseline, the information they are obtaining about their performance is particular to them and does not signify failure. Indeed, the profile above the baseline may be perceived as varying degrees of strength rather than strengths and weaknesses.

Tests of this type also, by their nature and use, make the important point that assessment is in the last analysis a matter of judgment, usually by people acknowledged to be experts. There is no extra-human agency (not even statistics!) that can enable people to pronounce definitively on the achievement of other human beings. This is a topic I shall consider further below.

SELECTION TESTS

I do not wish to spend much time on the subject of selection tests since it is not really germane to the theme of this book. Indeed, some tests that have greatly influenced education and life opportunities have deliberately tried to remove the effects of learning from their assessment of people. The secondary selection intelligence test in Britain is a notorious case of this approach. Other methods of selection that attempt to assess people's 'true' nature or ability include phrenology, graphology and astrology. (See Stones 1979, for a discussion of this phenomenon.) The advisors on and practitioners of these arcane rituals of separating the elect from the dammed resemble the priests who mediate between gods and believers. They interpret the signs for their patrons and advise on action on the basis of their interpretation.

Some selection tests are, of course, built on firmer foundations. Some tests of vocational aptitude, for example, make no pronouncements about whether the abilities of the person being tested are the result of native ability or of good teaching and learning. These tests are very similar to the diagnostic tests I have already considered. One might argue about the effectiveness of particular tests or items in them, but since they usually attempt to assess some aspects of current ability and not to make predictions on the basis of apparently unrelated criteria, they are much less vulnerable to criticism than intelligence tests.

TEST REFERENCE

Perhaps the most important point about selection tests for our present discussion is that they raise the question of test reference quite sharply. By test reference I mean the assumptions adopted to achieve the purposes of the testing. Two main approaches to the question are current: norm-referenced testing and criterion-referenced testing. Norm-referenced tests are designed to enhance the power of discrimination of test questions and success is measured by one's rank order in a list of scores of all candidates. In selection tests a slice is taken from the top of the list to decide who is to pass. The thickness of this slice frequently depends on things other than scholastic ability. In the selection testing for admission to secondary education in Britain, which was in widespread use in the 1950s and 1960s, the national average thickness of slice was 15 per cent of the children around the age of eleven. It was argued that this was the proportion of children in the population that were capable of benefiting from a grammar school education. This argument was essentially political sophistry to justify maintaining the existing level of funding and unequal educational provision, since the allocation to grammar schools varied considerably in different parts of the country.

In some parts of the country, where there was ample provision of grammar schools, the percentage went up to as much as 45, and the top slice comprised nearly half the children of those localities. The criterion for selection was thus really the number of places available in schools dubbed 'grammar schools' in a given location, and the tests were administrative devices for imbuing the selection process with some semblance of legitimacy in the allocation of scarce educational resources.

Norm-referenced tests, however, have a long history within schools even where selection is not an issue. Schools have traditionally taken performance in relation to the performance of others as the measure of a pupil's achievement. In some schools pupils were seated according to their ranking on the most recent test. The calculations made to obtain the gradings were frequently of dubious statistical validity, but apart from that there is a problem at the heart of norm-referenced testing that renders them of marginal interest to good teachers. The point is simple. What help is the calculation of a rank order on a test to the teacher or the pupils? Neither get any information about the learning that has taken place. The learning of the whole class could be abysmally low, so that being top of the class could still imply very poor accomplishment in specific fields of study.

Criterion-referenced tests do not purport to sort the sheep from the goats. They are, in fact, the type of test used by the teachers whose work we have been studying. The tests attempt to assess pupils' competence according to certain pre-established criteria. In the case of the teachers whose work I describe in this book, the aimed-for standard of competence would have been determined during the process of identifying objectives and in the task analysis. Thus the testing would be integrated with the teaching. In Britain criterion-referenced tests have recently become fashionable with politicians and, hence, also with their administrators, although they have been around for a long time. However, in the current wave of government enthusiasm for criterion-referenced tests, this integration is lacking. Even the fact that they are supposedly related to a common curriculum for schools cannot bring about this unity of teaching and the monitoring of teaching. While criterion-referenced tests are undoubtedly to be preferred by quality teachers over norm-referenced tests, they are subject to the same difficulties I have discussed earlier if they are imposed from outside. Schools awash with such tests, as many are, are likely to be less, rather than more, able to improve their teaching and the pupils' learning. This unfortunate outcome is a consequence not only of the bureaucratic impedimenta accompanying the tests but also of the low level of learning many of the tests assess, devised as most are to check delivery teaching. Checking delivery in the way one signs for the receipt of an unopened parcel is really all many such tests could hope to accomplish.

This is not to say all that tests produced internally are *ipso facto* satisfactory. All the pitfalls discussed above lie in the teachers' pedagogical path. It is the aim of this book to help teachers avoid the traps or overleap them.

WHOSE CRITERIA?

There may be criteria that tests of this type do fulfil, however. They may not always be made explicit; indeed, they may not always be consciously espoused by those setting them. The point is that criteria are set by people with different levels of pedagogical understanding, and of different interests, temperaments and motives. The case of criterion-referenced tests in Britain illustrates this question well. For many years a number of educationists had argued for the use of these tests on the grounds that they shift attention from the drawing up of rank orderings of pupils using norm-referenced tests to the actual achievement of pupils and its relationship with teaching. (See Stones 1966 for example.) Little progress was made towards their use, however, until politicians discovered them and introduced them into the educational system. On the face of it this was a positive step. But, as I have already implied, the criteria to which the proposed tests referred were not the same as those most educationists had in mind when they argued for their introduction. Indeed, one might reasonably suggest that criteria were operating that were connected not so much with pupil learning as with controlling the teachers. Obviously, such a crude assertion would not be made explicitly, but the signal to start the process was given fairly openly in a British government 'White Paper' in 1982 which foreshadowed the introduction of large-scale teacher appraisal programs and learning of facts (Department of Education and Science, 1983). As I wrote at the time, this type of externally imposed imposition of tests and teacher appraisal would be very familiar to teachers in the USA, who also suffer from such restrictions.

My point is that criterion-referenced tests as they are currently conceptualized and used may well achieve the opposite of what their early supporters intended. In the eyes of their promoters, however, they could succeed even if the pupils' learning they purported to measure was trivial. Thus, the setting of criteria for tests is a much more complex operation than may be realised. Whatever criteria one adopts, they will incorporate the values of the test constructors and the test promoters. This point is all too often overlooked by educationists, but it needs to be borne in mind by teachers for their self defence.

VALIDITY AND RELIABILITY

Whether or not a test actually assesses learning related to any particular criterion is referred to by educational testers as 'validity'. This is another concept that is more slippery than first appears. Although I personally espouse this view of validity, I believe that there are alternative views that will differ from mine according to the values held by others. Thus, according to a great deal of current political thinking, test validity would seem to be a function of the degree of success of the testing program in keeping teachers occupied in fairly low-level activities such as administering tests provided by outside agencies. I am fully aware that this notion of validity is not within the canon of thinking about testing technicalities, but I am convinced that it needs to be brought within the canon if only to alert test constructors with a genuine interest in fostering worthwhile, meaningful learning in pupils.

I said that 'validity' is a slippery concept, although I accept the notion that it should be seen as the extent to which a test measures what it is supposed to measure. Although there are many complicated ways of tackling the problem of assessing validity, employing statistical and psychometric techniques, I suggest that all too often crucial pedagogical factors are overlooked. It would be possible to demonstrate high test validity if its criteria of success were repeating exactly what teacher had said (The Gradgrind syndrome). As soon as one attempts to assess less trivial learning, things become more complicated. The work of many of the teachers we have considered earlier in this book make this point particularly aptly. How can one assess by conventional group testing such things as the quality of a melody, or a pupil's train of reasoning in making a judgment in a complex social situation or the elegance of a solution to a route choice in a forest? The answer, I suggest, is that it cannot be done by outside agencies. My position is that the best method of establishing validity is by the consensus of experts. Not, I stress, experts in statistics or test construction, but experts in the pedagogy of the subject being tested. Logically these experts would be the teachers.

I am not suggesting, however, that individual teachers should be totally responsible for idiosyncratic decisions about test validity. Clearly there should be moderation by colleagues. I did say a *consensus* of experts. Obviously, in addition, it would be obtuse not to make use of the knowledge of the experts in test construction. What is clearly needed is a teaching profession much better informed about methods of assessing pupil learning as well as other aspects of pedagogy. My last phrase is significant. Testing is part and parcel of teaching and pedagogy and can be of only doubtful help if it is divorced from them.

Reliability is normally taken to connote consistency in replication in different conditions. Test scores from one administration to another are checked to see if more or less the same outcomes are obtained. Scores awarded by different markers are checked for correlation to ensure inter-marker consistency. There is a clear assumption in attempts to produce tests that are reliable, that they are to have widespread and repeated usage. This view is a product of the psychometric movement whose bread and butter is the production of tests to cope with this widespread external usage. I should like to suggest that many aspects of the concept of reliability are of doubtful value in the encouragement of worthwhile pupil learning, mainly because of its detachment from practical teaching and the employment of procedures such as test-retest techniques that are artificial to teaching, not least because they are dependent on the measurement of variability of scores, whereas criterion-referenced approaches in essence try to remove it (Stones 1975b).

One aspect of reliability testing may be of use pedagogically. Inter-marker agreement can be very useful to moderate teaching standards. My interpretation of this process, however, is more in the nature of taking a second opinion than employing the statistical techniques commonly used in test construction. Teachers may, while setting their own objectives and devising their own test procedures, wish to subject their work to the scrutiny of peers to ensure that their work is not diminishing in rigour and effectiveness because of their lack of systematic contact with others in their field.

This approach to moderation is more productive than the more common marking of a few sample scripts, or even a whole set of scripts, by outside markers. Teachers whose work is being moderated learn from their colleagues in discussing specific courses and cases, and the moderators themselves also learn through their own involvement in the work of peers.

The points I have tried to make about validity and reliability both underline the view that testing cannot be totally objective in any non-trivial sense. In the final analysis the assessment of learning is a matter of judgment. Bringing in outside moderators recognises this and, recognising that human judgments can be flawed, makes explicit that the best we can do is to rely on a consensus of experts. Anyone who takes this view, as I do, needs, then, to accept its corollary, that in any system of integrated testing and teaching that is internal to schools and not imposed from without, the level of expertness in the teachers is crucial and needs to be developed to a high degree. The object of this book is to help as far as possible to achieve that state of affairs.

I realise that this line is diametrically opposed to the way things have traditionally been organised. The nearest approach in recent times in Britain has been the development of internal assessment by course work with external moderation. This approach could form the basis for a rational and pedagogically sound approach to the assessment of pupils' learning. Whether it will to any great extent depends on the resilience of teachers in the face of the barrage of external forces pushing them to abandon the complexities of pedagogy in favour of the certitudes of administering simplistic tests. It also depends in part on teachers' ability to subvert the system.

Many teachers are adept at subverting the system. They do their best to help their pupils pass examinations set by outsiders by hook or by crook, and if this involves them in training pupils to answer exam questions and to spot questions in forthcoming examinations, so be it. The very fact that it is possible, even with essay-type tests, to pass by reproducing material learned by rote, speaks volumes about the nature of the tests. Teachers might reasonably feel that if tests are like this, it is best to use methods appropriate to rote-learning to help pupils pass the exam while, at the same time, doing their best to get on with some worthwhile teaching. It is a tragedy of many school systems that many teachers spend most of their professional lives working like this.

The fact that many educationists wring their hands at the problem of producing methods of assessment that are impervious to 'teaching to the test' (See DES 1985 and Nickerson 1989) illustrates the point I have made earlier about the widespread limited thinking about the nature of and relationship between teaching and testing. Teaching to the kind of test that I am interested in, and which is employed in most of the case studies I am reporting, brings together teachers' concern to foster worthwhile transferable learning in their pupils and its assessment. Worries about teaching to the test are relevant only if the learning is simple and non-transferable (Stones 1986b). This is because learning from teaching by telling is by nature difficult to transfer to new situations and thus places a premium on memorization and its assessment. It tacitly accepts low-level learning as staple. Teaching that draws on pedagogical principles that foster conceptual learning produces transferable learning that is useful in novel situations. Any satisfactory test of that learning, by definition, would test complex understandings and transfer, so that, even if it were possible, 'teaching to the test' would be more reason for satisfaction than cause for concern.

A NEW PERSPECTIVE ON TESTING?

I have discussed approaches and problems related to the assessment of pupil learning as it is now and have made suggestions for methods of dealing with the problems. I shall now attempt to draw the threads together.

The most difficult problems are those related to the current dominant conceptions of teaching as delivery and of teachers as technicians. The main anxiety of politicians and administrators who control the teaching force seem to be to make teaching and testing teacher-proof. Managerial concerns, therefore, get much more attention than pedagogical ones. Currently, in Britain, in-service teacher education focusing on the management of schools attracts the lion's share of funding and pedagogy is rarely to be found in the prospectuses of the providing institutions. Entrepreneurially minded teachers flock to these courses. If teaching is no more than the delivery of a product, managerial and marketing skills are the ones that matter. Teachers are seen more as assistants in a retailing business than potentially skilled theorists in a dynamic collegial collective. Many teachers in Britain who find such a conception of their lot unappealing are making their views known in forthright terms, and the 'clipboard teacher' is their derogatory personification of the pedagogue as entrepreneur.

In the USA some teachers have been even more tightly controlled. In one school district school principals have gone so far as to prescribe the exact page in the basal reading books during every week (Peterson 1989). Peterson, in the same work, also provides an exemplar of a process endemic in British education: if you wish to improve pupil learning, tighten the testing screw. He reported the action taken by administrators in schools where the reading program was achieving poor results. Instead of reappraising the reading schemes they tried to resolve the problem by managerial and bureaucratic means. They ordered their reading resource teachers 'to become managers of massive record keeping systems that categorized pupils on the basis of their success or failure on basal tests.

Principals were told to focus their conferences with teachers on the reading test scores. Supervisors developed sophisticated pacing charts that had above-average pupils proceeding slowly through the basal texts and poor readers zooming through the material twice as fast so that they could "catch up"' (Peterson 1989: 296).

In reaction to what the teachers involved thought was the damaging influence of the use of basal readers and testing, they organised in resistance to it. After two years of 'real-life political controversy and pedagogical struggle' they made progress towards getting their views about pupil learning and the teaching of reading accepted, and innovative change within the classrooms became a real possibility.

The significant thing about this account is the conjunction of political and pedagogical activity. Gut reaction to unpopular methods of teaching imposed from above is unlikely to bring about long-lasting change. Activity based on analytical evaluation of those methods will strengthen the current case and is more likely to ensure its longevity.

The chances are, however, that the teachers whose action is described by Peterson were fighting with one hand tied behind their backs, pedagogically speaking. Teacher training in the USA is little different from the way it is elsewhere, and very few teachers are likely to have been inducted into the approach to pedagogical analysis and practice discussed in this book. I once likened the relationship between teachers and administrators who hand down tests and instructions to teachers about testing to that of the one-eyed king in the country of the blind (Stones 1975a). If I were to update this statement today I think I would be more sceptical about the acuity of the one-eyed king's vision than I was at that time and would look for other factors that might be propping up his rule.

All the points rehearsed in the last few paragraphs seem to me to point in one direction. For genuine progress to be made towards testing that goes beyond the assessment of rote-learning and teaching, two developments are essential. On the one hand teachers need to be rid of the bureaucratic incubus that turns them into hired hands, and on the other they need to be equipped with a body of pedagogical principles. A change of this nature would enable them both to establish their position as the experts, rather than the administrators, and to establish unimpeachable professional credentials. Most important, however, they would be able to use their knowledge and skills to promote worthwhile learning in the pupils. It may not be entirely fanciful to consider some of the straws in the wind, such as the revolt against basal readers and the sound of teachers voting with their feet against being treated like cogs in a bureaucratic machine, as the harbingers of change in teaching.

I hope I have not painted too lurid a picture of the current lot of teachers in their struggle with testing, since my interest is to promote change, not to induce surrender. Thus, I hope and believe that the work I now report will encourage experiment and reflection rather than resignation (in any sense) and dejection. Although the work was carried out before British teachers were subject to the draconian controls they currently groan under, similar approaches are by no means ruled out. These studies of teachers attempting to devise methods of testing for complex learning are relevant to the work of any teachers attempting in their own way to make sure that any assessment of their pupils' learning they may employ will assess learning that is worthwhile and transferable, while at the same time equipping the pupils to go through the hoops currently prescribed by those who temporarily hold sway over them.

9 Assessment of quality 2: a sample of studies

ENHANCIVE EVALUATION FOR THE IMPROVEMENT OF QUALITY

Readers are unlikely to have encountered this type of evaluation in texts on testing. The adjective itself is somewhat recherché. However, it does describe the essential nature of the assessment we are about to consider. 'Enhancive' evaluation is more comprehensive than any of the types of evaluation I have referred to above. It signifies the use of assessment procedures to identify pupil success and failure, whether summative, formative, diagnostic or ipsative. But it goes beyond that in its overt focus on teacher performance. Its overall aim is the enhancement of pupil performance by the enhancement of teacher performance.

Thus, in this discussion of enhancive evaluation, I shall not parade a series of exemplary test questions, but consider ways in which teachers with varied backgrounds and experience have attempted with varying degrees of success to assess their pupils' learning. Common to them all was that they were striving to assess meaningful learning that would transfer to new situations and to eschew involving their pupils in retrieving from their memories 'facts' delivered earlier. But the crucial distinguishing feature of the work of these teachers was the evaluation of their own teaching and testing that made the enhancement of their teaching and testing possible. The experience of each teacher grappling with this problem, whether successful or unsuccessful, has a lesson for all teachers.

Volleyball

I now consider the example of assessment that I discussed in Chapter 6 and which has elements of criterion – referenced testing, diagnosis and teacher learning. The skill being taught was the volleyball dig pass. The criteria for the successful demonstration of the skill were arrived at in the teacher's task analysis before the teaching. It was quite specific. The player would be able to:

. . . perform the dig pass, intercepting a ball thrown from the opposite side of the net and direct the dig pass to a player standing in a semi-circle whose diameter is 5 metres with an accuracy of 80 per cent. The test of accuracy is that the ball is received by the boy inside the semi-circle without its touching the ground, i.e. that he be in a volley position on receiving the pass.

The test involved the learner in fifteen trial digs which were recorded and appraised by the teacher.

The teacher also had a pre-teaching test which ascertained that the boy had some knowledge of the game from previous instruction and the necessary entry motor abilities but was not competent in the dig pass. In addition, through his experience in teaching volleyball, he was aware of the most common errors made by players and made a summary of the body positions and movements during the dig pass. The objective of teaching was, using the dig pass, to intercept the ball after it has passed over the net, changing a defensive action into a possible attacking action.

There can be little argument that this test of the skill is valid. Unlike many tests, it is an exhaustive test of the learning, not a sample. One might object that there should have been more and a greater variety of trials, and that, indeed, would have been a more stringent test. Nonetheless, the criterion had been set, and the test could hardly have been more valid. Whether or not it was reliable would have depended on the ability of the teacher to repeat the test and get comparable results or for others to have made comparable evaluations. The virtue of the video recording is that both types of reliability can be tested by its use. The use the teacher made of the test, however, is such that the question of reliability is of limited importance, as the teacher considers some of the possible causes of variability in his analysis of test results, their probable effects and how they might be controlled. The testing and the teaching were thoroughly integrated.

As I reported earlier, the objective was not fully attained and the boy achieved only 60 per cent success. The teacher wanted to know the reason for this failure. It is worth noting the nature of 'failure' here. Most conventional tests, especially norm-referenced ones, would consider 60 per cent a respectable score. The teacher analysed the learner's errors and then used his analysis to improve his teaching. This was the approach used in the development of the self-instructional program which I described earlier. In it I attempted by repeated tryouts and analysis of pupil error to identify deficiencies in the teaching that would need correcting.

The teacher analysed his errors in detail as I reported in Chapter 6. Later he made a very important point arising from his evaluation. He was so fixated on achieving the perfect dig pass that he failed to implement the intended procedures as he had identified them before the lesson. I shall consider this problem in more detail later.

The points we might note in the work of this teacher seem to me to be as follows. First we have an example of an experienced teacher bringing to bear his subject specialist knowledge, together with his understanding of psychopedagogical principles to guide him in a specific teaching task. Although the task is in the field of psychomotor skills, the points that emerge from a scrutiny of the assessment of the pupil's learning are of relevance in other types of teaching. We might note, particularly, that the learner is asked to demonstrate the new skill in action, not describe it. The fact that this may not seem surprising sheds light on methods of assessing skills not involving such obvious physical activity. We may reflect back to the discussion of problem solving. The learner in this case had to solve the problem of making a satisfactory dig pass in a new situation. Probably most teachers would consider asking for proof of competence in this kind of learning without a demonstration of the skill to be unsatisfactory. By the same token we might argue that to infer competence in cognitive skills by asking for a verbal explanation, written or oral, is equally unsatisfactory. The comment about low levels of feedback and reinforcement is familiar and a perennial problem. Finally, the test of pupil learning, through its integration with the teacher's planning and teaching and the teacher's reflection on both in the light of theoretical principles, had given an experienced teacher a new insight into teaching his specialist subject. This new insight laid the foundation for a cycle of improvement in his work.

History

The teacher whose work I discuss here is the student teacher we met in Chapter 5 teaching the concept of 'evidence' in the historical sense. Recall that she had been trying to teach the ideas of primary and secondary evidence. She attempted to assess the pupils' learning by presenting them with

> quite complicated examples of evidence and asking them to explain to me independently what sort of evidence they thought each example was. I had chosen, deliberately, tricky examples designed to test whether the the pupils had really grasped the concept. All the items presented were novel to the pupils and had not been used in the teaching.

I gave details of the lesson in my discussion of concept teaching (see p. 126) and explained there the confusion the teacher ran into in her discussion of the painting of Henry VIII and the Thracian treasures and will not go into these further.

The testing was carried out by oral questioning so that the teacher was able to probe, using follow-up questions, if she thought it necessary. In my view, the approach was fine but its implementation left something to be desired. This was brought home to the teacher in the exchanges with the pupils, particularly in the questions which revealed confusion in the pupils' minds. The important point to emerge was the lack of clarity and misunderstanding, by the teacher herself, on the classification of some of her test items as primary or secondary evidence. There is no doubt that without the analytical approach supported by the video recording and the commitment to enhancive evaluation the problem would not have been addressed. The teacher was aware of the problem at the time but was unaware of the precise reasons for the pupils' difficulties. Only later was she able to identify and clarify the nature of the problem and make ameliorative action possible.

It is likely, however, that if she had used a short answer test, either oral or pencil and paper, she might still not have fully grasped the reasons for the pupils' misunderstanding. The probing which accompanied the questions helped her to pinpoint the errors and to realise that the problem was not in the pupils' deficiencies but in the lack of clarity in her own thinking. This example serves to remind us that convenient standard forms of assessment may be all very well for administrators and may well please statisticians and psychometrists and yet be at heart inimical to pedagogy and pupil learning. The fact that oral methods permitting probing questions are difficult to employ in large classes does not invalidate the point. It merely poses starkly the question of what the tests are for. If the main criterion is, as I discussed above, administrative convenience or keeping the teachers off the streets, then use batteries of mass-produced tests. If the intention is to help pupils to learn effectively then it is necessary to think of other ways of doing things. If conditions in schools preclude that, it is better that teachers recognize this and make it clear to others as a step towards improvement of the conditions. In the meantime, methods such as this teacher used could be used on a sampling basis which tested a selection of pupils, perhaps in conjunction with other methods.

One other point from the work of this pupil teacher is particularly worthy of note. In the course of a single lesson she discovered an important error of understanding among the pupils and was in a position to take action. If remedial action had not taken place, all the future work of the pupils that drew on their concept of the nature of evidence would be distorted by this misunderstanding. It is a sobering thought to consider the multitude of occasions that misunderstandings of this type occur in the course of a person's formal education and the implications of these misconceptions for the way in which people are equipped to cope with their lives. The contemplation of this problem makes clear the urgency of the need to equip teachers with the skills to reduce the shortcomings of current approaches to pedagogy.

Written English

The assessment of written English has long been a vexed question. The main issues in contention have been marking by global impression after reading and the use of analytical methods based on pre-determined criteria for awarding marks. There is also a school of thought that argues that awarding marks for creative writing is to be deplored. This is not to suggest that pupils are to be denied guidance and feedback, just that no attempt should made to quantify their efforts.

The difficulty of quantifying merit in writing is well illustrated in the way marks in examinations of written English tend to be distributed. The raw scores of large-scale examinations in England involving thousands of pupils typically produce scores highly concentrated at the mean. I believe this bunching reflects the uncertainty in the minds of the markers, all experienced teachers and examiners, as to what the 'correct' mark for a piece of writing should be. To be safe they incline towards the average and leave the discrimination between the closely bunched marks to the statisticians.

It has been suggested that the 'true' mark for a piece of writing is the average of an infinite number of markers. This definition appeals to me for two reasons. One is that it recognizes the impossibility of ever achieving a 'true' mark (an infinite number of markers) and the other is that it implicitly acknowledges the subjective nature of marking work of this type. This subjectivity can be amply demonstrated by inviting experienced teachers to mark the same paper as other teachers and re-marking the same paper on a later occasion. Differences in marks awarded are guaranteed to diverge widely, quite enough to make the difference between 'pass' and 'fail' on specific papers. The only way of achieving 'consistency' of marking is statistically. I prefer the 'infinite number of markers' approach and believe that this view of testing could be applied much more widely than to the testing of written English.

The teacher to whose work I now turn was an experienced English teacher and was aware of the problems of assessing creative writing. He discusses a fundamental question that is often overlooked, namely that pupils often see their relationships with their teachers as those of candidate and examiner and the writing they submit as summative assessments of their learning (Britton *et al.* 1976). In the teacher's own words: 'This tendency to view the majority of writing done in school as final drafts for assessment by the teacher sees writing as a product rather than a process of learning and by-passes several important questions such as: what are the purposes of assessing written work? Is the way the written work is assessed necessarily the best way? What effect does assessment have on the writer's progress?'

He also makes an important point related to my earlier discussion of reliability. Because of the emphasis on product rather than process, most of the literature on assessment of pupils' writing focuses on reliability and has little to say about the effect on pupils of having their work assessed. Yet, as the teacher remarks: 'they [the tests] can have a crucial effect on motivation and the pupils' capacity to learn from the experience of writing and having their work commented on'. He quotes several workers in the field of teaching and testing of written English who stress the importance of the process aspect of teaching English, with the general message that the things that matter and that help pupils to improve their written English are not quantitative marks but qualitative comments that provide feedback about strengths and weaknesses. Very much in line with the arguments in this book, they stress the superiority of an approach that accentuates the positive and de-emphasizes the negative aspects of pupils' written work. In other words, the argument is for diagnostic feedback used judiciously to maximize reinforcement and minimize or eliminate punishing negative comments. After all, few pupils deliberately set out to produce badly written work. Castigatory comment on pupils' work, thus, cannot help their learning and can only serve some other function related more to the teacher's or the school's values and attitudes.

There seems to be a serious problem of social attitudes which the example of teaching written English highlights. Tests and marks are widely seen as the means by which learning is improved. Teachers and test constructors are seen as gatekeepers whose main function is keeping up 'standards' by excluding the undeserving. The onus on improving performance is thus thrown back onto the learner.

Teachers themselves are not immune from the obsession with marks. As the head of a department in a large secondary school I arranged with the staff that they would not award marks to the pupils' written English but that they should give them detailed comments by way of feedback. After some time I was approached by one or two pupils asking why I didn't award marks and could I do so. I discovered that at least one of the staff was awarding marks for written English despite our agreement not to. The attempt to provide helpful feedback was undermined by the obsession with unhelpful quantitative assessments that give little feedback to the pupils. Would it be too unkind to suggest that the preference for awarding marks rather than providing diagnostic feedback may not be unconnected with the ease of implementing the former and the thought needed to provide the latter?

The teacher whose work we are now considering was engaged in a fairly common project in English teaching, encouraging a group of five pupils chosen randomly from a class of thirty two, aged ten–eleven years old, to write imaginative descriptions, in this case, of an imaginary person. When it came to the assessment of the descriptions he was concerned to make the post-writing phase a 'positive rather than a punitive experience', with the aim of developing the ability in the pupils to evaluate their own writing independently. Merely giving them a mark out of ten would have been useless to achieve this. Thus, after writing he discussed the work with the pupils individually and as a group. He attempted to direct the discussion to go beyond the written work to the process through which the pupils arrived at it. He took a friendly and encouraging attitude and commended them on the strengths of their descriptions.

He was particularly concerned to introduce the post-writing discussion on a positive note and quotes some of the exchanges between him and the pupils. 'Yes, I liked that about his hair: "a few greasy strands of hair". I thought that was very good.' 'Yes I suppose that's one of the first things you'd notice about someone who works on a building site.' 'Some parts of it were very good. I like especially. . . .' Later analysis of the sequence in which these exchanges took place led the teacher to conclude that although the atmosphere of the classroom had been positive it was severely lacking as an example of formative assessment. To quote the teacher again: 'The reinforcers used [were] mostly unvarying and lacked specificity in the teacher's [his own] use of reinforcement with little attempt to connect the praise with the relevant aspects it was meant to reinforce'. Thus, while the pupils enjoyed the writing and the discussion, their learning was impaired because of the teacher's faulty use of feedback and reinforcement. In this case the teacher's attempt at formative evaluation in the post-writing discussion was less than perfect so far as the pupils were concerned but pretty effective for the teacher, a not unimportant outcome!

He also learned another important lesson from his analytical approach to the assessment of his pupils' learning that he would not have dreamed of if he had merely given them a qualitative mark. He found that although some pupils were able to appraise their writing in relation to the specific points raised in the pre-writing discussion, some were not. For example: following the teacher's question: 'Did you like what you wrote?' the following exchange took place. Pupil: 'No.' 'Why not?' 'I don't know really. I couldn't get it to mean what I wanted to say.' 'What do you mean?' 'I don't know really. It just didn't sound right.'

The post-writing discussion also revealed that the pupils were unclear as to what, in writing, constitutes a good description. They were, therefore, in no position to make an adequate appraisal of their own work. When asked how they might improve their written descriptions, they mostly focused on things they would leave out, and when asked whether they had looked over and revised their papers they said that they had but the 'mistakes' they corrected were formal or mechanical such as spelling.

The teacher considered that most of the problems he discovered in the pupils' learning were a consequence of his unsatisfactory pre-active work and the first part of his interaction with the pupils. Pre-actively, he had not clarified for himself the nature of the problems of teaching written composition and he had not satisfactorily identified the problems pupils experience when attempting written composition. In his words: 'Many of the problems encountered during the lesson grew out of a lack of insight into the subject with the teacher having failed to identify the problems confronting the learners'.

As a summative check on the pupils' learning, the teacher had the pre-teaching and post-teaching papers of all the pupils in the class typed and the typescripts marked by ten teachers. The five pupils he had taught in this way produced descriptions that showed improvement over the lesson period and were generally better than the other pupils'. The teacher, however, is realistically sceptical about what was achieved in this short period and makes various suggestions that might explain the effect. However, the important point that emerges from this account is summed up by the teacher, himself. 'Although it could be argued that the children certainly had benefited from the lesson such optimistic results could tend to hide many of the deficiencies shown during the subsequent analysis.' In these words he epitomizes the problem inherent in the use of global, summative ratings whether norm- or criterion-referenced.

In concluding the discussion of the work of this teacher, it is worth noting the resemblance between his post-writing session and the debriefing session of the orienteering teacher we discussed earlier. It seems to me that there is an important and neglected point here. Involving pupils in a discussion of the processes of their own learning is astonishingly little considered. There is little doubt that teachers and learners would benefit if it were given more attention.

Teachers' learning

I now turn to an example of teaching that applied the idea of debriefing to a small group of teachers and student teachers exploring systematic approaches to the teaching of art concepts. The teacher was the tutor we met before when we considered his objectives for teaching art concepts (see Chapter 3). He was a member of staff of a teacher training institution specialising in the teaching of art. His students were experienced teachers and student teachers, and their pupils were aged about ten years. The tutor was exploring with the teachers the effects of using the approach to teaching concepts outlined in the heuristic for the teaching of concepts discussed earlier. To this end he arranged for some of the teachers to teach their pupils short lessons in specific topics of art education using the guidelines in the heuristic and for others to teach without reference to the heuristic. All the lessons were video-recorded.

The teachers using the heuristic used it to guide their teaching; the others taught as they would 'normally'. Subsequent analysis revealed that the work of the first group, although using a variety of approaches, had certain constant factors. As the investigator put it, these commonalities comprised: '. . . conscientious analysis and structuring of teaching content [preactive leading to interactive phase of teaching]. Much of the success enjoyed

during the actual teaching could be traced to a rigorous task analysis . . .'
Further, the teachers:

> . . . conformed to the premise that in order to teach for understanding,
> less emphasis than usual would be accorded to skills of a mechanical
> type. . . . One effect of this change was for teachers to scrutinize
> the presentation of their material with more than usual care,
> striving for simplicity when introducing content and attempting to
> develop a theme, by degrees, towards a level of sophistication, e.g.
> progressing by stages. The emphasis upon building carefully graded
> pupil experiences, whilst taking account of pupil feedback, proved a
> salient feature of these teaching experiments. On the other hand a
> pronounced feature of the work of the teachers not using the heuristic
> was a plurality of aims which led to ambiguity in their ideas about what
> they hoped to achieve.

An interesting difference between the users and non-users of the heuristic
which bears on the question of evaluation of learning, was the presentation
of exemplars and practice. The former varied both while the latter in many
cases 'employed undeviatingly repetitive tasks, which, devoid of relief,
developed into unrelenting "slogging matches" testing the patience of
pupils and teacher alike'. The varied approach clearly is more useful in
terms of formative evaluation than the unvaried and has implications for
any subsequent summative evaluation.

The tutor reported several effects flowing from the use of the heuristic
for concept teaching on the teachers' approach to evaluation of pupil
learning. He considered that the task of ensuring that pupils had learned
what they had tried to teach was eased 'by (a) the presence of specified
objectives derived from task analysis (b) the systematic application of
psychopedagogical principles throughout teaching and (c) the stress upon
unambiguous demonstrations of pupil understanding. A review of the
"evidence" reveals that the schedule [heuristic]-users were conscious of
[its] value as a guide to assessment of teaching. As a consequence of each
teacher's being able to demonstrate the ability to teach systematically, whilst
responding to the needs of individual pupils, the final outcome of teaching
was seldom in doubt.'

Several considerations influenced the nature of the tests to assess pupil
learning. One was the inappropriateness of relying on verbal methods,
especially oral, with the inherent possibility of rote answers and imitation.
Verbal methods were, therefore, augmented by 'visually oriented activity'.
The concepts being taught by the teachers were tone in drawing and
painting, perspective, primary and secondary colours, and pattern. Some
of the ways in which the teachers using the heuristic assessed the pupils'
learning were to ask them to discriminate between novel exemplars of
the concept, to solve a problem involving the examplars in using the
concepts and principles they had learned, and to describe and provide

reasons for their actions. The pupils were also asked to demonstrate in practice that they had learned the principles meaningfully. This was achieved by such devices as asking them to place cut-out figures at the appropriate points on a landscape according to the principles of perspective and to demonstrate their understanding of tone by arranging tonal values in a scale and producing graded sets of tones in wash or pencil.

The evaluation of the teachers' teaching was achieved by means of a detailed scrutiny of all their written work related to the preactive, interactive and post-active phases of the teaching, together with the scrutiny of video recordings of the lessons, discussions with the teachers and the use of a questionnaire related to their experiences using the heuristic. This procedure resembled the way the teachers evaluated their pupils' learning with the addition of the access to the video recording. Perhaps an occasional joint scrutiny of recorded lessons by teachers and pupils would be an aspect of formative evaluation worth exploring.

Evaluation had three dimensions. First, all the teachers were able to assess their own teaching in respect of its success in producing meaningful pupil learning and in their employment of the pedagogical principles suggested by the heuristic. Second, they engaged in collective evaluation in which they compared their individual approaches to those of their colleagues tackling similar pedagogical problems. Third, they involved an 'expert outsider', the tutor, to provide his observations. These dimensions were not distinct in time but were interrelated and collaborative.

What are the salient points relating to evaluation arising from the work of these teachers? The general impression may well be the most significant. Although I have been able to provide only a glimpse of the total investigation, I suggest that it is enough to bring home to one the complexity inherent in assessing accurately the learning even of what may seem to be relatively simple skills and concepts. The assessing of art work by the production of test pieces is very common. Less common is the relating of the test pieces to theoretical principles. Indeed, 'theory' is often tested by conventional written exams, which are seen as more relevant to theory than practical work. The assumptions and misunderstandings lurking in the last two sentences have been the burden of a considerable part of this book. They snare and delude teachers and examiners into a simplistic view of learning and the assessment of learning. The complexity of both, as grasped by the art teachers, is not peculiar to their subject but common to all teaching and testing.

The assessment of the teachers' work was the main point of this investigation. While recognizing that the ultimate test of the teaching is the pupils' learning, it is clearly necessary to explore the nature of the teachers' activity and its relationship with how their pupils learn. In many investigations the linkage between teacher action and pupil learning has been explored using correlational techniques. I believe that these techniques are inappropriate for two main reasons. One is that they tend to treat the teacher as a 'black box' and do not examine the detailed nuances of individual teacher activity. The other is that correlational techniques depend on variability, whereas in criterion-referenced assessment of pupils or teachers the aim is to reduce variability. Ideally, pupil achievement would have low or zero variability since all would score 100 per cent in the criterion test. Similarly, in the crucial pedagogical skills, one would hope that teachers would invariably make the most effective moves. The aim, again, is to reduce variability. I am not talking here about 'dull uniformity', which is a catch phrase levelled almost as a reflex action by some educationalists when systematic approaches to teaching are proposed. As we have seen, the hallmark of pupil learning of the type proposed in this book in a wide variety of subjects, including the arts, is the expression of individuality in a context of basic competence. (See the discussion of the production of melodies or of the 'elegance' of problem-solving.) In the case of teachers much the same can be said as I suggested in my discussion of ipsative ratings in Chapter 8.

The overall picture from the work of the teachers and student teachers was that their objectives were achieved, and the pupils gave evidence of the learning intended. Apart from that crucial criterion, aspects of the teachers' work that were examined focused on the effects of using a structured approach to the teaching. The basis of the examination was the methods mentioned above. They provided a multidimensional attack on the problem of assessing teacher activity that considered theory and practice together. The use of video recording made this type of appraisal possible through the use of protocol analysis such as I have considered earlier. This approach contrasts strongly with the type of teacher appraisal that is currently so fashionable with its emphasis on simple check lists, its atheoretical approach and managerial orientation. It recognizes a complexity inherent in assessing teaching competence that is totally alien to the managerial simplisims. However, while the complexity of the problem is recognized, means of tackling it are also developed and employed.

It is perhaps apposite to close the discussion of this case study with a comment from the tutor *vis-à-vis* the relationship between this type of approach and the teaching of art. The perennial point of contention in this field is the extent to which systematic approaches are appropriate to such subjects. This is also an issue with the teaching of music, as I have discussed earlier. The art tutor considers that his results:

. . . suggest that the teaching of those concepts selected for study benefited from analysis, carefully sequenced presentation and subsequent evaluation according to the theoretical principles. In this way selected aspects of art content, frequently regarded as belonging to an anarchic area of experience, were seen to have as much to gain from the systematic application of psychopedagogical principles as those areas of the curriculum traditionally treated as more 'rational'.

Biology: the use of keys

Biology is one of the subjects that would probably be regarded as 'rational', in the words of the art tutor. Nevertheless the teacher in my next example, an experienced teacher of biology, was critical of unsystematic approaches to the teaching and testing of many aspects of the subject.

The teaching was a small-scale investigation over one lesson with two pupils about eleven years old. The topic she chose was the use of keys to identify specimens. Keys are algorithms that if used correctly will lead to the accurate classification of previously unknown specimens. The problem was that frequently the method of teaching employed is pedagogically inept in that the first specimen presented for identification is already known. Pupils therefore fail to see the usefulness of keys since they seem merely to confirm what they already know. This impression is likely to be reinforced when they find that they cannot use a key to identify novel specimens.

The teacher considered that probably the main problem of current approaches was the lack of clarity about the psychopedagogical nature of keys and their use. Although the logic of an algorithm leads one inevitably to the correct conclusion through a set series of steps which make few cognitive demands on the user, there is an inherent assumption of an essential prior level of knowledge. The prerequisites are that the user must understand the concepts manipulated when working through the steps and be able to identify and discriminate the features referred to in the key. Here is an example. It is taken from a key for identifying fungi (Lange and Hora 1963). 'Fruit body, cup-shaped or turbinate, with or without stipe, (go to page) 26.' Clearly a would-be user would not get far without a clear idea of what the various terms meant. Thus, the use of all keys, although a mechanical operation, depends entirely on prior meaningful learning in the field in which it is being used.

An adequate pedagogical analysis would distinguish between the concept of 'key' and its use and the concepts in the subject field the key related to. Thus a test of the use of a key would need to ensure that its results were not spuriously low because of a lack of understanding of the concepts in the field in which it was being applied. If the object of teaching in the study of fungi were the distinguishing features of particular classes, then the test of learning would be whether the learner could identify new exemplars of the concept. The key may be regarded as a guide to making this classification more exact by the identification and naming of the precise *specific* example, which would have been difficult or impossible without it.

A test of the ability to use a key must be free of the confounding factors of unfamiliar content. This might be accomplished by asking the learner to explain the logic of a key or to draw a schematic diagram depicting the logical steps. The best test, however, would be to demonstrate the use of a key in action. This is how the teacher decided to test the learning of her pupils.

She stresses that before teaching it was essential that the pupils had the necessary skills and concepts. Specifically they had to be able to discriminate the attributes referred to in any key used in teaching or testing, and they had to have a grasp of the concepts referred to in the keys. She ensured this prior competence by using familiar objects such as sweets, keys to locks and beans used for cooking. The test was intended to present the pupils with a real problem of identification using a key they had not previously encountered. The actual key used was one to identify different trees from the nature of the leaf buds. The concepts involved were commonplace: trees, twigs, round, pairs, single, spiral, red, brown, green, long, short.

In the event the teacher found that her assessment of the pupils' prior competence was faulty. The 'commonplace concepts' were not so commonplace after all. The pupil is presented with a twig of ash. The teacher reports: 'He was plainly disturbed by the distinction required of him'. The first criterion was ambiguous to him. He asks: 'Is that a pair or what?' and points to the buds. 'Would you say it was in pairs?' Is the problem that the pupil does not understand 'pairs', or is it that discriminating pairs on the specimen is beyond him? Whichever is the case, the test was not a good test of the pupil's learning of the use of keys because the irrelevant factor of uncertainty about arrangement in pairs was obtruding. The teacher concludes the report of her lesson as follows:

> Before giving a similar lesson I would give more thought to the production of a diagnostic test designed to encompass all the discriminations and conceptual knowledge that is a prerequisite of the new learning.

I must stress that this teacher was an experienced senior teacher in her school. She had taught this subject for some years and yet had not really come to grips with the complexity and intricacy of teaching the topic until she put her teaching under the microscope. If she had not tested the pupil in a face-to-face situation she would not have realized the nature of his difficulty but merely have noted that he failed on that question. Under normal conditions he would have gone on to subsequent work in the syllabus continuing to build up a learning deficit. In the use of keys this leads to the situation described by the teacher, in which even graduates will eschew their use and attempt to identify specimens by laboriously working through books of illustrations.

Mathematics

The advantages of clinical study of teaching and learning are illustrated in another case of a teacher with thirty years' experience of teaching mathematics. He taught a fourteen-year-old pupil over the space of three lessons with the aim I referred to in my discussion of objectives, namely that the pupil would be able to construct a graphical line representing a specific speed and would be able to read from the speed line related values for time in hours and distance in miles, both to notation of two decimal places. The teacher identified two important aspects of the clinical approach. One was that he was able to establish with some accuracy the entry competence of the pupil. The other was that he was more able to encourage the learner to use her own speech to guide her learning, for example by 'talking her way through the learning material in the construction of a graph'. He also asked her to explain what she was doing at many stages in the learning.

Discussing the assessment of the pupil's learning he stresses the complexity of the task and the interdependence of the identification and acceptance of objectives, the teaching itself and the evaluation. Throughout the lesson he was able to monitor the pupil's learning, and after the third lesson he asked the pupil to complete a homework assignment that required her to construct a graphical speed line unrelated to any previously taught. She was also asked to answer a questionnaire containing selected questions arranged in order of difficulty which required her to read related information from a number of graphical speed lines, some of them novel.

Formative evaluation in this teaching was, thus, very precise and flexible so that the teacher was in a position to make changes in his approach. He had also established baseline competence by giving the pupil pre-tests and, in addition, had taught the pupil for two years prior to this piece of teaching. The final assessment demonstrated a high level of competence by the pupil. Note the nature of the assessment. The pupil had to construct novel graphical speed lines and also answer questions involving novel material. Both elements of the test necessitated the transfer of learning. The teacher followed up with a test a month later, also using novel material, and found that the level of competence was sustained.

The teacher comments that he was able more easily to identify the strengths and weaknesses of his teaching than if he had been teaching a full class. It is, however, important to note that the key variable was not the one-to-one teaching situation, but the analytical pedagogical approach and the assessment involving transfer of learning. The pedagogical analysis had identified the three types of skill before the teaching and had planned to proceed from type C through type B to type A skills. Teaching and assessment were closely interrelated towards this end, and the crucial test was the demonstration of competence in the A type skill.

Orienteering

The work of the teacher of orienteering that I have discussed earlier provides interesting examples of assessment of entry competence, of formative evaluation and of summative evaluation. I should like here to repeat my earlier comment that this skill brought together in a unity several important elements in school learning that are often taught in isolation and with little perceived relevance by the pupils. Maths, the use of maps, the use of compasses and other skills come together and are applied in an amalgam of physical, intellectual and affective activity that is uncommon in conventional teaching.

The teacher produced a pre-test of the requisites for learning the concept of bearing. It was designed to test the following:

- Knowledge of right-angle turns and clockwise direction
- The cardinal points, NSEW and clockwise direction
- Intermediate cardinal points and turns greater or less than a right-angle
- Knowledge of 45 and 90 degrees rotation and anti-clockwise motion
- Understanding of 'an angle'
- The ability to estimate, measure and draw angles
- Knowledge of courses
- Knowledge of a bearing

The test was presented using a variety of approaches, all intended to be non-threatening mathematically. Like the work of many of the teachers discussed above, this diagnostic pre-test, intended to ascertain the pupils' readiness for the new learning, yielded some surprises. The teacher discovered that the pupils, while able to talk about angles, had only vague ideas about them. Asked to estimate the size of angles, they were not very accurate. This was an absolutely crucial piece of information for this teacher. Had it not been sorted out early it would have impeded the pupils' learning throughout until they acquired the concept haphazardly.

Later in the teaching, when they had left the classroom and the school grounds, the teacher devised an ingenious method of formative assessment. The problem was to ensure that the pupils were able to follow a bearing accurately. He arranged for a check point to be placed at the bottom of a slope which the pupils approached from the top. Thus, the check point could not be seen when one was approaching it until the last minute. At the top of the slope a tape had been placed at right angles to their path marked at 5-metre intervals with symbols. The point at which they crossed the tape would be a measure of accuracy in following the bearing. The exact location of the ideal crossing point had been identified by two expert orienteers; the nearer to the ideal point, marked 'G', the more accurate was the course they were following. A score for each pupil was obtained by expressing as a percentage the distance they had strayed from the true bearing by the distance from their point of departure to the tape. This measure gave the teacher a diagnostic check on the individual pupils to guide him in future teaching.

Note the essence of this measure. Ultimately the validity of the assessment rests on the views of the two expert orienteers and the teacher. This, as I have suggested earlier, is, in the last analysis, the most valid basis on which tests can rest. Having accepted that view, teachers can construct the means at arriving at useful methods of assessing pupils' attainment by the means most suitable to their purposes. The nature of the assessment is limited only by physical constraints of working conditions and the teacher's imagination. This teacher devised a method of ascertaining pupils' deviation from 100 per cent accuracy and a means of expressing the deviation in terms that were meaningful and useful to him and certainly comprehensive and acceptable to others. Add to that that in this particular case the pupils scored very well by 'normal' standards, with an average of almost 90 per cent success, who could ask for anything more?

The element in the summative evaluation that I find particularly appealing is one that I have referred to earlier. It is the measure of pupils' problem-solving ability that includes an element giving credit for the elegance of solution. In most aspects of human activity, one can usually achieve one's aims in several ways. A test of orienteering skills translates this idea of varied approaches into observable reality 'on the ground'. One can actually see people reaching the goal in different ways. Objectively one can tell whether or not the pupils reached the final check point. Objectively one can check the time taken. These are two obvious and necessary measures. Locating the control was awarded 20 points, time was awarded 100 points, and 30 points were awarded for elegance of solution. The last measure is clearly the subjective judgment of an expert. But so is the basis of the decision about the optimum path to take. The decision about time is more objective, but the number of points accorded for a good time will be decided by the teacher, having in mind the fact that the task is part of a competitive sport in which time is important. Thus the weighting of the various elements of assessment are affected by external factors which may or may not be relevant to the task being assessed. This is an important factor to be borne in mind in all assessment.

The recognition of elegance as an element in assessment has many of the attributes of ipsative assessment. Both are related to a minimum level of competence, in this case reaching the control point. Over and above this basic level of competence are different ways of achieving it. The element of time could be viewed similarly. The basic level of achievement is reaching the control point. Time taken and method of reaching control are individual matters. Note that the two elements of time and method of reaching the control may be accorded different degrees of importance by different assessors. One of them might consider time taken to be part of elegance, whereas another might prefer a rather longer time combined with a particularly ingenious approach to route finding.

These considerations apply to all attempts to assess human performance. Any subject taught in school is amenable to the approach discussed here.

The most important point at issue is that this type of assessment totally precludes rote-learning. Rote learning is learning without understanding and implies a fixed mechanical activity quite incompatible with the notion of individual variety of problem solution. The reason I find the idea of 'elegance' in assessment so appealing is that more than any other element it demonstrates a grasp of the principles relating to the activity being assessed. It is closely related to the idea of 'creativity', which is usually considered to be a 'good thing' and often has a somewhat mystical aura.

Music

My next example comes from the work of the teacher of music we discussed earlier. He was highly sceptical of the mystical view of creativity and explored the use of the systematic approach of psychopedagogy to the teaching of the composition of melody. On the basis of a pedagogical analysis of the problem of teaching musical composition to pupils with no particular bent towards music he identified the necessary skills and concepts involved in producing melodies. He considered that for anyone to learn the concepts and skills necessary for the composition of melodies one would need to be able to do the following:

Pitch

> Discriminate between high and low sounds
> Recognize the keynote, e.g. C, as first note of the scale
> Recognize the fifth note, e.g. G, in key of C
> Recognize the progression of the eight-note scale framework, i.e. stepwise ascending to eight notes
> Recognize the intervals of stepwise movement, (second) the third, fifth and the octave

Rhythm

> Discriminate between long and short sound durations (given pulse for each sound duration example)
> Recognize and perform crotchet, minim and dotted minim

Form

> Define bar lines as dividing sound progression into equal parts (see notation)

Notation

> Since the study adopts a literacy approach to teaching composition, the pupil will need to be able to recognise and understand the significance of certain musical symbols. The symbols should be drawn on the chalk board.

Recognize and understand the significance of:

Treble clef
The stave
Bar lines (see 'Form')
Crotchets (one beat)
Minims (two beats)
Dotted minims (three beats)

The checking of this prerequisite learning can be accomplished by the teacher (himself) in the form of questions, using the blackboard, chime bars or Casio (electronic) instrument. Any gaps in the prerequisite learning should be re-taught.

The teacher also considered it necessary to ascertain whether the pupils were already able to compose melodies. He therefore questioned them about melody and asked them to compose a simple melody. This additional check is similar to the one I described earlier in the chapter in relation to the program I used with teachers and student teachers. He thought it worth doing since some of the pupils may have had music teaching outside school.

After he had taught the concept of melody, the teacher needed to ascertain that the pupils had learned as he hoped they had before proceeding to the next stage, the actual production of melodies. He therefore compiled a test of concept learning which may be regarded as summative evaluation of the teaching thus far. It is also formative and diagnostic in respect of the teaching to follow, which aimed to take the pupils to competence in the production of melodies. It took the following form:

The teacher produced a melody in musical notation and asked the questions:
What do you see at the beginning of the melody?
What do you see at this point?
What bar is this in the melody?
What is significant about this bar?
What do you see at the end of the melody?

He followed this with two melodies in 2 and 3 time which included all the subordinate concepts essential to the melody. The first melody was performed by the teacher and pupils, and a test comprising eleven questions based on the melodies was given, including the following items:

What does the melody begin on? (Sub-concept 1)
What note values continue in bars 1–3? (Sub-concept 2, rhythm)
Why is the note value in Bar 4 different? (Sub-concept 2, rhythm)
What is the extent of the announcing phrase? (Sub-concept 2, pitch)
What note does the responding phrase finish on? Is this the best note to finish the responding phrase on?
What is the alphabetical name of this note? What else is in this note?

Note that this test has the feature of 'keying' that I referred to when I was discussing the test related to the teaching program. The words in parentheses at the end of the questions relate to the concepts that have been taught, and failure in any of the items can be linked to specific aspects of teaching, thus facilitating remediation.

When the pupils had demonstrated competence in this test they were ready to tackle the criterion task: the production of their own melodies. They were given ample time and asked to produce four to six melodies. The teacher asked for sample performances. In his words: 'The performances, which [were] taped . . . and the notational evidence act as the quintessential tools in the final assessment of the teaching programme'.

In this account of testing we have observed the assessment of type C skills, answering questions about melody; of type B, making analytical comment about specific melodies; and of type A, the production of their own melodies. We have also seen the use of diagnostic pre-tests, diagnostic formative evaluation and a summative post-test related quite precisely to the prespecified objectives and based on the teacher's pedagogical analysis and the use of his variant of the pedagogical heuristics discussed in previous chapters.

The main interest of this chapter is the way in which various teachers tackled problems of evaluation, rather than the actual performance of the pupils. However, it is worth commenting that the melodies produced by the pupils showed more 'elegance' or 'creativity' than those of pupils taught by less structured methods that are claimed to be more suited to the encouragement of spontaneity and creativity. These words are mine. The teacher's own comment is much more convincing and adds even more weight to the argument for this approach to teaching.

> Clearly, it would be a poor evaluation to simply state 'This is a good melody' or 'This is a bad melody' since there are no analytical criteria to say why. As the whole thesis of this study has been to adopt a systematic approach, it is clear that the evaluation should be the same.

He puts his words into action by giving examples of melodies produced by the pupils and analysing them in detail in relation to pitch, rhythm and form. It is thus possible for readers to examine the basis for his evaluation of the melodies produced. This analytical approach is particularly interesting in the assessment of a subject such as music which is often discussed non-analytically. It is highly relevant to the point made about the last case I discussed. Creativity and elegance of performance will not be found in people with no grasp of the underlying principles of the activity in which they are engaged. On the other hand rote-learning will be found in people denied such methods of teaching. This is what this teacher found in the performances of pupils who had been taught conventionally.

TESTS IN BRIEF

I should like to close this chapter with a brief consideration of ways in which other teachers have tested their teaching. Many of these we have encountered in earlier chapters. One of the most striking for me was the way the teacher of the Green Cross Code tested her teaching. From the gentle introduction in a quiet classroom where the pupils were learning the basic concepts, via the simulation in the playground using pupils on cycles as traffic, with other pupils acting as distractors, to the quite dramatic, almost hair-raising, transition on the video recording to a busy road with the children standing on the kerb, this piece of teaching was a salutary illustration of the need for accurate assessment. The final assessment of this skill was asking the children to go on an errand from school and observing them to see if they followed the code. There is little room for debate as to whether or not this method of assessment is valid. I think there is probably also little doubt that this method of testing is rarely used by other teachers. Testing that goes no further than questions and answer in a subject like this is an academic exercise we cannot afford.

My next example is less dramatic, but the same pattern of teaching can be observed. This teacher was teaching aspects of German poetry to seventeen–eighteen year-old students. Testing of C skills was done through question and answer. Testing of B skills was carried out by asking the students to listen to recordings and to distinguish a variety of rhythmic patterns. Type A skills were tested by asking the students to read aloud varying patterns of verse. The Achilles heel of his teaching proved to be the unsatisfactory nature of the pre-test. He says that the final test demonstrated that he had overestimated the entry competence of the students. He concludes ruefully in the case of one student: 'Insufficient time and care were devoted to making sure she could perform well before the lesson began. This was a case of an assumption being made too glibly; in my experience, this is a common fault and is probably the greatest single cause of ineffectiveness in teaching'.

I am not sure that I would entirely agree with second part of this assertion, but I have no difficulty in accepting the first part. Most of the teachers whose work I have studied have come to the same conclusion, usually when shortcomings in their teaching have been analysed after the fact. In the present case, the teacher assumed that the background knowledge of the students would be sufficient for him to present them with a definition of rhythm and that all he had to do was to tell them. After analysing the lesson he concluded that this was counter-productive and that he should have taught them using exemplars and non-exemplars to structure their learning so that they inferred the concept for themselves. His reason for presenting them with a definition was to save time. Undoubtedly there is a problem here – almost a chicken-and-egg situation. If effective formative and diagnostic evaluation were commonplace and teachers were continuously alive to the need for accurate monitoring of students' learning, mismatches between student competence and teacher perceptions of it would be much reduced. Until they are, the tension between 'covering the syllabus' and teaching with meaning will persist.

This need to 'cover the syllabus' is often argued by teachers working under external constraints. However, in the case we are considering, the constraints were in the mind of the teacher, who thought that giving the students a definition to memorize would be sufficient for them to learn the concept. This is an example of the near-universal fallacy in teaching I have discussed at length, that telling equals teaching equals student learning. His analysis taught him that it didn't more effectively than anything he might have read or been told. The same goes for his students. Both would probably benefit from his analysis. Unfortunately most of the millions of teachers on the planet, who are telling their students and getting through their set task like talking books, will never analyse their teaching or reflect on it when it has vanished into thin air, as speech has a habit of doing.

The outcome of his analysis forced him further back in his reflection on his lesson to the preactive phase, and he concluded that he had failed to identify at least two related sub-concepts: first, that in verse rhythms some words carry two stresses, a main and a secondary stress, and, second, that monosyllables may also carry a stress to fit in with the underlying pattern. He ascribed this failure to the fact that his pedagogical analysis had been unsatisfactory. We have been here before!

Pedagogical analysis and a systematic approach to teaching and assessment may not seem as appropriate in the primary class as in the teaching of older children. However, unless teachers' role is to be nothing more than child minders, they will be trying to teach their pupils something. Teachers worth their salt will also endeavour to teach well to enhance their pupils' learning. They will also wish to know how well they have taught. I do not see how these aims can be achieved without some form of structured approach. Perhaps I should stress here that I am talking about teachers' own use of tests related to their teaching, not the use of externally imposed tests.

This outlook informed the work of the next teacher. She was an experienced head teacher of infants, making a clinical study of the teaching of one child aged six. The object of the exercise was for her to put her teaching under the microscope to ascertain the applicability of the techniques and to identify the strengths and weaknesses of her teaching so as to help her improve her teaching generally and to help the staff of her school improve. This was the first step.

She chose to teach a subject on the curriculum, tessellation, which she conceived of as that 'certain regular shapes will fit together leaving no space'. Her teaching followed on a rigorous pedagogical analysis and used an approach to teaching the concept of tessellation using a variety of exemplars and non-exemplars and varying the salience of the criterial attributes. When it came to the test, she produced novel exemplars for the pupil to work with. The pupil was given the test a week after the teaching. Each item of the test was keyed to an aspect of the teaching in the way I have discussed earlier. All the items on the test involved the use of actual shapes and not merely answering questions. It went as follows (I quote the first four tasks):

1 Find the irregular shape.
   This tests objective 1 by asking the pupil to select the exemplar of an irregular shape from a set of non-exemplars.
2 Find the same regular shape.
   As in the previous question the pupil is asked to select an exemplar from a set of non-exemplars. This time it is intended to test the pupil's grasp of the concept of regular shapes.
3 Join the same shapes with a line.
   Now the child is asked to recognise the name of the shape. Since it was stated [earlier in her report] that this was not intended as a test of reading ability, the words were read out to the child before beginning the test. To avoid the risk of guessing, the shapes were presented twice, but a different order was used in the second array.
4 Will these shapes tessellate?
   The pupil is asked to tick those shapes which will tessellate. The word 'tessellate' was used rather than 'shapes that will fit together without leaving any spaces'. Therefore, by completing this question the child was, in effect, carrying our the actual task rather than repeating a statement which may have been learned in rote fashion. The child is presented with like-shapes, for example, squares with squares.

All the test items except the last demanded that the pupil demonstrate in action, by working with shapes, that he understood tessellation. The last question showed a picture of a portion of a brick wall and a football with panelled sections and asked the pupil: 'Where can you find these tessellated shapes?' It seems to me that this was a question of doubtful validity, since to my eyes the two pictures were obviously of a wall and a football, and I needed to know nothing about tessellation to make the correct answer. I suspect the same applied to the pupil. The question might just as well be phrased 'What are these pictures of?'

All other aspects of the test were fine. They involved the child in working with actual examples of material that might or might not tessellate. The exemplars of the concept were novel, so that success in the test items could not be achieved by rote-learning. The lapse in the last question was not that it allowed rote answers but that one could arrive at the right answers through cues that were irrelevant to the concept being tested. The price of validity is eternal vigilance.

Questions of validity also caused problems for a student teacher who was trying to teach pupils of eleven to twelve the concept of election. We met him earlier in the discussion of concept teaching, where he had some trouble with identifying criterial attributes. The first error he identified could be regarded as a deficiency in his formative evaluation. He reports:

> I was guilty of a serious error of omission just prior to my evaluation of the pupils' learning. After I had asked the pupils to tell me what the three criterial attributes of an election are, which they did successfully, I did not present them with exemplars and non-exemplars of the concept of an election to make sure that the concept had been meaningfully learned.

This omission led to trouble in his final test. He presented them with the names of various people and asked the pupils to classify them as elected representatives or not: the Queen, the Prime Minister, a local Member of Parliament and various other public figures. The pupils were usually able to discriminate accurately but when asked to explain their decisions they did not list all the criterial attributes.

He thought there were two possible explanations for this shortcoming. Either they did not know enough about the people they were asked to classify or they had not learned the concept. He leans towards the former explanation and opines that if he had provided more information about the people the pupils would have referred to all the criterial attributes. He admits, however, that if he had taught the concept properly the pupils would have realised that all the criterial attributes must be present for any of the individuals to exemplify the concept.

He mentions another possibility. The rubric of the question may not have made fully clear what they were expected to do. Instead of asking the pupils, 'Explain why you give the answer you do,' he should have framed the question 'and give all the reasons why you give the answer you do'. He concludes his report with the view that his test was deficient and he could not be certain if the pupils had learned the concept meaningfully. Validity was not proven.

Whether it was or not, and whether the pupils learned the concept or not, there is one very important outcome to this piece of teaching. This student teacher was taking an analytical view of his own teaching using ideas from theory of human learning to identify its strengths and weaknesses. He is aware of the problems of achieving validity in testing and of achieving meaningful learning of concepts and has notions about how to overcome the deficiencies in his teaching. Very large numbers of student teachers qualify every year without being able to tell a concept from a cauliflower and with little chance of ever learning the difference.

The difficulty in ascertaining entry competence with accuracy, even in clinical conditions, is easy to underestimate. The case of a tutor in geography in a college for teacher training makes this point quite graphically. His aim was to teach the concept of humidity to a first-year student specialising in the teaching of geography. The tutor had information about the student from his public examination record and also gave a pre-test to the whole group of students to check their general level of understanding and to isolate common areas of difficulty.

After the teaching and testing the tutor reported:

> Because of the nature of the pre-test, plus information gained from Geography Department records, a reasonably accurate picture of the student's competence had confidently been established. This confidence later proved to be unsound in two areas arising during the teaching. One of these areas was in relation to the difficulties that might be experienced by the student regarding fractions and percentages. The other main problem was in differentiating between common meteorological instruments. Neither of these problems had been foreseen by the assessment of prior competence.

Tutor: . . . so if you were a meteorologist or you were involved in some way with the weather . . . how would you find out how much water vapour was present in the atmosphere?

Student: . . . by the use of a thermometer, barometer.

Tutor: Well . . . perhaps through the use of a thermometer, a barometer wouldn't . . . why not a barometer?

Student: . . . a barometer . . . is that to measure the actual heat?

The tutor had noted the student's failure in questions on the pre-test that dealt with these two points. He had, however, misinterpreted the reasons for the failure. The first question involved the use of humidity tables, and the tutor ascribed the student's failure to reply to the questions as indicating his unfamiliarity with the tables rather than a lack of mathematical ability. In his answer to the test of discrimination among various meteorological instruments the student had put 'hydrometer' instead of 'hygrometer', which the tutor had interpreted as a spelling mistake rather than a lack of knowledge of the instruments.

The results of these errors of judgment by the tutor had been an overestimation of the student's beginning ability that influenced his subsequent work and possibly his final test score. The tutor was experienced in teaching both pupils and student teachers. He was also particularly interested in the psychopedagogical approach to his work. Thus, it is reasonable to assume that his error was not the result of incompetence or lack of interest and application. The comment one might make about the nature of the pre-test was that it was insufficiently analytical and that it should have had items that tested specifics more. The item on the use of humidity tables should have involved very simple calculations, but if ability to perform more difficult calculations was necessary, this should have been discovered by the pedagogical analysis and the assessment of the ability incorporated as a separate element in the pre-test. To rule out the possibility of spelling error in discriminating among different instruments, he might have asked the student to discriminate among pictures or among real objects linked with their names already printed. It is easy to be wise after the event, but only if you have some insight into the nature of the 'event'. This tutor had the insight and drew the message for future teaching. It is my hope that the message readers will receive is the complex nature of assessing human learning, which is quite at variance with most approaches to testing.

Another student teacher learned a different lesson through her experiences teaching the concept of exports and imports. In the report of her teaching she says that she aimed 'to draw on not only their cognitive skills, but also those of handwriting, map drawing, organisation and verbalizing skills; in other words, I aim to avoid the testing of the pupils' skills of remembering facts'.

In the event she realised that this plethora of aims was counterproductive. The final test was a pencil and paper test to attempt to assess the pupils' grasp of the main concept. She did not test any of the other skills she mentioned in her report. In particular, she did not test their map-drawing ability. However, a good deal of the lesson time was spent on drawing a map of Jamaica. She comments that she should have provided the pupils with duplicated maps instead. She thought the most important error was that while she was aiming:

> to test their knowledge of the concepts I was teaching – not their map-drawing ability . . . far too much time and importance was attributed to this secondary activity. They could still have used their own initiative in the construction of this diagrammatic representation of the concepts by . . . suggesting ways of doing it but not 'wasting' time on what was not so important in my teaching of those particular concepts.

In a profession where this problem is endemic the insight this student obtained into the relationship between her teaching and her testing of the children's learning was of considerable significance for her future development. Some people will object to the notion of such a single-minded approach focused firmly on the main aim of the teaching, on the grounds that it stifles creativity and individuality. To my mind the opposite is usually the case, and pupils are sold short because of the teacher's confusion of aims and lack of pedagogical clarity. This student teacher had learned that there is much to be said for a firm focus, and as we have seen from the work of many of the teachers discussed in earlier chapters, clarity and a systematic approach are usually more liberating than seat of the pants pedagogy.

In this chapter I have tried to draw attention to what I believe to be some of the key aspects of assessment of pupil learning. I have not attempted to provide model questions even though I have given some instances of test items. I have stressed the complexity of assessment not to dismay but to encourage an imaginative approach to test making. I use the word 'making' advisedly to distinguish it from test construction, which normally connotes pencil and paper testing. I have stressed the place of teachers' own judgment in determining test validity but warned against being misled by tests of insufficient sensitivity, especially in regard to diagnostic tests prior to teaching. In all the examples of teachers' work that I have discussed, the insight into the strengths and weaknesses of their testing has been their perceptions of the way it relates to their teaching. Those perceptions have been informed by their grasp of psychopedagogical principles and their teaching experience. Teachers acquire the latter willy-nilly. Their lack of the former has all too often put them at the mercy of professional test constructors with formidable talents in statistics but little if any grasp of pedagogy. I hope the chapter will help to equip teachers to shift the focus of attention in assessment from the movement of figures to the actions of humans trying to learn.

10 Cultivating quality

MOTIVATION: WELLSPRING OF QUALITY

One could argue that this chapter should have been the first. For clearly, all the talk in the world about the nature of teacher action to improve pupil learning will come to naught if the learners are disaffected and resentful or anxious and afraid. There is eloquent testimony in the writing of many educationists that argues a prior condition for all teaching and learning: the existence of a relationship between teacher and learner that is humane and based on mutual respect. (See, among many others, School of Barbiana 1970 and Kohl 1977). I accept this viewpoint and associate myself with it. However, it seems to me that it is also necessary to try to understand the processes that enhance learning and to maximize these and minimize those that impede learning. The two considerations of the need to employ systematic approaches to teaching and the development of a positive relationship between teacher and learner are, in fact, mutually dependent and supportive of each other. A systematic approach can help teachers to understand better the nature of their relationships with their pupils and to improve it. A supportive, humane relationship can help pupils and teachers to engage in pedagogical activity that enhances the learning of both.

The interdependence of the different aspects of the pedagogical relationship seem to me to be evident in the work of the teachers discussed in the preceding chapters; hence my decision to present that work first. We have, thus, already glanced at some of the important factors that influence pupil attitudes in specific learning situations. I shall now attempt to look rather more closely at the question of energising pupil learning which might reasonably be viewed as one of the key teaching skills.

The energising of pupil learning is commonly referred to as 'motivation'. Like so many labels in most fields of human activity the word has little explanatory value. A specialist dictionary of psychology refers to motivation as 'extremely important but definitionally elusive' (Reber 1985). It is thought of as an internal state driving the organism to action. Several different variations on this theme are proposed in explanation, but the main point is that no one motivator can be seen as the sole energiser. Physiological needs, innate reactions, learned predispositions and psychosocial factors are among the most prominent elements. A particularly important consideration is that motivation is closely related to emotion, which was the burden of my opening remarks. Unlike innate reactions, emotional states are not cyclical or regular but depend on specific situations and the way the situations are evaluated for their personal significance. In teaching, teachers are the main determiners of the learning environment that evokes emotional states in learners. It is a considerable responsibility for them to understand how to ensure that overall the learning conditions are experienced positively by their pupils.

There is one other important point. There is a very close link between the affective states of human beings and language. 'Fear' may label a very basic and primitive emotion – one that we can, perhaps, readily impute to non-human animals. But what about the way Margaret felt when the vicar's wife corrected her grammar? She sat 'abashed' (see Chapter 8). What about 'disaffection', a word I have already used in relation to pupils' emotions? What about such things as 'elation', 'contrition', 'remorse' and the innumerable subtle varieties of feeling to which most humans are prone? The point is that affective factors permeate the whole of the learning–teaching encounter, even though, on the face of it, it may seem essentially cognitive and verbal. The nuances in the use of language by teachers in all learning situations are all likely to carry an affective component, and this needs to be borne in mind constantly. The use of video recordings and systematic approaches to particular teaching tasks will help to reveal the way these processes operate in classrooms.

INTRINSIC OR EXTRINSIC?

The dictionary view of motivation cited above saw it as a state internal to the individual. This is a view that most psychologists would accept. However, this has not prevented discussion on the relative merits of intrinsic and extrinsic motivation from taking place. Intrinsic motivation, as the name implies, lies within the individual. In terms of school learning, intrinsic motivation would imply a self-sustaining desire to learn. Extrinsic motivation is motivation produced by outside forces such as high marks in tests.

I think there is a lack of clarity in the dichotomous view of motivation. I do not see how an internal state (motivation) can be external to the individual. As I see it, all motivation is internal. Sometimes its manifestation is a consequence of existing (learned) dispositions, and sometimes it will be manifested as a response to events in the immediate temporal or spatial environment. I am quite happy to talk about intrinsic and extrinsic *motivators*, since this allows one to talk about motivation being produced by outside or internal factors, the motivators. The state itself (internal) is the resultant motivation.

I don't think this point is nit-picking. It draws attention to the fact that intrinsic motivation is not a mysterious 'given' but largely learned and therefore strongly influenced by outside events at some stage in an individual's life history. It is unlikely that any person is born intrinsically motivated to work for hours at differential calculus or a computer keyboard or to write poetry. And yet large numbers of people, under no external influences, spend enormous amounts of time applying themselves to this type of activity. The more teachers can understand how people acquire such motivation, the better able they will be able to develop intrinsic motivation in their pupils.

REINFORCERS

It is probably better to talk about reinforcers and reinforcement than about external motivation, since they are the things that develop motivational states. Many reinforcers are within the teacher's grasp and, with understanding, can be used to develop interests that become an abiding part of the learners' fundamental attitudes. I discussed the role of motivation in human learning in my preliminary remarks on the subject in Chapter 1. The basic influences bear on learning in formal education but with considerable refinement and subtlety.

However, in all the talk about motivation and reinforcers in teaching, one makes a very important assumption. That is that the basic needs of the learners, such as need for food, shelter, warmth and so on, are satisfied and that praise, attention and encouragement, together with such things as satisfaction of curiosity and the competent execution of tasks, will act as reinforcers in the classroom. This may be a reasonable assumption so far as most readers are concerned, although even in affluent societies schools have among their pupils some whose basic needs are not fulfilled. Children from such backgrounds need different prescriptions from those this book can offer, but they are not pedagogical ones.

ARRANGING REINFORCEMENT

I caution you not to look up 'reinforcement' in a dictionary of psychological terms. If you do you will find problems at least as acute as those presented by 'emotion' and 'motivation'. None of the many usages of the term satisfy all psychologists, and some definitions are circular. We must, therefore, tread warily with a sceptical toe to feel our way. The dominant current use of the term explains little but enables us to talk about one of the most pervasive phenomena in the life of all animals. This is the so-called 'neutral definition' because it makes no presumptions about underlying processes. 'Reinforcement is any event, stimulus, act, response or information which when made to depend upon the response that preceded it, will serve to increase the frequency of that response' (Reber 1985).

Much of the research that has been influential in developing reinforcement theory has been carried out on non-human animals. While some of the very powerful basic principles of this body of theory operate in human learning, other principles are sometimes overlooked. The missing factor is that human beings are verbal animals whose actions are influenced by abstractions as well as by the satisfaction of basic pre-verbal needs. I have considered this earlier when I discussed language and concept formation. Provided we keep in mind the power of the abstract as well as the concrete environment to influence human learning, we can draw on principles derived from work with non-humans to provide insight into the way we encourage learning in the classroom.

One of the most important principles in this context was developed by Skinner (1954, 1962). This is the idea of successive approximations to the desired outcome by the learner, sometimes referred to as 'shaping'. This principle has been used to train animals to carry out quite complicated actions by giving hungry animals small amounts of food, first for quite gross activity that bears some resemblance to the desired outcome and gradually increasing the refinement of the activity necessary to produce the food, until eventually the aimed-for activity is observed. Pigeons have been trained to execute such improbable activities as turning in figures-of-eight and pecking buttons to provide a great variety of outcomes. In human learning these procedures are readily transferable to training very young children in basic skills such as putting shoes or socks on or tying laces. I am not suggesting that we should throw food to young children, as Skinner did to his pigeons, but that we arrange some event that is likely to lead to the repetition of the action we consider contributory to the outcome we are aiming for.

In the case of young children learning to dress themselves, one can easily imagine that a good reinforcer might be a parental cuddle or words of approbation. We are now considering the nature of reinforcers. What phenomena seem to be reinforcing of human behaviour? This takes us back to our struggle with the definition. There are so many possible reinforcers that depend on environmental forces, the physiology of individuals, their state of health, or their life history that the range is probably infinite. The challenge facing teachers and students of psychopedagogy is to identify effective reinforcers that are valuable in encouraging pupil learning.

There is a fair amount of agreement that approbation such as one might use with a small child applies very generally in learning. One other reinforcer that is widely accepted is the successful achievement of a task, perhaps solving a problem or the sheer delight in doing something well. The label for this phenomenon is usually 'competence motivation'. These two motivators are closely linked, although at first blush it seems possible to separate them. They should be closely linked in the thoughts of any teachers trying to reinforce their pupils. If they were not, teachers would be in the predicament of wishing to encourage children who are not succeeding in the learning tasks they have been set. It is not impossible to do this, however. Many teachers try to do this every day. But every one of those teachers is faced with the problem of encouraging pupils while avoiding reinforcing activity that is irrelevant or deleterious to the learning they are trying to develop. The more failure there is, the more difficult the teacher's task. It is a measure of the gross misapprehension by the majority of people in education that the opposite view seems to prevail and 'good' teachers get to teach 'good' pupils, rather than being allowed to direct their talents where they are most needed.

It therefore behoves teachers to do what they can to prevent pupil failure. This implies that they think before they teach, and, indeed, preliminary planning of learning activities is a crucial element in the skill of reinforcing to enhance pupil motivation. If planning is done competently the implementing of suitable procedures when the teaching is actually going on will be considerably simpler, whereas it may well not be possible if the mismatch between the teacher's activities and the pupils' state of expertise is extreme.

As we have observed in the discussion of the work of different teachers in earlier chapters, the mismatch often exists unperceived. Time and again we encounter the rueful comment that pupils' prior competence and readiness for the teaching were wrongly estimated by the teacher. Or that the analysis of the key concepts had been insufficiently thorough. When the prerequisite skills and concepts have been adequately learned, the next steps should not prove too difficult, and the chances of pupil success will be high. If the steps are too steep failure is almost inevitable. Apart from the cognitive gain from carefully graded progression through the sub-tasks of new learning such as I have discussed earlier *passim*, the affective consequences are clearly crucial and, equally clearly, the two interact. A learner failing is not only not equipped cognitively for the next stage but also impeded by the negative emotion resulting from failure. Which is just another way of saying success breeds success.

Ensuring success by arranging carefully graded progression of task difficulty cannot be done *ad hoc* in the heat of the moment. Prior planning will need to work out the optimum gradient, and that implies thought about the steps as they relate to the overall learning task. This, of course, raises the question of pedagogical analysis, and this, again, is one of the things most mentioned by the teachers we have met earlier when they have reflected on what they needed to do to improve their teaching. An adequate pedagogical analysis will produce pointers to the careful sequencing of the presentation of exemplars and non-exemplars in concept learning and also to the varying of the salience of criterial attributes, so that the pupils will experience success at all stages of the learning. In non-conceptual learning the task will be to present the stimuli to be paired, discriminated among, and generalised from, in a similar gradient of difficulty. This also aims to ensure that the learner experiences success regularly but that the difficulty of giving the correct response increases as competence increases. A very important element in the skill of reinforcing is thus a preactive skill: the skill of deciding beforehand how to arrange pupils' learning experiences so as to enhance the chances of successful progression through the learning sub-tasks.

In the interactive phase of teaching the actual deployment of reinforcement skills is still complex, even if the preactive planning has been appropriate. In new learning, it will be necessary to identify and react to all responses if possible. In most teaching situations it is impossible to do this on a one-to-one basis; a fact that lies behind Skinner's view that, as a reinforcing agent, the teacher is out of date (Skinner, 1954). Despite Skinner, there are still a lot of teachers around. And since the mechanisation of teaching seems no nearer than it did when Skinner delivered that opinion, I think it important that we examine the problem to see what can be done about it.

Skinner himself made an important contribution when he began to apply his ideas to teaching. In the early 1960s he had visions of improving teaching through the principles which he employed in experimental conditions with animals. He designed teaching programs in book form and for use with teaching machines based on these principles.

Although programmed learning had a phenomenal vogue in the 1960s, Skinner's position was constantly under attack from those who thought his attempt to apply principles developed from the study of the learning of rats and pigeons to human teaching and learning was too simplistic. To my mind the main error was to attempt to apply the principles to all types of human learning. As I suggested above, some of the earlier stages in learning certainly rely on principles such as those proposed by Skinner. But, as many psychologists would argue, much of human learning, being conceptual and dependent on symbols, cannot be explained or controlled in the same way. However, the crucial thing that Skinner brought to pedagogical thinking was his insistence on the careful preparation and pre-testing of the instructional material. The object of this careful structuring was to keep the level of success of the learner at a very high level and thereby keep reinforcement too at a high level.

Time has shown that the prototypical Skinnerian unit of instruction, just a sentence or two, has been unpopular with learners and teachers. It has also shown that writing programs is an unpopular activity with instructors and authors. It is so much more difficult than arranging schedules of reinforcement for pigeons. Ideas about the nature of concept learning have also undermined the purist Skinnerian position. However, there is little doubt that notions of careful structuring to facilitate reinforcement have permeated much of the thinking in the field of human instruction, which takes us back to my earlier comments on the virtues of preactive preparation.

It also points a way forward. Teachers skilled at reinforcing will have in mind the factors discussed above. They will take the necessary preactive steps to ensure a high rate of success by their pupils in the intermediate stages of learning and they will reinforce by approval or other means, such as making the facts of success clear to the learners or giving them the opportunity of other activity the teacher knows is reinforcing to the learners. In the process of new learning teachers should do their best to reinforce every correct step on the road to mastery. When competence in the new learning is achieved it can be maintained and consolidated by occasional reinforcement, a point based on Skinner's finding that random intermittent reinforcement is particularly effective in maintaining activity. Reinforcement of this type resembles what happens in classrooms when teachers encourage pupils at random by commending correct work when mastery is achieved. It is a different matter in the intermediate stages of learning. In normal classroom conditions it is impossible for teachers to reinforce every correct action by all pupils on the road to mastery by individual approbation.

This difficulty can be addressed by adopting some of the procedures used in the devising of instructional material, as in the teaching programs I mentioned earlier. It is assumed that success is reinforcing and the program is devised by repeated tryouts along the lines I described in the development of the program on teaching, until success is more or less guaranteed. Self-instructional material of this type can be used in classrooms, but teachers wishing to implement the principles could achieve similar results through carefully planned materials related to their teaching which the pupils could use to check their work and, assuming the learning gradient had been successfully devised, thus achieve success and the accompanying reinforcement.

The structure of one such program may exemplify the nature of an approach embodying many of the attributes of material that provides for self-monitoring with younger children. This was a short program to introduce children of around ten years old to the seventeenth-century Great Fire of London (Stones 1968a, 1971). The aim was to involve children in work that would convey the idea of simultaneity in the mass of activities that were taking place at the time, using various materials, some from contemporary sources and some specially prepared. Because things were happening all at once there was no one obvious main sequence of events. Therefore an attempt was made to allow the pupils to approach the material at different points according to their interests and to generate their own strategies in working through the material.

Choice of access to the material was afforded by a card with a menu of choices related to the main events taking place at the time. The key events and their main aspects were identified in the pedagogical analysis, and these made up the list of choices on the menu. They included such things as 'Why did the fire spread?' 'How do we know about the fire?' 'What was fire-fighting equipment like in those days?' After making a choice, the pupil was guided to the learning materials related to that choice. Having worked through the material pupils were presented with review material, similar to those discussed in the program on teaching, to which they have to construct responses. Having completed the exercises in the review material they are referred to a 'comparator', which provides feedback about the answers given to the review material. The nature of the answers was decided in the trying out process when the program was being developed.

The comparator is the key to the provision of feedback in this instructional material. It is based on an original pedagogical analysis and refined by try outs. Once it is prepared the teacher can use the material with some confidence that the pupils are in a position to monitor their learning and, because of the earlier trials, will be reasonably sure that the feedback will be reinforcing, since a learning gradient appropriate to the level of competence has been determined.

Feedback and reinforcement from the group and the teacher are also available, since the core program material refers individual pupils to the teacher if a pupil's suggestion seems to indicate that it is desirable. Reference to the group is built in when certain questions are suggested for group discussion, for example, the ethical problem posed by the behaviour of people who would not allow their houses to be pulled down to make a firebreak and thus allowed it to spread.

Another possible approach to providing regular feedback and reinforcement in large classes is to use the resources of the learning group itself. There is a long tradition of group work in reading in which a class is divided into a number of small groups in which pupils read in turn while the others in the group provide corrective feedback where necessary. There is also a tradition of peer tutoring in which pupils work in pairs, where the more competent pupils work with the less competent. This arrangement is not a return to the nineteenth-century monitorial system, in which selected pupils assumed the role of teachers of groups of other children. In general it involves pupils in working together, following the teachers' own introductory activities. Their main activity, as I have indicated, would be to provide feedback to one another. This would not be possible under normal classroom conditions, given the number of pupils. It seems to me that apart from the feedback to the pupils who may be having problems, the set-up is very similar to those in protocol work. The pupils are all engaged in interpreting the learning situation and thus consolidating the understanding of the successful pupil, as well as assisting the less successful pupils by providing ameliorative feedback.

There is evidence that the more competent pupils do, in fact, benefit from this kind of activity, as well as the less competent (Limbrick *et al.* 1985). Other variations on the theme of peer tutoring have produced similar results (Glynn 1985, Schunk 1987), and it seems that this method of dealing with the difficulties of providing feedback and reinforcement has much to offer. What is needed is more systematic exploration of its possibilities.

Involving pupils in peer tutoring does not just hand over responsibility to them. Teacher preparation needs to be at least as thorough as in any form of classroom organisation. Indeed, the more one moves from the delivery mode of teaching to the modes outlined in earlier chapters, the higher the degree of skill demanded of the teacher. By the same token, the skills demanded of pupils are more complex. Sponges need few skills, but active learners with a responsibility for their own development need a lot. Arranging environments that will facilitate the pupils' learning of those skills is more difficult than writing out lecture notes whose main detectable effect is exercising the teacher's vocal cords.

The idea of 'debriefing' that I discussed in previous chapters seems to me a potent development in involving the learning group in the control of their own learning. Recall that this involved pupils discussing with the teacher their performance in learning particular problem-solving skills. This was not just a session in which the teacher told the pupils what the correct answers were. In fact it resembled the work with protocols that I have discussed earlier. Just as the teachers have used video recordings of their teaching to help them reflect on their teaching, so the group used the way they had tackled problems in a session of group reflection on their learning. In the case of the orienteering group this involved a criterion of 'elegance' of solution. This group activity is a cooperative exercise of type B skills in which the principles underlying the activity are brought to bear on the pupils' own attempts to employ new skills.

Giving pupils a stake in their learning in this way is likely to be a powerful motivator, apart from the value of such sessions for their cognitive development. I believe it would also be very worthwhile engaging at times in preactive discussions appropriate to the age of the pupils, a form of teacher and pupil 'briefing'. Many of the teachers referred to in this book came close to this kind of activity in their attempts to ascertain the pupils' readiness for new learning. What would be needed in a briefing session would be to open it up to take in pupils' suggestions and questions rather than making it a one-way process as it tends to be at the moment. All the student teachers whose work is reported in this book had briefing sessions with trainee supervisors who were all experienced teachers, and this was reported repeatedly by the beginning teachers to be most useful.

I have developed this approach to great effect with student teachers studying psychopedagogy. Once they are familiar with the main principles and the way these principles relate to their practical teaching, they can become involved in the control of their own learning. They are learning to teach in the light of systematic pedagogical theory. Their learning experiences comprise an amalgam of practical teaching and group seminar discussion to lay a sound conceptual foundation. At an early stage the tutor introduces the use of video-recorded teaching as protocol material for the students to appraise in the light of their learned theory. Soon the student teachers are recording their own practical teaching and bringing the recordings to the group for scrutiny. They are then treating recordings of their own teaching as protocol material. This is what might be called 'group reflection'.

The affective side of this is extremely important. Apart from the benefits of group work of this type, a very important aspect is the way bringing one's work to the group, at first a potentially threatening situation, can become objectified so that the whole group is appraising 'the teaching' rather than an individual teacher's teaching. There is one further step in this set-up. As tutor I counsel the student teachers on their teaching in a group situation with video recording. My teaching is then open to appraisal.

The work of some of the teachers I discussed earlier indicates that techniques such as this would be possible with younger people. When pupils' views about teaching have been taken seriously they have made perceptive and helpful comments (Meighan 1977). It is very sad that many senior teachers were outraged at Meighan's suggestion that pupils might be consulted.

My own experience and that of the teachers whose work I have reported suggest that it might be worth bringing pupils even more centrally into the teaching–learning interaction by presenting teaching situations as cooperative learning encounters, such as are suggested by some educators dubbed 'progressive'. I shall discuss this question further in my last chapter.

Developments such as I have just described are quite antithetical to the classroom ambience characteristic of delivery teaching. There is every reason to suppose that they would have a very positive influence on the affective atmosphere of the classroom, and this would include the level of pupils' motivation. Classrooms with an emphasis on the type of pupil–teacher and pupil–pupil interaction I have been discussing seem to enhance motivation and enjoyment of learning (Fry and Coe 1980).

They would also bear strongly on another aspect of motivation. This is the effect of people's perceptions of the causes of success or failure in tasks they attempt. If it seems to them that failure occurs because of some inherent defect in themselves such as lack of 'intelligence', they are likely to expect future failure about which they can do nothing. Since nothing can be done to change the way they are, there is no point in trying. Failure breeds failure. If, on the other hand, they attribute their failure to lack of effort, they are less likely to expect failure in the future since there is something they can do about it, namely work harder. In the first case motivation suffers, in the second it probably will not (Weiner 1984).

Allied to this are the perceptions of learners about where the control over their learning conditions lies. If they have no part in the way their learning is structured, if the teaching is unresponsive to their individual needs, they are once again in a no-win situation. This time, however, motivation suffers, not because of defects within themselves, but because of a defective pedagogy. The inwardly directed negative affect associated with the former is replaced by negative affect directed at the pedagogical system. The former state evokes feelings of inadequacy and worthlessness, the latter evokes feelings of resentment and alienation.

There are other aspects to attribution theory, which is what I have been alluding to in the last few paragraphs. However, it seems to me that they are all functions of the nature of the pedagogy involved. Freire and other libertarian educationalists have realised this and tried to involve learners in more control over their learning (Smith 1982). Although the teachers whose work we are considering were not explicitly espousing such an approach, the logic of psychopedagogy moves them in that direction. Ideas about enhancing motivation permeate their work even when the main aim is to explore ways of teaching concepts or problem solving.

Thus, a pedagogy that takes into account, in a systematic and diagnostic way, what pupils' existing competencies are before embarking upon new learning is doing two important things. On the one hand it is taking action that will help to prevent any pupil from failing; on the other it is signalling to pupils that their needs are being taken into consideration and that they have some stake in their own learning. If this diagnosis were expanded into a 'briefing' such as I suggested, the pupils would be even more involved and in a position to influence their learning. The same can be said about the debriefing where the teaching and its outcome are analysed later by pupils and teacher. Note: this is not the same as going over the exam questions, as is often done in conventional approaches to teaching and testing.

The emphasis on criterion-referenced and diagnostic testing also contributes to the development of a positive classroom climate and pupil motivation. Both climate and motivation suffer when norm referenced tests are the staple. Norm referenced testing leads to severe discouragement for those pupils who have few academic successes in competition with their peers. It jeopardizes cooperative and group work such as I referred to above as assisting motivation. It undermines the solidarity of the class as a learning group and it does not encourage intrinsic motivation. Pupils work to beat others rather than because of an intrinsic interest in the work itself. (Ames 1984) Criterion referencing, especially if it has an ipsative orientation, is much more enhancive of intrinsic motivation.

Cooperative working, especially when the group is working on a group task, is particularly motivating. It has the effect of moderating positive and negative self-perceptions resulting from individual performance, and it reduces performance anxiety. There is also evidence that cooperative learning is more enjoyable than learning individually and that this tends to enhance intrinsic motivation for learning. (Ames 1984)

I am quite familiar with the arguments that pour scorn on the kind of classroom climate favoured in my remarks and the work of the people cited. After all, it goes, when the pupils leave school they enter a social and political jungle where competition is lauded and commercial aggression is a virtue. They should be trained for this and not for an unreal world of liberal fantasy. This argument serves to emphasise the value-laden nature of all considerations of pedagogy. One takes one's position according to one's values. This does not alter the fact that cooperative learning is more effective and enjoyable. There is a school of thought, I believe, that holds that learning should *not* be enjoyable so its adherents would not support cooperative learning on those grounds. I imagine, however, that nobody, whatever their values, would argue for ineffective learning. Paradoxically, it would appear, learning survival skills for life in a commercial jungle effectively could well be best accomplished in cooperative learning groups! I know of no research in this field. Perhaps the Harvard Business School might be interested.

Reinforcement and feedback

Throughout this discussion of reinforcement and motivation, questions about feedback have been implicit. Very often in discussions about teaching they are used as synonyms. As I said earlier, this usage is erroneous and the error is of considerable importance for any teacher trying to improve teaching and for anyone trying to investigate pedagogical theory and practice. Feedback gives learners knowledge of the results of their actions and is indispensable for learning to take place. The heuristic on pedagogical analysis reminds teachers of this and many examples have been given of teachers arranging feedback using different methods of implementing the basic principles. The teacher's speech is probably the most important mode of providing feedback because of its great flexibility and its role as a symbolling system.

This flexibility is particularly important in the delicate operation of maintaining motivation when the learner is not succeeding particularly well. Information that one has done well in a learning task is likely to be seen as reinforcing and will enhance motivation. Information that one has failed, although essential for learning to take place, can often be far from reinforcing. Instead of enhancing motivation it could well reduce it, since feedback in this case is viewed as a punisher, which is more or less the opposite of a reinforcer.

Teachers intent on improving pupils' learning will need to tread very delicately indeed in the way they use their understanding of the processes of reinforcement and feedback. If they use the insensitive but time-honoured method of rewarding success and punishing failure, they may well improve the self-regard and enhance the motivation of the successful but at least doubly de-motivate the pupil who does not succeed. I say 'doubly', because in addition to the fact of failure and the incurring of the teacher's displeasure, the experience of being blamed signals to the unsuccessful pupil that the fault lies within him/her and is not amenable to correction. Profoundly, for the teacher, it forecloses any consideration that the fault might lie in the teaching. It is a method likely to lead to pedagogical stagnation.

A skilful teacher will arrange things so that when pupils fail to learn they are not discouraged. The skill lies in providing genuine feedback about the causes of failure while at the same time providing reinforcement that acts against its punishing effects. This should help to deflect the attribution of the cause of failure from unalterable factors within the learners and enhance motivation through the knowledge that the pedagogical system is sensitive to their needs. There is no question of reinforcing mistakes. The skill lies in giving accurate feedback which helps the learners to diagnose their problems and to do better next time, while at the same time encouraging them in their efforts. Knowing that the teacher does not think any less of them because they have failed in a piece of learning is obviously more likely to enhance their learning and motivation than by piling punishment on top of failure. Sadly, however, schools all over the world daily operate this double-barrelled system of punishment.

I have faced this problem myself in my work with teachers and student teachers in the fields of practical pedagogy and the training of tutors of student teachers on practical teaching. The problem is the same with both groups. How to convey realistic feedback when a teacher or tutor counselling a student teacher on teaching practice has made what seem erroneous pedagogical moves in teaching or counselling. The way I tackle this problem is encapsulated in a heuristic guide for supervisors of student teachers (Stones 1984a) and mentioned in the heuristic guide referred to later in this chapter (p. 262). Briefly, one tries, through discussion, to lead the learner to make a self-appraisal of the teaching in the way one would make an appraisal of a protocol. One does not tell the teacher what the 'mistakes' were, but encourages analytical comments indicative of a realisation of the flaws in the teaching. When such comments are forthcoming, one makes positive comment that reinforces the teacher for the accurate appraisal of the teaching, while at the same time ensuring that the teacher gets helpful and accurate feedback about the teaching. In brief, one congratulates the teacher on identifying the weaknesses in the teaching.

There are several important points about this procedure. Video-recording is almost essential. Unless one has the facility to reinstate what happened in the lesson and even to re-run the tape several times, it is impossible to take an analytical look at what happened. Audio-recording would be better than nothing, but much is lost if the visual element is absent. It is important to control one's urge to tell teachers just what was right and what was wrong with the teaching. Give them time to make their own analyses. And if they do not identify any glaring weakness, it is still better to bite one's tongue and leave the subject for another time, when one will also have reflected on why a particular teacher was unable to make a satisfactory appraisal. One other point is to stress the need for analysis. As the music teacher whose work I reported remarked: it is poor evaluation just to say this is good or this is bad; there have to be analytical criteria to back up this appraisal.

I do not pretend that procedures of this type are simple; far from it. Nevertheless I have found that few teachers are totally unable to see any deficiencies in their teaching in such discussions.

But this work was done with teachers. What about work with pupils? I suggest that work such as was done by many teachers we have met in this book verges on this type of activity. Clearly the numbers of pupils involved creates problems not faced in the work of supervisors of teaching practice. In many of the cases I have reported, however, I suggest that the teachers were approaching this kind of activity. The debriefing session I reported and the careful arrangement of feedback both address the problem (p. 198). In these cases, as in practically all the cases reported, video-recording was available. In most developed countries most schools have the equipment for this type of work and in a few it has been used for recording teachers' teaching for subsequent appraisal. Very few, however, do this in connection with a coherent body of pedagogical theory and this is the vital thing. It seems to me that there is enormous potential for enhancing motivation by developing this kind of self-appraisal by pupils of their own learning.

I have discussed feedback when talking about cognitive skills and, of course, it is a phenomenon that provides a good example of the fact that the cognitive and the affective interpenetrate all the time. Economical learning necessitates careful structuring of the learning experiences of pupils. Optimally the structuring should be such that learners would have a range of experiences that would enable them to cope in any situations that necessitate the new learning. Errorless learning would be the ideal case here. It is also extremely unlikely to occur. But the ideal coincides with the ideal state of reinforcement and feedback. All feedback would inform learners that they were succeeding and should therefore continue along the same lines. At the same time the learners would be acquiring confidence through the reinforcing effects of success. In other words the affective and the cognitive effects of the optimally structured learning conditions would coincide. A superbly skilful teacher would approach this ideal state. However, in devising a heuristic for the guidance of lesser mortals we should still be advised to look for this capability.

The idea of errorless learning may raise a few eyebrows. As is well known, we learn by our mistakes. As with many folk sayings, there is a good deal of truth in this one. The point is, of course, that it relates to learning and not teaching. Or, if you prefer, learning without a teacher as opposed to learning with a teacher. In the latter case, the learning environment is quite deliberately structured; in the former no such structuring takes place. This structuring does not just protect learners from error, only to expose them to more error when the teacher's support is withdrawn. The skill of the teacher lies in arranging maximum feedback for the learners. The professional obligation to do this implies that the teacher will anticipate any information the pupils might get by way of feedback from making mistakes. The pupils could well be better prepared then for novel circumstances than pupils who had 'learned through their mistakes'.

There is one use of knowledge about the effects of reinforcement that diverges from the drift of my argument in this chapter. It stems from the behaviour modification movement. This is an approach that draws heavily on the work of Skinner and has focused on class management techniques. In this type of application there is little of what I would consider to be of a pedagogical nature. By and large the exponents of the approach take as their criterion of success the decrease of negative behaviour by pupils and the increase of time on task. Thus, if pupils are not disruptive and apply themselves to their work the conditions for success are satisfied.

While I accept the desirability of this kind of criterion I do not think that it carries much pedagogical weight. This is acknowledged by some practitioners who aver that their advice is limited to methods of class control and time on task (Wheldhall and Merrett 1987a). They consider that the teachers can supply the pedagogical component and do not address the complexities of learning that I have considered in earlier chapters. The obvious flaw in work that stops at this point is that it could be equally a prescription for pedagogical disaster as for success. Many teachers have cottoned on to the fact that an activity such as dictating notes to pupils is a copper-bottomed way of keeping them on task and quiescent. This is the apotheosis of delivery methods and a pedagogical cop-out. None of the teachers referred to in this book were of this ilk and would not be satisfied with advice that stopped short of addressing the more fundamental problems of teaching.

This is not to deride the contribution of people working in the field of behaviour modification. They have done us a service in that they have made very useful suggestions about methods of coping with problems of 'control', although critics argue that the concept of 'control' using behavioural techniques is inappropriate in principle and different kinds of relationships in classrooms would remove the problem and render the cure redundant.

MEMO FOR MOTIVATION

I should now like to draw together the threads of this discussion of the important aspects of the pedagogy of motivation as they appear to me and present them in the form of a reminder of the key principles to have in mind when thinking about motivating pupils. Unlike the other heuristics, which dealt with aspects of learning that are to some extent amenable to discussion separately, considerations of motivation, reinforcement and punishment relate to all types and conditions of learning. They should permeate all planning and interactive aspects of teaching and never be far from any teacher's mind.

But even if a teacher achieves the level of application suggested in this counsel of perfection there could still be problems. One of the most common findings in the work I have done over the years with many teachers is that they all misjudge the level of reinforcement they use in their teaching. This mismatch is realised only after the event, when teachers have made video recordings of their teaching. I therefore suggest that any teacher wishing to try out the memo on motivation make a recording of the teaching for subsequent analysis.

I hope the discussion in this chapter so far will enable the reader to see the implications behind the relatively bald statements of desirable teaching attributes in the heuristic, so that the reader will be able to apply the suggestions in a variety of situations. It is well to remember that the appraisal of teaching in this way is a type B skill in my category system and is, therefore, a complex skill. It would be useful to view the recording with a colleague, so as to increase the chances of identifying key aspects of the teaching. Student teachers, particularly, would be well advised to discuss the teaching, before it takes place, with a tutor. Afterwards the tutor's input would be to focus attention on the critical incidents in the teaching as they related to the items in the memo. Whether neophyte or experienced teacher, one can benefit greatly from collegial appraisal of recordings, always bearing in mind the pedagogical guidelines that focus on the deep structures of teaching and steering the discussion away from surface chat about the cosmetics of the teaching.

HEURISTIC FOR MOTIVATION

This list sets out in brief the key teacher activities that are likely to enhance pupil motivation. Not all the items will be relevant in all situations, and the list is intended to be not prescriptive but suggestive. If recordings are available it is illuminating to view the recording with the heuristic in mind and possibly rate the teaching so as to produce an ipsative evaluation. In this way the strengths and weaknesses of a specific piece of teaching are identified without making any comparisons among teachers.

A   Preactive

1 Make a pedagogical analysis of the teaching objectives to arrange a learning gradient sufficiently gentle to ensure that the pupils achieve high levels of success.
2 Plan for feedback to follow pupils' activities at a very high level. This would probably involve the use of methods other than the teacher's own actions or words.

B Interactive

3 In all new learning reinforce every correct response at first. When learning is established shift to a random variable schedule. (Basically this involves taking care to reinforce each time at the beginning and remembering to reinforce from time to time later).

4 Arrange to reinforce by methods other than the teacher's actions: e.g. peer approval, experience of success, satisfaction of curiosity. (This could well be a consequence of good planning at 1 and 2)

5 Involve the whole group in reinforcement by encouraging cooperative work.

6 Provide for vicarious reinforcement by including a whole group in encouragement of effort and correct (or near correct) attempts.

7 Recognize punishers and, ideally, avoid them altogether. Never punish for mistakes in learning. Instead examine your teaching.

8 Ignore undesirable behaviour consistently, unless harmful to others, and engage other students in activities to deflect their attention from misbehaving pupils.

9 Reinforce any positive behaviour on the part of pupils acting generally negatively.

10 Ensure that feedback planned in item 2 is reinforcing. (The suggestions made earlier about reinforcing the identification of errors by the pupils themselves is applicable here).

C Evaluative (much more rare than in content teaching)

11 Attempt to assess pupils' enthusiasm for the activities involved in the teaching. (Difficult; but careful observation of class activities, involvement in the work and the extent to which the pupils maintain an interest outside the class are possible indications).

The acid test of a good, affective classroom climate would be to allow the pupils free choice as to whether they would attend or not. But this test itself depends on other considerations prior to the planning or execution of the teaching. The best teaching in the world would not inspire or motivate pupils who thought that what the teacher was trying to teach them was completely irrelevant. It can be argued that part of a teacher's job is to help pupils to see the relevance of their studies, but it could hardly be thought that this should apply in all circumstances. The questions of 'relevance' takes us outside the realm of theory and practice of teaching into such fields as philosophy and politics. *Force majeure* may work against what teachers think is appropriate. In such cases teachers may have to make the best of a bad job and do their best to make their teaching interesting to the pupils. They may also do their best to change the way things are. In both cases they will be working with the good of their pupils in mind. And that is what matters.

MOTIVATION IN PRACTICE

Feedback to the teacher

Before considering questions of motivation in specific cases of teaching, I should like to refer back to my remarks at the beginning of the book about the use of video recordings of classroom events. As I pointed out there, and as has been evident in the work of teachers we have been considering, recordings provide a unique source of feedback to teachers, and feedback is as important to teachers as to any other learners. In the case of reinforcement, feedback of this type is particularly useful. This is because of the subtle nature of the exchanges involved. The exchange quoted on p. 203 when Margaret was 'corrected' by the parson's wife, although fictitious, illustrates the point beautifully. I commented on the irony in the novelist's account and on the subtlety of the emotion implied by the words that she sat 'abashed'. In the context of the exchange the irony refines the connotations of the word 'abashed' even further, adding an element of amusement to Margaret's reaction. The affective element in her reaction is so complex that it virtually defies description.

The novelist's imagination has preserved in print her insight into human interactions which enlightens and enlarges our understanding of human relationships. Countless such exchanges are taking place constantly, mostly little appreciated and often undetected. Exchanges in teaching are no exception. They are multifarious, multifaceted, extremely complex and very often unobserved by teachers. Attempts have been made to chart these interactions, but, being made *in vivo* by the use of coded check lists of types of classroom interactions, they are very crude measures (see for example Flanders 1970). This is not to denigrate the work done on classroom interaction. In their time these techniques broke new ground and paved the way for more sophisticated techniques. Recording of interactions using the Flanders system is often done by noting what is happening every few seconds. However, if one views a videotape of a teacher–pupil interaction one can often find material with profound significance for the teaching within the space of one or two seconds. In addition the recording actually reinstates the important aspects of the interaction, not merely such things as 'teacher questions pupil' which is the type of information noted in many records of classroom interactions. There is also the crucial difference that one can view the tape as often as one feels the need. Further, the recording has the visual as well as the verbal component of the interaction, and this is important as I have suggested and as studies of non-verbal elements in teaching demonstrate. (Neill 1986) In the same way as one reads a text, such as I have done with the Gaskell extract, one can read and re-read the recording, each time uncovering nuances that were lost in the ephemeral classroom situation.

By using two cameras and special effects devices one can add an extra dimension that is totally impossible in life. One can view the teacher through the eyes of the pupils and at the same time see the pupils from the teacher's viewpoint. It is thus possible to monitor very closely the actual interactions of teacher and pupils. In small group work and in individual teaching the recording of interaction is particularly effective, but even with full class teaching, useful recordings can be made. In the discussion that follows some of the teachers made use of this type of recording; some made use of one camera. Some also transcribed the verbal exchanges, so that the material available for analysis was considerable.

The amount of material and its richness creates its own problems and also points up its value. This kind of work is in its infancy and can already be seen as an important source of information about the nature and complexity of teaching. There is so much information in just a few minutes of pedagogical interaction that in very little time one can accumulate enough material for months and years of analysis. In the next few pages I shall consider what is possibly the most promising use of analyses of this type; the analyses carried out by teachers of their own teaching. It should be remembered that the teachers were not making a special study of reinforcement but trying to teach concepts, skills and problem solving. In the process of analysing the recordings of their teaching, questions relating to feedback and reinforcement arose and clearly influenced the outcomes of the lessons, demonstrating in practice the integrality of the affective and other aspects of learning. Finally, in this preamble to the examples, I should like to remind readers that although many of the comments made by the teachers are critical of their teaching, the outcomes of all the teaching were as good as those achieved in 'normal' teaching, and many much better. The novel aspects of the reports are, first, that they were made at all and, second, that they were analytical and based on a body of principles related to psychopedagogy.

Feedback and reinforcement

My first example illustrates very well the way in which different aspects of pedagogy integrate. It is taken from the report of the teacher teaching the 'dig pass' in volleyball I discussed earlier. I commented on this in Chapter 6, on learning psychomotor skills. I should now like to report in more detail the way in which the affective element influenced the teaching. I can do no better than let the teacher speak for himself.

> Because the boy did a couple of successful attempts, I quickly moved on instead of giving him adequate practice and verbal reinforcement through praise. Looking at the section of video where I gave the boy

practice, the amount of praise and information given in the form of feedback is minimal. What I also feel I was doing at this stage of the lesson was that I was trying to ignore or extinguish actions that were resulting in poor direction; these tended to relate to actual body position such as the body not being in line with the desired direction of the ball. The use of the legs at this stage was very good, but no comment was made because I was concentrating on achieving good direction. So, as well as ignoring or trying to extinguish bad body direction, I was also failing to confirm the good leg action the boy was producing.

To further compound this negative action of mine during the dig exercise where the boy is moving to make the dig pass the use of verbal cues and praise is once again lacking. Because of my expectation of the perfect dig pass I underestimated the quality of some of the digs produced in the move because they did not reach my expectation and therefore I did not reinforce what was approximating the correct action. To give an example of this, after the first two digs of that exercise, possibly due to no praise or comment, the standard deteriorated and I had to review an earlier sub-skill of where to make contact with the ball. The first dig after this revision was a good example and was acknowledged by me and the standard improved once again.

Note his recognition that he had failed to provide reinforcing feedback that progressed gradually from the reinforcing of actions showing some promise of being correct to the aimed-for performance. He ascribed this error to the fact that he had in mind a perfect performance. This error is one of the difficulties in the 'show and tell' approach to physical skill teaching. Note also the effect: the standard deteriorated.

As a result of his analysis of his teaching he was able to pinpoint the most important shortcomings and look ahead.

It is, therefore, necessary for me now to review the sub-skills of the dig pass with the pupil, this time offering more reinforcement and praise and to spend far more time on actual practising of the skills.

An exchange from a very different field, this time the work of a student teacher, illustrates the same fixation on the desired outcome at the expense of attending to positive steps on the way to achieving it. This is a teacher we have met before teaching about an industrial dispute, a British rail strike.

Teacher: Who's suffering? [From the effects of the strike]
Pupil: The public.
Teacher: Who else might be suffering?
Pupil: ASLEF [the railworkers' union], everybody will be suffering. People have no transport and British Rail are losing money.
Teacher: Yes (very halfheartedly), who else might be suffering?

The person who is suffering in this conversation is Billy —— as he puts forward several creditable answers and gets no feedback at all except for a half hearted 'yes'. Billy suffered more than anyone else in my blinkered persistence at getting to what I thought was the desirable answer. It's to his credit that he kept on offering answers.

This teacher has realised at the outset of her career that she is suffering the tramline syndrome. That is, with her eyes on the goal, she pays little attention to the landmarks on the way. Like the volleyball man, for her, only the answer she wants will do. Fortunately she realises this and recognises the effect this has on pupil motivation. Billy's good nature compensates for her rigidity. This pattern of pupil–teacher interaction probably occurs millions of times every day, but few teachers have the insight and the opportunity provided by video or other feedback to realise this and see its implications for their own teaching.

Video feedback can help teachers acquire deeper insights into their teaching even when teaching in a one-to-one situation. This is illustrated in the work of an experienced teacher trying to help an eight-year-old boy with letter reversal problems in reading. The pupil had had only two and a half years in school and, had attended at least five different schools, including six months in Ireland, where he had to try to learn Gaelic. He could read only one or two words that he had learned by the look and say method.

The teacher had planned the work carefully and had in mind the suggestions made in the heuristic for motivation. He also had in mind the need to give the pupil time to respond to questions. This is the 'wait time' I have mentioned earlier (p. 103). Despite the simplified conditions and his attempt to wait at least three seconds for the pupil to respond, the recording revealed that in his teaching he frequently did not.

Too often I did not wait three seconds. For example, I began speaking too early when I asked him why he had chosen the wrong bee (picture used in a test of visual discrimination). Our voices sounded simultaneously, John immediately deferred to me and I took over.

The teacher would not have realised what had happened without the recording. He was also able to reflect on the pupil's affective reactions.

A study of the video tape shows that John enjoyed the lesson; his non-verbal communications show this even more clearly than his verbal responses.

The teacher was able to see the activity that led to the boy's enjoyment. He saw that he had successfully implemented some of the suggestions made in the heuristic.

John was rewarded not only by having his successes immediately identified but by having each one approved by me. The approval was not routinely given, but was strengthened by strong non-verbals as well.

This point contrasts with the common complaint of reinforcement that is routine and often nothing more than oral punctuation in the teacher's discourse.

As a general comment on the teaching, the teacher thought that the systematic use of feedback and reinforcement had produced a high level of enthusiasm, intrinsic motivation and task involvement. As a result most of the time was active learning time, and a great deal of work was accomplished 'that made a significant contribution to John's final level of achievement'.

Another teacher working with similar aims in mind, this time with a group of pupils, had a similar experience. He is the teacher teaching creative writing I referred to earlier. He had a pre-writing session which might be thought of as resembling the 'briefing' session I mentioned earlier (see p. 255). In his words:

> Working with a small group it was very easy to supply the necessary feedback, especially during the pre-writing phase. The teacher's manner was pleasant and the frequency of smiles and nods reinforced all the correct responses. Although the teacher attempted to reinforce each and every correct response at first, subsequent re-analysis of the video tape shows very little evidence of this. By far the most common way of reinforcement appears to be the teacher's repetition of the child's correct response showing acceptance.

He actually finds that on every occasion a pupil answers a question he just repeats the pupil's answer. He remarks:

> Although this could be seen as reinforcing in the earlier part of the lesson, it is doubtful if at the end of the lesson it was viewed as such by the pupils, especially when careful analysis of the video recording shows that the teacher did exactly the same with incorrect responses.

This teacher has put his finger on some important aspects of reinforcement. Repeating a pupil's answer is often considered a reinforcer. It signifies 'acceptance'. One needs to be very careful before accepting such blanket assertions. What the teacher is saying, in effect, is that sometimes it is and sometimes it isn't. His analysis suggests that at first his repetition of the answer might be seen as a reinforcer, but after a while it loses its impact and becomes mere verbal punctuation. Moreover, the fact that the teacher does the same whether the answer is correct or not could well be confusing to the pupils. There is clearly a pedagogical problem here that needs the teacher's urgent attention.

His analysis is the first crucial step to solving the problem as his comments demonstrate. All the comments are the teacher's own speaking of himself in the third person.

Teacher: What does the word 'soiled' mean?
Michael: Sown.
Teacher: Sown – what do you think then?
Emma: It's got patches on.
Teacher: It's got patches on – it could have.

The teacher relies heavily on the tone of voice and facial expression. In this case the teacher repeats the child's incorrect response. Although the tone of voice was obviously very different, implying uncertainty rather than acceptance, it must cast a doubt on assuming that simply because the teacher repeats the pupil's response, the child accepts this as being reinforcing, especially when such repetitions occur with such frequency as in this recording.

The teacher revealed other aspects of his use of reinforcement through the analysis of the recording; in particular, an important and unrealised discrimination in the way he treated different pupils. He gives an example (all the comments are the teacher's own, given in the third person):

Teacher: What would you say?
Matthew: What they look like.
Teacher: What they look like – all right. (Teacher turns to the board and writes 'look like'). Fine.

The teacher accepts Matthew's first response, writing it on the blackboard. Similarly with Michael and Emma, who both respond quickly during the first minute. However, when Helen responds to a question after two minutes (into the episode)

Teacher: What else would you describe, Helen?
Helen: The ears.
Teacher: The ears. Michael?

The teacher accepts the answer and moves immediately on to Michael. Similarly with Renee who does not respond until after three minutes.

Teacher: Renee?
Renee: Smooth skin.
Teacher: Smooth skin. (Nods to Matthew).
Matthew: Rough skin.
Teacher: Good boy.

This was Renee's first contribution, yet the teacher offers no praise or reinforcement, but offers immediate praise to Matthew. Analysis of the video-recording shows that Matthew, Michael and Emma received a highly disproportionate share of the reinforcing comments. . . . . As the lesson progressed Matthew, who received most reinforcers, could be seen to grow in confidence.

The teacher goes on to suggest that if he had made similar reinforcing comments to the others they might have become more involved. This bears on one of his main objectives, to involve the pupils in a pre-learning briefing. I will discuss this aspect later. He provides more detailed comment on the way he used reinforcers and attempted to avoid punishment, all of which would be most useful feedback for his future guidance. I cannot go into this detail here but can report his summing-up of the result of his reflections.

> Although on balance there were few negative responses and the proportion of positive to negative reinforcers [he means punishers] was high, it could be argued that a teacher skilled in reinforcing would have (a) taken preactive steps to ensure a higher rate of success by all the pupils, (b) have planned for reinforcement by means other than the teacher's approval alone and (c) have displayed a more varied strategy both in the level and frequency of his use of reinforcers.

A student teacher considering her lesson on scale to pupils of thirteen–fourteen years of age is clear about the difference between feedback and reinforcement. She is also aware of the importance of feedback to the teacher from pupils' responses. She exemplifies this in two comments.

> The feedback to the teacher was not taken up in enough depth. For example, when Andrew said that a football pitch was seven metres long, this should have said a lot and this point should have been investigated. He obviously had no idea of measurement, and this point needed further explanation. Again, important feedback came from the pupils at the end of the lesson when the pupils were asked to use their own words to describe scale and Andrew answered 'the actual size'. This showed that he had obviously not understood the concept and another explanation was required. Important feedback came from Carl, who showed that he was understanding the concept quite well. It was assumed from this that the rest of the pupils also understood the concept, but this, in fact, was not the case.

We have considered the work of this teacher earlier. She had realised that her pedagogical analysis had been unsatisfactory and that this had led to a problems with her teaching and in turn to faulty pupil learning. She faced the dilemma I have mentioned before; because the pupils were not learning very well there was little progress to commend. As she put it:

> In evaluating the lesson it became apparent that there was very little actual reinforcement, particularly in the case of teacher approval or praise for an action. In only one instance was direct praise given for a correct answer. The lack of this type or reinforcement arose because it depended upon another type of reinforcement, that of success for the pupils.

She ascribed the cause of this problem first to the inadequate pedagogical analysis, and later, in the interactive phase, to the fact that she had gone from stage to stage in her planned lesson without systematic formative evaluation. Consequently some of the pupils were moved on before they were ready and dropped further and further behind instead of making progress. This is the point she illustrated above.

She seems aware of the double-edged nature of learning failure. If approval depends on success, and if there is no success, there is no approval. She considers that in a future lesson 'it should be remembered that teacher approval and praise may be expressed for pupils' attempts and not merely for success'. This point is a variant on the one I discussed earlier. It is the question of reinforcing small steps in the right direction and gradually increasing the demands on the learner before reinforcement is provided. There is no doubt that this teacher had identified the main problem in her teaching. Her faulty pedagogical analysis had produced a too-steep learning gradient for some of the pupils and this, coupled with a lack of clarity in her analysis of the concepts, had led to their unsatisfactory learning.

Her analysis does not make clear whether, by her comment that she should reinforce the pupils' attempts, she had in mind the principle of successive approximation to the target learning. Encouraging effort is well and good and helps to create a positive learning atmosphere. However, unless encouragement is coupled with a systematic progression towards the learning of the new concepts or skills, the teacher and the pupils will wind up in the pedagogical sands, happily getting nowhere.

The reasons why teachers at times misread the feedback they get from the pupils are varied and subtle, like most teaching–learning interactions. Some insight into this complexity may be found with the help of the following account by a teacher teaching the concept of symmetry to pupils aged ten–twelve years. It starts just after the beginning of the lesson.

> Almost immediately a somewhat discordant note creeps into the lesson. One pupil (Alison) dissents from the main consensus of opinion. The problem appears to be that while we can all agree that lines of a specific exemplar are parallel, Alison did not perceive that pattern was produced. Instead of taking this opportunity to identify precisely what the pupil's difficulty was (several reasons suggested themselves in retrospect) the teacher opted for relying upon 'authority of position' by restating the observed phenomenon as 'fact'. Unfortunately, the challenging of an idea was seen as threatening the progress of the lesson. It was seen as a possible source of confusion in the minds of the other pupils also. Instead of sorting out Alison's difficulty, the teacher broke a basic rule. 'Backed up' by strong pupil support (non-verbal) he forged ahead. Reinforced by 'correct-thinking' pupils, the teacher was content to

restate that a circumstance was 'so', missing a potentially useful insight.

Here we see another example of the tramline syndrome, with a teacher unable to deviate from his chosen course when all that he understood well about formative evaluation and diagnosis was overwhelmed by the reactions of the majority of the pupils. It is interesting and salutary (not least to him) that this teacher, by no means authoritarian, falls into the prototypical role of instruction by assertion. His discomfiture on realising what had happened redeems him in our eyes, but it is worth remembering that his regretted action is little different from standard delivery teaching.

The teaching as a whole, however, was not of that type. The careful attention to planning, the assessment of prerequisite ability and the thought given to the provision of exemplars and non-exemplars all contributed to a useful learning experience for the pupils. 'The use of reinforcement', he says, 'permeated the thinking behind the schedule [heuristic] and its implementation made this apparent'. Feedback was predominantly oral by the teacher. But he also encouraged the pupils to use their own speech in response to his cuing. The idea behind this was to help them clarify their thinking and to help provide feedback to the teacher. His use of feedback, in his view, was closely related to his cuing, which was aimed to foster pupil independence.

He also had his non-verbal behaviour analysed by a colleague. It was very positive overall, with no punishers and much smiling and encouraging body posture. This had its effect on the pupils, who grew relaxed and enjoyed the lesson.

As I have suggested earlier, the use of video-feedback could well be a powerful adjunct to teaching for many reasons other than for teachers to view their own performances. However, the overriding principle is not to use video to provide feedback but to use one's imagination. In the case of the teacher teaching rhythmic patterns, the misleading convention of clapping slowly or quickly to indicate long and short notes was replaced by the use of a tone generator. At one stage in the search for methods of producing suitable feedback to indicate length of notes, this teacher and one or two colleagues used, first, a kymograph to produce a trace on a rotating drum to produce a visual display of length of 'clap' taking 'clap' to be the pressing on a lever in long or short actions. This was later replaced by a similar device showing a trace on an oscilloscope screen which produced traces of different lengths on a screen that acted as an analogue of the notes. Feedback was thus provided visually for what is essentially aural training.

This example emphasises the crucial role of the practitioner in developing practical pedagogy. A time-honoured but flawed piece of teaching method, clapping, was first revealed as flawed by examining how it was working in practice as an analogue of long and short notes. An attempt to produce a genuine analogue that young children could operate themselves led to experiments with a kymograph. This in turn led to the use of the button attached to an oscilloscope producing an electronic visual display. This, linked to a tone generator, can produce both visual and auditory information about length of note. These developments were evoked by the interplay of theoretical pedagogical analysis, the need to produce an accurate analogue and feedback, the teacher's own experience of teaching the subject, and technical developments that made available new methods.

I should like to stress quite strongly that this use of developments in electronic technology in this small piece of teaching is very different from the way they are normally used. The normal use of new gadgetry is as an adjunct to delivery-type teaching. Lessons, for example, are put on videotape. In this instance, and in all the instances of the use of recorded material I have discussed, the technical apparatus subserves a pedagogical intent. In the case we are discussing, new apparatus made new approaches possible. However, only the teacher's ingenuity and grasp of pedagogy, in this case with particular reference to the need for accurate feedback, led first to the identification of the need and then to the way that need could be satisfied. A systematic analytical approach to pedagogy makes demands on a teacher's creativity.

In the case of the music teacher teaching musical composition, audio-tape, musical notation on the chalkboard, a keyboard and the teacher's speech were used in conjunction to provide continuous monitoring of the pupils' responses. The lessons were carefully structured to provide more or less continuous feedback. Starting with the teaching of the subordinate concepts, the teacher led the pupils along a gentle learning gradient, checking their learning at key points. As the teacher explains:

a) The teaching is divided into units, each concerned with a sub-ordinate concept in one particular area of the melody.
b) A line divides the teacher activity and the pupil activity. The pupil activity is a response to the teacher's initial teaching strategy.'

The line the teacher refers to is one he mentions in the prefatory material relating to the remarks being reported here. He explains that in his version of the heuristic for teaching concepts he has a vertical line down the page with the the teacher strategy on the left and the pupil responses on the right. The teacher tests the pupils' grasp of the concept being taught immediately. This is the way he guides his organisation of continuous feedback to the pupils.

c) The teacher explains or establishes features of the concept while the pupil, as a correct response, identifies these features. 'Identifies' . . . means that the pupil demonstrates the feature to the teacher. He listens and performs the feature to ensure that learning has taken place.

d) This explanation and identification is an exemplar of the feature of the subordinate concept. However, it is possible for the pupil to repeat the correct answer without understanding the reasons why. This is true of much teaching and ignores the pupils' need to discriminate between right and wrong exemplars of the feature. Thus, after the exemplar has been taught, the use of non-exemplars offers a check that the understanding of the subordinate concept has been achieved by the pupil.

e) If the pupil successfully discriminates the non-exemplar from the exemplar, then it is time to complete this teaching unit with a test of the unit.

Each subordinate concept is dealt with in the same way, until all the units are complete. In this way, the pupils will have understood the overall concept and will be able to attempt composition of their own. Successful identification of each unit will serve as immediate feedback for the teacher. . . .

The teacher goes on to make some useful points in relation to the use of the heuristic. Recall that he was teaching musical composition and specifically the concept of melody and the composition of melodies. He recommends that teachers following the heuristic should prepare ancillary material such as notes, melodic fragments and test papers to exemplify the concepts being taught. He proposes the use of audio-tape recording for later evaluation of the teaching. Audio is not preferred to video, but it was more feasible in his circumstances. A final point is that it is best to avoid detailed prepared scripts since, in his words, they 'offer too much of a tramline approach to the teaching'.

The careful pre-structuring of the teaching to provide a gentle learning gradient and the very regular feedback to the pupils led to a high level of success and involvement by the pupils.

The same applies to the teacher of orienteering. He also provided much ancillary material to implement his teaching. In fact the same applies to all the teachers whose work I have discussed. Being reminded by the pedagogical analysis to consider the type of learning involved and the means of presenting stimuli and providing feedback, apart from all the other elements, ensures that one prepares some type of adjunctive material to one's discourse. It would take a very insensitive person to enter in all the columns of the analysis 'teacher talk' as the pedagogical agent.

As with many of the other reports, there is so much pedagogical richness in the record of the teaching of orienteering that it is difficult to know what to single out. As the teacher comments:

> A pleasing feature of the schedules at the interactive stage is that they do not inhibit or restrict the method in which the lessons were presented. In fact the heuristic device to analyse the teaching activity prompts the teacher to consider a variety of approaches, methods and materials. The teaching of bearings meant that I had to devise and construct apparatus and situations because the subject is rarely covered at primary or middle school level.
>
> The schedules [heuristics] did not provide me with guidance on these matters. This does not detract from them; rather it is an advantage, leaving the teacher free to present the lesson as he or she considers best.

As I reported in Chapter 4, this teacher constructed a variety of devices to present stimuli to provide feedback. These devices are used to provide a logical progress of increasing difficulty with feedback regularly provided and cuing gradually faded. Examples are carefully graded: 90 degrees, then approximately 180 degrees, 45 degrees, 270 degrees, 360 degrees, 135 degrees and finally 270 degrees so that the level of difficulty in estimating a particular bearing is increased. A calibrated disc was available for the pupils to use to check the accuracy of their estimates and thus provide instant feedback.

I have already alluded to the way the degree of accuracy of the pupils' ability to follow a bearing in the forest was assessed. The same approach was used in the teaching phase. The pupils had to travel along a bearing in the forest. Just before each check point they crossed a tape on the ground with cards numbered from one to ten pegged along the tape at regular intervals. The pupils had to note the number on the card they arrived at on crossing each tape. When all the group had finished they compared results and the answer corresponding to the correct bearing was revealed, thus providing feedback. This exercise was repeated so that the pupils would get further information about the way they were performing.

Several variants on this theme were employed, some involving pupils' guiding the teacher and each other in following bearings. In this way a complex matrix of learning interactions was developed comprising teacher and pupil activity, systematic and regular feedback and group support: all ingredients for a very positive and productive learning atmosphere, as indeed, it proved to be.

FEAR OF THE FULSOME

In my work with large numbers of teachers attempting to implement psychopedagogical principles I have found great concern about the danger of overdoing the praise and encouragement. Time and again, however, I have found, and they have discovered, that they reinforce far less than they imagine. I have never once experienced a teacher whose actual reinforcement exceeded the intuited amount of reinforcement. As we have observed many times, the usual comment about reinforcement is that it was sparse or inadequate or spurious. The message seems to be that fear of the fulsome is misplaced and that classrooms by and large are unrewarding places for pupils. And the message from that observation is that learning would be much improved if teachers overcame their inhibitions, threw caution to the winds and increased the amount of reinforcement they dispensed to the pupils, not forgetting that a little has to go a long way, given conventional class sizes.

BRIEFING AND DEBRIEFING

My final comment returns to an earlier theme and introduces a note of qualification to my last remark. This comes from the report of the teacher of rhythm in German poetry. It sounds a note of warning, without invalidating the points made in the last paragraph.

> It ought to be said that reinforcement of learning can do little to help if the lesson itself is badly constructed, for example if the entry competence has been misjudged [as his was]. In such a case, encouragement can take on a ring of desperation and falseness which causes pupils to react by withdrawing commitment, despising or resenting being encouraged to do the impossible. Thus the major source of reinforcement is the successful negotiation [with the pupils] of the learning programme. It is the teacher's job to arrange this.

This is the kind of thing I have referred to as a 'briefing session'. The Green Cross Code teacher did it using brainstorming techniques; the music teacher used a very full interactive assessment of existing competence. It is all of a piece with the points made about debriefing. It is a greatly neglected approach that offers much in the way of enhancing intrinsic motivation.

So does the debriefing session I referred to in the discussion of problem solving in the orienteering work. There the pupils and teacher discussed different ways of solving the problem of optimum route choice in a particular section of forest. This group reflection on a learning experience has positive implications for motivation of future learning. Currently, 'reflection' for teachers is the fashion. Collegial reflection on the part of the pupils seems to me also of importance. When pupils are given the opportunity to become involved in commenting on their own learning experiences and on the teacher's teaching, they have often proved extremely responsible and provided a very useful perspective for the teachers. (Meighan 1981) Feeling that one has some sort of influence over one's own activity is one of the most potent influences in developing intrinsic motivation. And by general agreement, intrinsic motivation is the essential ingredient in quality learning.

11 Quality quality

'IN MY END IS MY BEGINNING'

I started this book by reversing the title of a British Government White Paper, *Teaching Quality*. I end with a reversal of one of T.S. Eliot's best known lines. I suggest that both Eliot's original (from 'East Coker', *Four Quartets*) and my version are apposite to the study and practice of teaching. I don't suppose for one moment that Eliot had aims and objectives in mind when he wrote, 'In my beginning is my end'. Nevertheless, his words fit well the rationale of quality teaching as, I believe, does my version. The two in combination suggest a cycle. Whether it is a closed cycle which repeats itself or an ameliorative recursion with change and development built in depends upon the quality of the teaching that drives it.

I hope that the discussion in this book has been sufficiently helpful in clarifying the key questions in the theory and practice of teaching to enable readers to ensure that their pedagogical cycles are open and developmental in the way I proposed at the outset. The aim is a form of teaching in which formative and diagnostic evaluation are *systemic*. Teaching of this kind combines theory and practice in open ended research and teaching in which change and development are an integral part (Stones 1986a).

The book itself, having indicated its goals in the first chapter, now aspires to reflect back on its beginning to examine to what extent the intervening discussion has thrown light on the problems raised. Thus its end has a new beginning. If my task has been accomplished with a reasonable measure of success the reader will be more aware of the nature of the problems and the possible ways of resolving them in any future thought or action in teaching.

'HE WHO CAN, DOES. HE WHO CANNOT, TEACHES'

About a century ago, in his *Maxims for Revolutionists*, George Bernard Shaw coined the above aphorism about a century ago. A few years ago, Shulman took it as his text for the 1985 presidential address to the American Educational Research Association (Shulman 1986). Shulman saw the expression as a gross calumny on the profession and mounted a sustained attack on Shaw and a defence of teaching. He also made proposals for improving teaching, including some which relate to the general line I have taken in my discussion. However, I believe that he has misapprehended some important points that need addressing for a truly effective defence of teaching. Since the misapprehensions are widespread in the public at large and also within the academic community, I should like to consider them briefly in order to clarify the impediments to the development of quality teaching. I hope that by so doing I shall be able more effectively to suggest approaches to removing them. I stress that although the focus of my remarks is the points raised by Shulman, I do not wish to detract from the general drift of his argument. However, in view of the widespread influence of the article subsequent to publication, I think it particularly important that we examine those propositions that might weaken the case for the view of teaching Shulman advocates and which I accept with some qualifications.

The first point I consider is Shulman's assumption that Shaw wrote the words 'in a fit of pique'. This assumption seems to me not only almost certainly untrue, but also probably counterproductive. The image of teaching and teachers since the advent of large-scale public education has been a poor one. To fail to recognise this and to impute malign intent to comments such as Shaw's is to underestimate the problems the study of teaching faces. Consider, for example, the case of teaching in institutions of higher education, both as a discipline worthy of study in its own right and as a medium for informing their own students. Few, if any, university faculties of education have departments of teaching or teaching studies. There are very few institutes, internationally, devoted to such studies. (See *The World of Learning* 1990.) Ironically, often where teaching *is* studied, there is little connection between the study of teaching theory and its manifestation *in vivo*. Little attention is given in any institution of higher education to the training of its teaching staff.

Many teacher training institutions in the USA do not see it as their job to research into teaching or to make a study of pedagogy. In Britain university teaching and research staff commonly disavow any particular expertise in the study of teaching (Stones 1989b). A recent British Government initiative to fund research in teaching via the Economic and Social Research Council is in the tradition of short-term funding, and although the funds available are large in comparison with previous dispensations, they are pitifully meagre compared with those disbursed to more glamorous projects in the hard sciences and educational projects with hardware connections such as CCTV and, currently, computers.

The attitudes towards teacher education in Britain that I discussed earlier also indicate the lowly status of teaching as a subject worthy of study and research. The attack on teacher training *per se* has been so sustained and virulent that the Universities Council for the Education of Teachers issued a statement signed by sixty-nine senior professors of education refuting these attacks (UCET 1990). In most anglophone countries there have been government moves to relocate teacher training in the schools in some form of apprenticeship training. Is it surprising that the status of teaching among the academic faculty is almost universally lower than virtually all other fields of study? Lanier and Lytle (1990) write about the de-intellectualization of teacher education in the USA and see it as 'a marginal part of the university community, criticized for its lack of rigor, but discouraged from trying to be anything else'. The Shavian contempt for teaching is alive and well a century on.

Shulman does not escape the transmission trap. He argues: 'As we have begun to probe the complexities of teacher understanding and the transmission of content knowledge, the need for a more coherent theoretical framework has become rapidly apparent'. The phrase 'transmission of content knowledge' is a variant on the 'delivery teaching' I have discussed earlier. It is of paramount importance that any 'coherent theoretical framework' that is developed sees the idea of transmission of knowledge for what it is: a recipe for rote-learning. Teachers cannot 'transmit knowledge'. They can transmit words which may or may not lead to change in hearers' or readers' concepts in the subject of study. This is not nit-picking about the use of terms. It is a fundamental problem. The view of teaching as transmission of knowledge sees teaching as talking; as explaining; as delivering. It accepts as proof of learning reciting, answering questions by verbalising, whether orally or in writing, and giving back to the teacher what the teacher dispensed earlier. This is the view of teaching held by many academics, by the public at large and by the majority of administrators and politicians in the field of education. In effect, it forecloses discussion about pedagogical theory almost by ignoring it, or by regarding it as something outside the practice of teaching.

It seems to me to be of the utmost importance that this view of teaching be rejected by teachers and researchers in teaching and pedagogy and that no opportunity should be lost in discussion and practice to promote alternative views, including approaches such as the one discussed in this book and exemplified by the work of the teachers involved.

There is one other important question not addressed by Shulman. It is the fact that institutions for the preparation of teachers in most countries also, tacitly at least, espouse the delivery view of teaching. As a consequence the Shavian view of teaching is really unchallenged. 'Doing' any of the disciplines to be found in institutions of higher education is clearly more difficult than talking about them. Thus the problem of theory development alluded to above is compounded by the fact that the key workers in the field, the teachers, are not equipped by their training to make a contribution. If this had not been the case, this book would not need to be written. As it is, the work reported in it is very much in line with the kind of work advocated by Shulman. However, it goes further than Shulman in its adoption of a systematic programme of pedagogical inquiry.

Shulman suggested compilation of case studies of teaching in order to shed light on the way teachers work, in the belief that this would help develop theory. This view has become fashionable in recent years, but I believe the way it is generally propagated is deeply flawed. To free teaching from the incubus of its delivery image, it is crucial to address the issue of the nature of the theory held by teachers. The craft knowledge acquired by teachers in their work in classrooms can be useful as we have seen. But it cannot be sufficient. Piling up case studies of delivery teaching will be of limited value. For genuine progress to be made towards the construction of useful pedagogical theory it is necessary to go beyond the recycling approach to theory building. Teachers need, and many want, help to go beyond present practice to break into this closed pedagogical circle, thereby to enhance the possibility of turning it into the ameliorative recursive cycle I have referred to at the beginning of this chapter.

It would be foolish to ignore international differences in the nature of the attitudes towards, and the provision made for, teacher training when considering the feasibility of the integrated approach to teaching and research I have discussed in this book. In countries where entrants to the profession are ill qualified educationally, the type of work I have described would be more difficult, and, in some cases, would necessitate drastic adaptation. Lanier and Lytle (1986) in the USA refer to the 'persons with low measures of academic talent [who] are allowed to dominate the field'. In many non-industrialized countries under-educated staff and under-resourced teacher training systems change the parameters of the approach. I do not think, however, that the difficulties in either case invalidate its general principles. They do increase the responsibility of workers in higher education, and especially teacher training, to help develop problem-solving skills in the teachers. On the other hand, case studies of teaching *as it is*, with no attempt at pedagogical intervention, in such widely different circumstances, could tell us a lot about local educational provision – but little if anything, about general pedagogical principles.

PROBLEMS OF PEDAGOGY

In this section I consider some of the difficulties encountered by the teachers and student teachers whose work I have reported. However, I should like to stress most strongly that the problems were not those of failing teachers but were found within a context of teaching that was generally of a high level and productive of insightful teacher learning. The latter is the important thing. In all but a few cases the teachers themselves, in retrospective analyses, identified the problems and were able to make proposals for remedial action for pupils and teachers. The key to this ability was the teachers' understanding of pedagogical theory. Time and time again this message came through from teachers who could never have made the analyses had they depended on 'craft knowledge'. This particularly applies to the student teachers. My purpose in considering the difficulties they encountered is to point to some of the common problems so that others might benefit from their experience.

Many problems currently faced by teachers might well be considered to be non-pedagogical in nature. 'Control' (of pupils) figures large in many discussions of teaching and might be held by some to be an important pedagogical skill. In the nineteenth century corporal punishment was esteemed as a method of control. Currently, methods based on behaviour modification are in vogue. Neither of these approaches addresses the central question raised in this book: teaching for meaningful, transferable learning. In the teaching of pupils in normal schools both methods of control are essentially aimed at facilitating the teacher's talking to the pupils.

Much the same could be said about some other aspects of teacher activity that commonly attract attention and are often to be found in schemes for appraisal of teaching. Clarity of diction, quality of writing on the chalkboard, poise and use of questions are among some of the favourite constituents of appraisal schemes. There is no evidence that any of these schemes are able to separate the good from the bad teachers, for reasons I have rehearsed before. Other questions that have attracted researchers' attention are equally futile. A great fuss was made in the 1980s about the relative effectiveness of informal and formal approaches to teaching, and 'teaching style' became a buzz word. The buzz has subsided now, but new ones follow. 'Reflection' is a case in point, but others are sidling in. 'Metaphors' about teaching, 'images' of teaching, teachers' 'stories' are on the starting blocks at the moment, and I am unsure which one to put my money on. Whichever takes the lead in the next year or two, one thing is sure, and I *am* prepared to bet on this, it will have no impact on the way teaching is.

A little reflection on the nature of human learning is all that is needed to understand my readiness to make this prediction. The best diction in the world is no help if the teacher is talking nonsense. Nor is it if the message is totally unconnected to the pupils' current level of understanding. Time on task, another passing fad of the 1980s, is irrelevant if the task is pedagogically nonsensical. The same applies to 'formal' and 'informal' teaching styles, even if we accept for the moment that the terms are not vacuous. All of these passing fancies tacitly accept the prototypical delivery view of teaching. None of them addresses the fundamental questions relating to the way teachers can structure the learning environment in new ways that will help pupils to learn concepts or psychomotor skills or develop transferable problem-solving skills. Most of these fancies do not even mention such things.

'Pedagogy' and 'teacher as researcher' are also currently in vogue. I have been discussing these concepts throughout this book and thereby, I hope, have made explicit the way I conceive them. Unfortunately, the terms are frequently used without such exegesis, so that the processes to which they refer are vague and could be related to trivial teaching activities with no potential for enhancing pupil learning.

I have tried to avoid vacuity by paying attention to what I believe are the more fundamental aspects of teaching, not as it is now, but as it could be. In the work I have discussed in previous chapters I have considered cases of teachers' grappling with the gulf between the delivery or transmission view of teaching and the view that tries to bring to bear theoretical notions relating to human learning. I should like now to recapitulate what seem to be the most significant issues that have emerged.

Delivery as regression

In many cases, despite the fact that the teachers or student teachers were committed to a psychopedagogical approach, there was, at times, a regression to delivery methods. Significantly this took place at moments of stress or frustration. Consider the case of the teacher teaching the concept of symmetry referred to in Chapter 10. A pupil has a difficulty in understanding and says that she cannot see a pattern in the example. The teacher, feeling threatened by the dissenting voice and thinking it might confuse the other pupils, does not attempt to establish the nature of the pupil's problem but restates with more authority that it *is* a pattern. He says it is so, and the pupil's problem is unresolved.

Another example is the student teacher who was given the task of teaching historical materialism (Chapter 5). Given the scale of the pedagogical task and her insecurity in the grasp of psychopedagogical principles, she retreated into a delivery mode and proceeded to 'tell' the pupils. Unfortunately, she was further stressed by the fact that the lesson was to be video-recorded. The result was a verbal outpouring, both oral and written on the chalkboard.

It is not my intention to disparage the use of teachers' spoken language in teaching. As I have argued throughout, language is the most powerful instrument in developing abstract thought and reasoning skills. Its use by a teacher as a constant in concept learning is crucial. The delicate precision required for careful guiding, cuing, and providing feedback and reinforcement is impossible without language. But language cannot be used in such ways unless it springs from a firm grasp of pedagogical principles and those principles imply active learners and two-way interaction, not passive receivers and one-way transmitters. Both teachers referred to here realised this truth after the event. This was the positive outcome to their experience. In their end was a new beginning. Unfortunately many teachers never have that insight. Unfortunately millions of pupils never recoup lost opportunities for learning because of that missing insight.

Covering the syllabus

Part of the reason the student teacher teaching historical materialism decided to adopt a delivery approach was that she thought it the only way to accomplish the task she had been given in the time that was available. Teachers often argue for this view when one suggests approaching teaching in the way I have done in this book. As I have already suggested, student teachers are often sceptical about the need for such (as they see it) time consuming and elaborate activity. The apprenticeship they have served in watching hundreds of teachers 'delivering' has produced concepts about teaching quite other than the one being suggested to them. Some experienced teachers react similarly, although probably for somewhat different reasons. In addition to *their* apprenticeships in school, they have their own experience and habits and ways of doing things, and it may be somewhat uncomfortable to entertain radically different ideas about something they may have been doing for many years.

External examinations and tests also produce pressures and constraints that force teachers into methods they believe will enable them to 'cover' the content of the syllabus. In extreme cases drill methods that amount to little more than the crudest rote-learning are employed. The teacher 'gets through' the material. The pupils learn nothing of value and probably little of the content they were intended to learn.

'Covering the syllabus', 'doing' a topic', 'getting through' an assignment and, a recent British official variant, 'visiting' an aspect of the curriculum are all expressions in general use. Discovering just what they signify to various groups of teachers would be an interesting research topic. However, one thing is virtually sure, and that is that they all involve notions of some form of telling, delivering or transmission. Pupil learning may or may not take place. While it may not be made explicit, pupil learning is usually at best a secondary consideration (Stones and Morris 1972, Stones and Webster 1984, McCulloch 1979).

The fact that the saving of time by adopting delivery methods is at the cost of pupil learning is attested in the post-teaching comments of several of the teachers in the cases we have considered, as well as those of many of their colleagues who worked along the same lines. We encountered it in the teacher teaching volleyball, the two referred to earlier in this chapter and the one teaching German poetry, who took the typical approach of starting from a definition and later realised that in trying to save time he had failed to achieve what he had intended. Time had been wasted, not saved. Several others came to the same conclusion with aspects of their teaching.

The teaching of the Green Cross Code is a striking example of the futility of 'time-saving' delivery teaching. The conventional talk by a policeman saves considerable time as compared to the work of the teacher we considered. Viewing the videotape of her teaching illustrates starkly the futility of *telling* young children and the complexity and potential of adopting a more time-consuming (but less child-consuming) approach.

The work of the teachers discussed here, and that of many of their colleagues, makes it clear that the combined pressures of their own experiences as pupils and teachers and of external demands for them to tick off items on a check list as having been 'done' are very real. Their conceptualisation of teaching was firmly entrenched and resistant to change even if they were sympathetic to what was being suggested. Telling them about psychopedagogy orally or in writing could be only part of the process of developing new ideas about the nature of teaching. To achieve that demanded a variety of approaches. Discussions in small groups, in dyads, sometimes using protocol material from a variety of videotaped lessons all contributed. But the thing that clinched their acceptance of the value and desirability of this novel approach was their own experience of teaching in the light of psychopedagogical principles. Thus my own experience working with these teachers epitomizes the general line taken in this book.

As to covering the syllabus: an objectives-oriented approach such as I have proposed emphasises general principles not specific content. Specific content is hard to justify unless it subserves the learning of general principles and problem-solving ability. Thus, the listing of topics to be dealt with by the teacher as a pedagogical device needs to be questioned Such questioning involves value judgments, as is clearly attested by such things as the current debate into the 'content' of the British National Curriculum in the fields of English, history and science between the 'facts' faction and the 'concepts' camp. The value of the hierarchical and analytical approach suggested in Chapter 3 is that it forces one to examine the basis for the proposed inclusion of any particular topic in a syllabus. The examination will most likely reveal that many topics traditionally included are apposite to the achievement of our aims, but their adoption will be based on explicit criteria that we believe will help us to achieve our aims. Shakespeare will be included in the English syllabus not because we think pupils should know about Shakespeare but because we believe study of his work will bring about changes in pupils' attitudes and understanding that we value. Particular events and episodes in history will be included because they exemplify general historical processes, not because it is considered a good thing to be able to memorize their dates and the names of the people involved. Similar things can be said of other fields of study.

Topics that contribute little or nothing to our understanding of general principles and trends are difficult to justify as part of a syllabus to be covered. In nineteenth-century Britain generations of children learned, in geography lessons, the names of capes and bays around the coast. It would be a bold person who advocated the same today in a discussion of the geography curriculum. This is an obvious point to make, but is it so much different from the 'capes' and 'bays' of history, such as the dates of kings and queens or presidents that still persist in some curricula? In science and mathematics some topics are included in syllabuses and 'covered' by teachers to little effect. Recent investigations of the understanding of teachers in these fields have revealed considerable ignorance of some of the most important general principles and concepts (Kruger *et al.* 1990). In an international study of understanding of scientific concepts widespread ignorance was discovered and also widespread primitive superstition. Yet most of the people surveyed are likely to have covered syllabuses which included science (Sagan 1990).

The point is that it is not possible to keep heaping up specifics in curricula. Nor is it helpful merely to exchange an old for a new topic, since this approach still maintains a 'collection' view of the curriculum which limits the number of subjects by the amount of time available. If, however, we adopt an approach which focuses attention on general principles the collection approach is replaced by one that develops and changes organically. A hierarchical objectives approach to teaching will maintain the most general aims related to principles relevant to contemporary bodies of knowledge, while specific and short-term subordinate objectives change their character or become obsolete following developments in current knowledge and thinking. This process resembles the development of science; new developments leading to new specifics may shed new light on the existing generalities and eventually transform them. Growth is, thus, inbuilt.

The 'covering the syllabus' syndrome is more attuned to the 'collection' view of the syllabus. 'Doing' the specifics is fulfilling one's commitments. As the teachers who suffered from this complaint reported above, if the aim is the teaching of general principles, 'delivering' all the specifics is no guarantee that worthwhile learning has occurred.

Meaningful, transferable learning is more likely to take place if the teachers select and programme the specifics according to principles based on concept learning. Judicious selection could reduce the number of specifics actually to be 'covered' and still stand a good chance of resulting in more productive learning. However, if external constraints, in the form of tests or examinations, place a premium on learning of specifics, it may be that a teacher would feel obliged to teach the specifics instead of general principles because of those external pressures. It is a sad consequence of the dominant current conceptions of teaching that many teachers find themselves, in this situation, teaching an array of 'facts', not because the facts contribute to general understandings, but because external forces so decree.

It is a matter of professional judgment in particular conditions just how individual teachers resolve the problem of conflicting demands. In many cases the problem of covering the syllabus may be more apparent than real, as was probably the case in the examples cited above; and, as the teachers realised, the constraints may well be in the minds of the teachers rather than in external factors. However, unless teachers are familiar with notions other than those of delivery teaching, they will not be in a position to achieve that realisation. Not being aware of the alternatives restricts their professional freedom at least as much as the external imperatives for delivery teaching.

Tramlining

'Tramlining' became the term used by the teachers I worked with to refer to the fixation on predetermined outcomes or detailed lesson plans. It is not an uncommon phenomenon (Shavelson and Stern 1981). It is manifested in the inexorable progress by the teacher through a set series of steps in a lesson come what may. It is frequently asserted that this problem is a consequence of taking an objectives-oriented approach to teaching. This assertion was not supported by the experience of the teachers involved. This is not to say that tramlining did not occur; it did. But when it did it was not a consequence of the systematic approach related to the identification of teaching aims and objectives. More often that not it followed when teachers lost sight of the aims and the heuristics derived from them.

Tramlining is, in fact, antithetical to the spirit and the letter of the approach advocated here. The continuous monitoring of the current state of the learners' skills and concepts advocated and the suggested means of doing this rule out the following of rigid routines. The teachers who found themselves in tramlines in their teaching realised this and were able to discern where the problem lay. Let us consider a few examples.

The volleyball teacher's comments bear on the general problems related to delivery teaching. There were elements of the 'covering the syllabus' problem. Instead of a gradual approach cuing and guiding, he 'progressed too quickly and spent too long on explanations'. He thought he 'should have introduced practical exercise'. In a comment on the specific point of tramlining he recognises his error, realising that because he was so fixated on the idea of the perfect dig pass he failed to monitor the boy's learning with sufficient sensitivity and take the necessary action to ensure that it progressed satisfactorily.

There are clear connections between covering the syllabus and tramlining. This teacher's anxiety to achieve the perfect action channelled him into focusing on the elements of the skill and regressing to the show and tell approach because it seemed to offer a quick solution to his problem. His subsequent analysis told him where he went astray and enabled him to decide what he should have done to have ensured more effective, and in the long run quicker, learning by the pupil. It reminded him of the commonplace in folk wisdom 'more haste, less speed'. The self-prescribed remedial action was that what he needed to do was to take more time and, by encouraging the learner when he produced less than perfect results, lead him to a gradual refinement of the action and an increase in confidence and competence. He made other suggestions, as I detailed in Chapter 6, connected with cuing and guiding. All these actions would have had the effect of taking him out of the tramlines, increasing the flexibility of his approach and making him more sensitive to the needs of the learner.

The work of the art tutor I have reported in earlier chapters bears closely on the same point. In this case those teachers using the heuristic guide to concept teaching avoided tramlining, while those not using the guide were really stuck. As I reported earlier, the former varied their cuing and guiding and presentation of exemplars while the latter 'employed undeviatingly repetitive tasks, which, devoid of relief, developed into unrelenting "slogging matches" testing the patience of pupils and teacher alike'. The heuristic helped the teachers to monitor the pupils' progress and so avoid the tramlines in which the other teachers got stuck.

The case of the student teacher teaching about primary and secondary evidence gives us a vivid impression of the forces confining teachers to the predestined route. Some of the pupils seemed confused. She tried to clarify things but did not stay for an answer and continued:

> However, I determined to proceed with the next stage in my plan which was to show the pupils completely different and somewhat complicated examples of primary evidence and I told the pupils that I wanted to find out whether they had understood the differences between the two sorts of evidence. *Here problems became evident but I ploughed on with the lesson.*

The insightful and honest report of the student teacher teaching about an industrial dispute illustrates beautifully a typical tramlined exchange. I referred to it in my discussion of reinforcement. Her comment bears repeating:

> Billy suffered more than anyone else in my blinkered persistence at getting to what I thought was the desirable answer. It's to his credit that he kept on offering answers.

Anyone who has observed teachers teaching will recognise the tone of the half-hearted 'yes' she produced in reply to Billy's answer. It is more in the nature of a mild reproof for not guessing what is in the teacher's mind. Instead of adjusting to the pupil's answers and exploring their nature, the reasons any particular answer was made and the logic behind it, the teacher performs like an automaton that responds only to the appropriate pre-programmed signal: the 'right' answer.

Finally, in this section, let us consider the remarks by the teacher of musical composition. He is discussing his variant on the concept-teaching heuristic. He is making suggestions for teachers preparing to teach composition along the lines he adopted.

> Although the schedule [heuristic] is a detailed and systematic guide to the teaching of composition, the teacher should make preparations in the way of notes, melodic fragments and test papers before embarking on the schedule. These need not be scripts but examples of the content to be taught. A tape recording of the lessons [tape section three] will serve as a better evaluation tool than detailed prepared scripts, which offer too much of a tramline approach to the teaching.

This is a point I have made before. Detailed lesson notes could well be the enemy of flexible and sensitive monitoring and diagnostic formative evaluation. All too easily they become scripts to deliver rather than guides to inform one's pedagogy.

Misconceptions

Underlying many of the teachers' problems referred to so far was a misunderstanding of the pupils' grasp of concepts. Not the concepts the teachers were trying to teach, but the concepts they were using in their discourse with pupils in introducing new learning. Consider the example referred to in Chapter 10. The pupil replies to the teacher's question, relating to creative writing 'What does "soiled" mean?' with the word 'sown'. The teacher says: 'Sown – what do you think then?' addressing another pupil who replies: 'It's got patches on?' Clearly neither pupil's concept of 'soiled' had much in common with the teacher's, but the teacher moved on along his tramline. I presume the first pupil's reply sprang from his reasoning that soil had something to do with gardening and if something was soiled it was committed to the earth, 'ensoiled' as it were. The second pupil presumably took the teacher's reply as a qualified positive, latched on to the sound 'sown' in its needlework sense and had a go at giving the teacher what he wanted. The teacher repeats this reply and adds 'it could have' and moves on to another pupil.

Within this short exchange some very interesting things occur. The first pupil makes a stab at guessing what the teacher wants. It is not entirely an uninformed guess. There is an element of logic in it. There is also an element of logic in the second pupil's answer in its relation to the first answer. However, it is moving further away from the original problem. The teacher, intent on getting the correct answer to the question, overlooked the obvious discrepancy between the pupils' understanding of the term and its conventional one. I leave it to the reader's imagination to conjecture on the conceptual content of the word 'soiled' for the three people in the exchange and the implications for future exchanges related to the topic.

There was more to the exchange than the points just discussed. A glance back to the discussion of the same episode that would look at the non-verbal interaction and the provision of feedback by the teacher would illustrate another complication. No doubt one could return again and again to that episode, and almost certainly any random selection of a few minutes of teaching could reveal similar complexities if looked at with an analytical eye and through a pedagogical lens.

The example I gave earlier of the student teacher teaching 'scale' also illustrates a mismatch between pupil and teacher ideas, but in this case the problem is not one of complete misunderstanding but of inaccuracies and vagueness on the part of both pupil and teacher. Recall that the pupil in question thought that a football pitch was about 7 metres long. Probably only football *aficionados* know the exact length of a pitch, so this is not the issue. The grossness of the error does not indicate ignorance about football but about the measurement of length. In this case the pupil's answer revealed the problem. Another problem was revealed when the teacher used a photograph of her dog as an exemplar of scale. She showed it to one pupil and asked:

Teacher: Now, Andrew, you've seen my dog. Do you think this looks like her?

Pupil: No, Miss.

As she comments, the photograph 'did not achieve the desired result and might have caused some confusion in the pupils' minds'.

Thus two of the exemplars that she had hoped to use, a drawing of a football pitch and a photograph, foundered; one because of pupils' misconceptions of the relationship between measured length and their experience of the size of the pitch, the other, I suggest, through the teacher's own lack of clarity about the concept of scale. The former problem was a case of misjudging the beginning competence of the pupils which could be tackled by teaching to bring them up to the appropriate level. The latter problem demands a re-think by the teacher about the concept of 'scale'. In later discussion the validity of photographs as exemplifying scale was queried, and she took this point. In her appraisal she suggested that a series of photographs of individual pupils of different degrees of magnification would have made the point. This does resolve the problem at one level but it is not clear whether she resolved the problem of the validity of using two-dimensional representations (photographs) of three-dimensional objects.

The concluding remarks in her report reveal that she had been sensitized to the problems of mismatch between pupils' understanding and her own and her appraisal of theirs.

The concept of scale is far more complex than it was first envisaged. This is where the main fault of the lesson lay. Ideas need to be broken down into terms that the pupils could understand and are familiar with. The pupils gained some understanding of the concept but not enough depth. It would be necessary in future to move more slowly, firmly establishing each point before moving on to the next, to encourage more active pupil participation and to clearly define the concept that was being taught.

Beginning competence

The student teacher whose work we have just considered realised subsequently that her misconceptions about pupil level of understanding had its roots in her unsatisfactory pedagogical analysis. This was compounded by deficiencies in her assessment of beginning competence. She remarks: 'Although a pre-test was given it was merely to try to ascertain the degree of difficulty the pupils could cope with and it did not contain any of the subordinate concepts that would be necessary to the lesson'.

The problem of assessing beginning competence is one of the most common problems the teachers had. Almost universally they ascribed any failure here to their unsatisfactory pedagogical analysis. When their analyses were satisfactory and their pre-tests were truly diagnostic they were sometimes surprised by the mismatch between their intuitive views of pupil capability and the actual level of pupils' concepts and skills. The teacher of orienteering was surprised to discover from his diagnostic pre-test that the pupils could not estimate angles accurately. They were also ignorant of some map-reading skills. Neither of these deficiencies would have come to light until it was too late if he had not used pre-tests. He recommends that teachers wishing to avoid disappointment in their teaching make good use of pre-tests.

The biology teacher teaching the use of 'keys' to identify specimens endorses this view strongly. I considered her experience when I discussed approaches to assessment. I mention her again to remind the reader of the case and to report her conclusions after she had analysed her teaching. She writes:

> This study has emphasised the importance of prerequisite learning. Every time a key is used none of the prerequisite discriminations and concepts should be taken for granted.

Sentiments such as these were repeated time and again by teachers taking this analytical approach to pedagogy.

Cumulative deficit

The work of these teachers, with their often acute analyses and frank appraisals of their own teaching, gives one great pause to think. They are among a very small number taking a systematic and analytical approach to teaching. Because of their study of psychopedagogy they are almost certainly much better informed, pedagogically speaking, than most of their colleagues. Yet all of them were able to point to specific aspects of their teaching that fell short of their intentions and led to pupil learning that was also deficient. Since it is likely that some of the pupil misconceptions and learning deficiencies were crucial elements in the bodies of concepts and skills the teachers were trying to teach, the deficits would almost inevitably lead to difficulties with subsequent learning unless remedial action were taken. The cumulation of such deficits over a school lifetime by most learners implies an underfulfilment of potential learning of enormous proportions.

The reason that this underfulfilment is unappreciated by most people, including most teachers, is, in my view, a direct consequence of the trivial amount of attention given to developing useful and rigorous pedagogical theories and practice. The teachers and student teachers in the cases I experienced, and which are exemplified by those in this book, detected the flawed learning and the misconceptions precisely because they had taken a systematic theory-based approach to their teaching. For the same reason they were able to prescribe for themselves ways of improving their teaching and remedying the pupils' learning deficiencies. Even the experienced teachers teaching sequences of lessons achieved insights they had not previously obtained. The student teachers made considerable progress in restructuring their original stereotypical view of teaching and, for the same reasons as the experienced teachers, were able to identify pupil misunderstanding and prescribe appropriate remedial action, often with considerable acuity.

These teachers, in the process of identifying learning deficits, seem to me to be opening up exciting possibilities of reducing cumulative learning deficits. Given the conditions for employing this type of approach to teaching more generally, and taking the view that all learners suffer learning deficits, the possibility arises of teaching capable of developing general levels of learning achieved in the past only by an exceptional few.

I am aware of the panacean tone of these comments. However, I do not feel overly defensive about this. Unlike most specifics for the universal improvement of the human condition, the suggested method of approaching teaching makes no claims to perfection or exclusivity. It is available to all to test and has already been thoroughly tested over many years by many teachers and in many different conditions. It also has, in my view, a basis in rational and testable theory. It is open to, indeed it encourages, change since it takes an open ended developmental point of view.

I shall return to some of these points later in the chapter. In the meantime I should like to consider some of the other common problems that this approach to teaching enabled teachers to detect in their own teaching.

Reinforcement

In my earlier discussion of reinforcement I referred to the 'fear of the fulsome'. I had in mind the difficulty experienced by practically all the teachers I worked with in expressing overt approval of pupils' work and efforts. Among my sample of British teachers none considered that they had been too commendatory when they viewed and analysed their teaching. When any comment was made about their reinforcement it was almost always to express surprise and frequently dismay at the paucity of their encouragement of pupils. This finding was so much the staple in the teaching we viewed and analysed that I felt justified in making the extrapolatory assertion that 'classrooms are for most pupils unrewarding places'.

I suspect that this problem may have a greater cultural loading than most teacher activities. Some recordings of US teaching seemed, on superficial viewing by some of the British teachers among those whose work I am reporting, to verge on the fulsome, while the opposite seems to be the case when Scottish teachers are compared with English teachers. I present this observation as a topic worthy of investigation rather than established fact.

I have been at pains to refer to viewing and *analysing* recordings of teaching when considering teachers' reactions to their reinforcement in the classroom. The point of this is to stress that a concern with the *quantity* of reinforcers is unlikely to give a totally accurate picture. As I have suggested earlier, transcripts of teaching interactions can give a very inaccurate picture of reinforcement and feedback when shorn of the non-verbal element and the tone of voice. Further, the social context of the exchanges and the history of the relationship between the teacher and the taught all influence the effect of the teacher's contribution to the exchange.

Apart from the sheer paucity of commendatory comment, the main problems to emerge were as follows. The commendatory words become routine and little more than punctuation. 'Good', 'Fine' and 'Yes' are common examples. The notorious flexibility of 'Yes' manifested itself frequently. 'Yes' sometimes meant 'No', sometimes 'Continue'. Sometimes it asked a question. Sometimes it expressed doubt. Similar comments could be made about other words which in cold print might seem to constitute reinforcers. Even the frequently recommended practice of repeating the pupil's answer as a reinforcer can turn into its opposite, as was illustrated in the teacher teaching creative writing (see p. 268). His repeating of the pupils' answers had become nothing more than a habit, a sort of verbal tick providing a signal of an impending shift of attention to another pupil and a loss of interest in the pupil who had just responded to his question.

Problems relating to intrinsic motivation relate to questions I have already discussed about mismatch between pupil and teacher perceptions and the misappraisal of pupils' beginning competence. Both student teachers and experienced teachers found that at times they misjudged the level of understanding of their pupils, almost universally overestimating their grasp of concepts necessary for the new learning. As a consequence the pupils had difficulties in coping with the learning and lost interest, thus exacerbating their learning difficulties.

As I have mentioned earlier in connection with other questions, neither of the problems relating to reinforcement would have been detected without the use of analytical techniques wedded to the use of video-recording. The recording makes the analysis possible, but it is insufficient on its own. The theoretical insights enabled the teachers first to identify the problematic elements in their teaching, to probe into their nature and to make provisional suggestions for their remediation. In most cases the teachers concluded that their difficulties sprang from inadequate preactive work and particularly from unsatisfactory pedagogical analysis.

Conceptual analysis

The problems relating to intrinsic reinforcement I have just mentioned were frequently a consequence of faulty analysis of the conceptual structure of the learning the teachers were trying to encourage. This failing also affected the efficacy of the teachers' work aimed at teaching bodies of concepts and problem-solving skills. I have already given examples of teachers' problems in this area. The main problem seemed to be in the hierarchical analysis of general principles into their subordinate principles and bodies of concepts. This procedure is a difficult one at all levels. I have found the same problem among teachers at university level, who, we might reasonably assume, are likely to be the most knowledgeable in their fields of study. All the teachers whose work I have reported were graduates in some field of study and all found the conceptual analysis a challenging operation. But in their reflections on their teaching they commented repeatedly on the need for a thorough analysis of the nature of the concepts they were trying to teach. Where they had been perfunctory in their analysis, they came to grief in various parts of their teaching and were able to trace the problem back to that neglect. To some extent the difficulty in analysing the conceptual structure of content may be a consequence of its unusualness. I am not aware of any other work on teaching that has built this type of activity into it. Thus all the teachers were faced with an activity that was particularly unusual and demanding. Not surprisingly, there were differences in the type of output from the analyses the teachers produced. In many of the examples I instanced I, personally, would have produced analyses that differed from those of the teachers. I commented on some of these in my discussion of pedagogical analysis. However, the great value of this work is that by explicating the way they perceived the conceptual structure of the matter to be taught, the teachers made it available to scrutiny and discussion by others and also preserved it for their own use in examining its relevance to the teaching they recorded, thus testing it in practice.

My experience over almost two decades of working with teachers attempting analyses such as these has persuaded me of the futility of the hortatory calls to systematize teachers' *pedagogical content knowledge*. Even if the teachers know their subject inside out, there is no guarantee that they will be able to make a useful analysis of its key principles and concepts. Recall, for example, the work of the biology teacher, the music teacher or the teacher of orienteering. They were all experienced teachers, all well versed in their subjects, but, without some input drawing their attention to work in the field of conceptual analysis they would *never* have developed the type of pedagogical content knowledge they did.

None of the teachers I worked with then or since has found this type of analysis anything but difficult. To my knowledge, nothing like it goes on in the teaching or research faculties in universities or other institutions of higher education. This lack is a further indication of the universally gross misconceptions about the complexity of human learning and teaching.

Thus the exhortations to emphasise pedagogical content knowledge in teacher education are essentially vacuous and will continue to be so until attention is given to its more systematic explication and the exploration of its role as a mediator between practice and theory. This cannot be done merely by writing about it or conducting short-term forays into classrooms to see how it is done. Progress will not be made without cooperative systemic explorations by teachers and researchers over the long term.

Pupils are reasonable

Teachers analysing their teaching in the light of their recordings and their preactive work become aware of the fact that what seems learner ignorance and an inability to comprehend the obvious very often turns out to be something quite different. I have already referred to the kind of thing I have in mind. Faced with teacher obscurity and sometimes even teacher error, pupils do not always resort to guessing what the teacher wants. Witness the boy trying to reason out the nature of primary and secondary evidence who was handicapped by the teacher's misunderstanding. Or the girl who wanted more evidence from the art teacher about what he was teaching, only to be rebuffed by his falling back on his authority position instead of attempting to clarify his explanation. Or the child who brought her hands slowly together to try to change the length of her clap. Or even the pupil who suggested 'sown' as a synonym of 'soiled'. The picture does emerge that there is a logic in most pupils' 'errors' that needs much more careful attention than it normally gets. Error and correctness are rarely polar opposites in these situations. A sensitive awareness of this fact, coupled with a rigorous analysis of the conceptual structure of the content being taught will enable teachers to capitalize on these 'mistakes' to explore the nature of the learning more thoroughly.

This suggestion applies to both pupil and teacher error. In all the four cases I have just mentioned, there was an element of teacher error. In all cases, had the teacher spent time in discussing with the pupils the nature of the discrepancy between their understanding, there would have been more scope for elucidation and arousal of interest and motivation than occurred when the teachers just continued on their way to the terminus. The decision as to how to avoid being shunted into a siding in such discussions is a difficult one, but should be borne in mind.

The question of the child's clapping error raises an interesting point that bears on most of the misunderstandings these teachers experienced. It is the use of convention in teaching. The slow clap conventionally signifies a long sound, whereas in reality the sound is the same length whatever the speed of the clapping. I have mentioned other uses of convention, for example in cartography; and in writing and print we find the most important conventions of all, the arbitrary substitution of one symbol, the graphical, for another, the auditory. The questions of symbolization and arbitrariness are hardly ever dealt with at any stage of education, and yet they are among the most powerful conventions in human intercourse. These questions arose out of the discussion of the teachers' analyses, but no systematic work has been done to explore the question. It seems to me that such an exploration would be most interesting and probably productive in our attempts to explore the nature of teaching.

ADDRESSING THE PROBLEMS

Since I have suggested throughout the book possible methods of tackling the problems I have just been discussing, I shall not go into detail about them here but try to summarize their main features.

Cultivating learning or delivering facts?

Undoubtedly the most important aspect of any attempt to improve current teaching quality must be the total rejection of the delivery or transmission model of teaching. As I have pointed out, it seems to be so bred in the bone that even liberal calls for change, such as Shulman's, fall into the same mould. Until the mould is well and truly shattered, progress is unlikely.

Calls for change are ten a penny. Action is as rare as snow on Midsummer Day. In Britain, report after report from the Government Inspectors' (HMI) documents bemoan the high incidence of rote-learning that goes on in schools. The same can be, and often is, said about most other countries. In the USA there is a high incidence of exhortation from leading members of the American Educational Research Association calling for teachers to teach for understanding and to go easy on teaching facts for memorizing (Simon 1980, Cole 1990). These exhortations, however, co-exist with a proclivity for teacher educators to fall in line with current values and mount the delivery wagon.

Exhortation for teachers to be reflective is also currently very fashionable. As editor of a refereed journal concerned with teacher education, the *Journal of Education for Teaching*, I find that a very large proportion of all submissions I currently receive contain the word 'reflection' in the title. But what is there for delivery teachers to reflect on? And how does one reflect on teaching anyway? These questions are rarely considered.

I have addressed these question in earlier chapters, and the theme is central to the concerns of this book. The words of the teachers analysing their own teaching are a living example of the reflection on teaching that is currently so much in vogue. However, unlike the bulk of the writing about such reflection, this is explicitly related to actual practical teaching by teachers able to articulate the rationale of their teaching and diagnose its strengths and weaknesses. This ability to explain the processes of one's teaching to others is not commonly found when 'expert' teachers are asked to communicate to others the secret of their success (Brown and McIntyre 1988, Cole 1990, *inter al.*).

The great problem with these exhortations is that they implicitly accept the *status quo*. They call for an end to rote teaching yet accept current approaches as though all is needed is a slight change of direction by teachers, a sort of fine tuning, and all will be well. The call for case studies and reflection in this pedagogical context is deeply conservative and more likely to perpetuate low-level teaching and learning that to replace it with the more complex teaching and learning called for.

Breaking the mould

Thus the work I advocate to break into this closed circle of sterile pedagogy is not more strident exhortation but deliberate attempts to intervene. We have had far too much exhortation and quite enough observation of teachers delivering the curriculum. Instead we need serious attempts to integrate theory and practice in which researchers and teachers work together in the way I have described in this book. And if this sounds like just another exhortation, at least it is based on a solid foundation of many years' collaboration with teachers which has led to their producing the kind of learning being called for. Indeed, the entire spirit of this approach is the avoidance of rote teaching and the espousal of joint exploration of ways of enhancing the meaningful learning so earnestly desired by British Government Inspectors and AERA luminaries.

The work I have described in these pages seeks to achieve these ends by the close collaboration of practising teachers, student teachers and researchers in what I referred to earlier as 'systemic research' (Stones 1986a). Teaching is seen as a form of action research. Every lesson is a pedagogical exploration in which theory from psychopedagogy combines with the teachers' practice and the understanding they have acquired from past experience of teaching. The work is open ended, as I have said earlier.

Using the techniques I have discussed, particularly combining the use of video-recording and the theoretical pedagogical constructs in the scrutiny of teaching as protocol material, facilitates collegial cooperation and the development of the ability to reflect on one's performance. This experience is particularly useful to student teachers in training in helping them to shake off their stereotypical view of teaching as telling, delivering or transmission.

But the approach must be systematic as well as systemic. Thus the work needs to be planned and implemented with care and an eye to future development. Video-recording is a powerful tool but it needs to be controlled. Obviously it can be used only sparingly, or the teachers will be overwhelmed in a week by the sheer weight of tape. It may well, therefore, be best programmed when it is possible for colleagues to collaborate in scrutinising the recording. But all teachers would benefit greatly from occasional use of recordings of their own teaching as protocol material for them to appraise in the light of pedagogical principles. In this way useful, theory-related, reflection can be developed systematically rather than in the unspecified ways implied in many exhortations for reflection.

A key element in the approach is to clarify the objectives of the teaching. As I argued in Chapter 2, this activity does not automatically result in the pupils' memorizing collections of unrelated facts. Rote teachers will set rote objectives, and delivery teachers lists of objectives to deliver. The fact that, in the past, curricula objectives have been couched by some people in such modes does not invalidate their use. The teachers in this sample, time and again, commented in their reflections on their teaching that more precision in their objectives would have improved their work, or that to a large extent their success owed a great deal to their taking time over their objectives. As the biology teacher teaching vector-carried disease found, specifying objectives precisely and systematically enables one to construct a pedagogical analysis that incorporates theoretical insights and a programme of action in a way that the vague objectives set out in the syllabuses of external examining bodies could not.

There was universal agreement among the teachers that pedagogical analysis was crucially important to the success of their teaching. Repeatedly, shortcomings were seen as a result of error or lack of rigour in their analyses. Their findings and convictions strengthened my view that this procedure is the vital link between theory and practice.

I should like to remind readers, however, that the pedagogical analysis is vastly different from some other procedures for planning teaching. Often all that the latter involve is deciding on a path to follow in instruction that is frequently of a delivery nature. Pedagogy rarely enters into these analyses. Pedagogical analysis, on the other hand, requires skill in conceptual analysis, in identifying the nature of learning in a given task, in deciding how best to arrange teaching to maximise the learning and how best to evaluate learning, making sure that the learning assessed is genuinely transferable. I am assuming, here, that it is unlikely that a teacher would wish to teach a lesson entirely devoted to rote-learning, although this could be possible.

The knowledge and use of pedagogical analyses was entirely the consequence of the interventionist approach adopted. No amount of case studies of 'normal' teaching or the codification of craft knowledge is likely to have provided evidence or information about the use of pedagogical analyses by the teachers. To think otherwise is another example of the misconception of teaching as a simple operation that one learns by doing. As it is, none of the teachers knew anything about this approach at the outset. They were, therefore, in no position to realise its great utility without the intervention of a theoretically oriented researcher/tutor. Further, they would not have been able to make a pedagogical analysis without an understanding of pedagogical theory.

In the event, cooperative work among colleagues with the intervention of the tutor/researcher and study of the principles of psychopedagogy equipped them to make their analyses. However, they would not have fully understood the benefits of pedagogical analysis if they had not tried it in practice. When they had had experience of teaching based on pedagogical analyses their reactions were of the nature of those I referred to earlier. In the words of the art tutor: 'Much of the success enjoyed [by the teachers and student teachers he had worked with] during the actual teaching could be traced to a rigorous task analysis'.

On p. 296 I commented on the inability of 'expert' teachers to explain the secret of their success. Leaving on one side for the moment the question of 'expertness', I suggest that this apparent inarticulateness is a consequence of the teachers' lack of a body of pedagogical theory. It is not merely that they lack the jargon, but that they have not had the appropriate experience to have acquired the necessary conceptual structures and pedagogical skills. Operating, as those teachers are likely to be, within a conventional view of teaching as an undifferentiated practical skill to be learned on the job, they have no means of analysing their practice in terms useful to others. By the same token, they are also unlikely to be able to articulate to themselves, in any insightful and systematic way, the reasons for success or failure in their teaching. In other words, despite their expertness, they will not be able to 'reflect' on their teaching.

The concept of 'expertness', however, is one that could be challenged. In general, discussions invoking the practice of 'good' teachers are based on a norm-referenced model and a view of teaching as it currently is. Without entering into a discussion of the shakiness of this foundation for the idea of 'expertness' (see Stones 1984a, Stones, 1989a and b, Stones and Morris 1972), one might question the notion of 'expert' that does not include the ability to relate one's activity to some body of theory and to communicate it to others. Candidates for expert teacher status drawn from a body of such people might be nothing more than the best of a bad bunch. I do not wish, by these remarks, to denigrate the efforts and skills of the many dedicated individuals in our schools, but to draw sharply to the attention of readers the hollowness of much of the writing about reflection. Current discussions about reflection on action or in action ought to concern themselves with reflection on or in practice *and theory*.

The work that I have reported in this book has been aiming to do that over many years, and I believe that progress has been made. I think this applies particularly in connection with teacher acceptance of and enthusiasm for the idea of a systematic body of rigorous theoretical principles to which they can relate their practice and to which they themselves can contribute. They feel their eyes opening to larger horizons and they like it.

Shaping the new

As I have mentioned on several previous occasions, every one of the teachers whose work is reported in this book and all their colleagues, both novices and veterans, conducted pedagogical investigations of various degrees of size and complexity. All of them analysed their experiences and produced a report on them. This was reflection on and in theory and practice of pedagogy. It was the outcome of systematic intervention into teaching in the light of theory. A striking feature of the work was the way the teachers felt that the heuristic guides liberated rather than constrained their work. This effect is the opposite of that argued by those who see systematic approaches to teaching as inhibiting and the death of creativity. The reverse seems to be the case. The teacher who developed the exciting idea of looking for elegance in problem solving was one who explicitly referred to the help derived from the heuristics. He had leaped ahead in his teaching and his thinking about teaching, as compared with the exhortations of writers such as I referred to at the beginning of this chapter.

Another development, still in embryo but nonetheless real, is the idea of involving the pupils themselves in reflection on their learning. This is to be seen in the briefing and debriefing sessions. I see no reason why the techniques for teacher learning and development discussed in these pages should not be raised with the pupils themselves to the extent that this seems appropriate.

The general point underlying such developments is that if one operates from a body of practice-related theoretical principles, one draws on a distillation of a wide range of experience, both of practical teaching and of pedagogical theory. This experience, being so wide-ranging yet integrated and concentrated, enables one to tackle a variety of new and old pedagogical problems with a good chance of success and with the possibility of finding new and creative ways of solving them. If, on the other hand, one operates with no unified body of theory, one is constrained almost inevitably by a disparate collection of past experiences much less rich in possibilities for finding ways of solving pedagogical problems. This argument is all of a piece with the general line taken throughout this book on the way learning should be. By the same token, I suggest, this is the way teaching should be.

THE PROBLEMS AND THE POSSIBILITIES

The problems are many, the possibilities are virtually limitless. Elsewhere, I have suggested that we are currently at the paleopedagogical stage in our understanding of human learning and teaching (Stones 1989a). We have hardly begun to understand either. People have achieved fame and fortune and made distinguished careers for themselves by training rats, dogs, or circus animals to perform tricks that most children can learn to do in minutes. Other people have spent weeks attempting to simulate the most trivial piece of human learning using some of the most sophisticated computers currently available. The regard in which this type of work is held contrasts sharply with the way teaching is usually regarded.

Why the discrepancy? I suggest that the major factor accounting for it is the point I have repeated many times that because the type of learning that is peculiarly human, namely cognitive learning, is based on language, the shadow of thought is confused with its substance. Speech is equated with thought. Words cover a conceptual vacuum. By the same token, if all one has to do to teach is to tell, it is clearly more difficult to teach animals without speech than children with it.

Humanity's first step out of the paleopedagogical age will not be taken until it is generally realised that there is more to teaching than telling. Considering teaching as intervention in human learning to change human thinking, rather than as delivering a product vaguely labelled 'the curriculum', could well be a bigger step for mankind than Neil Armstrong's lunar footfall. Probably the human skills required to develop systematic ways of enhancing human thinking will be greatly in excess of those used to deliver the astronaut to his destination.

The payoff would be equally disproportionate. If only a fraction of the cumulative learning deficit I referred to earlier could be reduced, the lives of an enormous number of people would be enriched. If it could be reduced considerably, the potential is mind-boggling.

FOR A FUTURE OF QUALITY

Despite the extravagance of the last few paragraphs, I do not believe I am a millenarian. Future developments in pedagogy do not await a supernatural manifestation. The potential for their realisation is in our own hands and minds. The cases I have considered are in some ways a puny contribution to the process, and I make no great claims for them. But they are indicative of the possibilities for development and the routes that might be worthy of exploration. The implementation of the approach I have described and advocated is dependent upon a number of shifts in attitudes and practices which I have alluded to and which I should like now to recapitulate.

The first will be no surprise. The delivery view of teaching is so prevalent in the English-speaking world today, in the language used about teaching as well as in much of its practice, that it is probably the greatest single obstacle to the development of a form of teaching fit for human beings.

Closely linked with this view is the idea that on-the-job teacher training plus a modicum of theory is adequate to produce competent teachers. The kind of theory intended is unlikely to have *any* pedagogical content remotely resembling anything I have discussed in this book. It is more likely to be concerned with subject matter. Might I recall for you the findings we repeatedly found, that subject matter specialists were rarely able to make a conceptual analysis of their chosen fields and that printed sources on the pedagogy of various subjects are virtually non existent.

On-the-job training involves the neophyte watching the expert and attempting to do likewise. This is another manifestation of the simplistic view of teaching now canonised by the British Government's decree that teacher trainers can refresh their teaching merely by going into schools for 'relevant experience'. For any worthwhile progress to be made towards improvement in teaching, attitudes such as these need to be abandoned for those that unify 'relevant theory' with 'relevant practice'.

Thus my next desideratum is for far greater attention to be paid to pedagogical theory and practice. Pedagogy has come a long way from the days I first used the term in the early 1970s as the title of the courses I was running for beginning and experienced teachers. In those days it was scarcely mentioned, and when it was it had the connotations of an arid academicism. It is much more acceptable these days. However, one needs to be careful to clarify the way one is using the term, since its boundaries are very fluid and its constituent concepts vague. I have tried to clarify my use of the term in this book and have also narrowed its focus to the psychological aspects of teaching. I believe that this is reasonable since psychology is the discipline *par excellence* concerned with the nature of human thinking, learning and emotional life. However, I do not dispute the claims of other disciplines to an important role. But theory must demonstrate its practical relevance and utility to teaching to merit consideration as part of pedagogical theory. The great deficiency of much education theory in the past has been its virtual irrelevance to teaching (Stones 1989b). Not surprisingly it has disappeared from the curriculum of many teacher training institutions.

It is essential, in my view, that theories from psychology be reinstated into teacher training courses. Not by bringing back the old discipline, but by its rising from its ashes reborn in a new form as psychopedagogy. I have made my attempt to encourage this renaissance but make no claims to exclusivity. We need pluralistic approaches, dialogue and dialectic to enhance developments in the field. However, the proving of whatever nostrums are advanced is in the practice. Only if they demonstrate their efficacy in developing conceptual learning and problem solving in a variety of fields, in motivating pupils and in being capable of development in connection with practical teaching should they be entertained.

This commitment to meaningful learning and problem solving, in a psychopedagogical context, precludes the type of approach characteristic of conventional courses in educational studies in training institutions. When these courses were prevalent in Britain, delivery approaches were widespread and coexisted with the apprenticeship approach to practical teaching. The reborn pedagogy must eschew this dichotomy. It should take the form of an interventionist discipline, bringing theoretical insights from appropriate sources to bear on real teaching problems. Those sources will include such disciplines as psychology related to human learning, concepts from the fields of subject study and the teachers' own experience and accumulated know-how.

Approaches to teaching of this sort will facilitate another indispensable element in a rigorous pedagogy: the marriage of the work of teachers and that of theorists and researchers. The offspring of this liaison would be the systemic pedagogical research I referred to earlier. The boundaries between research and teaching become blurred and teaching itself becomes a form of action research and an open ended process of recursive amelioration such as I have described earlier. Teachers become aware of the complexity of teaching. They realise its challenging nature and interest far beyond the bounds of the appeal of transmission teaching. Teachers with this type of experience will be able to make a worthwhile approach to reflection.

For developments of this type to take place the teacher training institutions need to take pedagogy far more seriously than they have done hitherto. The dilemma many such institutions face at the moment is the void produced by the disappearance of courses in the educational disciplines that bear on teaching. In practical terms the institutional pressures are all against the developments I advocate. Tutorial staff themselves are likely to be ignorant of many of the phenomena I have discussed in this book. As I said some years ago, a bootstrap operation is called for (Stones, 1984a). I know this is easier said than done. One way forward would be to concentrate on the nature in which teaching practice is conceived and attempt to introduce into it some of the notions of pedagogy I have been discussing. I do believe, however, that often the biggest obstacles in situations such as these lie in people's minds rather than institutional structures. If the will is there, the way will be discovered.

Apart from the pedagogical insights and improvement in teaching that the work I have described has enabled teachers to achieve, it also provides two other important messages for teachers and teacher educators and may facilitate bootstrap operations. The cooperation of the in-service experienced teachers working with the student teachers on initial teacher training was a powerful learning relationship for both. The student teachers gained from the experience of their non-judgmental mentors, and the experienced teachers gained from the freshness and different insights of the recently graduated student teachers. They both gained from having to justify action and proposals for action by analytical reasoning in connection with very specific teaching situations. The analysis was not that which is commonly found in student–teacher supervisor interviews, but was focused on the deep structures of pedagogy that have been discussed in this book.

The group 'counselling' using video recordings of their teaching by both groups was also a very powerful learning encounter. The establishment of an atmosphere of supportive openness combined with frankness and sharp appraisal of each others' teaching takes time to achieve, but it is essential in order to obtain maximum benefit from the discussion. The routine use of TV equipment and the willingness of the university tutor to be subjected to the same process in connection with *his* role also helped. The aim is to objectify the teaching that is the subject of appraisal, so that whichever of the teachers is on the screen the personal threat is diminished and the ideal of discussion focusing on *the* teaching rather than the teaching of specific teachers is approached. Given time, I have found that this can be achieved so that the unusual situation is reached in which groups of teachers are discussing each others' teaching which is available for all to see with few inhibitions. With this stage reached, cooperating teachers from schools and visitors to the institution have been routinely absorbed by the group with no difficulties.

I believe there is one other point of considerable importance to be derived from this work. As I have said, many of the teachers involved had subject specialities. The middle school, primary and infant teachers were more generalist. Some of the experienced teachers came from teacher education themselves but were subject specialists, not people from the 'education disciplines'. None of them had any prior knowledge of psychopedagogy. Nevertheless, through working in the ways I have outlined, entirely through workshop reading and practice-related activities, with *no* lectures, they were able to get sufficient insight into the principles of teaching as investigative pedagogy to be able to continue working. Further, they found this way of working congenial and fruitful in this way as I shall show later. Of particular interest is the reactions of people from other teacher training institutions. They were subject specialists and they became particularly enthusiastic about the approach. Some went back to their institutions and introduced psychopedagogy and the idea of systematic exploration of teaching into their own courses (Evans 1983).

Among the new pedagogical insights these teachers gained were those that bear directly on the question of pedagogical content knowledge. The teachers were specialist in different fields of teaching. Ideas about pedagogy and exploratory teaching changed their ideas about the teaching of their chosen subjects. Pedagogical content knowledge was developed where there had been little or none of a systematic nature before.

Finally, I suggest that the teaching I have discussed in these pages has raised some interesting questions about the way we view pupils. The practice of debriefing after teaching raises questions similar to those raised in publications such as those of Freire (1972) and the School of Barbiana (1970). This is the idea of making the learners party to their own learning. The difference is that the involvement of the learners as partners is augmented by the theoretical insights that can be introduced by the teacher. Why not acquaint the pupils with some idea of the rationale of the learning activity the teacher is asking them to engage in? I have referred to teaching in which the pupils are clearly doing their best to cooperate with the teacher but are in the dark about what is going on. Giving teachers what they want is a well recognised phenomenon; why not give the pupils a few clues as to how they might be able to do that effectively?

We might approach this by introducing some ideas to the pupils about how human beings learn. The suggestions I made above for building on the briefing and debriefing sessions could be extended to include some aspects of psychology related to human learning. Psychology is now on the syllabus of some secondary schools. Why not approach it not as a 'subject' to be taught by delivery methods, perhaps augmented a little by a few experiments, but by integrating it with the subject matter they are striving to learn? Why not introduce psychology to the pupils as it impinges on the most interesting 'subjects' they could study: themselves? Why not make those ideas fully systemic by inviting the pupils to help in the process?

If this suggestion seems impossibly impractical, consider one possibility. If the teachers implement the procedures of reflection themselves they will be employing what I refer to as B type skills, in which they appraise human activities in the light of theoretical principles. In my discussion I have focused on the teachers' teaching, since this is the concern of this book and little work has been done to extend this to pupils. However, some of the teachers did make use of protocols in their teaching, and this involved the pupils' appraising their own or their peers' actions in the light of principles the teacher had been trying to teach. Activity of this type was using the principles with the pupils; what was not done systematically was to make explicit to them just what the principles were. It may not have been possible to do this with all the pupils, especially the younger ones, but there seems to me to be much to be said to support the idea of the systematic involvement of pupils in the study of their own learning, to the extent that the teacher judges they are capable of benefiting from it. In case of teacher uncertainty, I would always advocate bringing the pupils into the process.

In an interesting way, then, via the route of hard-headed systematic exploration of pedagogy, we converge with many of the ideas advanced in the past by 'progressive' educators. With a difference. What I am suggesting involves what most of them lacked, namely a rigorous, theory-informed pedagogy that is explicated and explicable to others and not dependent upon the presence of a guru. Sitting with a guru is little different from Sitting with Nellie (Stones and Morris 1972) to learn to teach. The learning of neither teachers nor pupils will progress with such a foundation. The externalising of pedagogical principles tried in practice makes them available to all and will, to my mind, make the learning of teachers and pupils much more effective and enjoyable. I hope the experiences of the teachers whose work has taught me so much will help readers to receive the same benefit.

VALEDICTION

I should like to conclude with a selection of some of the reactions of the teachers and student teachers to the work they did. The comments were spontaneously included in the course of the reports in which they appraised their teaching. Their comments were, thus, not off-the-cuff remarks but based on their thinking while compiling and writing up their reports. I am aware that it is commonplace in reports of research introducing student teachers to new methods in teaching to find student enthusiasm for the innovation. In part it may be a form of Hawthorne effect. It may well be a form of giving teacher what he wanted. Naturally I demur from this assessment in the case of the way the teachers evaluated the utility of the work reported here. However, I also suggest that there are several factors that support this view. The shortest time any of the participants was involved in it was one year, and in the case of all the experienced teachers it was much longer. The Hawthorne effect would thus have had time to dissipate, and the time spent was long enough for them to make a genuine test of the approach in action. In addition, in the early stages some of them made their scepticism quite clear,although they changed their ideas later. They were not asked to make these comments but were asked to conclude their reports with an appraisal of the teaching they had undertaken. Nevertheless, should readers wish to take with a grain of salt what follows I feel confident that they will soon realise it is not really necessary.

My first example comes from a graduate student teacher who had been teaching about compound words.

The whole experience was both enjoyable and valuable to me, it is one I should like to attempt again. Self-criticism is a valuable exercise in itself, but more so if one learns from one's mistakes. The only point that I, as a student teacher, would wish to make is that I feel that not enough time has been spent both in the study and the application of the theoretical ideas from psychopedagogy *and that represents on my part a move from reception to a feeling if not a strong belief to one that suggests that perhaps it does provide the framework for putting theory into practice which after all is what teaching is all about.*

Another student teacher teaching the concept of 'leisure' comments as follows:

> I think that all the favourable points during the lesson could be attributed to the various schedules studied in *Psychopedagogy*. In particular, the 'concept teaching' chapter and task analysis were invaluable. . . . Thus any future teaching which I undertake will be more formally structured and analysed due to the in-depth study of this teaching exercise. Obviously, due to pressures of time, not every lesson could be as highly structured, but the main principles will be utilized.

The next student teacher had taught a series of lessons about small animals. The pupils had to collect and record information about them to develop an understanding of them and to overcome some of the pupils' negative feelings about the animals. It was an exercise in teaching problem solving.

> The exercise was very valuable and useful to me . . . [it] allowed me to practise problem-solving theory in practical teaching and highlighted the tremendous problems which can occur. . . . I realise that using theory in practice produces qualitatively better teaching.

The student teacher teaching primary and secondary evidence:

> Thus, I feel that the exercise has been a useful although slightly painful eye opener on just what is involved in the seemingly straightforward task of teaching concepts like primary and secondary evidence.

The following contribution comes from a student teacher who was initially very sceptical:

> To conclude, I think that the teaching experiment has been a helpful, enlightening and important feature of my teacher training. Initially, I was a non-believer. I couldn't see the relevance of psychopedagogy to myself as a teacher. I now realise that this was due to my lack of understanding of the subject. Rather than admit this, my natural defence mechanisms foolishly dismissed the subject as being unimportant and futile. Now, however, I am certainly more knowledgeable about the subject and having myself had the 'pleasure' of watching a recording of myself teaching I can also see how it can be applied to an actual teaching situation by aiding and advising how to correct problems that may occur. Teaching is often regarded as a vocation, you are either born a teacher or you are not. I doubt very much whether this is true, but if it is then a teacher can still improve his methods and techniques by following a more psychopedagogical approach. If I had done so more carefully my teacher effort would most certainly have borne more fruit.

An experienced teacher and college tutor concluded:

Very briefly, this is an extremely valuable exercise for any teacher at any level. It seemed to me to underline the significance of work at the pre-active phase. The clear identification of pupil and teacher objectives, the establishment of the necessary entry behaviour and the congruence of the analysis of objectives with the pedagogical analysis are the determinants of the quality of work, especially if that work is evaluated in terms of pupil learning.

A biology teacher commented that the heuristic guides would be valuable:

> as a method for the teacher to exert quality control on the process/ products of her lessons [and] as a method of quality control for the teacher's learning and development.

The art tutor, whose work with in-service and student teachers I referred to in earlier chapters, produced a lengthy comment with specific reference to the heuristic on the teaching of concepts. I report a selection of his main points, emerging from a study of the teaching of various art concepts comparing teaching using psychopedagogical methods and 'normal' teaching.

> Feedback from the study has taken the form of written notes, video tapes, questionnaires and, not least, hours of discussion with teachers in training and service. The conclusions of the study show that psychological principles, in the form of STOC [the heuristic for concept teaching], have a contribution to make to teaching.
>
> The problem of arriving at pedagogical guidelines has been com- pounded by a parallel subject dilemma. The need to correct an imbalance between the weight accorded to craft [psychomotor] activities and the neglect of art concepts which constitute a theoretical basis for those craft skills, is long overdue in my opinion. I also believe that the Schedule for the Teaching of Concepts presents a means of dealing with this imbalance in the form of a system of guidelines based on an analytical approach to teaching in which the emphasis is upon understanding of conceptual content. I suggest that the schedule represents an alternative model which would challenge the 'closed circuit' in teacher education and reverse the tendency towards conservatism which is a characteristic of the profession.
>
> It is my proposition that teacher education in art would benefit from a more systematic approach than is currently practised, involving the analysis of content, structuring of teaching and assessment of the outcomes of that activity. It might be that in STOC we have a tool purpose built to perform that very task.
>
> It is my intention to continue to apply the schedule's principles to

teaching experiments with the long term view of incorporating the schedule into an Art PGCE (initial teacher training) programme.

It is my belief that STOC, in addition to providing a means of evaluating the effectiveness of the student teachers' teaching, also provides the supervisor with guidelines for his own behaviours. Further, I believe the implications for teacher education are clear and that a strong case can be argued for involving STOC at all levels of professional development.

The teacher of orienteering also wrote at some length about the efficacy of the approach. Again, I attempt to identify the salient comments.

Intuition played no part in planning the lessons as throughout the psychological principles relating to human learning were applied. The learning system . . . enabled me to produce effective learning situations.

He goes on to suggests ways in which he would modify his approach on a future occasion. He continues:

However, none of the alternations or refinements detract from, invalidate or provide evidence of the impracticability of the approach and the schedules [heuristics], rather, because of them I was able to evaluate my teaching to become more efficient and effective. Further, through my daily work in mathematics, science and geography, I have become more aware of the interrelatedness and comprehensiveness of the schedules for different contexts.

Any reservations about the approach . . . lie not in the guidance of the heuristic devices but rather in the reluctance of the practising teacher to make use of the guidance.

I found the model for specifying the types and levels of objectives to be very helpful in generating the objectives. In particular I found the heuristic device for analysing specific teaching tasks to be very beneficial.

As I reported in Chapter 10, this teacher also expressed pleasure at the way the heuristics did not inhibit or restrict him; rather they prompted him to explore a variety of approaches in a systematic way.

He concludes his remarks by posing questions 'Would the pupils wish to continue solving problems in orienteering given a free choice?' and 'Would I continue to teach using the approach specified?' The answer follows:

I am pleased to report that the pupils are achieving success in orienteering. To be more successful, however, they must now learn the second basis of navigation, that of knowing how far one should travel in a particular direction. We both possess the motivation, and because this study has widened and deepened my understanding of the psychological principles relating to human learning I have the means successfully to attain the objective.

THE FUTURE IN THE PRESENT

Finally I return to where I began this chapter, on the hortatory appeals for the development of the kind of work I have described in this book. The key developments advocated are teaching for learning with understanding, and for changes in teacher education to enable teachers to teach like this (Simon 1979, Hopkins and Reid 1984, Hogan 1988, Solomon 1987, Cole 1990, McNamara 1990, HMI reports various years). Shuell (1990) suggests that problem solving holds promise as a 'metaphor' of learning and teaching. Shulman epitomises appeals such as these in the paper I referred to earlier, where he looks ahead to the way he would like teaching to be in the future.

> I envision the use of case method in teacher education, whether in our classrooms or in special laboratories with simulations, video disks and annotated scripts, as a means for developing strategic understanding for extending capacities towards professional judgment and decision making. These methods of instruction would involve the careful confrontation of principles with cases, of general rules with concrete documented events – a dialectic of the general with the particular in which the limits of the former and the boundaries of the latter are explored.
>
> (Shulman, 1986)

Since I have been doing the kind of work appealed for in the many and varied exhortations since the early 1970s, I cannot help sharing the sentiments they express. The notion of teaching as problem solving, in my experience, is not metaphorical, it is practical. Shulman's vision is no mean description of that work, some of which is discussed in this book. And, as I mentioned in the first chapter, I am continuing to develop it with head teachers working with colleagues in whole school staff development. But that's another story.

Let one of the teachers from this present study have the last word. He is the music teacher, also a jazz musician, and takes teaching seriously. Like the teacher of art, he is critical of the vague talk about creativity in such subjects and is forthright in his comments.

> So far in this study there has been a hint of dissatisfaction with many approaches in music education. The unsystematic nature of many discussed is the main area of concern. Though many may claim to be developing the concepts of the learner, the aims and schedules of the teaching programme are often so vague it leaves one wondering how they can succeed. It is one thing to get into print by stating 'all

the children to compose', but it is another explaining to the teacher just how to do this. The lack of true direction reported in this study would suggest that many teachers have given up; wanting to 'create' but not knowing how to.

He found that the systematic approach taking composition as a type of problem solving helped to remedy this difficulty.

With reference to this study, it can be seen by systematic evaluation that unexpected results were observed. These could be modified in future work of this nature. Pupils did things that were not expected. The use of unison melodic progression and the interval of the fourth are examples of this unexpectedness.

The value of this approach is that it has shown, in practice, some evidence of successful concept learning at a high-level. It has also been shown that, although it is not the only approach to the teaching of composition, the systematic approach used here ensures a clear set of results in that the pupils' melodies are good models of their type, doing exactly what is required and not including erroneous or irrelevant assumptions in the form of compositions. Those offered by other methods have been proved to show the latter.

If teaching is to become effective and accountable, it needs an approach such as this. It is not expensive to instigate, nor is it time consuming once initiated.

One man's vision is another man's *déjà vu*.

Appendix

THE CASE STUDIES

The work of the following student teachers and experienced teachers has been referred to in the text. Several hundred others not directly referred to also influenced and are continuing to influence my thinking. I acknowledge the work of all of them with thanks.

Starred items are M. Ed. dissertation titles held at the University of Liverpool, Sydney Jones Library. All items are mimeo.

Alarcão, I., Teaching English as a foreign language to student teachers
Andrews, P., Social studies: the concept of an election
Ashworth, P., Metalwork: flat cold-chiselling
Bescot, P., Geography: the concept of scale
Blackburn, J., French language, oral questioning
Boultwood, A., Social studies: democracy
Breen, J., Social science: historical materialism
Bretherton, R., Poetry: metrical rhythm in German poetry
Carrick, G., History: the bog people
Cartwright, S., Social studies: the concept of democracy
Dodd, A., Social studies, politics, the concept of an election
Dudley, J., Trade: imports and exports
Edgar, D., English grammar
Edwards, Social studies: the concept of 'a tourist'
Ellis V.A., (1983) Infant teaching: the applicability of psychopedagogical techniques to the teaching of rhythmic patterns to young children*
Ellis, V.A., Infant teaching: tessellation
Erskine, B., (1982) Art: psychopedagogy in the teaching of art concepts*
Erskine, B., Art: pattern
Erskine, B., Art: tone
Evans, D.J., (1982) Music: the applicability of psychopedagogical techniques to an aspect of aural music training*
Evans, H.C., Geology: reading a geological map
Evans, H.C., Student teacher counselling on practice teaching: a diary
Fraser, J., Biology: the use of keys
Fraser, J., Biology: concept of cell
Fraser, J., Biology: concept of vector-carrying disease
Hegarty, K., Road Safety: teaching the use of the Green Cross Code
Hegarty, K., Mathematics: the concept of rectangles,
Hodkinson, C., Drawing: plans in drawings

Hollingworth, A., History: the use of evidence

Kayes, J., Psychomotor skill: the volleyball dig pass

Martland, J., (1980) Orienteering: an empirical study of the application of psychological principles to the teaching of orienteering*

Martland, J., Motor skill training: catching a rugby ball

Merrick, J.B., Geography: humidity

Morris, G., English: teaching creative writing

Anon. Industrial relations: a rail strike

Paterson, R., Economics, the concepts of wage and salary

Pollington, C.H., Music: accent

Pollington, C.H., Music teaching appreciation

Pollington, C.H., (1982) Music: an investigation into the psychopedagogy of teaching simple musical composition*

Quinlan, R.R., (1983) Reading comprehension: the teaching of reading comprehension in junior schools: the application of psychopedagogical principles*

Quinlan, R.R., Reading: psychopedagogy applied to contextual cuing in the development of word attack skills

Quinlan, R.R., Reading: reversals and inversions

Reay, L., Social studies: leisure

Scott, A., Social studies: democracy

Seviour, A., History: the concept of 'immigrant'

Silvano, W., Sociology: deviancy

Taylor, M., Mathematics: line graphs

Tillston, M., English: compound words

Troy, A.E., Metalwork: soldering

Watson, B., English: writing a description

Williams, E., Probationer teacher counselling

Young, R.J., (1981) Reading: the implications of theory and research for the teaching of reading comprehension*

Processes, Teacher Satisfaction and Pupil Affect: a Meta-Analysis, San Francisco: Far West Laboratory for Educational Research.

Gliessman, D. (1972) *The Nature and Use of Protocol Materials*, Preliminary paper for Task Force '72, Washington, DC: US Department of Health, Education and Welfare.

Glynn, T. (1985) 'Contexts for independent learning', *Educational Psychology* 5(1): 5–15.

Gottleib, E. E. and Cornbleth, C. (1989) 'The professionalization of tomorrow's teachers: an analysis of US teacher education reform rhetoric', *Journal of Education for Teaching*, 15(1): 1–12.

Grimmett, P. P. (ed.) (1984) *Research in Teacher Education: Current Problems and Future Prospects in Canada*, Centre for the Study of Teacher Education, University of British Columbia.

Grove, J. W. (1988) 'The intellectual revolt against science', *The Skeptical Inquirer* 13–1: 70–75.

Hartley, D. (1990) review of Carr (1989) 'Quality in teaching: arguments for a reflective profession' in *Journal of Education for Teaching*, 16(3): 319–20.

Hextall, I. (1988) 'Educational changes in England and Wales: the impact of the New Right', in Gumbert, E. B. *Making the Future: Politics and Educational Reform in the United States, England, the Soviet Union, China and Cuba*, 59–76, Georgia: Georgia State University.

Hogan, P. (1988) 'Communicative competence and cultural emancipation: reviewing the rationale for educational studies in teacher education', *Oxford Review of Education*, 14: 185–97.

Hopkins, D. and Reid, K. (1984) 'Master's degree in Education', *Journal of Further and Higher Education*, 8(1): 10–17.

Kagan, D. M. (1988) 'Teaching as clinical problem-solving: a critical examination of the analogy and its implications', *Review of Educational Research* 58(4): 482–505.

Kagan, D. M. (1989) The heuristic value of regarding classroom instruction as an aesthetic medium, *Educational Researcher*, 18(6): 11–18.

Kohl, H. (1977) *On Teaching*, London: Methuen.

Krathwohl, D. R., Bloom, B. S. and Masia, B. B. (1964) *Taxonomy of Educational Objectives: Handbook II: the Affective Domain*, London: Longmans, Green.

Kruger, C., Summers, M., and Palacio, D. (1990) 'INSET for primary science in the National Curriculum: are the real needs of teachers perceived?', *Journal of Education for Teaching* 16(6): 133–46.

Landa, L. N. (1976) 'The ability to think – how can it be taught?', *Soviet Education*, March, 4–66.

Lange, M. and Hora, F.B. (1963) *Collins Guide to Mushrooms and Toadstools*, London: Collins.

Lanier, J. E. and Lytle, J. W. (1986) 'Research on teacher education' in Wittrock, M. C. (ed.) *Handbook of research on teaching*, 3rd edn, New York: Macmillan.

Leinhardt, G. (1990) 'Capturing craft knowledge in teaching', *Educational Researcher*, 19(2): 18–25.

Leytham, G. W. H. (1970) Review of Stones, E. (1968) 'Learning and teaching: a programmed introduction', *British Journal of Educational Psychology*, 40: 90–3.

Limbrick, E., McNaughton, S. and Glynn, T. (1985) 'Reading gains for under-achieving tutors and tutees in a cross-age peer tutoring programme', *Journal of Child Psychology and Psychiatry*.

Liston, D. P. and Zeichner, K. 1987 'Reflective teacher education and moral deliberation', *Journal of Teacher Education* 38(6): 2–8.

Liston, D. P. and Zeichner, K. (1990) 'Reflective teacher education and action research', *Journal of Education for Teaching*, 16(3): 255–74.

Luchins, A. (1942) 'Mechanization in problem-solving: the effect of *Einstellung*', *Psychological Monographs*, 54(6).

Luria, A. R. (1961) *The Role of Speech in the Regulation of Normal and Abnormal Behaviour*, Oxford: Pergamon.

McCulloch, M. (1979) *School Experience in Initial B.Ed./B.Ed.(Hons) Degrees Validated by the Council for National Academic Awards*, London: CNAA.

McLaughlin, D. (1991) 'National examinations in teacher education in Papua New Guinea: political and pedagogical dimensions', *Journal of Education for Teaching*, 17(1): 17–28.

McNamara, D. (1988) 'Objectives or aspirations?', *Education Section Review*, Journal of the Education Section of the British Psychological Society.

McNamara, D. (1990) 'Research on teachers' thinking: its contribution to educating student teachers to think critically', *Journal of Education for Teaching*, 16(2): 147–60.

Mark, R. (1990) 'Pedagogical content knowledge: from a mathematical case to a modified conception', *Journal of Teacher Education*, 41(3): 3–11.

Martland, J. R. (1983) 'An empirical study of the application of psychological principles to the teaching of orienteering', *Journal of Education for Teaching*, 9(1): 77–96.

May, W. (1990) 'What's in music and art textbooks?', *Communication Quarterly*, 12.3, Spring, 1 and 4, Institute for Research on Teaching, Michigan State University, East Lansing.

Medley, D. M. (1987) 'Criteria for evaluating teaching' in Dunkin, M. J. *The International Encyclopedia of Teaching and Teacher Education*, 161–9, Oxford: Pergamon.

Meighan, R. (1977) 'Pupils' perceptions of the classroom techniques of postgraduate student teachers', *British Journal of Teacher Education*, 3(2): 139–48.

Meighan, R. (1981) *A Sociology of Educating*, Eastbourne: Holt, Rinehart and Winston.

Montessori, M. (1964) *The Montessori Method*, translated by Gorge, A. E., New York: Schocken.

Mugford, L. (1972) 'A new way of predicting readability', *Reading*, 4(2): 31–5.

Neill, S. R. S. J., (1986) 'Children's reported responses to teachers' non-verbal signals: a pilot study', *Journal of Education for Teaching*, 12(1): 53–64.

Nickerson, R. S. (1989) 'New directions in educational assessment', *Educational Researcher*, 18(9): 3–7.

O'Hear, A. (1989) 'Teachers can become qualified in practice', *The Guardian*, 24 January, London.

Pavlov, I. P. (1941) *Selected Works*, Moscow: Foreign Languages Publishing House.

Pavlov, I. P. (1955) *Lectures on Conditioned Reflexes*, translated Gantt, W. H., London: Lawrence and Wishart.

Perkins, D. N. and Salomon, 'Are cognitive skills context bound?' *Educational Researcher* 18(1): 16–25.

Peterson, R. (1989) '"Don't mourn – organise": teachers take the offensive against basals', *Theory into Practice*, 28(4): 295–9.

Reber, A. S. (1985) *Dictionary of Psychology*, Harmondsworth: Penguin.

Reid, J. F. (1966) 'Learning to think about reading', *Educational Research*, 9(1): 56–62.

Robinson, F. P. (1946) *Effective Study*, New York: Harper Row.

Rogers, C. G. (1987) 'Attribution theory and motivation in school', in Hastings, N. and Schwieso, J. *New Directions in Educational Psychology: 2 Behaviour and Motivation in the Classroom*, 195–213, Lewes: Falmer.

Rowe, M.B. (1974) Relations of wait-time and rewards to the development of language, logic and fate control: Part 1 – Wait time, *Journal of Research in*

Science Teaching, 11: 81–94., Part 2 – Rewards, *Journal of Research in Science Teaching*, 11: 291–308.

Sagan, C. (1990) 'Why we need to understand science', *Skeptical Inquirer*, 14(3): 263–9.

Samuel, R. (1989) 'History's battle for a new past', *The Guardian*, 21 January, London.

Sandels, S. (1975) *Children in Traffic*, London: Elek Books Ltd.

Sanders, D. P. (1981) 'Educational inquiry as developmental research', *Educational Researcher*, 10(3): 8–13.

Sapir, E. (1963) *Language*, London: Harvest.

School of Barbiana (1970) *A Letter to a Teacher*, Harmondsworth: Penguin.

Schon, D. A. (1983) *The Reflective Practitioner: How Professionals Think in Action*, New York: Basic Book.

Schunk, D. H. (1987) 'Self-efficacy and motivated learning' in Hastings, N. and Schwieso, J. (1987) *New directions in Educational Psychology: 2 Behaviour and Motivation in the Classroom*, Lewes: Falmer.

Seaborg, G. T. (1990) 'The crisis in pre-college science and math education', *Skeptical Inquirer*, 14(3): 270–5.

Shavelson, R. J. and Stern, O. (1981) 'Research on teachers' pedagogical thoughts, judgments, decisions and behavior', *Review of Educational Research*, 51: 455–98.

Shuell, T. J. (1990) 'Teaching and learning as problem-solving', *Theory into Practice*, 29(2): 102–8.

Shulman, L. S. (1986) 'Those who understand: Knowledge growth in teaching', *Educational Researcher* 15(2): 4–14.

Simon, B. and Simon, J. (1957) *Psychology in the Soviet Union*, London: Routledge and Kegan Paul.

Simon, H. (1980) Invited address to Annual Meeting, American Educational Research Association, Boston.

Sinclair, J. (ed.) (1987) *Cobuild English Language Dictionary*, Glasgow: Collins.

Skinner, B. F. (1954) 'The science of learning and the art of teaching', *Harvard Educational Review*, 24: 86–97.

Skinner, B. F. (1962) *Cumulative Record*, London: Methuen.

Smith, B. O., (1969) *Teachers for the Real World*, Washington DC: American Colleges for Teacher Education.

Smith, M. P. (1982) *The Libertarians and Education*, London: Allen and Unwin.

Soltis, J. F. (1984) 'The nature of educational research', *Educational Researcher*, 13(10): 5–10.

Solomon, J. (1987) 'New thoughts on teacher education', *Oxford Review of Education* 13(3): 267–74.

Sparkes, A. C., Thomas, J., Templin, T.J. and Schempp, P.G. (1990) 'The problematic nature of a career in a marginal subject: some implications for teacher education programmes', *Journal of Education for Teaching*, 16(1): 3–28.

Stolurow, L. M. (1965) 'Model the master teacher or master the teaching model', in Krumboltz, J. D. (ed.) *Learning and the Educational Process*, Chigago: Rand McNally.

Stones, E. (1966) *Introduction to Educational Psychology*, London: Methuen.

Stones, E. (1968a) 'Strategy and tactics in programmed learning', *Programmed Learning*, 5(2): 122–8.

Stones, E. (1968b) *Learning and Teaching: a Programmed Introduction*, Chichester: Wiley.

Stones, E. (1968c) Tutors' Handbook to *Learning and Teaching: a Programmed Introduction*, Chichester: Wiley.

Stones, E. (1971) *The Great Fire of London*, London: Macmillan.

Stones, E. (1975a) 'Black light on exams', *British Journal of Teacher Education*, 1(3): 299–303.

Stones, E. (1975b) 'How long is a piece of string? The assessment of practical teaching', in *How Long is a Piece of String?*, London: Society for Research into Higher Education.

Stones, E. (1979) *Psychopedagogy: Psychological Theory and the Practice of Teaching*, London: Methuen.

Stones, E. (1983) 'Never mind the quality, feel the ideology', editorial in *Journal of Education for Teaching*, 9(3): 207–9.

Stones, E. (1984a) *Supervision in Teacher Education: a Counselling and Pedagogical Approach*, London: Methuen.

Stones, E. (1984b) *Psychology of Education: a Pedagogical Approach*, reissue of Stones, E. (1979) *Psychopedagogy: Psychological Theory and the Practice of Teaching*, London: Methuen.

Stones, E. (1986a) 'Towards a systemic approach to research in teaching: the place of investigative pedagogy', *British Educational Research Journal*, 12(2): 167–81.

Stones, E. (1986b) 'Teacher appraisal and student learning'. Paper to the British Educational Research Association conference on teacher appraisal, Sheffield, mimeo.

Stones, E. (1986c) 'Collegial appraisal for the enhancement of pupil learning', in Stones, E. and Wilcox, B. (eds), *Appraising Appraisal*, British Educational Research Association.

Stones, E. (1989a) 'Pedagogical studies in the theory and practice of teacher education', *Oxford Review of Education*, 15(1): 3–15.

Stones, E. (1989b) *Ritual and Reality in Psychology and Teacher Education*, Eighth Vernon-Wall lecture, London: British Psychological Society.

Stones, E. (ed.) (1990) *A New Agenda for Teacher Education*, report of international invitational colloquium, Birmingham, mimeo.

Stones, E. and Anderson, D. (1972) *Educational Objectives and the Teaching of Educational Psychology*, London: Methuen.

Stones, E. and Morris, S. (1972) *Teaching Practice: Problems and Perspectives*, London: Methuen.

Stones, E. and Webster, H. (1984) 'Implications for course design of failure and retrieval rates in initial teacher education', *Educational Research*, 26–3: 172–7.

Stones, E. and Wilcox, B. (1986) (eds), *Appraising Appraisal*, British Educational Research Association.

Tennyson, R. D. and Cochchiarella, M. J. (1986) 'An empirically based instructional design theory for teaching concepts', *Review of Educational Research*, 56(1): 40–71.

Travers, R. M. W. (1981). 'The magic of educational research', in Grimmett (1984) (ed), *Research in Teacher Education: Current Problems and Future Prospects in Canada*, Centre for the Study of Teacher Education, University of British Columbia.

Tripp, D. H. (1985) Case-study generalisation: an agenda for action, *British Educational Research Journal*, 11(1): 33–43.

Tuma, D. T. and Reif, F. (eds) (1980) *Problem-Solving and Education*, New Jersey: Lawrence Erlbaum Associates, Inc.

Universities Council for the Education of Teachers (UK) (1990) Press release 26 June 1990: mimeo.

Verloop, N. (1989) *Interactive cognitions of student teachers: an intervention study*, Arnhem: National Institute for Educational Measurement.

Vigotsky, L. S. (1962) *Thought and language*, Cambridge, Massachusetts: M.I.T.

Walter, C. (1974) *Reading Development and Extension*, London: Ward Lock.

Weiner, B. (1984) 'Principles for a study of student motivation and their application within an attributional framework', in Ames, R. E. and Ames, C. (eds) *Research on motivation in the classroom: volume 1 student motivation*, London: Academic Press.

Wheldhall, K. and Merrett, F. (1987a). 'What is the behaviourist approach to teaching?' in Hastings, N. and Schwiesco, J. *New Directions in Educational Psychology 1: Behaviour and Motivation in the Classroom*, Basingstoke: Taylor and Francis.

Wheldhall, K. and Merrett, F. (1987b) 'Troublesome classroom behaviours' in Hastings, N. and Schwiesco, J. *New Directions in Educational Psychology 1: Behaviour and Motivation in the Classroom*, Basingstoke: Taylor and Francis.

World of Learning, The (1986) London: Europa.

Zeichner, K. (1990) 'Changing directions in the practicum: looking ahead to the 1990s', *Journal of Education for Teaching*, 16(2): 105–132.

Index to case studies

Subject index

abstraction:
and classification 19; in human learning 19; transforming effect of 18

acid test: of classroom affect 263; of concept learning, identification of novel exemplars 111; of theory, practice as 15

affect in learning 18–19

aims: of learning, transferability as 143; relationship of affective and cognitive 38 153; in teacher planning 33; in teaching 33

aims: *see also* objectives

algorithms, and problem solving 167, 170

American Educational Research Association 295

analysis *see* pedagogical analysis *see also* reflection

appraisal: objectification of 256; uninformed approaches to 2

approbation, as reinforcer of human behaviour 250–1

arbitrariness: and language in concept learning 24; power of in symbolisation 24

assessment: of art teaching 231; of 'delivered' learning 8; and ipsative tests 212; judgmental nature of 212; and video-recording 231

attitudes, measurement of 38

attributes: criterial, and concept learning 21–5, 105–6; and language in heightening salience of 107–8, 121; noncriterial in quality teaching 103–4

attribution theory, and motivation 256–7

beginning competence, teacher misapprehension of 74, 105–6, 233

behaviour modification 261

biology, the use of keys, test of 232–4

briefing, and motivation 257

briefing and debriefing 276; and improvement of teaching quality 302–3; and reflection 299–300

British National Curriculum 32

case studies: discussed in this book and problems of pedagogy 280–95; iterative in research on teaching 31–2; and pedagogical theory 32; protocols not models to be emulated 129–30; of teaching; as closed circle 280; critique of 280

case studies index 313

classification in human learning, and abstraction 19

classroom affect, acid test of 263

clinical teaching 32

commodification of education 2

concept learning: acid test of, identification of novel exemplars as 111; compared with learning motor skills 134, 143; counterpositioning of exemplars and non-exemplars in 108–9, 118; and criterial attributes in 21–5, 105–6; experience of the world essential for 91; and language as crucial in 23–4, 91; language as key factor in 23, 109; links with learning motor skills 146–7, 159–61; and non-criterial attributes 21; non-exemplars in 22; and pedagogical theory 27; and symbolisation in 23; use of exemplars

Author index